What They <u>Didn't</u> Teach You About the American Revolution

Other books by
Mike Wright

What They <u>Didn't</u> Teach You About World War II

What They <u>Didn't</u> Teach You About the Civil War

City Under Siege: Richmond in the Civil War

What They <u>Didn't</u> Teach You About the American Revolution

Mike Wright

3/28/2001
DeHoff

PRESIDIO

Published by Presidio Press
505 B San Marin Drive, Suite 300
Novato, CA 94945-1340

Library of Congress Cataloging-in-Publication Data

Wright, Mike, 1938–
     What they didn't teach you about the American Revolution / Mike Wright.
          p.   cm.
     Includes bibliographical references (p.324) and index.
     ISBN 0-89141-668-4
     1. United States—History—Revolution, 1775–1783—Miscellanea.
     I. Title.
     E209.W77   1999
     973.3—dc21   99-19699
                                             CIP

Printed in the United States of America

Lin:

Had we but world enough, and time.
—Andrew Marrell; To His Coy Mistress

And the next generation:

Michele Ann Wright
Teresa Joanna Wright

What a glorious morning for America!
—Sam Adams, April 19, 1776

The Revolution was effected before the war commenced. The Revolution was in the minds and hearts of the people.... This radical change in the principles, opinions, sentiments, and affections of the people, was the real American Revolution.

—John Adams, 1818

Sacred cows make the tastiest hamburger.

—Abbie Hoffman, remembered on his death, 1989

I have sworn upon the altar of God, eternal hostility against every form of tyranny over the mind of man.

—Thomas Jefferson, letter to Dr. Benjamin Rush,
September 23, 1800

Contents

Acknowledgments

Friends and librarians, guides and mentors, I thank you all and acknowledge your support in so many ways. To Bob and Richard Kane and E. J. McCarthy of Presidio Press; thank you for your continued support and encouragement.

But mainly to my wife, Lin. She aids my research and suffers with my deadline-induced stress. She reads every version of everything I write—every book and every article; she corrects, agrees, disagrees, and criticizes. Still, somehow, she remains loyal through rewrite after rewrite. We met when I was asked to help her turn her doctoral dissertation into a book. We never got around to that. Instead, we turned that first meeting into both a labor of love and a love of joint labor.

Thank you.

A Chronology of the War

1597: British Transportation Act approved
1607: Jamestown, Virginia, settled
1608: Samuel de Champlain founds Quebec for France
1609: British Pilgrim separatists move from Amsterdam to Leyden, the Netherlands. Two ships headed from England to Virginia wrecked in the Bermudas, inspiring Shakespeare's *The Tempest*
1610: Don Pedro de Peralta establishes Santa Fe, New Mexico, for Spain
1619: First boatload of women arrives at Jamestown. First elected assembly in America. First Africans sold in Jamestown. First Thanksgiving celebrated near Jamestown
1620: Puritans establish Plymouth Plantation, Massachusetts
1622: Slide rule invented
1625: Dutch found New Amsterdam
1627: 1,500 London children kidnapped and sent to Virginia
1629: English capture Quebec from French
1636: Harvard University founded in Massachusetts
1638: First printing press set up in America
1642: English civil war. Three hundred thousand die in China flood. Massachusetts enacts law mandating parents educate their children
1643: New England Confederation
1645: Navigation Acts passed
1666: Great fire of London. *Père* Jacques Marquette arrives in Canada
1669: Death of Rembrandt
1670: Hudson Bay Trading Company granted charter
1681: Matches invented. William Penn granted land patent in North America. La Salle sails Mississippi River
1688: Lloyds coffeehouse in London becomes insurance center
1689: King William's War
1690: First paper money in America. In Boston, John Harris publishes first newspaper in America; it's suppressed after one issue

1692: Salem, Massachusetts witchcraft trials

1693: College of William and Mary founded

1702: Queen Anne's War

1704: First regular newspaper published in America, John Campbell's *Boston Public Advisor*

1739: War of Jenkins' Ear

1740: King George's War (War of Austrian Secession)

1742: First performance of Handel's *Messiah*

1744: First "baseball" game (rounders) played in England

1746: Benjamin Franklin begins his research into electricity

1752: Gregorian calendar adopted

1756: French and Indian/Seven Years' War. Composer Wolfgang Amadeus Mozart born

1764: Sugar Act passed

1765: Stamp Act annulled

1767: Townshend Acts passed. Mason-Dixon Line established

1770: Boston Massacre

1773: Boston Tea Party

1774: Coercive (called the Intolerable Acts in America) Actspassed. Thomas Jefferson writes *Summary View of the Rights of America*. British Loyalists leave America for England and Canada

1775: Battles of Lexington and Concord, Massachusetts. England declares Massachusetts in state of rebellion. First American abolition society founded. American Revolution begins

1776: Declaration of Independence written. Washington wins Battle of Trenton

1777: Howe defeats Washington at Battle of Brandywine, Pennsylvania. Articles of Confederation adopted (ratified in 1781). Winter at Valley Forge

1778: France recognizes American independence. Gates defeats Burgoyne at Battle of Saratoga, New York

1781: Washington defeats Cornwallis at Battle of Yorktown, Virginia

1783: Treaty of Paris ends American Revolution. United Empire Loyalists (Tories) settle in Canada

1786: Shays Rebellion

1787: U.S. Constitution written. Northwest Ordinance written

1788: Rhode Island rejects Constitution. New Hampshire ratifies

Constitution, making adoption formally effective. Final Congress of Articles of Confederation adjourns

1789 Mutiny on the Bounty. French Revolution begins. Pennsylvania legislature repeals ban on public performance of stage plays. First Congress of Constitution convenes in New York City. First Congress's first bill proposes raising of revenue; its first measure is a taxbill. George Washington sworn in as first U.S. president

1789: Congress submits twelve proposed amendments to the Constitution

1790: Congress votes to build capital city on the Potomac River. First U.S. census

1791: Bill of Rights approved

Introduction

What is it that so fascinates us about the American Revolution? It is a seemingly simple question but one without a simple answer. The Revolution is (1) a glorious period, (2) a glamorous period, and (3) a period that changed our lives, no matter that we weren't around at the time and may not recognize that our lives were changed.

Glorious? Maybe, maybe not. The Revolution was a fraternal and civil war that may have pitted at the most one third of us (those who wanted the colonies to separate from Britain) against another third (those who wanted to remain with Britain), with the rest (the final third) not caring one way or the other. For all, lives were disrupted, government was altered beyond imagination, and homes and existence were, at the least, threatened.

Glamorous? The eighteenth century saw people die of diseases that today can be cured with less than a dollar's worth of medicine. A medical treatment often used in the eighteenth century was also commonly used in ancient Egypt—"trephination," in which a surgeon used a cylindrical saw to cut a hole in your skull to release bad vapors. The surgeon, incidentally, doubled as your barber, which is why barber poles are made of red and white stripes, white bandages and red blood.

It was a time when the air was polluted, not by man-made chemicals but by animal-made excrement. A town's sewage system often consisted of a shallow ditch flowing through the streets. From second-story windows residents blithely threw out the contents of chamber pots, giving rise to the saying "Will you give the wall?" because it was safer to walk as close to the houses, as close to the wall, as possible. Human smell wasn't much better, because bathing wasn't all that common in the eighteenth century. Troops in the Revolution were actively discouraged from taking baths; it was felt bathing would be too relaxing and, thus, injurious to a soldier's health. Imagine whole towns smelling of unwashed bodies, roadways peppered with excrement, and open sewage flowing by your house. Realize, too, the town's sewage system became a trough for animals, which themselves became tomorrow's meal for humans. The waste trickled down to become drinking water thick with mud and disease.

The American Revolution was more than Washington standing up in a boat while crossing the Delaware River in the middle of a winter's storm. It was more than Thomas Jefferson taking quill in hand to write the Declaration of Independence. It certainly had nothing to do with myths surrounding those characters we have dubbed the Founding Fathers. The American Revolution was a time that changed the government of the colonies and changed the world, and that is why it is so interesting, why it is so important. If the Revolutionary era was neither glorious nor glamorous, perhaps what so fascinates us is that it was a time of massive changes.

This is not the American Revolution of powdered wigs and the minuet; such wigs were worn by, and the dance danced by, those above the middling class. Rather, what follows is the history of people—men and women—salted down with toughness and wisdom, individuals who, as the saying goes, had "been up the creek and over the mountain." It was not an army that won the Revolution; it was a population.

Those we call the Founding Fathers are, as a certain Mr. Shakespeare put it more or less a century and a half earlier, such stuff as dreams are made of. But at the moment of their birth, they were neither dream nor myth. The myths they became were begotten by hard reality, the very stuff of life.

What follows includes some dark and delicious details of history. These are stories—"roughness, pimples, warts, and everything," as Oliver Cromwell once said. Along the way, in telling these stories we hope to have a little fun, because we humans truly are a funny species.

It is almost as if we are taught that the American Revolution sprang godlike from the conjoined heads of Jefferson, Franklin, Adams, and Washington. Not only was there no such "godlike" springing, it took decades and the will and work of thousands of people throughout the colonies to tear apart and then rebuild a government.

A long and often fractious relationship evolved between the

American colonies and their mother country. Yet, despite a troubled relationship, most colonists not only regarded the British government as the best the world had to offer, they firmly maintained that they were part of that world. They were an ocean away from London, but New Haven, Connecticut, farmers believed they were as true Englishmen as their cousins in East Anglia; Charleston, South Carolina, merchants were as British as those in Manchester; and sailors out of Boston, Massachusetts, were certain they were no less than those sailing from Bristol.

The story of the American Revolution is more than the battles. The true story is what caused this love of all things English to change, what caused residents of Williamsburg and Philadelphia and Boston to alter their definition of "my country" from Virginia or Pennsylvania or Massachusetts to mean "The United States of America." This change, this alteration, was a long time coming.

What follows is a series of essays, presented in only a general chronological order. They are short takes on parts of our history that we may never have been taught before. Much of the material was there all along, but for whatever reason—perhaps in a rush to move on to the "important events"—a lot of the really interesting moments in our story were never mentioned. We make no claim to this being a definitive work. Rather, we hope it will entice the reader into doing further reading. After all, books are a marvelous invention.

CHAPTER ONE

Prelude to Independence:
Revolution, Dogma, and Stamps

Why do I have to know about the past?
You gotta look to the future.
—Teenager, December 31, 1995

I was among the first who embarked in the cause of our common country [and] I
have never left your side one moment but when called from you on public duty....
—George Washington, March 15, 1783

George Washington grew marijuana on his farm at Mount Vernon, Virginia. It's not known whether he smoked pot, much less inhaled it, but the Father of Our Country* did raise the weed that two hundred years later became something of a symbol of rebellion as well as a major cash crop in the United States.

For many years Washington grew tobacco on his plantation and for a while at least he also grew hemp—the marijuana plant. At one point in his farm diary he wrote of ordering his gardeners to separate the stalks of the hemp plants from the flowers. The stalks contain fiber for making rope. Dried flowers and leaves of the hemp plant are the source of the drug cannabis.

We don't know whether George kicked back and lit up a doobie, but there is evidence that like others we glorify as the Founding Fathers, Washington experimented in many of life's ways. The lives of thousands who fought and died for independence reenforce our knowledge that these men and women were real people who took real risks and created a real miracle.

---

* In a letter to Washington dated March 19, 1787, Henry Knox referred to the soon-to-be first president of the United States as "The Father of Your Country."

1

That miracle went beyond flag waving and holiday celebrations and hamburgers on the backyard grill. Very simply, the miracle they created invented a world we can either remember and retain or forget and forgo.

On October 31, 1753, young Major George Washington of the Virginia militia rode out of Williamsburg with a warning for the French commandant along the Ohio River. With him he took as interpreter Jacob van Braam of Holland, a schoolteacher who supposedly spoke flawless French but who in reality did not. Certainly not flawlessly. Washington's first military command consisted, all told, of just seven men, one of whom was an interpreter who couldn't interpret.

Fifty-two days out of Williamsburg, almost five hundred miles from the Virginia capital, Washington marched into French-held Fort le Beouf, near present-day Waterford, Pennsylvania. George not only was far from home, but he was in over his head.

Fort le Beouf was packed with troops and bristling with cannon. Wearing the bright red dress uniform of the Virginia militia—he'd taken it along for just that occasion—Washington presented himself before the fort authorities. He gave Coulon de Villers, the garrison's commander, Governor Dinwiddie's demand that the French withdraw from the Ohio Valley. The elderly Frenchman waved off "the summons you sent me to retire," saying, "I do not think of myself obliged to obey it."

His message delivered and rejected, all that young Major Washington could do was return to Williamsburg. It was January 16, 1754, when George Washington stood again before Governor Dinwiddie, tired and worn out from a harrowing journey. He didn't have long to rest. Within a week of returning from his journey, Washington was ordered to train an army to secure the Ohio territory. In somewhat conflicting orders, Dinwiddie told Washington to "act on the defensive, but in case any attempts are made to obstruct the works or to interrupt our settlement by any persons whatever, you are to restrain all such offenders, and in case of resistance to make prisoners of or kill and destroy them." His orders specified that Washington should "conduct yourself as the circumstances of the service shall require and to act as you shall find best for the furtherance of His

Majesty's service and the good of the dominion." This time Washington was to be a lieutenant colonel with a lot more than six men to command.

On May 24 he arrived at a spot called Great Meadows, about ten miles from Uniontown, Pennsylvania. The area was nearly all marsh; still, he called it "a charming field for an encounter." He ordered his men to set up camp.

Three days later, frightened members of a garrison who'd been building an English fort at Pittsburgh met Washington and his troops. More than a thousand men had surrounded them, the workers reported, and they were lucky to get out alive. The would-be fort builders were ready to head back to Virginia. Not so George Washington.

After all, with him was the Indian chief Tanacharison, whom the English called Chief Half King. The chief told Washington about a French party camped at Chestnut Ridge, not far away. Attack them, Half King pleaded, before they attack you. Washington was persuaded; the colonials and the Indians would "go hand in hand and strike the French."

On May 28, forty American colonials and a small band of Indians swooped down on the French camp, ignoring the fact that England and France officially were at peace. In the early hours, through a "heavy rain, and a night as dark as it is possible to conceive," Washington attacked. "I was the first man that approached them," Washington said, "and the first whom they saw, and immediately upon it [they] ran to their arms and fired briskly till they were defeated."

Washington and his militia troops opened fire on one side of the camp. When the French tried to run out the back way, so to speak, the Indians were waiting for them.

A letter from Governor Dinwiddie to the Earl of Albermarle in England sanitized the ambush:

> Col. Washington, with forty Men, march'd out that Night, and about six next Morning join'd the Ind's and march'd out. One of the Ind'n Runners tract [tracked] the Feet of the French and came up to their Lodgment about nine. The

French seeing our People, got undr Arms, a skirmish ensued, w'n we lost one Man and had two wounded; the French had 12 killed on the Spot and 21 taken Prisoners, w'ch I have in Prison in this city [Williamsburg].

Washington caught the French by surprise, but still they managed to get off a few stray shots at their attackers. "I heard the bullets whistle," he wrote of his first campaign under fire, "and, believe me, there is something charming in the sound." When King George II heard about Washington's remark, he commented, "He would not have said so if he had been used to hear many." Washington himself admitted, "I fortunately escaped without any wound."

Within minutes the battle was over. Nine Frenchmen were dead. One man was wounded and twenty-two others were about to be taken prisoner, when one of them, Ensign Joseph Coulon de Jumonville, walked toward Washington to surrender. As Jumonville neared the young Virginian, Half King rushed up and hit the Frenchman in the head with a club, killing him instantly. Now the death toll among the French was ten.

One French soldier apparently was answering a call of nature at the time of the attack and managed to escape. He took the news back to the Forks—the triangle where the Ohio, Allegheny, and Monongahela rivers meet. The French had taken over the English construction project and were building Fort Duquesne, named after the Marquis Duquesne, governor general of New France.

Jumonville carried with him letters showing he was on a mission of peace to warn off British and Virginia troops. He was, according to his orders, a *parlementaire,* a commander with orders demanding Washington peacefully withdraw. However, his private, unwritten orders called for him to snoop around any British or American settlement or fort in the Ohio Valley. These orders made him not a diplomat but, since he wore no uniform, a spy.

French troops quickly headed toward Washington's party, and when word reached Washington he quickly turned back toward Great Meadows and went to work building up his defenses. He didn't have much time and rapidly completed what he called "a small palisadoed fort," naming it Fort Necessity. The term was as accurate as it was ironic. Looking at the inadequate fort his young ally was building, Half King and his men faded into the forest.

On July 3, in the middle of a rainstorm, the French struck with a force of six hundred soldiers and a hundred Indians. Within an hour, thirty of Washington's men were dead and another seventy were wounded. The colonials were close to being annihilated.

Fort Necessity had been poorly conceived. On one side, Washington had cleared a space of about sixty feet away from the palisades. It wasn't enough and left the French an area of wooded land from which they shot downhill into the fort. The battle took place in a driving rain and Fort Necessity proved to be a catch basin, with water rapidly pouring into defensive ditches Washington had built. Men sloshed around in water made bloody by the dead and dying. On top of that, the roof of the hastily built magazine leaked, and soon the powder inside was virtually useless. By then, less than a three-day supply of food remained, and at this point Washington did about the only thing he could do; he broke out kegs of rum and gave his remaining troops a hearty drink. "It was no sooner dark," Dr. Adam Stephen reported, "than one-half of our men got drunk."

That night the French called on Washington to discuss terms of a surrender. *"Voulez-vous parlez?"* Washington agreed to talk but insisted the negotiations be in the open between the two sides. One of the two men sent out to talk with Captain de Villiers was George's erstwhile interpreter, van Braam.

Because England and France were not actually at war, de Villiers said, he would be lenient. He warned that if Washington refused the offer and continued to resist, the French could not guarantee what would happen; he claimed four hundred more Indians were on their way to Fort Necessity to fight on the French side. De Villiers exaggerated a bit—only one hundred were on the way—but he got his point across. Washington realized he had little choice and agreed to the terms, but he wanted them put in writing. It was early in the morning of July 4, 1754—twenty-two years before that more famous Fourth of July—when van Braam returned with two copies of the written agreement. They were in French and the paper was "wet and blotted" by the rain.

Washington could neither read, write, nor speak French; so it was left up to Jacob van Braam, and he was, after all, working three languages in his mind. He was Dutch, the agreement was in French, and he had to translate into English. Not to mention that everybody, literally, lacked sense enough to come out of a shower of rain.

Bad handwriting, wet and blotted paper, poor translation. Whatever. The agreement Washington signed did not say that he had "killed" a diplomat; instead, it said he had "assassinated" him, something entirely different in political circles. De Villiers, of course, was delighted with it all, and in his report he congratulated himself: "We made the English give us in their own hands, that they had committed an assassination on us, in the camp of my brother. . . ."

Later in the day Washington's men buried their dead, thirty all told—despite modern investigative techniques, their graves have not been located. The Americans patched up seventy men who were wounded. They burned much of their baggage, anything they couldn't carry or weren't leaving under French guard. Then they marched out with one small field piece, a swivel gun they were permitted to take with them to use in the event of an Indian attack.

As the Americans left, the French marched into the fort and raised the fleur-de-lis. Among the material left by the colonials were several kegs of rum, which de Villiers quickly smashed to keep out of the hands of his troops. His men destroyed the weapons Washington's men had left and tore down most of the palisade posts. Then he set the fort on fire.

In attacking the French troops George Washington ordered the first shots of the first global war. In Europe it was known as the Seven Years' War; in the colonies it was the French and Indian War. That war led to Britain's attempt to tax Americans, which led to the American Revolution, which led to Washington's fame as soldier, which further led to his becoming the first president of the United States.

Simply put, George Washington began the war that brought him to glory, and out of it came America's independence.

The French and Indian War ended outside Montreal in an area known as the Plains of Abraham. The area took its name from an early owner, Abraham Martin, a onetime sea captain who farmed the land more than 150 years earlier. Both Britain's James Wolfe and France's Marquis de Montcalm died in the September 1759 battle on the Plains of Abraham. The British victory at Montreal shocked Europe and sent England into ecstasies.

The Seven Years War continued two years longer—on the seas, in the West Indies, in Asia, and in Europe. The end saw a humiliating defeat for France. With the signing of the Treaty of Paris in February 1763, territory around the world changed hands. It amounted to the nearly total disappearance of French influence in North America. Except for a couple of small islands off the Newfoundland coast, France lost all of its New World possessions—Canada went to England, New Orleans went to Spain. Spain ceded to Britain its claims to Florida. From Hudson Bay in the north to St. Augustine in the south, the Atlantic to the Mississippi, England reigned over America.

For a while.

On October 25, 1760, before the official end of the French and Indian/Seven Years' War, short, dark, and thick-bodied King George II died at the age of seventy-seven. It was 7:15 in the morning. A royal page "heard a thud," rushed in, and found the old king dead. Long live the new king! George II's son, Frederick Lewis, Prince of Wales, had died in 1751, so the new Prince of Wales, George II's grandson, became king of Great Britain. George III was twenty-two years old when his grandfather passed on to that great throne room in the sky.

In America, George III was known as a tyrant. In England, some of his subjects (including his own family) believed he was insane. In truth, the troubles felt on both sides of the Atlantic Ocean may have been due to King George III's urinary problem.

George III suffered what the English at the time referred to as "the Royal Malady." It would be two hundred years before the mystery of the Royal Malady was apparently solved. In 1966 two British physicians assembled the evidence—the king's history of recurrent, spasmodic abdominal pain, his neurologic and psychiatric symptoms, and, importantly, the color of the royal urine.

Apparently, King George III suffered from erythropoietic porphyria. It's more commonly called Günther's disease and more graphically referred to, for reasons we'll explain, as the "pink pee." It is a rare but very damaging disease that results from a nearly complete absence in the body of the enzyme uroporphyrinogen III cosynthase. The disease is marked by a weltlike rash, unsightly scars, and the appearance of facial hair at the same time the sufferer is losing head hair. There is a fluorescent red staining of the teeth and the individual's urine is discolored to a bright pink. For periods of time the individual appears insane.

That pretty much describes George III as he progressed through life. The first noticeable occurrence of the Royal Malady came in 1765, five years after he took the throne and ten years before fighting broke out in the American colonies. It was at the height of the Stamp Act crisis, and the crisis and the malady likely exasperated each other. The king had numerous attacks of the malady and, in 1810, his son took control as Prince Regent, relinquishing power only when George III's urinary problems apparently eased up and what had appeared as insanity abated.

For most of his life up to the point he became king, George III lived with his mother, Princess Augusta. His former tutor was a Scottish peer, John Stuart, the Earl of Bute (pronounced "boot"). Bute was also said to be Princess Augusta's lover, which, of course, confused matters.

George III's father, Frederick, never got to be king because his father, George II, lived so long. Frederick left his son a letter, to be read by Princess Augusta after her husband's death. In it he urged the young George—only thirteen at the time of his father's death—to "retrieve the glory of the throne." The man who would never be king told his son who would that "I shall have no regret never to have wore [*sic*] the crown if you but fill it worthily." Princess Augusta agreed: "Be a king, George," she told him, "be a king," hoping he would reverse the crown's loss of power and, while sitting by his side, she would share everything such power carried with it.

One of the first things George III did after putting on the crown, not unexpectedly, was to name as his new prime minister Lord Bute. His former tutor. His mother's alleged lover. The man historian John C. Miller refers to as "the most hated man in the [British] kingdom." In becoming prime minister, Bute replaced a man who may have been the most loved politician in the kingdom, William Pitt, the namesake not only of Fort Pitt, but of a town called Pittsburgh.

Much of Britain, including the colonies, had loved William Pitt. Much of Britain, especially the colonies, now hated Lord Bute. But it was to Bute the new king turned, and the more public sentiment turned against George's mother's lover, the firmer the king's attachment to him grew.

Bute had a disgraceful, incompetent, and thankfully short stint as prime minister. Two years after he took office, he was forced to resign.

By 1770 George III had gone through minor attacks of the malady and a series of prime ministers. In that year Frederick Lord North took office. Apparently North was the man the king had been seeking and the man the American colonists had dreaded. He made Bute look good. By the time North left office, he had lost most of his friends on both sides of the Atlantic. On the American side, however, it no longer mattered who was British prime minister, because by the time Lord North was gone, so were the colonies.

Colonial American troops and their Indian allies contributed to winning the French and Indian War, but it was the British regular soldier who did most of the fighting. All you had to do was ask the British, and they'd tell you why. English regular soldiers, they claimed, were the best in the world. Colonial troops were totally ignorant of military affairs, ill disciplined, lazy, and lacked even rudimentary knowledge of camp sanitation, which led to a high rate of illness among any other troops who came near them. Colonials were rough, untutored, and not fit for the company of English gentlemen.

America's Indian allies were worse, according to British General Jeffrey Amherst. Native Americans were a pack of "lazy, rum-drinking people, and [of] little good." General John Forbes classified Indians as "more infamous cowards than any other race of mankind [with a] natural fickle disposition." After all, they hid behind trees to fight guerrilla fashion.

Some English officers who weren't quite so dense under their tricornered hats learned to modify standard battle tactics used on the European continent. That tactic consisted of lining 'em up, marching 'em toward the enemy, and then either shooting 'em down or being shot down. Generally this British army acclaimed the best in the world marched head-on until the soldiers were only literally yards from the enemy and then they'd blast away, while the enemy blasted right back. In Europe, of course, they fought on good, decent plains. Field conditions in the American wilderness were radically different from those of England, France, or Germany, where hiding behind a tree to fight was considered the cowardly thing to do.* Eventually, some English soldiers learned to deliver aimed fire, not just fire in volleys; however, this method of fighting never became standard procedure for the English during the Revolutionary era.

Still, someone in the English military establishment *must* have felt some admiration for Americans as soldiers. After all, during pre-Revolutionary wars, the British army recruited American frontiersmen and used them as rangers. One problem was that many of the colonials they recruited were indentured servants. The British military didn't bother to reimburse the indenture-holders, which obviously angered American indenture-holders. Taking their property, Americans believed, was "an unconstitutional and arbitrary Invasion of our Rights and Properties." At times, when army recruiters went looking for help, angry mobs harassed the English and made it difficult to get enough "volunteers." When the British military in the colonies failed to recruit adequate numbers of short-term troops, London was forced to send regular regiments to America to fight in colonial wars.

According to the English belief, not only did their regular soldiers have to do most of the fighting during the French and Indian War, ungrateful America didn't have enough public buildings to use to house the troops. That meant that they either had to be put up in tents—and this certainly wasn't their favored option, given a climate colder than the British were used to—or to quarter the men in private houses. This brought up an argument over whether troops should be quartered in private homes without the owners' consent. The dispute grew more rancorous as time went on, and eventually it wound up among the colonists' chief objections voiced in the De-

* For more on this, see Chapter Ten.

claration of Independence. A few years later the same objection became the Third Amendment to the Constitution.

So the English army recruited indentured servants without paying their masters, they forced colonists to house regular army troops in private homes, they impressed food and other property with no reimbursement made, and they bullied colonial legislatures. Sure, with all that in mind, Americans certainly would remain loyal. Then London tried to tax the American colonies to pay for what British troops were doing to them. In the House of Parliament and among the king's ministers, the British government became increasingly bored with the colonists' constant clamor over their "rights as Englishmen."

So, Britain's regular troops held their own abilities in high esteem and believed both the American colonists and their sometimes Indian allies were shiftless, lazy, and untrainable. The colonists, however, learned something about the regulars.

So, they learned that the vaunted British soldier could be beaten.

The French and Indian War—Britain's Great War for Empire— gave the English people an expanded world empire and left it with a staggering debt. To handle that debt, Britain turned to its American colonies. After all, the London government felt, the war had begun in America, and most of the land fighting had been here with British regular troops. Why not have Americans pay for it?

In an effort to administer this new empire efficiently, King George III and company began enforcing the Navigation Acts. Officially they were known as the Acts of Trade and Navigation and were enacted over a 122-year period between 1645 and 1767.

The Navigation Acts changed somewhat over time but what had remained fairly consistent was the lack of imposition. The ordinance first ordered products of New England's whaling industry to be shipped to England only in ships manned by English seamen. Later it prohibited the importation of French wines, wool, and silk into England, Ireland, or the colonies.

Effectively, this meant that any goods originating on the European continent went to England first, where a profit was taken and fees and handling charges were included in the cost. Finally they were transported to the American colonies in British ships. The only good part of the Navigation Acts was that they were rarely enforced.

When the English began colonizing America, they brought with them that quintessential British animal, the sheep, but the Navigation Acts forbade the exportation of American wool in woven form. Hats made from the American beaver were a coming thing in English and French fashion, but the Navigation Acts also prohibited the colonists from transporting hats from one colony to another, to England, or to anyplace else. Raw materials—that is, beaver pelts or wool—had to be shipped back to England on English vessels, where they would be processed in English factories. This obviously prevented an American manufacturing system from developing, while it abetted English shipping and manufacturing companies.

The Navigation Acts also barred the small colonial hat industry from using Negro apprentices, which undoubtedly was a good thing for Negro apprentices, even if the English didn't mean it the way it turned out. Making hats involved the use of mercury, and over time, hat makers literally went crazy from breathing the fumes, giving rise to the saying "He's mad as a hatter."

Among the several Navigation Acts, the Molasses Act levied prohibitive taxes on sugar and molasses imported into the colonies from French and Dutch Islands. Once again, however, it wasn't strictly enforced, which was good; otherwise the New England rum industry would have been destroyed. If it *had* been enforced, it likely would have stopped the obscene but highly profitable Triangular Trade. This was sort of a sordid if perpetual-motion machine of trade whereby the West Indies produced molasses and sugar, which were shipped to New England, where it was made into rum, which was used to buy slaves in Africa, which were traded in the West Indies for more molasses and sugar. While slavery was strongest in the South, the northern colonies earned their fortunes on the backs of black men, women, and children stolen from Africa. Every year New England shipped out more than two million gallons of rum as part of the Triangular Trade. Teaching us about the Triangular Trade was one of the few things our history teachers seemed to have gotten right. They failed, however, to mention a strange relationship between slavery and that most New England of all products, Boston beans. New Englanders made fortunes by raising beans that were shipped to the West Indies to be used as cheap food for slaves.

Some of America's most revered Revolutionary figures were slave holders. Take South Carolina planter and merchant Henry Laurens. He was an avid if not radical agitator. During the prewar period of 1740 to 1750, Henry Laurens bought and sold slaves in what he thought of as a straightforward business manner. In a letter written to his supplier, Laurens commented in a rather matter-of-fact manner:

> Please to observe that prime People turn to best Account here. . . , the males [are] preferable to the Females & and that Callabars* are not at all liked with us when they are above the Age of 18, Gambias or Gold Coast are prefer'd to others, Windward Coast next to them.

By 1763 Laurens expressed qualms that some in his generation "would not pursue the African Trade." In 1776 Henry wrote his son John that

> my Negroes, all to a man, are strongly attached to me; hitherto not one of them has attempted to desert; on the contrary, those who are more exposed hold themselves always ready to fly from the enemy in case of a sudden descent. . . .
>
> You know, my dear son, I abhor slavery. I was born in a country where slavery had been established by British kings and parliaments, as well as by the laws of that country ages before my existence. I found the Christian religion and slavery growing under the same authority and cultivation. I nevertheless disliked it. . . .
>
> Not less than twenty thousand pounds sterling would all my Negroes produce if sold at public auction tomorrow. I am not

---

* Possibly those captured in Kalamo, in what is now Zambia.

the man who enslaved them; they are indebted to Englishmen for that favour; nevertheless I am devising means for manumitting many of them, and for cutting off the entail of slavery.

In the Continental Congress, when the word *independence* first crept into the discussion, Henry Laurens was shaken to the point of uncontrollable tears. Laurens later became president of the Congress, succeeding John Hancock.

Between 1526 and 1870, nearly ten million slaves were bought or stolen from Africa, then shipped from Africa to the New World. Strangely enough, where it lasted longest wasn't the place to which most slaves originally were shipped. Brazil received 3,647,000 black slaves, Spanish America received 1,552,000, more than 1,665,000 went to the British Caribbean, while French America bought 1,600,000. Traders shipped a million black slaves to Dutch America, and 28,000 were stolen and transported to the Danish West Indies. Beginning in 1619, British North America, including what is now the United States, bought 399,000 black slaves.

Almost from the beginning, blacks were considered separate and inferior. The first blacks brought to North America were sold as ordinary indentured servants, but the English knew from the beginning that their fate would be different. The Spanish and Portuguese used blacks as slaves, and racial prejudice, ignorance, and fear created a basis for a different, harsher treatment of black "servants" than of white.

In October 1763, King George III tried to stop the white settlers' western movement. He proclaimed that until further notice, no colonial government could grant, and no white man could take, land beyond the sources of rivers that flow into the Atlantic. It didn't work. With land already taken along the ocean shore, more and more settlers moved farther and farther west.

Robert Walpole, who in 1721 became Great Britain's first true prime minister, had objected to the Navigation Acts, believing that unrestricted trade would bring in more gold than taxes would. By

1763, gold was just what the British treasury needed. England's debt from the French and Indian War amounted to over 133 million pounds. Much as it would in the United States in the 1990s, in the 1760s the words *national debt* caused panic in Britain.

At the time Americans paid an average of $1.20 per year in taxes, all made up of levies on imports. That is, they were indirect taxes. In England, taxes were twenty-five times as high, which made it difficult for the English to understand the Americans' objection to their lower taxes.

The Sugar Act of 1764 was also known as Grenville's American Revenue Act, named for George Grenville, a personal friend of Lord Bute, who, you may remember, was a very personal friend of George III's mother. Thanks to Bute, Grenville became First Lord of the Admiralty and Chancellor of the Exchequer, where, as historian Mark Boatner puts it, he "did much to hasten the American Revolution."

It was under Grenville that the first overt symptom of alienation between England and America was seen: the Stamp Act. Reaction brought an end to what is known as the period of "salutary neglect," with king and Parliament, in effect, neglecting to enforce the Navigation Acts.

Parliament passed the Stamp Act in order to raise £60,000 a year in America. Britain reckoned it would cost upward of £350,000 a year to maintain troops in the colonies; £60,000, it was felt, wasn't much for the Americans to pay considering they would be protected from both internal and external forces.

The Stamp Act required fifty-five various types of printed material—everything from handbills and broadsides, newspapers and prayer books, playing cards and dice—to be taxed and a stamp affixed, indicating that the levy had been paid. A stamp for dice, for example, cost ten shillings; for a college diploma it was two pounds, and if you got a grant from the governor, six pounds.

The Stamp Act was seen as the first direct tax on the American colonies. It would affect most directly the most vocal and powerful segments of colonial society—lawyers, publishers, merchants, shipowners, speculators, and those who sat around playing cards or throwing dice. In other words, it would hit hardest those groups who were likely to object to it most. It may have been this simple fact that did in the tax and started the American Revolution.

Not everybody objected to the Stamp Act. Some rather powerful people applied to distribute the stamps—men such as Richard Henry Lee of Virginia, from whom later came the call for independence from Britain, and Benjamin Franklin, and from him would later come the cry that the tax was unjust.

Simply put, Lee and Franklin realized that there was money to be made in distributing the stamps—£300 a year plus patronage privileges—and they both wanted in on it. At first. When Lee realized most of his fellow colonists opposed the tax, he claimed he hadn't recognized the grave meaning of the Stamp Act. Actually Lee lost the post to an ally of the speaker of the Virginia House of Burgesses and immediately began harassing anyone who proposed to obey the law. "My mind has been warmed" to fighting the tax, Lee said, "and I hardly know where to stop."

When Franklin realized the American people opposed it, he told Parliament that there wasn't enough money in the colonies to pay for the stamps.

One of the defining moments in this prologue to revolution came when a young member of Virginia's House of Burgesses spoke out against the Stamp Act. The problem is, today we're not sure what he said. Patrick Henry had been admitted to the legislature only nine days before he rose to introduce a series of resolutions against the Stamp Act. Most of the older members of the House of Burgesses had left for the day. As historians Edmund and Helen Morgan put it: "What Henry said and what the Burgesses did are clear in legend but cloudy in history."

While the average Burgess at the time owned 1,800 acres of land, Patrick Henry owned only 600, and unlike most others in the House, Henry's land had not been inherited. In fact, Patrick Henry was something of a carpetbagger, as the term would have it in the next century. Henry still lived in Hanover County but bought land in nearby Louisa County in order to have the Louisa seat in the House. Even then, it cost him financially. He spent six pounds to buy rum for voters on election day; another two pounds went to have the rum taken to the polls.

More than half the leaders of the House of Burgesses had gone to college, most of them matriculating down the street from the colonial capital at the College of William and Mary; most House members also came from Virginia's first families. Patrick Henry was neither of a first family nor was he college educated. He was self-schooled, and after failing as a farmer, and twice failing as a store-keeper, Patrick Henry turned to law. It was nothing short of a miracle, many believed, that Patrick Henry became a certified attorney. He was seen as something of a lively young playboy from the West, adept in dancing and music and a bit of a wit. What he wasn't was trained as an attorney, so he set about reading a law book. That's "a" law book. Singular. One book, obviously not an impressive education.

In order to obtain a license to practice law, a would-be attorney had to be examined by four practicing lawyers. All four would be chosen by the candidate himself, so that automatically gave the would-be lawyer a break. They would not sit as a board but interview the applicant separately. At least two practicing lawyers had to sign the applicant's license in order for him to pass.

One lawyer that Patrick Henry chose as an examiner was Robert Carter Nicholas, who immediately realized candidate Henry didn't know much about the law. However, Nicholas said he'd sign the application if the young man promised to study more law. Since Patrick Henry had read only one law book, *Coke upon Littleton,* studying "more law" wouldn't be difficult. He agreed.

Next on Henry's lawyer list: George Wythe, under whom Thomas Jefferson later read. A few questions, and Wythe also realized Patrick Henry hadn't much of an idea what the law was all about. Unlike Nicholas, however, Wythe refused to sign the license and quickly showed the would-be attorney the door.

Henry went to work on John Randolph, who initially was inclined to treat the applicant the way Wythe had. The two men spoke briefly, which was all that Randolph needed to realize two points: (1) Henry was lost as far as the law went, and (2) the young man had something going for him. Henry could, John Randolph perceived, put up a strong argument. "You have never seen these books," Randolph said, pointing to shelf after shelf of law books in his private library, "yet you are right and I am wrong." Randolph believed that if Patrick

Henry studied more than just a single textbook and worked hard at it, he could become a valuable member of Virginia's legal brotherhood.

Actually, it was a brotherhood that almost didn't exist. Lawyers charged such exorbitant fees and wielded such power that there were frequent outbreaks of violence against them in the Carolinas and New Jersey. They were denounced as "serpents, seven times more devouring than [the Stamp Act] who in their daily Practice are as Private Leaches [*sic*], sucking out our very Hearts Blood." Virginia almost outlawed lawyers, which some might argue would still be the best approach. Many members of the Virginia House of Burgesses were ill trained. Like Patrick Henry, they would read one or two books on law and consider themselves attorneys. In the late seventeenth century the royal governor complained that the Burgesses spent most of their time reviving old laws written by ill-trained lawyers. The governor wanted lawyers outlawed, but the assembly refused, probably because many of the members were lawyers themselves.

In any event, Patrick Henry talked both John Randolph and his brother Peyton into signing his lawyer's license. The brothers, according to Jefferson, did so with as much reluctance as good manners permitted. Still, Patrick Henry was now an attorney.

He was also, for a while, a slave holder; he inherited a half dozen from his father. When his house at a spot called Pine Slash burned down, Henry sold his slaves to pay for his store. He lost that money as well when the business failed.

Patrick Henry was tall but rather stooped and, early in life, had red hair. By the time he began practicing law, his hair was so thin, he generally wore a wig. His clothing was cheap and, unlike paintings showing him as flamboyant, Henry was anything but and generally was a bit unkempt. His mouth was too wide, and his forehead was noticeably wrinkled under blue eyes. He was said to be appealing, but that may have been more from personality and charm than good looks or grooming. In his early years he roamed the area around Virginia's Pamunkey River. While other boys his age went to school, Patrick Henry went hunting for ducks, geese, and deer. He was tutored at home by his Scottish father and an uncle, the Reverend Patrick Henry, who together taught young Patrick Latin and Greek. Actually, he pretended to be far less educated than he was, and it even fooled Thomas Jefferson for a while. "Naiteral parts," Henry would say, "is better than all the larnin' on yearth."

The Hanover County courthouse, where Patrick Henry practiced law, sits across the road from a tavern the young man once owned, which may or may not be a coincidence. The tavern is about eighteen miles north of Richmond and now houses a dinner theatre.

It was in that courthouse that Patrick Henry leapt into prominence. An Anglican minister, the Reverend James Maury, sued Hanover County. Reverend Maury had earlier been Thomas Jefferson's tutor.

It was the so-called Parson's Cause, involving an old law that set a minister's salary in terms of the value of tobacco. It was a reminder that clergymen were paid by the colony. In 1748 the Virginia House of Burgesses fixed a clergyman's salary at sixteen thousand pounds of tobacco a year—worth about four hundred pounds in British sterling at the time. If town officials (that is, vestrymen) did not pay that much, they could be sued for damages. The king had ratified the law, and after that only he could undo it.

Eight years later, tobacco output was down, and the Burgesses regretted being so generous to the clergy. With crops even worse in 1758, the assembly amended the law to force clergymen to accept the colony's depreciated paper money at the rate of two pence for every pound of tobacco—that is, two pennies. That meant Reverend Maury and his fellow preachers got only about a third of what the law originally guaranteed them.

A clergyman took the issue to court, won, and was awarded damages amounting to double his regular pay. Hearing that, Maury filed a similar suit in the Hanover County courthouse.

Courts then being about the same as courts are now, it took a year and a half to come to trial. When it did, in November 1763, Maury won his case. The court ruled that the king had signed the original law but had never agreed to its repeal; therefore, the town council—the vestry—had acted illegally in not paying Maury as much as it should have. So far, so good, for Reverend Maury. The court set a second hearing to assess damages.

In a quirk of the law, while the vestrymen would have to pay Maury's salary, Hanover County deputy sheriff Thomas Johnson would be fined for not collecting the quota of tobacco the reverend was due. Johnson couldn't find any of the area's more distinguished attorneys to take his side of the argument, but Patrick Henry said he would. Henry was only twenty-four years old and figuratively was untried and was literally inexperienced. He did, however, have the advantage of being the presiding judge's son.

On the morning of Reverend Maury's damages hearing, wealthy planters from the area crowded the courtroom to root for their money, so to speak. Nearly two dozen clergymen were there as well. Patrick Henry's preacher uncle wasn't among them. Like Patrick, his uncle was one of the so-called "new lights" from the Great Awakening. Patrick himself had reveled in the Great Awakening, especially in the flamboyant oratory of the preachers who took their message throughout the colonies. While the established Anglican Church disliked this flamboyancy, it greatly impressed young Patrick Henry.

Patrick had asked his uncle not to attend the penalty hearings. "I shall be obliged to say some hard things of the clergy," he'd warned, "and I am unwilling to give pain to your feelings." He lived up to his warning.

Not only was Patrick Henry's father the judge at the hearing, the jury picked that morning had not come from gentlemen of the town, as was usually done. To find jurors, Parson Maury later complained, the sheriff "went out among the vulgar herd" hanging around the village green. Among that herd was Patrick Henry's cousin and a couple of other "new lights."

Maury's attorney was a three-hundred-pound Irishman named Peter Lyons. Noted for his refined courtroom manner, he praised the Anglican clergy and called on the jury to award Maury £300 in back pay. Then it was Patrick Henry's turn, and at first his words came slowly. So slow, indeed, were his arguments following the eloquent Lyons that people began looking away from Henry. Even the judge seemed shamed by his son's lack of speaking ability. Not for long, however. Henry seemed to change, to glow with an inner fire. He stood taller and walked about more gracefully. His words took on a chilling polish.

Patrick Henry said the king and the people had a binding contract, and that same king was duty bound to protect his people. The Two Penny Act of 1758 was a valid law. In nullifying a law passed by the Burgesses, the council—that is, the crown—had been guilty of "misrule or tyranny." When that happened, the king ceased being a father of his people and degenerated into a tyrant.

Peter Lyons rose from his chair: "The gentleman has spoken treason, and I am astonished that your worships can hear it without emotion or any mark of dissatisfaction." Around the room there were other cries: "Treason! Treason!" All of which would sound familiar to Henry later in life.

Then Henry took on the Anglican clergy. A parson, he said, should set an example for unselfishness; he should not want more than his parishioners. Did a clergyman who grasped for more serve God or himself? "Do they feed the hungry and clothe the naked? Oh, no, gentlemen." Shame, Henry cried, shame on pulpit greed.

These rapacious harpies would, were their power equal to their will, snatch from the hearth of their honest parishioner his last hoe-cake,* from the widow and her orphan children her last milch cow! The last bed—nay, the last blanket—from the lying-in woman!

Clergymen had come to support Reverend Maury but now rose and left the courthouse, whether in shame, disgust, or fear isn't clear. Henry continued for another hour. He concluded by saying the jurors were not required to award *any* damages at all to Reverend Maury. They could, however, if they so chose, give him something nominal, say, a farthing.

After Patrick Henry's stirring argument, there really wasn't much doubt how the jury would vote. The members adjourned outside for a brief conference, then returned to the courtroom to announce their decision. Awarding Parson Maury only a farthing would be too

---

* A corn cake, originally prepared by slaves during breaks while in the field. They were cooked on the blades of hoes used for weeding, thus the name "hoe-cake."

insulting, they announced. Instead, they gave him *four* farthings, worth a total of about a penny. Judge Henry gaveled the session closed, and spectators carried his son the attorney out of court on their shoulders.

The Parson's Cause made Patrick Henry's legal career. Within a year he had nearly two hundred clients, rich and poor. Treason? Far from it. Not now; he was the people's hero. Two years later there would be another cry of treason against Patrick Henry, and once again he would be proclaimed the people's hero.

Patrick Henry was a brand-new member of the House of Burgesses when he rose to speak in favor of a series of resolutions that he'd introduced against the Stamp Act. It was May 30, 1765, and only thirty-nine of the House's 116 members were present. A few spectators watched from a lobby, one of them—an unidentified Frenchman in Williamsburg—stood next to young Thomas Jefferson, taking notes. His is the only known written eyewitness account of one of America's most famous moments.

It would be fifty years and a revolution away before anyone tried to reconstruct what Patrick Henry said that day and what later happened. That reconstruction would be by Henry's early biographer, William Wirt, who claimed that Henry was the first to speak out against King George.

In a letter to the *Weekly Register* on February 13, 1818, John Adams "recommended these hints to the consideration of Mr. Wirt, whose life of Henry I have read with great delight." Patrick Henry, wrote Adams with more than a hint of jealousy, "did not 'give the first impulse to the ball of independence,'" as Wirt claimed. It would be years, Adams said, "before the name of Mr. Henry was heard beyond the limits of Virginia."

William Wirt's version has Patrick Henry speaking in harsh but eloquent words.

> Resolved, That the first adventurers and settlers . . . brought with them [all] the Privileges, Franchises, and Immunities that have at any Time been held, enjoyed, and possessed by the People of Great Britain.

These rights, Wirt quoted Henry as saying, "have been confirmed" by two royal charters.

> Resolved, That the Taxation of the People by themselves or by Persons chosen by themselves to represent them . . . is the distinguishing Characteristic of British Freedom. . . .
>
> Resolved, [that the people of Virginia] have uninterruptedly enjoyed the Right of being thus governed by their own Assembly, in the Article of their Taxes and internal Police. . . .
>
> Resolved, therefore, That [the people of Virginia] are not bound to yield obedience to any law or ordinance whatever designed to impose any Taxation Whatsoever upon them, other than the Laws and Ordinances of the General Assembly. . . .

As he got down to the point, Wirt wrote, Henry "exclaimed in a voice of thunder, and with the look of God: 'Cesar had his Brutus, Charles the First his Cromwell, and George the Third. . . .'"

House Speaker James Robinson interrupted with a cry of "Treason! Treason!" But Henry completed his sentence: "—may profit by their example!" And looking at Robinson, he added, "If this be treason, make the most of it!"

This is the version we remember from those fleeting moments of high school or college history, but it may not be quite accurate. According to that visiting Frenchman, Patrick Henry took a much more even—and apologetic—tone. Years later Thomas Jefferson corroborated much of what the visitor wrote down in 1765.

The Frenchman's account turned up in the Newport, Rhode Island, *Mercury* on June 24. In it he claimed that as Henry spoke, he'd taken notes on the flyleaf of an old law book:

> May the 30th. Set out Early from Halfway house in the [sedan] Chair and broke fast at York, arived at williamsburg at 12, where I saw three Negroes hanging in the galous [gallows] for having robbed Mr. Waltho [Nathaniel Walhoe, Clerk of the Council] of 300ps. I went immediately to the Assembly which was seting, where I was entertained with very strong Debates Concerning Dutys that the parlement wants to lay on the Amer-

ican Colonys, which they Call or Stile stamp Dutys. Shortly after I Came in one of the members stood up and said he had
read that in former times tarquin and Julus had their Brutus,
Charles had his Cromwell, and Did not Doubt but some good
American would stand up in favour of his Country, but (says he)
in a more moderate manner, and was going to Continue, when
the speaker of the house rose and Said, he, the last that one of
the members of the house was loyal Enough to stop him, before he had gone so far, upon which the Same member stood
up again (his name is henery) and said that if he had afronted
the speaker, or the house, he was ready to ask pardon, and he
would shew his loyalty to his majesty King G. the third at the
Expence of the last Drop of his blood . . . but, again if he said
any thing wrong, he beged the speaker and the house pardon.
some other Members stood up and backed him, on which that
afaire was droped.

The day Patrick Henry spoke, whether with fire or apologies, the
shorthanded House apparently approved his resolves—the Virginia
Resolves as they came to be known—and put them on the record.
More or less. Not all of them showed up in the actual journals of the
House of Burgesses.

By the following day Henry had left town. More conservative members of the House of Burgesses had rushed back in, looking for ways
to have the vote expunged. Apparently they found it. Peter Randolph, a distant relative of Thomas Jefferson's, found a precedent
in the records, and when a fuller House—without Patrick Henry present and with some others changing their minds—convened on the
afternoon of the 31st, it changed Henry's resolves. According to the
Frenchman's account:

> May the 31st. I returned to the assembly today, and heard
> very hot Debates stil about the Stamp Dutys. The whole house
> was for Entering resolves on the records but they Differed much
> with regard the Contents or purport thereof. Some were for
> shewing their resentment to the highest. one of the resolves
> that these proposed, was that any person that would offer to sus-
> tain that the parlement of Engl'd had a right to impose or lay

any tax or Dutys whats'r on the american Colonys, without the Consent of the inhabitants thereof, Should be looked upon as a traitor and Deemed an Enemy to this Country. there were some others to the same purpose, and the majority was for En-tring these resolves, upon which the Governor Disolved the assembly, which hinderd their proceedings.

The Frenchman apparently got the dates wrong. Part of what he records as occurring on May 31, according to other accounts, took place on the 30th, meaning he may have written the whole thing several days after the events. That, of course, could have altered his memory and changed his interpretation of the events.

There are even questions of how many resolves Patrick Henry introduced and how many were passed that first day. Governor Francis Fauquier, who wasn't present for the May 30 debate, wrote in a letter to London that four resolves were passed. He added that a fifth resolve failed because it was "thought the most offensive" and claimed that some House members had two other resolves ready to go, but didn't offer them in the heated debate, certain they would not be approved.

Burgesses records show no mention of the Stamp Act under May 31, and the next time there's any mention of them, only four of Patrick Henry's Virginia Resolves of 1765 show up on the record. When Henry died, however, he left behind a paper on which five were written. Four of them are, more or less, as they stand in the journals. The fifth, according to the Henry papers, reads:

> Resolved Therefore that the General Assembly of this Colony have the only and sole exclusive Right and Power to lay Taxes and Impositions upon the Inhabitants of this Colony; and that every Attempt to vest such Power in any other Person or Persons whatsoever, other than the General Assembly aforesaid, has a manifest Tendency to destroy British as well as American Freedom.

It is this fifth resolve that was the most important. Only the colony's legislature could tax that colony; no one else, nobody else—be it king or Parliament—could tax Americans except Americans.

25

However it happened, however many resolves were actually passed, Patrick Henry's reputation exploded. From that moment on he was known as a fire breather who would, and did, take on King George III. A few weeks later the Virginia Resolves—including the nobody-taxes-us-but-us clause—found their way into newspapers around the country. And the pot of Revolutionary stew began to simmer.

The best known portrait of Patrick Henry isn't of Henry at all. It was painted sixteen years after the statesman-orator died, by an artist who based the picture on one of Captain James Cook. It was said Henry looked something like Captain Cook. Several years later, a real portrait—a miniature—of Henry was discovered. He looked nothing like the captain.

In Boston, on August 14, 1765, a crowd hanged in effigy the man who had been appointed stamp distributor for Massachusetts, Andrew Oliver. He was Lieutenant Governor Thomas Hutchinson's brother-in-law. Hanging beside the effigy of Oliver was a boot with a devil crawling out of it—it represented Lord Bute, King George III's former minister, whom the crowd believed to be one of the Stamp Act's instigators. Hutchinson ordered the sheriff to tear down the effigy, but the officer said that he couldn't; the crowd was so large that he wouldn't even try. Later the crowd did the job itself, taking down the effigy and boot and carrying them past the house where Governor Sir Francis Bernard was meeting with his council. "Forty or fifty tradesmen, decently dressed" made up the mob. They marched down to a dock where Oliver had recently constructed a building, rumor had it, that would be the tax office. The mob tore down the building, then they paraded to Oliver's house. The would-be tax collector and his family weren't there but had left friends to defend his house.

In something akin to street theater, the crowd beheaded and abused the effigy, broke all the windows in Oliver's house, and dragged the headless effigy to nearby Fort Hill, where they stomped on it and burned it in a bonfire. The crowd returned to Oliver's house, where it beat down the doors and smashed a mirror said to be the largest in North America.

That was too much for Governor Bernard. He ordered the colonel of the colonial militia to beat an alarm. The colonel refused, saying that any drummer who tried to sound an alarm likely would have his drum smashed. Besides, the colonel added, he doubted he could find a drummer willing to try; they were all in the crowd smashing Oliver's house.

When Governor Bernard realized how things were going, he took refuge in Castle William, a fortress in the middle of Boston harbor under protection of British regular troops. Lieutenant Governor Hutchinson, however, tried to protect Oliver. He and the sheriff went back to the tax man's house and attempted to disperse the mob. Pelted with rocks and stones, Hutchinson and the sheriff ran off into the night.

The following day a group of citizens called on Oliver, demanding he resign his post. Oliver hadn't even received his commission, and he had no stamps; but he agreed to write London, requesting permission to quit.

Eleven days later another crowd gathered. Half broke off to march on the home of the well-known Tory William Story, who was deputy register of the admiralty court. They attacked his house and destroyed most of his private and public papers.

The second half of the mob went looking for the comptroller of customs, Benjamin Hollowell. He wasn't home, so the mob smashed his windows, tore down the shutters on his house, broke through the doors, smashed his furniture, and carried off his books and papers. Thoughtfully, they also emptied out his wine cellar for him.

The two halves of the mob reunited in front of Thomas Hutchinson's empty house. The lieutenant governor had been warned that the mob was coming, so he and his family had a quick afternoon tea, then left. The mob slashed paintings on the walls and battered in the walls themselves. They broke windows and doors, burned furniture, and tore out every partition in the house. They stole money and personal belongings, they ripped out wainscoting and roof tiles and left the house a total wreck. They even removed the cupola from the top of the house and destroyed fruit trees in the garden. They ransacked Hutchinson's papers dealing with the Stamp Act and pitched into the night air a manuscript Hutchinson had been working on for years, a history of the Massachusetts Bay Colony. The mob burned much of everything it could find.

Patriot Josiah Quincy Jr., wrote that it was "really amazing. I could not think that so much work could be done by 20 skillful men in 50 hours—all in the Dark." And he added:

> O ye Sons of Popularity: beware lest a Thirst of Applause move you groundlessly to inflame the Minds of the People. . . . Who, that sees the Fury and Instability of the Populace, but would seek Protection under the ARM OF POWER? . . . Who that beholds the Tyranny and Oppression of arbitrary Power, but would lose his life in the Defence of LIBERTY?

John Adams also was worried by the mob action. To be treated as Oliver had, Adams wrote in his diary, was "a very atrocious violation of the Peace and of dangerous Tendency and Consequence."

In September 1765, as time for enforcement of the Stamp Act neared, Virginia's Richard Henry Lee (who, it will be remembered, once wanted to be Virginia's stamp commissioner) launched a series of protests. To further desecrate an effigy of George Mercer (the man who had beaten Lee out of the job of tax collector), Lee hung signs around the mannequin's neck, proclaiming "Money is my God" and "Slavery I love." The effigy was placed in a hangman's cart and accompanied by a group of costumed men, who actually were Lee's own slaves. Acting as both judge and confessor, Lee had the effigy hanged, not once but twice in two days. Then he burned it.

This all occurred before George Mercer even arrived in America, so he was rather surprised when he reached Williamsburg two days before the tax was to take effect. It was a time when the meeting of the colony's general court crowded the normally sleepy town, and as Mercer arrived, he was met by a crowd before he could even make his way to his lodgings. Immediately they demanded he resign from a job he hadn't yet begun. Asking for time to consult friends, he walked to a nearby coffeehouse. The antitax crowd followed closely behind. Among his friends at the coffeehouse was Virginia's acting governor, Francis Fauquier. When the mob—the "mercantile people," Fauquier later put it—prepared to seize Mercer, Fauquier stepped forward, took him by the arm, and walked him to the governor's mansion, the governor's palace, as it's called today.

By the following morning Mercer's mind was made up. He resigned without ever taking office. That left Fauquier with the stamps but no stamp distributor to enforce the law. "I will do my duty to His Majesty," he wrote Parliament, "and save the stamps from being destroyed . . . tho' I can by no means answer for the success of my endeavours. . . ."

In Pennsylvania, as much to bolster his own place in politics as anything else, Benjamin Franklin nominated his crony John Hughes to be distributor of stamps. Hughes wrote a friend, Anthony Wayne (the same "Mad Anthony" Wayne of the coming war) that the appointment had given the colony's proprietary party, which Hughes and Franklin opposed, "no small pain." By early September, however, Hughes had begun receiving suggestions that he resign. He wrote Franklin in London that

> you are now from Letter to Letter to suppose each may be the last you will receive from your old Friend, as the Spirit of Flame of Rebellion is got to a high Pitch amongst the North Americans; and it seems to me that a sort of Frenzy or Madness has got hold of the People of all Ranks, that I fancy some Lives will be lost before this Fire is put out . . . [When] a Mob is on foot, my Life and Interest may fall a Sacrifice to an infatuated Multitude.

Patrick Henry's Virginia Resolves sounded "an alarum [*sic*] bell to the disaffected," and Massachusetts summoned its sister colonies to send delegates to a congress in New York City to discuss and debate the Stamp Act. Only nine colonies responded. Still, Americans were moving toward union, and the Stamp Act Congress of October 1765 was an important step. In tones somewhat less vehement than Patrick Henry's Virginia Resolves, delegates passed a set of resolutions asking Parliament to repeal the Stamp Act.

Benjamin Franklin, meanwhile, had been working both sides of the street, so to speak. He argued in London against the act, but his enemies claimed Franklin had actually been the architect of the Stamp Act. Not only had he pushed through the name of a close friend to be tax commissioner, but when a first attempt to repeal the act was rejected, Benjamin Franklin went out and bought stamps for his own printing company. Hearing this, an angry mob back in Philadelphia threatened to burn down his house. Franklin's wife, Deborah, sent their daughter to New Jersey, then barricaded herself inside with guns and ammunition.

Eventually Franklin realized that the Stamp Act would be the defining cause for the American colonies, and he worked to have it repealed.

Benjamin Franklin worked as a London lobbyist for several colonies, eventually becoming an agent for all of them. In February 1766, Franklin appeared before Parliament. Speaking against the Stamp Act, he answered 174 questions over a four-hour period. True, some of the questions were "softballs," lobbed at him by an ally, but others were not.

Q. Are not the Colonies, from their circumstances, very able to pay the stamp-duty?

A. In my opinion, there is not gold and silver enough in the Colonies to pay the stamp-duty for one year. . . .

Q. Do you think it right America should be protected by this country, and pay no part of the expense?

A. That is not the case. The Colonies raised, clothed, and paid, during the last war, near 25,000 men, and spent many millions.

Q. Were you not reimbursed by Parliament?

A. We were reimbursed what, in your opinion, we had advanced beyond what might be reasonably expected from us; and it was a very small part of what we spent. Pennsylvania, in particular, disbursed about £500,000, and the reimbursements, in the whole, did not exceed £60,000. . . .

When asked if he still held Parliament in the same respect he had, Franklin answered:

A. No; it is greatly lessened.

Q. To what cause is that owing?

A. To a concurrence of causes; the restraints lately laid on their trade, by which the bringing of foreign gold and silver into the colonies was prevented; the prohibition of making paper money among themselves; and then demanding a new and heavy tax by stamps; taking away at the same time, trials by juries, and refusing to receive & hear their humble petitions.

Q. Do you think the people of America would submit to pay the stamp-duty, if it was moderated . . . ?

A. No; they will never submit to it. . . .

Q. If the stamp-act should be repealed, would it induce the assemblies of America to acknowledge the rights of Parliament to tax them, and would they erase [the Virginia] resolutions?

A. No, never. . . .

In an effort to nullify the Stamp Act, semisecret colonial societies sprang up. The largest—and it had branches in every colony—was the Sons of Liberty. They took the name from an antitax speech made by Isaac Barré in the British House of Commons. Barré was a military officer and member of Parliament, where he championed the American cause.

Wilkes-Barre, Pennsylvania, is named after Barré and John Wilkes, whose name loomed large in the Revolution as a symbol of the "rights of Englishmen." A distant descendant of John Wilkes looms large in the blacker annals of history: John Wilkes Booth, the man who assassinated Abraham Lincoln.

On February 7, 1765, Isaac Barré attacked the proposed Stamp Act and referred to his American cousins who opposed it as "these sons of liberty." The name stuck. Sometimes these radicals did more harm than good and quite frequently did it violently. Samuel Adams recruited members for the Boston branch of the Sons of Liberty largely "from the wharfingers [wharf owners or managers], artisans, and shipyard workers of North Boston."

Two hundred years before similar actions by Vietnam-era protestors, Adams's Sons of Liberty burned the records of the British vice-admiralty court. Often actions performed by the Sons were not very different from those of modern-day street gangs. The Sons were so powerful that not many people openly objected to their actions, and they literally got away with murder.

They didn't invent the practice, but Sons of Liberty made liberal use of tar and feathers and in riding their opponents out of town on a rail. The punishment itself went back to the Middle Ages, where it was used by followers of England's King Richard. British mobs used tarring and feathering to intimidate anyone they disliked, and America's Sons of Liberty took up the practice. As adopted by the Sons, and shown in a famous painting that depicts events surrounding the tea controversy, anyone accused of "Paying the Exciseman"—the tax man—might be stripped of his clothing, have hot tar poured over him, and be plastered with feathers. At the very least, the tarred and feathered victim wound up with third-degree burns that took weeks or months from which to recover. Sometimes victims died of their injuries.

In Boston, among other things, the Sons of Liberty had publicity working for them. Benjamin Edes, the editor of the *Boston Gazette*, was an active member in the group. In addition, they had Ebenezer Macintosh (or McIntosh), widely known "a common street brawler." He was a "colorful, impressive" man who was given to wearing a blue and gold uniform, strutting around with a cane, and using a speaking trumpet (an eighteenth-century bullhorn) to yell out his orders. The crowds gave him the mock title "First Captain General of Liberty Tree." A month after his "coronation" as captain general, Macintosh was being called "governor." Samuel Adams and James Otis manipulated Macintosh into recruiting his South End mob as supporters of the Patriot cause. It didn't take too much manipulating, since it was from this group that the British navy frequently pressed sailors into unwilling service. Macintosh and his South End mobsters, under the guise of the Sons of Liberty, burned royal officials in effigy, trashed Tory-owned houses, and finally ran the royal governor out of town.

In 1770, a North Carolina group calling themselves Regulators protested against the western counties' underrepresentation in the colonial legislature. In several small incidents the Regulators took back a horse that had been seized by authorities when its owner refused to pay taxes, and they shot up the home of a colonial official who opposed them. It came to a head in 1771, when Governor William Tryon defeated a virtually unarmed army of about two thousand rebels. Tryon had six of the rebels publicly hanged, then forced the sixty-five hundred residents of Hillsboro to swear allegiance to the Crown. Many of the defeated Regulators migrated westward and became known as the Over the Mountain Men in what later became Tennessee.

Hoping to stop smuggling, which is to say, hoping to collect taxes on goods being brought to America illegally, the armed schooner *Gaspee* was stationed in Narragansett Bay, Rhode Island. "A dispatch from Boston confirms our worst fears," a witness remembered merchant John Brown saying, "Montagu intends to patrol Narragansett Bay." John Montagu was the fourth Earl of Sandwich, and in 1772, First Lord of the Admiralty.* He had ordered a crackdown on smuggling around the coves and inlets of Narragansett Bay, which meant cracking down on virtually half the population of Rhode Island, because smuggling was their main occupation.

Montagu hand-picked Lieutenant William Dudingston. "Given the chance," Dudingston told the sandwich-making Montagu, "I will seize smugglers and treat them for what they are—pirates." As soon as he reached American waters, he began making the colonists' ships dip their colors in salute to every British gunboat. Any ship failing to salute His Majesty's ships would have a shot fired across its bows. That was bad enough, but Dudingston wanted to put an end to the smugglers' livelihood.

John Brown didn't take kindly to that and decided to do something about this brash British lieutenant. Brown outfitted a fast boat;

---

* Captain Cook later named what are now the Hawaiian Islands after him, calling them the Sandwich Islands. The sandwich itself was named after Montagu, who, according to the *Oxford Universal Dictionary,* in 1762, "once spent twenty-four hours at the gaming-table without other food than beef sandwiches." Such is fame.

manned it with veterans of the area, who knew every nook and cranny and reef around Providence; and sent it out into Narragansett Bay as if it were loaded with contraband, which, incidentally, it was not. The idea was to lure the *Gaspee* into an area unfamiliar to its crew.

Dudingston fell for it, suddenly finding himself the hunted instead of the hunter. On June 9, he accidentally grounded the *Gaspee* at a place now called, appropriately enough, Gaspee Point. The schooner hit so hard, the British officer realized he had no chance of floating his ship until the next high tide; all he could do was wait.

Less than an hour after sunset the crew heard the sounds of muffled oars and realized they might be boarded. What they didn't realize was that John Brown had eight boatloads of conspirators ready to attack—not Brown, however. It seems he was too fat to fit in a boat and carry out his own plan. But never mind, there were enough willing hands to do the job. At least sixty colonials boarded the mud-stuck *Gaspee* and attacked the crew. They nearly broke Dudingston's arm when they forced him belowdecks. When he reached for a pistol, the boarders shot Dudingston in the groin.

After taking everything they wanted from the British vessel, the colonials carried the profusely bleeding Dudingston ashore and set his ship on fire. As the ship burned to the waterline, crowds in nearby Providence cheered.

A board of inquiry was set up to locate the culprits and send them to England for trial. In London the King's Privy Council authorized a reward of £500 for information leading to the capture of the leaders in what they termed "Colonial acts of piracy." But no witness ever came forward to collect the reward. The closest Rhode Island's royal officials came to arresting anyone was when they took depositions from three men who admitted playing minor roles in the burning of the *Gaspee*. Everyone else, it seems, had an almost total loss of memory of events of that night.

The Royal Navy, however, was certain it could catch the criminals and sent one of its largest ships of the line to Newport to transport the men to England. In fact, the ship's commander, Sir James Wallace, thought he'd found out who likely had led the attack, local resident Abraham Whipple, so Wallace sent a message: "You, Abraham

Whipple, on June 9, 1772, burned His Majesty's vessel the *Gaspee*, and I will hang you at the yard-arm."

To which Whipple replied: "Sir, always catch your man before you hang him!"

Wallace never did, and a year after the *Gaspee* was burned, the commission gave up the chase and adjourned in frustration. John Brown, Abraham Whipple, and five or six dozen other men had defied the British navy.

The *Gaspee* affair caused consternation on both sides of the Atlantic, gaining some friends for the colonists' cause, and losing others. For Loyalists who had worked to enforce the Navigation Acts, the cause now seemed lost. As the Rhode Island collector of customs put it: "There's an end to collecting a revenue and enforcing the acts of trade." Which is just what the Americans had hoped for.

CHAPTER TWO

Founding Fathers, Part One:
A Farmer, a Lawyer, and a Sage*

There never was a good war or a bad peace.
—Benjamin Franklin

Trying the effects of electricity on paralytic persons ... a young boy's sight was perfectly restored. ... I observed the iris to contract and dilate as well as ever.
—*Boston Weekly News-Letter,* May 28, 1752

Thomas Jefferson once proposed that the United States hold annual elections on February 29. Obviously, everyone makes mistakes.

A farmer, a lawyer, and a sage. Thomas Jefferson was all three, plus a surveyor, a musician, a lover of fine wine, a lover of women, an architect who never finished his own home, and a politician whose voice was so weak he could barely be heard. In addition, he was a writer and a revolutionary. As president, Thomas Jefferson went against his own principles. He believed in small government, strictly adhering to the Constitution; yet, as president he more than doubled the size of the country by a purchase which may be unconstitutional.

He was born on April 12 (old style, April 2), 1743, at Shadwell, in Virginia. It was the smallest but most important of his father Peter Jefferson's tobacco plantations, only four hundred acres. Peter Jefferson had bought the land for the price of a bowl of punch, and it's still called "the Punchbowl Tract."

Tom's mother, Jan Randolph, was a member of one of the most distinguished Virginia families. Her family, Jefferson wrote in his Au-

---

* From *1776*. Music and lyrics by Sherman Edwards, book by Peter Stone. Copyright 1969.

tobiography, "trace their pedigree far back in England and Scotland, to which let every one ascribe the faith and merit he chooses." Jefferson's father's ancestors were Welch.

Peter Jefferson was a successful farmer, a surveyor, and a member of the Virginia House of Burgesses. He was virtually uneducated—"quite neglected," his son wrote—but Peter Jefferson saw to it that Tom had all the advantages of the family's position: books, horses, the good life at several plantations, and a classical education.

The elder Jefferson died in 1757, when Tom was only fourteen, "leaving my mother a widow, who lived till 1776, with six daughters and two sons, myself the elder." On his father's death Thomas Jefferson was left 2,750 acres of land and two hundred slaves. From the start the man who later wrote that all men are created equal was more equal than most others. Thomas Jefferson was among the richest men in the country.

"Mr. Jefferson was six feet two and a half inches high, well proportioned, and straight as a gun"—the words of Captain Edmund Bacon, who worked as Jefferson's Monticello overseer for twenty years. "He was like a fine horse," Bacon continued.

> He had no surplus flesh. He had an iron constitution and was very strong. He had a machine for measuring strength. There were very few men that I have seen try it that were as strong in the arms as his son-in-law, Colonel Thomas Mann Randolph; but Mr. Jefferson was stronger than he.

Admitted to the bar in 1767, Jefferson quickly became a successful attorney, perhaps as much due to family connections and friends as to any ability. Two years later he was elected to the House of Burgesses and served in every succeeding assembly for eight years. As a freshman lawmaker Jefferson had his kinsman, Richard Bland, introduce a bill allowing the emancipation of slaves. Bland "was denounced as an enemy of his country."

The man who wrote some of the most stirring antislavery words in our history obviously had trouble assimilating his own message. Throughout his life Thomas Jefferson waffled on the issue of slavery. In 1769, the same year he proposed that slaveholders be allowed to emancipate their slaves, Sandy, a mulatto carpenter slave Jefferson had inherited from his father, stole a horse and ran away. Jefferson placed an ad in the *Virginia Gazette,* offering a reward for Sandy: "He is greatly addicted to drink, and when drunk is insolent and disorderly, in his conversation he swears much, and in his behavior is artful and knavish." Sandy was caught and three years later Jefferson sold him for £100.

A year after Sandy ran away, Jefferson acted as attorney on behalf of another mulatto slave who had run off. The man claimed his grandmother had been the daughter of a slave father and a white woman; Virginia law had it that the status of a slave was determined not by color but by the status of the mother (in this case, white), and that the mother's descendants also should be free. In defending the man, Jefferson used words he would virtually repeat six years later: "Under the law of nature, all men are born free, and every one comes into the world with a right to his own person, which includes the liberty of moving and using it at his own will." This was too radical for the time and place, and he—and certainly his client—lost. The opposing attorney, the lawyer for the slave owner, was Jefferson's old mentor, George Wythe.

On New Year's Day 1772, Jefferson married Martha Wayles Skelton, a young widow later described by their granddaughter, Ellen Randolph Coolidge, as "very beautiful . . . a little above middle height, with a lithe and exquisitely formed figure . . . a model of graceful and queenlike carriage." Jefferson's great-granddaughter, Sarah Randolph, wrote that Martha had hazel eyes, auburn hair, and exquisite skin.

Less than a year after Tom and Martha married, her father, John Wayles, died, leaving his daughter and therefore his son-in-law, Thomas Jefferson, 135 slaves. One of them was Elizabeth, or Betty, Hemings. Apparently Betty had been John Wayles's concubine with whom he had at least two children, James and Sally Hemings, who also were part of the Martha/Tom inheritance.

Betty Hemings had an African mother (her name is unknown) and an English father, a sea captain, who apparently stopped off just long enough to impregnate her. Former slave Isaac Jefferson described his mother, Betty, as "a bright mulatto woman," adding that her daughter "Sally [was] mighty near white."

The Jeffersons' marriage appears to have been happy but marked perhaps by more pregnancies than the somewhat frail Martha could physically handle. She died in 1782, at the age of thirty-three, after bearing six children (only two survived to adulthood) and suffering several miscarriages.

Moments before Martha died, Jefferson was "led from the room almost in a state of insensibility." When his family got him into his library, he fainted. It would be weeks before Jefferson could resume even a semblance of a normal life. Finally his sense of duty to a new nation pulled him out of his grief. In 1784, he became America's first minister to France. It was in Paris that he apparently became sexually involved with one of his slaves. This became the longest-lasting blot on Thomas Jefferson's life and one we still find abhorrently compelling.

In 1787, Jefferson's slave Sally Hemings accompanied his daughter Polly to France. At the most, Sally was fourteen, and apparently not your average fourteen-year-old black slave. When Abigail Adams met Polly and Sally's ship in England, to say the least, the outspoken Abigail was surprised as hell; she thought that Polly was being accompanied from Virginia by a middle-aged woman. Instead, she found the escort was the teenage Sally, an adolescent beauty.

Sally Hemings's mother, Betty, it will be remembered, was half white and half black. If Sally's father was John Wayles, that made Sally three-fourths white and one-fourth black. As late as the 1960s she would have been legally listed in her home state of Virginia as "Negro." Jefferson would later refer to Sally as a "quarteron," his version of the word "quadroon." Importantly Sally was a half sister to Jefferson's late wife, Martha, and looked very much like her, her color not much darker than Martha's. Isaac Jefferson remembered Sally as "handsome, [with] long straight hair down her back." Nature and Jefferson's libido apparently got together in Sally Hemings's bed.

The first public report of a Jefferson-Hemings affair came on September 1, 1802. In the *Richmond Recorder*, hack political writer James Thomson Callender claimed that

> it is well known ... that the man, whom it delighteth the people to honor, keeps and for many years has kept, as his concubine, one of his slaves. Her name is Sally. The name of her el-

dest son is Tom. His features are said to bear a striking though sable resemblance to those of the president himself. The boy is ten or twelve years of age.

Callender, whom Jefferson biographer Dumas Malone described as "a traitorous and truculent scoundrel," himself described Sally as a common slut "from which the debauchee, that prowls for prey in the purlieus of St. Giles, would have shrunk with horror."

Apparently no newspaper of the day dared send a reporter to Monticello to check out Callender's tale; however—sight unseen—newspapers in Boston and Philadelphia claimed that Jefferson's daughters were "weeping to see a *negress* installed in the place of their mother."

The anti-Jefferson Massachusetts State Legislature even used the miscegenation claim as one of many charges when it staged a mock impeachment trial in 1805. At the time Jefferson indirectly denied the charges.

At first Jefferson's friend Abigail Adams rejected the charges and was "really mortified" by Callender's claims. Later, she believed them and scolded Jefferson:

> This Sir I considered a personal injury. This was the Sword that cut asunder the Gordian knot, which could not be untied by all the efforts of party Spirit, by rivalship by Jealousy or any other malignant fiend.

Historian Fawn Brodie revived the story in 1974's *Thomas Jefferson: An Intimate History,* quoting oral tradition handed down among Sally Hemings's descendants. Novelist Barbara Chase-Riboud's story of Tom and Sally—lust running rampant between mansion and slave quarters—was scorned by many.

Jefferson supporters seemed to see him as pristine and above sex, not just with a slave, but with anyone other than his wife. Dumas Malone offered the theory that it wasn't Thomas Jefferson who fathered Sally Hemings's children but Tom's favorite nephew, Peter Carr.

Now, however, newly performed DNA tests apparently prove that Sally Hemings shared her bed (and the parenthood of at least one child) with Thomas Jefferson. Tufts University professor of pathology Eugene A. Foster "analysed DNA from the Y chromosomes of five male-line descendants of two sons of [Thomas Jefferson]'s paternal uncle, Field Jefferson" along with that of the sons of two of Sally Hemings's children, Thomas Woodson and Easton Hemings Jefferson. Altogether Foster conducted tests on fourteen male descendants of Jefferson's and Hemings's families.

The Y chromosome is passed unchanged from father to son and, except for occasional mutation, "can reveal whether individuals are likely to be male-line relatives." According to Foster, his evidence shows that "it is at least 100 times more likely [that] the president was the father of Easton Hemings Jefferson than if someone unrelated was the father."

Easton was Sally Hemings's last child and was born in 1808, six years after James Callender's article claiming Tom Jefferson had fathered a child by Sally. In fact, Easton was born three years after Massachusetts's mock impeachment trial, which used Callender's charges as "evidence."

Dr. Foster admits that he cannot "completely rule out other explanations of [his] findings." After all, since the Y chromosome must come from the male, and because Thomas Jefferson's only recognized son died at birth, there is no male-line relative. In Foster's own words: "We have not provided absolute proof of anything. What we have done is throw the weight of probability very strongly in one direction." Interestingly, the child James Callender claimed was Jefferson's offspring likely was not related to Jefferson, according to Eugene Foster.

The DNA evidence is more than enough for some who appear ready to erase Jefferson's name from the Declaration of Independence, tear down Monticello, and turn the Jefferson Memorial into something akin to a pizza parlor. Annette Gordon-Reed says such reconsideration is about time too. The New York Law School professor, the author of *Thomas Jefferson and Sally Hemings: An American Controversy*, believes that "If people had accepted [Callender's] story, [Jefferson] never would have become an icon." She adds that "I don't think he would have been on Mount Rushmore," much less the American nickel.

For some African American critics, the DNA evidence is testimony that Jefferson was, at best, a hypocrite; after all, in the 1780s—about the time he began his relationship with Sally Hemings—he backed away from a leadership position in the antislavery movement. He expressed fears that emancipation would lead to racial mixing and amalgamation. For many white historians, however, this new evidence merely underscores Jefferson's tortured position on slavery—a personal contradiction and something of an internal game of emotional hide-and-seek.

History may not find it comfortable to forgive Jefferson, but it is equally difficult and uncomfortable to apply modern mores and standards to two-hundred-year-old events. Jefferson was, after all, a product of his time. Any marble pedestal he sat on, we built for him.

Thomas Jefferson never freed Sally Hemings. That was arranged by his daughter after his death. His defenders say that because of existing Virginia law, a freed slave had to leave the state within a year of manumission. The master of Monticello—Sally Hemings's owner and lover, the father of at least one of her children—could not bring himself to do that. Tom would have had to deprive himself of one he loved, Sally Hemings. Jefferson's daughter, however, petitioned the state legislature to allow Sally to remain in the state. She died in 1835.

As a practicing lawyer, Jefferson also served as justice of the peace and parish vestryman. However, he seemed almost afraid to speak before large crowds and had, it was said, a "morbid rage of debate." Instead, he began making a name for himself as a writer. He wasn't much of a military man, and his closest tie to being a soldier was as a lieutenant in the Albermarle County militia.

Jefferson gave up practicing law in 1774. It was the same year he wrote his *Summary View of the Rights of America,* a widely read and widely acclaimed attack on the British Crown. His name did not appear on the *Summary,* but it soon became known that he was its author. By the end of the year it had been reprinted in both Philadelphia and London, twenty-three pages in all. At the time of its writing Thomas Jefferson was not yet set on independence from the mother country, but thoughts he used in the *Summary* later became part of the Declaration of Independence.

It was more radical than most other pamphlets of the time. There were inaccuracies, and Jefferson later tried to correct them. Jefferson's chief biographer, Dumas Malone, says it was "written in the white heat of indignation against the coercive acts of the British government."

> We are willing, on our part, to sacrifice everything which reason can ask, to the restoration of that tranquility for which all must wish. On their part, let them be ready to establish union on a generous plan. Let them name their terms, but let them be just. . . .
> The God who gave us life, gave us liberty at the same time; the hand of force may destroy, but cannot disjoin them. This, Sire, is our last, our determined resolution.

In Boston, in 1721, community leaders argued whether to inoculate the town's citizens against smallpox. It was a relatively radical idea and drew on some of the hysteria that rocked Salem with witchcraft charges thirty years earlier. Inoculation was seen by some as something of the black arts. Mobs tarred and feathered those whose beliefs didn't match their own. Proponents and opponents even took out their frustration on their opposite numbers' dogs, killing family pets to spite those on the other side.

Among the town leaders favoring inoculation were members of a well-to-do family named Boylston. A member of that family would become the mother of one President of the United States, the grandmother of another, and the revered ancestor of a family whose prominence stretched into the twentieth century. Susanna Boylston was twenty-two years old when her family led the fight for inoculation against smallpox. She was thirty-five when she married a not so prominent farmer and seller of malt, John Adams of Braintree, now Quincy, Massachusetts. Not *the* John Adams. Susanna and John Adams's son, John Adams the Patriot, was born in 1735, the first of three children.

The younger Adams was contemptuous of the thought that a man's place in society should be determined by his lineage, but he once admitted that his father's marriage into the more prominent Boylston family lifted his own family out of small town obscurity. In that position John Adams became an important lawyer in the Boston area, a prime mover for independence, a major voice in securing a peace treaty with Britain, the first vice president, and the second president of the United States.

In today's television-driven politics, Adams might not have gotten very far. He was shorter than average, more than just a little on the chubby side, pretty much bald, and he irritated the hell out of a lot of people, even, he admitted, his friends.

Violence came quickly and not unexpectedly in the quarrel between Britain and the colonies. There were several instances of American crowds and British troops arguing, fighting, and killing. In 1765, mobs rioted against the Stamp Act in Boston, Rhode Island, and Connecticut; in New York, Philadelphia, Williamsburg, and Charleston. More followed. In many cases they were given a semi-religious air.

In Connecticut young boys enacted a kind of mummer's play. That is, stumbling and staggering and acting out a mock religious liturgy. Instead of the usual object of worship, they substituted names: "We beseech thee, O Cromwell, to hear us." Instead of "O holy, blessed, and glorious Trinity," they substituted "O Chatham [that is, William Pitt], Wilkes, and Franklin, have mercy upon us!"

In Dumfries, Virginia, a crowd mounted an effigy of the stamp master backward on a horse, with a copy of the Stamp Act "tied round its neck with a halter." Then, in partly religious language, they scolded the effigy, caned it, whipped it, then hanged and burned it.

In North Carolina an effigy of the stamp master was displayed alongside that of a wife murderer, letting the crowd draw the desired conclusion that one was as bad as the other. In New York, on the night of November 1, 1765, crowds began carrying effigies of Stamp Act notables but ended the night by "destroy[ing] several bawdy houses." Go figure.

Often, to evade prosecution, radical newspaper accounts of disturbances substituted the word *boy* for *young men*. The traditional Pope's Day—November 5—was marked with parades celebrating the attempt in 1605 to assassinate King James, Guy Fawkes's infamous gunpowder plot. In America the celebration changed into something quite different. Those in authority, no matter what religion, often were knocked about, their homes and dignity violated, and effigies of the individuals were dressed in breeches* of the type worn by babies. In Boston Pope's Day usually turned into a brawl between South End and North End gangs, with rocks, stones, and barrel staves used as weapons. Newspaper accounts usually referred to the participants as "children," "young People, Servants, and Negroes," or "negroes & other servants." "Child" was more an expression of kinship, than age.

On August 11, 1766, British troops and American colonists clashed in New York. Local leader Isaac Sears was wounded when the redcoats destroyed a liberty pole patriots had set up. Sears was a well-known smuggler whom New Yorkers had nicknamed "King Sears." He was the leader of nearly every New York mob action for a decade. When word of the clashes at Lexington and Concord reached New York, Sears led a group of more than 360 patriots in seizing arms and ammunition from the British arsenal and taking over customshouses.

For years the British military tried to capture Isaac Sears, but they never could, and he continued working for independence and smuggling English goods into the colonies. In 1786, while on a business trip in China, Sears caught a fever and died. He's buried in Canton, China.

Benjamin Franklin was a major force in having Parliament repeal the Stamp Act. In testimony before the House of Commons on February 13, 1766, Franklin convinced Parliament that what the American colonists objected to was "internal" taxes. It was, as historian Edmund S. Morgan writes, "a dangerous piece of deception with unfortunate after effects."

Tories sneered at the idea that the colonies could get together on anything, but in October 1765, representatives met in New York to work jointly against the Stamp Act. Not all colonies sent represen-

---

* During the later French Revolution, wearing trousers became so important that the term sans-culottes, "without gentlemen's breeches," came to signify the working class, and thus a radical affiliation.

tatives, however. New Hampshire, North Carolina, Georgia, Nova Scotia, and Virginia were never represented at the Stamp Act Congress, and several delegations—South Carolina, Connecticut, and New York—were not given permission to sign any agreement that might be reached. The Pennsylvania Assembly finally appointed delegates after a bitter struggle in which members voted fifteen to fourteen to join the Congress.

On October 19, the Stamp Act Congress adopted a moderate proposal made by John Dickinson of Pennsylvania to be submitted to the British government: A Declaration of Rights and Grievances. It was far less radical than Patrick Henry's Virginia Resolves, less than the action demanded in Massachusetts by James Otis. It was, however, the first time the colonies came even close to seeing eye to eye on the need for concerted resistance against Britain's encroachments on colonial rights.

Every one of the royally appointed stamp-tax collectors resigned. Only in Georgia, because of its strong royal governor, Sir James Wright, did stamped documents hit the marketplace. Even Wright wasn't very enthusiastic about the stamps, and six days after the stamps went on sale, he stopped all business requiring their use.

On March 18, 1766, Parliament repealed the Stamp Act, and initially people cheered. In New York they declared a joint celebration: repeal of the Stamp Act and the king's birthday. The New York legislature even voted to build a fifteen-foot-high equestrian statue of King George III.

The statue lasted less than a decade. On July 9, 1776, after the Declaration of Independence was read to a crowd, the Sons of Liberty looped ropes around the statue and pulled it to the ground. Someone sawed off the king's head and stuck it onto a stake; the rest of the statue was dragged off to be melted down for bullets. Isaac Bangs was on hand for the ceremonial dethroning.

> In it were 4,000 pounds of lead, and a man undertook to take 10 oz. of gold from the superficies, as both [king] and horse were covered with gold leaf. The lead, we hear, is to be run up into musketballs for the use of the Yankees, when it is hoped that the emanations from the leaden George will make as

deep impressions in the bodies of some of his redcoated and Tory subjects, and that they will do the same execution in poisoning and destroying them as the superabundant emanations of the folly and pretended goodness of the real George have made upon their minds, which have effectually poisoned and destroyed their souls . . .

It was estimated that forty-two thousand bullets could be manufactured from the statue, in order that, as Ebenezer Hazard of New York put it, "the bloody-backs could have melted Majesty fired into them."

On the same day Parliament repealed the Stamp Act, it approved the Declaratory Act asserting Parliament's and the king's right to make laws binding on the colonies. That set John Adams wondering "whether [Parliament] will lay a tax in consequence of that resolution." As he soon found out, the answer was yes. They were called the Townshend Acts.

Charles Townshend was the second son of the Third Viscount Townshend. He had been adamant that the Stamp Act remain. His lively speeches in Parliament and equally lively activities outside chambers earned him the nickname "Champagne Charlie." William Pitt believed that Townshend was a weak leader, and he tried to oust Champagne Charlie from parliamentary control as chancellor of the exchequer. It didn't work. Townshend set out to prove that Pitt, now Lord Chatham, was wrong; Champagne Charlie would push through another American tax. Only this one, because Franklin and others had claimed the colonies objected only to internal taxes, would be different.

The Townshend Acts passed easily on June 29, 1767, fifteen months after the Stamp Act was repealed. The new law imposed duties on various imports and took away the colonial legislatures' single control over royal governors; now it would be Parliament, not the legislatures, that would pay the governors' salaries. The Townshend Acts also tightened up the colonies' slack system of customs, set up admiralty courts that could try smugglers without a jury, and made it easier for customs officials to obtain Writs of Assistance, which would make it easier for British officials to obtain search warrants.

• • •

The 1766 brawl in which mob leader Isaac Sears was wounded came about when the New York Assembly refused Governor Sir Henry Moore's request to provide funds to house British troops. A new law provided for quartering troops in inns, alehouses, and unoccupied dwellings. A second quartering act legalized quartering of troops in occupied homes and buildings.

Tension mounted between American citizens and British troops. In 1768, during an argument with a British naval officer, a Rhode Island man was killed.

In August, Massachusetts Governor Sir Francis Bernard (pronounced BURR-nurd) received word that British troops were being sent to Boston. Afraid the city might revolt if the troops arrived unannounced, Bernard leaked the information. The leak, however, only made things worse for Bernard; it gave Patriot leaders time to prepare for the soldiers' arrival. Rather than forestall opposition, the governor's miscalculation helped spread it.

Immediately lines were drawn between British regular troops and American radicals. It didn't help when a British officer came upon a group of slaves and shouted, "Go home and cut your masters' throats." Captain John Wilson of the Fifty-ninth apparently had been struck by the incongruity of slaves in a society proclaiming so loudly for liberty. Wilson told the slaves: "I'll treat your masters, and come to me to run my Sword thro' their Hearts."

Years later John Adams recalled the military activity of the soldiers in Boston. They paraded daily in Brattle Square outside his house, waking his family with "the Spirt Stirring Drum, and the Earpiercing fife."

Protests continued, and in January 1770 redcoats and Patriots battled on New York's Golden Hill. Some thirty or forty bayonet-wielding soldiers battled citizens armed with cutlasses and clubs. No deaths, but both sides counted several who were seriously wounded.

February 22, 1770, was a school holiday in Boston, and "many hundreds" of young boys "collected before the Shop of [Loyalist] Mr. Lillie . . . and a carved head upon a Pole was fixed before his Shop Door." The mob then accosted another Loyalist, Ebenezer Richardson, and chased him to his house. The boys tried to break in, and

Richardson opened a window and fired his musket into the crowd. One youngster, eleven-year-old Christopher Seider, was hit and killed.

His death became the occasion for a giant ceremonial funeral and parade, and "a vast Number" of boys let out of school for the occasion preceded his coffin along the way.

On March 2, 1770, three British soldiers stationed in Boston did what soldiers of most armies have done, went looking for part-time work. In this case they went to a ropewalk. Boston, being a naval town, had several ropewalks, where men made ropes for ships and boats.

At this ropewalk a free black journeyman taunted the soldiers, and a fight broke out. One of the participants in the fight was a man named Sam Gray, and he would be heard from again.

When they lost at fisticuffs, the soldiers returned to their barracks for reinforcements, then went back for revenge. A dozen hands at the ropewalk, along with a dozen or so workers from neighboring establishments, once more defeated the redcoats. The soldiers said they would be back to avenge the insult.

On the afternoon of the fifth, a group of British soldiers left their barracks and beat up several citizens before they could be driven off.

About nine o'clock that night, Boston church bells suddenly began to clang in alarm. Members of a lawyers club, John Adams among them, were meeting on the town's south side, and when they heard the bells, they assumed Boston was on fire. Fire was not an unlikely event, considering that nearly every house and shop was made of wood and open fireplaces were used not only for heating but for cooking as well. Ten years earlier, fire wiped out most of the buildings from Milk Street to King Street, from the present Devonshire Street to Kirby Street, then the water's edge. When church bells rang out as they did that Monday evening, organized volunteers rushed to the scene. They carried leather buckets with them—the law mandated that every house have a leather fire bucket ready—to help douse the fire. Volunteers would man wheeled pumper engines strategically located throughout the city. It was a foregone conclusion that a home fire likely would destroy the house, so many running to a fire carried bags to help victims remove whatever belongings they could.

Grabbing their hats and cloaks, the lawyers ran off to help fight the expected flames. This time, however, the cries of "Fire, fire!" weren't meant to help put out a conflagration. If anything, they were meant to encourage one. Instead of a fire, the lawyers learned that British soldiers had fired into a crowd of American citizens. It was the Boston Massacre. Three Boston-area citizens had been killed. Two others would die from wounds, and a half dozen more were wounded by British soldiers. John Adams later observed that the men who lost their lives that night were "the most obscure and inconsiderable that have been found upon the continent."

The three who died at the scene were James Caldwell (whom, today, we'd classify as homeless, but who was, Samuel Adams claimed, a young mariner schooling himself "in the art of Navigation"), Samuel Maverick (a seventeen-year-old apprentice to ivory turner Isaac Greenwood, Maverick lived with his widowed mother at her boardinghouse), and a runaway slave who, two centuries later, became a celebrity, Crispus Attucks. John Adams referred to Attucks as "Michael Johnson," and apparently that's what the man called himself at the time. A year before, however, an advertisement ran in the *Boston Gazette:*

> RAN-away from his Master, William Brown of Framingham, on the 30th of Sept. last, a Molatto Fellow, about 27 Years of age, named CRISPUS, six feet two inches high, short curl'd Hair, his Knees nearer together than common; had on a light color'd Bearskin Coat.
>
> Whoever shall take up said Run-away, and convey him to his abovesaid Master, shall have Ten Pounds Reward, and all necessary charges paid.

Apparently the runaway slave was never captured; the reward was never claimed. At the time there were more than 5,200 free blacks in the Boston area, and it's likely that the runaway slave found a home among them.

Attucks, or Johnson, generally was known as "the mulatto" and apparently was half white and half Negro or Indian. Perhaps all Indian, since some accounts say he was a full-blooded member of the Natick tribe living near Framingham. He himself claimed to have come from New Providence in the Bahamas. After the shooting on March 5, Attucks became known as the first martyr of the American Revolution. Maybe he wasn't a martyr. He may have been not so much a hero as a half-drunk bully who was caught in the middle of it all.

The martyr-bully-drunk known as Johnson-Attucks was variously described as "stout" and "towering"; he stood at least six feet two and was massively built. He was said to be either in his late twenties or his late forties, which is to say we really don't know. Early that evening he was eating supper at Thomas Symmonds's (or Simmons) victualing house, what today would be called a diner. Off-duty British troops often used it as a hangout. Hearing the church bells chime, Attucks ran out into the night to join the crowd, a group of twenty to thirty sailors; most carried some kind of club or other weapon. They were, an observer claimed, "making a noise." Along the way Attucks found himself a cordwood stick about the thickness of a man's wrist.

Of the approximately three hundred members of the British army's Twenty-ninth Regiment, only thirty-six were five feet ten or taller; only four men were as tall as six feet. The average man of the Twenty-ninth was over thirty years old, medium height, and Irish. Crispus Attucks would have looked like a giant to the soldiers.

The regiment had arrived in Boston the previous October 1, marching into town with "Drums beating, Fifes playing, and Colours flying." Regular soldiers wore red coats, while drummers had yellow jackets. The ordinary infantrymen wore black white-laced three-cornered hats, while the elite troops, the grenadiers (as the name implies, originally they threw grenades or hand bombs) wore tall, distinctive, miter-shaped bearskin hats. Honoring King George III and his German family, grenadiers wore on the front of their tall hats emblems honoring the House of Hanover—a badge with a white horse and a motto that read: *Nec aspera terrent* ("They fear no difficulty"). In addition to their yellow coats, drummers (many of whom were black) wore bearskin capes with badge and motto.

At their necks officers wore crescent-shaped gorgets, a final remnant of the time when officers rode into battle wearing armor. Across their shoulders officers wore crimson sashes; they had swords on waist belts, and carried in their hands espontoons, ceremonial half-pikes. Grenadier officers carried carbinelike light flintlock muskets called fusils.

In all, an impressive sight, just as it was meant to be.

What really happened the night of the Boston Massacre is unclear. The results, however, are not. March 5, 1770, was a clear, cold night, with upward of a foot of packed snow on the ground. Patches of ice were broken into sharp shards where the snow had melted during the day and refroze. Near the center of old Boston was the town house, where the council and governor met; it corresponded to a city hall today. Nearby was the customs house, where the colony's official records were kept. The Main Guard, headquarters of the British forces in Boston, was to the south. Guards stood on either side of the building. Private Hugh White, of the Twenty-ninth Regiment, stood his post about thirty yards away, in a sentry box at the corner of King Street and Royal Lane.

Outside Private White's box at the customs house, the beginnings of a mob stood taunting the young soldier with barrel staves and clubs. One young man, a wigmaker's apprentice named Edward Garrick, yelled at Captain-Lieutenant John Goldfinch, one of White's officers who was passing by. "There goes the fellow that won't pay my master for dressing his hair," Garrick called out. Goldfinch walked on without replying. The British officer was a stingy, shifty man, Garrick screamed, and perhaps most important to the ensuing events, Garrick said Goldfinch was no gentleman. The sentry and the apprentice got into an argument over that point: Was Captain-Lieutenant Goldfinch a gentleman? The argument was a frivolous start to a deadly event.

It was dark outside the sentry box—it would be four more years before Boston installed streetlamps—and Private White dared Garrick: "Let me see your face."

"I am not ashamed to show my face," the apprentice said, and stuck his head into the sentry box. Not too smart. White hit Garrick with the butt of his musket. Dazed and crying, the young man ran off, crying that he'd been attacked. He ducked into a nearby shop doorway, and another guard, a sergeant, slashed at him with a bayonet. Together Private White and the sergeant walked back to the sentry box, taunted all the way with cries from a crowd of Garrick's fellow apprentices: "Bloody back!" and "Lousy rascal" and "Damned rascally scoundrel lobster son of a bitch." The louder they shouted, the larger the crowd grew.

Meanwhile, the man Edward Garrick had accused of not paying his bills and not being a gentleman was not far away, trying to calm things down. Captain-Lieutenant Goldfinch saw a group of British soldiers swatting away at snowballs another mob was throwing at them and ordered the troops back to their barracks. As the soldiers withdrew, the crowd threw more snowballs and cried out, "Cowards! Afraid to fight!"

Merchant Richard Palmes was a short man in a light greatcoat. He tried to act as a mediator between the troops and the crowd, which had begun small but now likely numbered more than four hundred. Palmes stopped a group of British officers and said he was surprised to see the troops out of their barracks after eight o'clock.

"Pray," one soldier asked Palmes, "do you mean to teach us our duty?"

"No, I do not," Palmes replied, "only to remind you of it."

As more snowballs flew through the air, an officer told the crowd to go home. Any soldier who had injured any citizen, he said, would be punished.

But the crowd continued to yell and throw ice-encrusted snowballs at the troops. Palmes again tried his hand at mediation. "Gentlemen," he said to the crowd, "you hear what the officers say, and you had better go home."

Some did, but others wanted to continue the action. "Let's go to the Main Guard," someone cried, and the mob swarmed down a nearby alley, huzzahing and beating the walls with their clubs. They stopped outside the Brazen Head, a shop owned by Tory William Jackson, who earlier had refused to sign a nonimportation agreement. Jackson himself wasn't home but was having dinner with his mother, who ran a boardinghouse.

Captain Thomas Preston of the Twenty-ninth Regiment, in fact, was one of Mrs. Jackson's boarders. Preston was a forty-year-old Irishman whose face was pitted from smallpox. A musician who regularly performed at Boston events, even the radicals called him "a sober, honest man and a good officer." On the night of the massacre, Preston was officer of the day.

Lieutenant James Basset, the Twenty-ninth's officer of the guard that night, had just turned twenty. He'd been commissioned through family influence at the age of twelve but had little experience.

It's unknown who was doing it—the Sons of Liberty likely had a hand in it—but church bells continued to peal and, in answer, the crowd continued to grow. Actually there were at least three crowds that night. One was busy jostling Private White, a second was taunting the officers at Murray's Barracks, and a third was gathering in Dock Square, where a mob of more than two hundred swirled and eddied. There were repeated cries of "Fire!"

The twenty-year-old owner of Boston's London Book-Store, Henry Knox, saw what was happening and approached Private White, urging the young soldier not to fire on the citizens. If he did fire, Knox said, he would die for it.

It didn't work. "Damn them," the soldier said to Knox. "If they molest me, I will fire."

Not all of the British troops forcibly quartered on Boston citizens were disliked. Private Hugh White's landlady back on Royal Exchange Lane was worried about the poor boy, so she asked a young neighbor, Jane Whitehouse, to check on White. Apparently Hugh had earlier, as the military term puts it, "fraternized with the enemy." He and Jane were well acquainted. As Jane ran up to Hugh, the young soldier reached out an arm to stop her. It was not safe there; the private told her, "Go home, or you'll be killed."

The noise along King Street increased, and there were more cries of "Fire!" Officers Basset and Preston went up on the roof of a nearby building just to make certain there really was no fire. What they saw was their sentries being harassed and endangered. Mobs of club- and rock-carrying men railed at the young guards. Another officer of the Twenty-ninth, Captain Jeremiah French, was in the British Coffee House on King Street when the crowd rushed by. Like Preston and Basset, he climbed to the roof of the shop to get a better view. French was shocked at what he saw and later testified that the mob contained no less "than 300 or 400 people."

The size and temper of the crowd apparently even shocked the leadership of the Sons of Liberty. They began mixing with the crowds, trying to persuade the people to return to their homes, but they had little effect. Earlier they had roused the crowd to a high fever, and now the mob refused to leave. Among the cries and shouts, one call frequently was heard coming from the mob: "Damn you, why don't you fire? You dare not fire. Fire and be damned." They believed the troops would not fire, because it technically was not a riot.

As Shakespeare put it: "Ah, there's the rub." It was not a riot unless some official said it was a riot. Under Massachusetts's riot act, based primarily on England's riot act, if there were twelve or more men armed with weapons or clubs, or fifty unarmed men, a civil officer (anyone from a magistrate to a constable would do) could call on the crowd to disperse. This civil officer, then, would figuratively if not literally "read them the riot act," a definition of which has little in common with today's saying, "read 'em the riot act." Once a civil officer read this proclamation, the crowd was required to disperse within an hour; if they did not, they would be liable to forfeiture to the king of all their lands and goods, they would be flogged with up to thirty-nine lashes, and they would be given a year's prison sentence, during which they would again be flogged every three months.

To top it off, when the hour they were given to disperse expired, other citizens, including the military, would be authorized to seize and hold any members of the mob still hanging around. And—once again, here lies Mr. Shakespeare's "rub"—a citizen or soldier injuring or even killing a recalcitrant mob member was not liable for the incident—no criminal liability, no civil liability.

So, the theory goes: A justice of the peace reads the riot act to the mob; the mob gets an hour to disperse; after the hour's up, the area becomes something of a free-fire zone, with troops not held liable for anything they do to the crowd.

The growing mob in Boston that night felt certain the British guards would not shoot them no matter how they were taunted; they even said just that—"Why do you not fire? Damn you, you dare not fire. Fire and be damned."

After all, no official had appeared to "read the riot act." When justice of the peace James Murray tried to reach the mob and do his duty, he himself was attacked; the crowds abandoned their snowball assault on the guards long enough to pelt Murray with the missiles and send him scurrying down Pudding Lane (now Devonshire Street).

Other justices of the peace tried unsuccessfully to do their duty. In an earlier incident, two such men, Richard Dana and Samuel Pemberton, were attacked. They weren't going to try again.

There's a modern aphorism that might apply to the Boston mob: If an automobile and a locomotive race toward a railroad crossing, in case of a tie, the train wins. No way can a relatively small car match a multiton train. In this analogy the army was the train; the mob was the car.

The streets of Boston echoed to the knell of church bells, the beat of drums, and cries of "To arms! To arms! Turn out with your guns!" The Boston mob that March night was certain the British soldiers would not fire on them unless someone read the riot act, and the mob wasn't about to let anybody read the act. That's where the two sides tied, so to speak. One side had rocks and clubs and snowballs and were certain they would not be shot. The other side had muskets and bayonets and were afraid they would be attacked. Tie game, citizens lose.

Henry Knox tried "everything in his power to prevent mischief on this occasion." When he couldn't keep the mob away from Private White, Knox approached Captain Preston. "For God's sake," he said, "take care of your men. If they fire, you die."

"I am sensible [i.e., aware] of it," Preston replied, and rushed to rejoin his men, who were beginning to load their muskets, to charge the firing pans, and to ram the cartridges home. Meanwhile, the crowd noise rose—calling, jeering, cursing, and crying out—and still the church bells pealed.

Preston ordered Private White to join him and march back to the Main Guard, but the crowd continued to press around them. "Damn you, you sons of bitches, fire," the mob chanted. "You can't kill us."

Preston ordered the guard to form a roughly semicircular single line, one end at a hitching post next to a corner of the customs house, and the other on the street side of the sentry box; and while it's not certain exactly where each individual was, the guards in general were about a body's width apart.

Captain Preston stood in front, between the soldiers and the mob; if the guards fired then, the captain himself likely would be hit. He shouted and tried to convince the crowd to disperse. The mob advanced "to the points of the Bayonets . . . endeavouring to close with the soldiers." The crowd was so large and so near the soldiers "you could not get your hat betwixt them and the bayonets." Whatever civil authority that could have saved the day stayed in hiding.

"Why do you not fire?" "Damn you, fire." "You dare not fire." "Fire and be damned." The soldiers thrust (the term is "payed") at the crowd with their bayonets.

"Do not run, my lad," Sam Gray said, clapping Joseph Hinkley on the back. "They dare not fire." Gray, who had been part of the original ropewalk battle three days earlier, pushed through the crowd, giving others the same message. But Gray was flushed with exuberance, possibly buoyed by too much alcohol and probably weighted down with too little knowledge of reality. Certainly, the guards would not use what today authorities refer to as "excessive force."

Twice Captain Preston was asked if his men had loaded their muskets, and twice he said yes. When asked if he intended to order the soldiers to fire, Preston replied, "By no means, by no means."

Someone in the crowd threw a club at the soldiers, striking Grenadier Private Hugh Montgomery hard enough to knock the guard onto his back. Another version says Montgomery was hit by a piece of ice, fell back, and slipped on the ice when he tried to stand. When Private Montgomery stood up, he was angry and frustrated. Captain Preston may have cried out, "Do not *fire!* Do not *fire!*" but if he did, Private Montgomery apparently mistook his words and pulled his weapon's trigger. The musket fired, but no one seemed to have been hit. Someone—either Crispus Attucks or former peacemaker Richard Palmes—swung wildly at Montgomery with a club, hitting the soldier on the left arm. The attacker then struck at Preston. Grenadier Montgomery thrust his bayonet at the attacker, who ran off. Right into another group of soldiers, and their bayonets began flicking at him—his arms, his chest—until finally he was stabbed once in the upper arm and a second time on the side of his chest.

Montgomery's shot caused the crowd to push back a bit, away from the guard's semicircular line. Private Matthew Kilroy raised his musket to fire, but a member of the mob, Edward Gambett Langford, cried, "God damn you, don't fire." Kilroy apparently didn't take aim, but he did fire, and Samuel Gray, who had been standing with his hands in his pockets, fell to the pavement. He had, according to another member of the mob, a hole in his head "as big as my hand."

A third shot, then two more, and more. In uneven bursts, not volley fire, eleven men were shot; three died instantly, one only a few hours later, and a fifth several days later. Six others were wounded and survived.

Colonial propagandist Samuel Adams claimed Crispus Attucks not only did not start the dance of death that night but, rather, was himself attacked by the guards. Attucks, Adams said, "was leaning on a stick when he fell, which certainly was not a threatening posture." Another eyewitness later testified that Attucks had lunged, cudgel in hand, for the soldiers and was hit twice in the chest. The witness was Andrew, a slave owned by Boston selectman Oliver Wendell. Andrew believed that Crispus Attucks was one of the primary agitators. "This stout man," he testified, "held the bayonet with his left hand, and twitched it and cried, kill the dogs, knock them over. This was the general cry; the people then crowded in." The court asked who the "stout man" was, and Andrew replied, "I thought, and still think, it was the mulatto who was shot."

James Caldwell, the homeless youth and would-be sailor, was hit twice, one bullet passing through his body and a second lodging in his shoulder. Young Samuel Maverick ran away as fast as he could, but he wasn't fast enough, and a ricocheting bullet struck him in the chest. Robert Paterson was shot in the wrist as he tried to raise his hand. Patrick Carr was crossing King Street when a shot "went through his right hip & tore away part of the backbone & greatly injured the hip bone." Edward Payne was shot in the right arm as he calmly stood in his own doorway. Kit Monk was standing with his friend James Brewer, when Monk seemed to stumble. "Are you wounded?" Brewer asked. Monk said, "Yes," but Brewer didn't believe him; "You are only frightened," Brewer said.

Even with bodies lying in the street, people didn't believe the soldiers had shot into the crowd, or if they had shot, it was with blank cartridges. The bodies weren't really bodies, but people "had been scared and run away, and left their greatcoats behind them."

The soldiers reloaded and recocked their muskets. "Stop firing!" Preston shouted. "Do not fire!"

The crowd began pushing toward the dead and dying lying in the street. Benjamin Burdick looked down at the dead body of Crispus Attucks and said to Captain Preston, "I want to see some faces, that I may swear to another day." "Perhaps, sir, you may," the captain said.

The scene in front of the customs house cleared rapidly, the bodies of the dead and wounded carried off. Gray's corpse was taken to Dr. Loring's house, but the door was locked, and his body was left on the steps. Carr was still alive and was taken to a house in Fitch's Alley, and someone went for a doctor. The large body of the man who called himself Michael Johnson, but who became known as the runaway slave Crispus Attucks, was heavy. Volunteers struggled with difficulty to bear him to the Royal Exchange tavern across the street from the customs house. James Caldwell's body was dragged away and eventually would be taken to Faneuil Hall along with Attucks. Young Samuel Maverick was coughing up blood and was helped to his mother's boardinghouse; he died a few hours later.

Captain Preston formed up the soldiers and marched them off to the Main Guard, where he put them in a formation known as "street firings," designed to permit small groups of soldiers to control large mobs. If a guard fired his musket, he would move to the rear, and a second man would take his place, fire, then he, too, would move to the rear.

Throughout the night there were cries in the street, "To arms! To arms!" Drums continued to be beat, summoning the militia; church bells changed from frantic pealing to doleful tolling, but there were no other incidents that night. The Boston Massacre was over.

Almost immediately the Sons of Liberty began using the Boston Massacre for propaganda. Artist John Copley's half brother, Henry Pelham, quickly produced a drawing of the scene. It can be labeled only an interpretation; there are too many things that are incorrect for the drawing to be called anything else. Just as soon as Pelham drew the scene, Paul Revere stole it. And once again that's the only word that can be used: stole. In turning it into a money-making engraving, Revere didn't even give Pelham credit for the drawing, not to mention paying him for it when it appeared as an engraving in the *Boston Gazette* a week later.

Paul Revere soon took the black-and-white drawing and vividly colored it, using a lot of red in doing so. He wrote a verse telling the Patriot version of the event:

> Unhappy Boston. See thy Sons deplore,
> Thy hallow'd Walls besmeared with guiltless Gore:
> While faithless P-n [Preston] and his savage Bands,
> With murd'rous Rancour Stretch their bloody Hands,
> Like fierce Barbarians grinning o'er their Prey;
> Approve the Carnage and enjoy the Day.

The engraving shows seven British soldiers, neatly lined up, being ordered by Captain Preston to fire. There were eight musketmen, but for some reason the eighth is left out. In Revere's version of the incident, British soldiers shoot completely innocent Bostonians. Muskets blaze away, but the crowd is docile, hopeless innocents retreating backward, except, of course, for the two men who apparently are dead and three others who are wounded and are being carried off by friends. Colonists' bodies are bleeding, but there's no sign of the clubs they carried; they're actually trying to stop the soldiers' bullets by holding up their hands. A mongrel dog calmly looks at the soldiers, and the scene is clouded with musket smoke.

Actually, there isn't much about the engraving that is correct. A sign on the right says BUTCHER'S HALL, and there was no such place. It claims two people (Christopher Monk and John Clark) were mortally wounded; they were wounded but both survived. Crispus Attucks, who may or may not have been Michael Johnson, and who later was called the first martyr of the American Revolution, is not even pictured in the etching.

> The Patriot's copious Tears for each are shed,
> A glorious Tribute which embalms the Dead.

The drawing Paul purloined and engraved turned out to be a money-maker for Revere. It became perhaps the most effective piece of propaganda in the Revolution. Forget the errors the artist and engraver each made. British troops had killed American citizens who were peacefully rioting!

A broadside printed later listed the names of those who had died:

AMERICANS
Bear In Remembrance
The HORRID MASSACRE
Perpetrated in King Street, Boston
New-England,
On the Evening of March the Fifth, 1770
When five of your fellow countrymen,
Gray, Maverick, Caldwell, Attucks,
and Carr,
Lay wallowing in their Gore!
M U R D E R E D!
And SIX others badly wounded!
By a Party of the XXIXth Regiment!
Under the command of Capt. Tho. Preston

Another broadside in the March 12, 1770, issue of the *Boston Gazette* shows five black coffins with the initials of those who died in the massacre.

In his engraving of the massacre, Paul Revere claimed the British soldiers might find a legal loophole, but he warned:

[Know that] fate summons to that awful Goal,
Where Justice strips the Murd'rer of his Soul;
Should venal C-ts [courts] the scandal of the Land,
Snatch the relentless Villain from her Hand,
Keen Execrations on this Plate inscrib'd,
Shall reach a Judge who never can be brib'd.

Slowly, after the shooting the mob drifted off, which surprised leaders of the Sons of Liberty. They had already sent out express riders to neighboring towns, rousing inhabitants out of their beds and urging them to rush to Boston's defense. Now, with the crisis momentarily over, many who had armed themselves and were on their way to town were stopped; there was no further danger that night. A barrel of oil had been sent to Beacon Hill to be set on fire to draw more help. Now it, too, wasn't needed and was removed.

With Boston quiet for the moment, Governor Thomas Hutchinson sent for the town's selectmen—that is, the justices of the peace—to take depositions from eyewitnesses. Lieutenant Basset and Captain Preston were brought before the hastily assembled group. It was 2:00 A.M. One witness swore that he had been within two feet of Preston when the muskets went off, and that Preston had given the order to fire. Another witness agreed that Preston not only had ordered his men to fire but cursed them when they didn't immediately react to his command. Other witnesses claimed the captain had said "fire," but they weren't certain whether it was part of an order such as "do not fire." By 3:00 A.M. the justices had heard enough. They released Basset but ordered Preston arrested. Later in the morning the eight soldiers who had fired on the crowd surrendered and were also jailed.

In the weeks following the massacre, the Sons of Liberty virtually controlled Boston. That "Matchiavel of Chaos," Samuel Adams, had long predicted trouble if the British army garrisoned Boston. The blood of those killed in the massacre still stained the King Street snow, while Adams drew up plans to press his advantage; he clearly wanted to drive the British troops out of Boston.

Mercy Otis Warren, the sister of one Patriot leader and wife of another, wrote of the Boston Massacre: "No previous outrage had given a general alarm, as the commotion on the fifth of March 1770." It created, she added, "a resentment which emboldened the timid" and "determined the wavering."

Newspaper reports of the massacre circulated quickly. The *Boston Gazette* ran a headline: BLOODY WORK IN BOSTON. A black border of mourning surrounded the report of the deaths. The *New Hampshire Gazette* picked up the Boston report:

> The Streets of BOSTON have already been bathed with the BLOOD of innocent Americans! Shed by the execrable Hands of the diabolical Tools of Tyrants!—O AMERICANS! this BLOOD calls aloud for VENGEANCE!

• • •

Other newspapers, however, treated the shooting with more caution. The *New York Journal* published a concise factual report but did not use the word "massacre." The editor even added that "as a Printer, he is of no Party, but equally at the Services of all."

On March 16, a dispatch boat left for London. It carried with it reports of the rowdiness and shootings, along with depositions of antimilitary and anticustoms activities. In London these reports were gathered into a pamphlet by radical leader James Bowdoin: *A Fair Account of the Late Disturbances at Boston.* In it Bowdoin assumed that as he put it, the "Horrid Massacre" was the result of sinister plots by the soldiers and military commissioners. He claimed erroneously that "a number of guns (cannon) were fired from the Custom House." The *Account* carried several of the depositions gathered by officials in Boston, including one by customs employee Thomas Greenwood, who blamed the citizens of Boston; however, a footnote was added by the town committee, urging that "no credit ought to be given to his [Greenwood's] deposition."

From New England to Georgia, preachers told their congregations about the shootings, and colonists soon believed that the British had made a cold-blooded attack upon the innocent citizens of Boston.

On the night of the massacre John Adams was thinking more of his family than of mob action. Rushing out of his lawyers' meeting, he passed through the center of the city, where he saw a company of British soldiers with fixed bayonets. They were marching toward where the problem seemed to be.

Adams, however, hurried home; his wife, Abigail, was expecting another child.

The next morning Adams was sitting in his office, when James Forrest, a local merchant, knocked on his door with a message from Captain Thomas Preston. The officer was having trouble getting an attorney to represent him and wanted Adams to serve as his legal counsel. Actually it was Acting Governor Thomas Hutchinson's idea that Adams and Josiah Quincy represent Captain Preston.

Preceding by two hundred years the words every lawyer in every television soap opera mouths, John Adams said, "Counsel ought to be the very last thing that an accused Person should want [i.e.,lack] in a free Country." Always, he added, "the bar ought to be independent and partial, under every circumstance."

With the first sign of unrest, Hutchinson had tried to calm the crowd. He immediately went to King Street and stood on the balcony of Town House to tell the crowd that "the law shall have its course." He added, "I will live and die by the law." Hutchinson's actions may have saved Boston from a massacre far more serious and deadly than it had been.

It's not certain why Hutchinson wanted Adams to defend the soldiers. It may be that he'd seen Adams in court before, or it could have been meant as a trick. If Adams, at the insistence of the Sons of Liberty, turned down the job, it would be proof the Patriots were putting politics above the law and indiscretion above justice. In any event, Adams and his partner, Josiah Quincy, agreed to defend the redcoats. They were opposed by a team of more experienced lawyers headed by the solicitor-general of Massachusetts, Samuel Quincy, Josiah's more conservative older brother.

Loyalists arranged to have the town of Boston pay for the prosecution of Captain Preston and the soldiers. Defense attorney John Adams turned down a retainer, but then, in asking him to defend Preston, conservative merchant James Forrest had offered him only a retainer of one guinea. Now a guinea is a pound. In Boston at the time, £100 was the equivalent of about $135, which makes the offered one guinea retainer worth about $1.35.

With public sentiment running the way it was, Samuel Adams and the Sons of Liberty believed cousin John didn't have much of a chance, and they pressed for an early trial. Hutchinson, on the other hand, tried to delay things. Samuel Adams and the boys won, perhaps because a "vast concourse of people" marched into court and demanded the judges push the thing along.

John and Samuel Adams, although second cousins, were at opposite ends of the same political party. John had been educated as a lawyer and, generally, tried to work within the system. Samuel studied law to please his father, it was said, but gave it up to please his mother. Sam was a republican in principle and manners, once saying that independence from Great Britain "had been the first wish of m[my] heart seven years before the war." When John took the defense of British troops after the Boston Massacre, Samuel warned, "This affair will end the political hopes of the little man from Braintree."

Nearly every colonial American town had a "liberty tree," which served as a rallying point for anti-British rallies and provided limbs from which to hang in effigy government officials who might not share the patriots' feelings. It was also a place where notices could be nailed and complaints made about king and Parliament. In towns where there was no conveniently located large tree, the people improvised. They planted "liberty poles," which, just as the name implies, were wooden poles dedicated to the cause of liberty.

The March 8 funeral services for the massacre victims centered around Boston's liberty tree, and nearly all of Boston turned out. A solemn procession took the four coffins (the fifth victim, Patrick Carr, died six days later) around the liberty tree and to the Old Granary Burial Ground. An estimated twelve thousand people marched in the cortege. Considering that Boston's population at the time was only about fifteen thousand, the crowd was enormous. William Billings, a tanner by occupation but a composer by choice, wrote a song for the occasion: "By the rivers of Watertown, we sat down / Yea, we wept, as we remembered Boston."

In defending the soldiers, John Adams told the jury, "Facts are stubborn things; and whatever may be our wishes, our inclinations, or the dictates of our passions, they cannot alter the state of facts and evidence." The big question in prosecuting Captain Preston was whether he actually ordered his men to open fire. Jane Whitehouse, Private Hugh White's friend, testified that it was not Preston; she said that the order came from someone standing behind the soldiers, someone dressed in dark-colored clothes. A sailor, James Waddel, corroborated Whitehouse's story; it was a "person like a gentleman walking behind the soldiers dressed in blue or black velvet or plush." It was this "gentleman" who had yelled "Fire!"

No one knew who this gentleman in "blue or black velvet" was. He may have been an ancestor of that conspiratorial "gunman" who appeared later at the grassy knoll in Dallas and whose cousin was seen firing from across a motel in Memphis and who even showed up in Roswell, New Mexico.

John Adams apparently succeeded in packing the jury with British sympathizers. Juror Philip Dumaresq candidly declared that Captain Preston was "as innocent as a Child unborn," adding that he "would never convict [Preston] if he sat to all eternity." Juror Joseph Barrick was an avowed Loyalist who later left the country when the British evacuated Boston. William Hill was a baker whose chief customer was the Fourteenth Regiment. And juror Gilbert Deblois even helped the captain by lining up witnesses to support Preston's version of the nonmassacre.

Of the British soldiers who fired on the Boston mob, Adams and his law partner and Josiah Quincy got four acquitted. Two others were convicted of manslaughter but escaped serious punishment under the old English custom known as the "benefit of clergy." That is, they were allowed to mitigate their sentence simply by reading a verse from the Bible. They were branded on their thumbs and discharged from the army.

John Adams's defense of enemy troops likely would have ruined his chances of political office in today's world. Luckily for our independence, eighteenth-century Americans seemed to have forgiven him.

As for Crispus Attucks, unlike Samuel Adams, who called him a hero, Cousin John said that it was Attucks who "appears to have undertaken to be the hero of the night; and to lead this army with banners, to form them in the first place in Dock square, and march them up King Street with their clubs." It was Attucks "whose very look was enough to terrify any person" who "had hardiness enough to fall in upon them, and with one hand took hold of a bayonet, and with the other knocked the man down." It was Attucks "to whose mad behavior, in all probability, the dreadful carnage of that night is chiefly to be ascribed." It was not British soldiers, John Adams claimed, who caused the Boston Massacre. Rather, it was Patrick Carr "from Ireland and . . . Attucks from Framingham [who sallied] out upon their thoughtless enterprises, at the head of such a rabble of negroes &c, as they [could] collect together."

Crispus Attucks became, first, a footnote to history, then a martyr, either a patriot who landed a blow for freedom or, as Adams called him, a "discontented [ghost] with hollow groans." Perhaps it was an impulsive act by Attucks. Perhaps it was the work of a drunken bully. Perhaps, even, he was a brave man. Nothing about Crispus Attucks is certain.

Had it not been for Samuel Adams, the Boston deaths might have remained a local affair. The shabby yet intense master propagandist that he was, Samuel Adams would not let it rest. He forced the removal of the Fourteenth and the Twenty-ninth Regiments from Boston city into Castle William in Boston harbor, where the two units became known as "Sam Adams's Regiments."

With his thundering oratory about the Boston Massacre, Samuel Adams convinced Boston that a gang of toughs were martyrs. Thanks to him, March 5 became a hallowed anniversary in Boston to be sung and celebrated, and in other colonies, to become another step toward revolution.

John Adams seems often to have been a bitter, certainly cynical, and envious man. When the First Continental Congress gathered in Philadelphia, Adams said: "We have not men fit for the times. We are deficient in genius, in education, in travel, in fortune—in everything." He believed that the history of the American Revolution would be a lie from one end to the other, told in simplistic language, the latter part of which turned out to be true. This version of history, Adams claimed, would have Benjamin Franklin smiting the earth with his electrical rod and George Washington springing out of the ground. Together Franklin and Washington would fight the war and conduct the diplomacy. The rest, Adams and Jefferson included, would just go along for the ride.

On July 30, 1815, ex-President Adams wrote ex-President Jefferson, claiming that the Revolution was "a radical change in the principles, opinions, sentiments and affections of the people," which began "in the minds and hearts of the people." If that is so, even John Adams didn't believe it early on. He's often quoted as saying only one-third of the American people favored independence from Britain, that another third opposed the idea, and that the final third didn't care; they just wanted to be left alone by both sides. In truth, of course, no one knows how many people actually favored independence.

His presidential election in 1798 over Thomas Jefferson was by a margin of only three electoral college votes. Four years later he lost to Jefferson by eight votes. They were the only two presidents to sign the Declaration of Independence.

There's been much made of the Adams-Jefferson on-again off-again friendship. When they were first friends, Adams recommended that Thomas Jefferson write the Declaration of Independence. Later, after they'd become political enemies, Adams claimed that Jefferson had plagiarized the Declaration from the Mecklenburg Resolves.

On May 31, 1775 (May 20, under the old-style calendar), a committee met at Charlotte, North Carolina, in Mecklenburg County and drew up twenty resolutions for delegates to present to the Continental Congress. In those resolutions, or resolves, according to local legend, North Carolina citizens declared themselves "a free and independent people." In 1819, the *Raleigh Register* printed what it claimed was a copy of the resolutions, saying the Mecklenburg document had been the inspiration for the Declaration of Independence. That's when John Adams accused Thomas Jefferson of plagiarism.

By then Adams disagreed with almost anything Jefferson said, past or present. He wrote Reverend William Bentley, claiming that "Mr. Jefferson . . . must have seen it [the Mecklenburg document], in the time of it, for he has copied the spirit, the sense, and the expressions of it *verbatim*, into his Declaration of the 4th of July, 1776."

It was years before a full copy of the Mecklenburg Resolves was discovered, and when it was, it was realized that at no time was the word "independence" used. Records of the Mecklenburg meeting, and the resolves, had been destroyed by fire in 1800. The version the *Raleigh Register* printed twenty years later came from the memory of one Joseph Graham, a Revolutionary War officer who had lived in Mecklenburg County during the time the resolves were written. He was sixty years old when he began writing down North Carolina history *as he remembered it,* and what he remembered wasn't always as things happened. Graham was familiar with the Declaration of Independence, and apparently he became confused as to which came first.

Before the apparently genuine article was discovered in 1847, Jefferson himself declared it a "spurious document." Both the North Carolina state seal and flag declare the Mecklenburg Declaration of Independence to be genuine, and the state proclaims May 20 a state holiday. Outside North Carolina, however, the document's authenticity is still questioned.

Benjamin Franklin was in London during the Boston Massacre. It was June when he got word of the shooting deaths, and he believed the incident would serve to harden king and Parliament's resolve to deal sternly with the colonies. Earlier, he'd written the Reverend Samuel Cooper, claiming the British policy of maintaining a "standing army . . . among us in time of peace, without the consent of our assemblies" was a grievance almost as serious as the government's claim that it had the right to tax the American people.

Benjamin Franklin was a sage, often a humorous one. His fictitious alter ego, Poor Richard, is noted for many sayings still popular today: "Three may keep a secret if two of them are dead"; "Early to bed and early to rise, makes a man healthy, wealthy, and wise"; "God helps them that help themselves." Two hundred years before the claim became famous among joggers and other athletic enthusiasts, Poor Richard said, "There is no gain without pain."

Perhaps the biggest pain in Franklin's life (aside from a continuing sore toe due to the gout) was his relationship with his illegitimate son, William. The story of a parent being estranged from a child isn't unusual. What is unusual in this case is that they were separated by a war for independence.

William Franklin was with his father during those famous lightning experiments, although William wasn't as young as he's usually depicted in paintings. William went to London with Franklin when Benjamin became a colonial agent. It was then that his father described William as "a tall proper Youth, and much of a Beau." He became acquainted with Lord Bute, who appointed the then thirty-five-year-old "proper Youth" royal governor of New Jersey.

William and his father were political opposites. At one point Benjamin wrote William about the young man's position.

> I don't understand it as any favor to me or to you, the being continued in an office by which, if all your prudence, you cannot avoid running behindhand, if you live suitably to your station. While you are in it I know you will execute it with fidelity to your master, but I think independence more honorable than any service, and that in the state of American affairs which, from the present arbitrary measures is likely soon to take place, you will find yourself in no comfortable situation, and perhaps wish you had soon disengaged yourself.

William disagreed and continued as New Jersey's royal governor. On June 16, 1776, the Provincial Congress of New Jersey kicked him out of the governor's mansion and declared him an enemy. Continental forces held William prisoner in an abandoned mine at East Windsor, Connecticut, and severely mistreated him. His wife was not allowed to visit him and she died while Franklin was held captive. In October 1778, William Franklin was finally exchanged for John McKinley, the president of the revolutionary Delaware government.

From 1767 to 1769, Massachusetts Chief Justice Thomas Hutchinson and his brother-in-law Andrew Oliver, the provincial secretary, wrote several letters to their longtime friend in London, Lord Hillsborough. In them Hutchinson, who became governor, and Oliver, who became lieutenant governor, suggested that the town of Boston was near rebellion and that British troops were needed to secure the area.

Somehow Benjamin Franklin got hold of the letters in 1772. Apparently they were given to him as examples of the type of tougher policy being urged on Parliament. Franklin sent the six Hutchinson letters and four from Oliver to the Speaker of the Massachusetts House, Thomas Cushing, saying that

> There has lately fallen into my hands part of a correspondence. I have reason to believe it laid the foundation of most if not all of our present grievances.

I am not at liberty to tell through what channel I received it. I have engaged that it shall not be printed, nor copies taken of the whole or any part of it. Confident that you will respect these provisions, I send you enclosed the original letters in handwriting that is well known.

I can only allow these letters to be seen by you, by the other gentlemen of the Committee of Correspondence, and a few others. After being some months in your possession you are requested to return them to me.

Respectfully,

B. Franklin,

Agent for the Massachusetts province

What Franklin wanted, likely, was what was done soon: The letters were turned over to the newspapers. Hutchinson had urged that Parliament send a brigade of troops to Boston to arrest the leaders of what he saw as an increasingly restless mob. He added that "there must be an abridgement of what are called English liberties."

Samuel Adams first read the Hutchinson letters to a secret session of the Massachusetts House in June 1773. Later that summer colonial newspapers began printing them. To say the least, they outraged the people of Boston, and the colonial assembly demanded the recall of both Oliver and Hutchinson. In London the question arose over who had leaked the letters to the colonies. Two prominent men, banker William Whately and John Temple, even fought a duel over the issue. Luckily neither man was seriously injured, and a few days later, Christmas Day 1773, Franklin came forward and admitted that it was he who had obtained the letters.

Benjamin Franklin was sixty-eight years old at the time and, as he put it, "old and heavy, and . . . a little indolent." Now he was in trouble.

He was ordered to appear before the king's Privy Council in an area of Whitehall Palace known as the "cockpit" since the days of Henry VIII, when it literally was the scene of cockfights. The room was sparsely furnished. Arrayed in front of him were the chancellors sitting at a long table. They were the only ones allowed to sit. No matter that Benjamin Franklin was aging, overweight, and frequently suffered from gout, he stood.

It was one of the few occasions when Benjamin Franklin wore a wig, but it was expected of him and he did it. He stood before the council as straight as an "old and heavy" man could, wearing a brown velvet suit.

The charges against Hutchinson were "baseless . . . and vexatious and seditious," Solicitor General Alexander Wedderburn said on behalf of the government. He blamed virtually all of England's colonial problems on Franklin, calling him "the true incendiary . . . and abettor" of the Boston committee of correspondence now busy inflaming the colony. Boston radicals, Prosecutor Wedderburn claimed, had learned "the lessons taught in Dr. Franklin's school of politics," and then gone on to repeat them. Governor Hutchinson had become the target because he had challenged teacher Franklin's lessons. According to Wedderburn, Franklin was so sure that the colonies would break from England, instead of sounding like a colonial agent, that Franklin was already using "the language of the minister of a foreign independent state." Perhaps in the spirit of the room's original sight of bloodletting, Wedderburn turned to the thirty-six chancellors sitting in front (a thirty-seventh chancellor, Lord North, arrived late and, like Franklin and the audience, had to stand). Wedderburn continued:

> I hope, my lords, you will mark and brand the man for the honor of this country, of Europe, and of mankind. Private correspondence has hitherto been held sacred in times of the greatest party rage, not only in politics but religion. He has forfeited all the respect of societies and of men. Into what companies will he hereafter go with an unembarrassed face, or the honest intrepidity of virtue? Men will watch him with a jealous eye; they will hide their papers from him, and lock up their escritoires (writing desks). He will henceforth esteem it a libel to be called a man of letter, this man of *three* letters.

The audience applauded wildly, for in hearing of "this man of *three* letters," the classically trained spectators realized Wedderburn referred to a play by the Roman Plautus in which a thief was called a *"trium litterarum homo."* The prosecutor was charging Franklin with being nothing more than a common thief.

For a solid hour Benjamin Franklin stood there, and for a solid hour Wedderburn poured invectives down on him. Franklin neither spoke nor changed expressions the whole time. When it was over, he turned around and walked out the door. For the British government it was a "complete triumph." The following year the British government disciplined Franklin and took away his position of deputy postmaster general for America.

The Massachusetts legislature had petitioned Parliament to recall Hutchinson. Who was recalled, however, was not Hutchinson, but Franklin. In 1775, for the first time in eighteen years, he returned to America.

Benjamin Franklin lived in England so long that some Americans thought that he was a Tory, a closet one at least. His verbal torture in the parliamentary cockpit changed their minds. Franklin reached Philadelphia on Friday evening, May 5, his return announced by the "ringing of bells."

Two days later William Franklin learned that his father was back home. William thought the Hutchinson letters were innocuous. He was leaning more and more to the Tory side. By the time William learned of Franklin's arrival, his father had already become a member of the Second Continental Congress.

On June 7, 1776, Richard Henry Lee of Virginia moved the following resolution:

> That these united colonies are and of right ought to be free and independent states; that they are absolved from all allegiance to the British Crown, and that all political connection between them and the state of Great Britain is and of right ought to be totally dissolved.

With that Lee rushed back to Williamsburg, where the Virginia House of Burgesses would continue to debate the issue. His resolution can be divided into three parts: (1) The colonies should declare their independence from Great Britain, (2) these united colonies should form alliances, and (3) Congress should prepare a plan of confederation. Naturally Congress did what all political bodies do; it formed committees to study the three points.

One committee was selected to draw up a document declaring America was free of Britain, which is to say that while it wasn't 100 percent certain Congress *would* vote for independence, if it did, it wanted to have a statement ready for king, Parliament, and the American people. To this committee were named Pennsylvania's venerable Benjamin Franklin (who, at age seventy, declined to do the actual writing, saying it wasn't in his nature to put to paper anything other than light extemporania),* conservative Robert Livingston of New York (he favored eventual independence but felt the time was not quite right for it), and Roger Sherman of Connecticut (a self-taught former cobbler who would go on to sign what perhaps are America's four greatest documents—the Articles of Association of 1774, the Declaration of Independence, the Articles of Confederation, and the Constitution). And of course John Adams and Thomas Jefferson. As Adams later remembered it:

> The sub-committee met. Jefferson proposed to me to make the draught.
> I said "I will not."
> "You should do it."
> "Oh! No."
> "Why will you not? You ought to do it."
> "I will not?"
> "Why? . . ."
> "Reason first—you are a Virginian, and a Virginian ought to appear at the head of this business. Reason second—I am obnoxious, suspected and unpopular. You are very much otherwise. Reason third—you can write ten times better than I can."

Jefferson was distracted by his wife's illness back in Charlottesville, but he virtually locked himself in his room and got down to work. "I turned to neither book nor pamphlet while writing the Declaration," he claimed, although many of the opening words were taken directly

---

* Thomas Jefferson, in his *Biographical Sketches of Famous Men,* quoted Franklin as saying, "I have made it a rule . . . whenever in my power, to avoid becoming the draughtsman of papers to be reviewed by a public body."

from Richard Henry Lee's resolution. And much of the principles and language came from John Locke's *Second Treatise of Government*, written in 1690, which had been virtually memorized by Thomas Jefferson.

Meanwhile Congress declared itself a committee of the whole and debated the issue of independence. Several delegates opposed the idea: James Wilson and John Dickinson of Pennsylvania, Robert Livingston of New York (even though he was on the committee writing the Declaration of Independence), and Edward Rutledge of South Carolina. Of these four, only Wilson and Rutledge eventually signed the Declaration.

Just a year before, Dickinson had pushed through Congress the so-called Olive Branch Petition. The petition came after the armed clashes at Lexington and Concord, Bunker Hill, and the Boston Tea Party. Dickinson wanted to pay for the tea destroyed in Boston (an idea with which Benjamin Franklin agreed) and was willing to concede Parliament's right to regulate trade in the colonies. The Olive Branch Petition was a final attempt to settle the colonies' grievances with the mother country.

In writing the petition, Dickinson tried to skirt Parliament and go directly to King George. It was a windy statement, almost begging (or so it seems more than two hundred years later) to be edited, and contains one of the longest sentences ever written:

Most Gracious Sovereign:

Attached to your Majesty's person, family and government, with all devotion that principle and affection can inspire, connected with Great Britain by the strongest ties that can unite societies, and deploring every event that tends in any degree to weaken them, we solemnly assure your Majesty, that we not only most ardently desire the former harmony between her and these Colonies may be restored, but that a concord may be established between them upon so firm a basis as to perpetuate its blessings, uninterrupted by any future dissensions to succeeding generations in both countries and to transmit your Majesty's name to posterity, adorned with that signal and lasting glory that has attended the memory of those illustrious personages, whose virtues and abilities have extricated states from dangerous convulsions, and by securing happiness to others have erected the most novel and durable monuments to their own fame. . . .

Richard Penn, a staunch Loyalist and descendant of Pennsylvania founder William Penn, hand-carried the Olive Branch Petition to London. For all the good it did. George III refused to see Penn or to receive the petition.

It had taken more than a month for the petition to go from Philadelphia to London, and when it finally arrived, it got there at just about the same time as word of Bunker Hill reached London. George III also learned that the colonists were forming an army— George Washington had been named as its head—and that Americans were about to invade Canada.

Even John Dickinson couldn't have been too hopeful that his Olive Branch Petition would work. At the same time he was writing the appeal to return to the former harmony, he was working with Thomas Jefferson on another plea, the *Declaration of the Causes and Necessity for Taking Up Arms*. It was an indictment of Parliament for having "attempted to effect their cruel and impolitic Purpose of enslaving these Colonies by Violence, and have thereby rendered it necessary for us to close with their last Appeal from Reason to Arms."

As John Adams said of the congressional proceedings that summer of 1775, they had something approaching a "whimsical cast" to them. On the one hand, they begged for peace, while on the other they prepared for war. Perhaps more than a "whimsical cast," it showed that Congress could not yet make up its mind if it wanted to free itself from England.

It is easily argued that the Declaration of Independence was a white man's document. Jefferson's words and actions were contradictory toward slavery. He owned slaves. He bought and sold slaves. He advertised for runaway slaves. He had slaves lashed.

In his *Notes on Virginia,* Jefferson "advanced," as he put it, "a suspicion . . . that the blacks, whether originally a distinct race, or made distinct by time and circumstances, are inferior to the whites in the endowments both of body and mind." He wrote that even after a century and a half in which whites "have had under our eyes the races of black and red men, they have never yet been viewed by us as subjects of natural history."

Jefferson commented on what he saw as "the preference of the Oran-utan [orangutan] for the black woman over those of his own species." He had never seen an orangutan and possibly took it from its original meaning, "wild men of the woods."

Notes on Virginia was written in answer to inquiries made to him by the Marquis de Barbé-Marbois, then secretary of the French legation in the U.S. capital, Philadelphia. He wrote and revised them during the winter of 1782 to 1783, and they were first published (anonymously) in Paris in 1784, two hundred copies, all misdated 1782.

Of blacks, Jefferson said:

> They have less hair on the face and body [than whites]. They secrete less by the kidneys, and more by the glands of the skin, which gives them a very strong and disagreeable odor. This greater degree of transpiration, renders them more tolerant of heat, and less so of cold than the whites. . . .
>
> They seem to require less sleep. A black after hard labor through the day, will be induced by the slightest amusements to sit up till midnight or morning.

Jefferson believed that blacks were "at least as brave, and more adventuresome," but added, "This may perhaps proceed from a want of forethought, which prevents their seeing a danger till it be present." As for blacks and sex:

> They are more ardent after their female; but love seems with them to be more an eager desire, than a tender delicate mixture of sentiment and sensation. Their griefs are transient. Those numberless afflictions, which render it doubtful whether heaven has given life to us in mercy or in wrath, are less felt, and sooner forgotten with them. In general, their existence appears to participate more of sensation than reflection. To this

must be ascribed their disposition to sleep when abstracted from their diversions, and unemployed in labor.

Love among blacks, Thomas Jefferson wrote, "is ardent, but it kindles the senses only, not the imagination." Religion, he added, "produced a Phyliss Whately [poet Phillis Wheatley]; but it could not produce a poet."

Wheatley, however, was very much a poet, whose work was considered one of the wonders of the age. Brought over from her African homeland in 1761 when she was seven or eight years old, she was sold as a slave to a Boston tailor and merchant, John Wheatley. His wife named her Phillis after the ship she arrived in. Phillis Wheatley published her first poem in 1770, and three years later she published a book of poems, *Poems on Various Subjects*. By 1774, Wheatley was internationally known, with France's Voltaire referring to her "very good English verse." In 1773, Benjamin Franklin visited Wheatley in London. "I went to see the black poetess," he wrote, "and offered her any services I could do for her." On October 26, 1775, Wheatley wrote George Washington, sending along a poem celebrating his appointment as commander in chief of the Continental army. Her poem expressed the hope that "your Excellency would be successful in the great cause you are generously engaged in."

> Celestial choir! enthron't in realms of light,
> Columbia's scene of glorious toils I write.
> While freedom's cause her anxious breast alarms,
> She slashes dreadful in refulgent arms . . .
> Proceed, great chief, with virtue on thy side,
> Thy ev'ry action let the goddess guide.
> A crown, a mansion, and a throne that shine,
> With gold unfading, Washington! be thine.

In "An Hymn to the Evening," Wheatley showed a flair for lyrical imagery:

> Soon as the sun forsook the
> eastern main

The pealing thunder shook the
heav'nly plain;
Majestic grandeur! From the
zephyr's wing,
Exhales the incense of the
blooming spring,
Soft purl the streams, the birds
renew their notes,
And through the air their
mingled music floats.

John Paul Jones was a Phillis Wheatley fan. Jones, who considered himself no mean poet, was on board the *Ranger* when he wrote a Boston friend: "I am on the point of sailing—I have to write you— pray be so good as to put the Inclosed into the hands of the Celebrated Phillis, the African Favorite of the Muse and of Apollo— should she reply, I hope you will be the bearer." Jones was commissioned by William Whipple of Portsmouth, England, with whom he remained friendly, to buy several pairs of gloves for Phillis Wheatley while the admiral was in France.

Thomas Jefferson wasn't the only one not to recognize Wheatley's talent. The year her book of poems was published, someone in London bound it in skin stripped from a black slave.

Jefferson was not the only member of the Declaration writing committee ever to own slaves. Benjamin Franklin had owned "a Negro couple" but decided to sell them not so much out of moral reasons but because the woman "behaves exceedingly well" and the man had been hired out at a profit to a local printer, "but we conclude to sell them both the first opportunity; for we do not like Negro servants." Later he wrote, "The labor of slaves can never be so cheap here [America] as in Britain," adding, "Anyone can compute it." Besides, "the number of purely white people in the world is proportionably very small." Why, he asked, "increase the sons of Africa, by planting them in America, where we have so fair an opportunity, by excluding all blacks and tawneys, of increasing the lovely white and red?"

• • •

In Jefferson's original draft of the Declaration of Independence he wrote a strongly worded attack on slavery. It didn't make it through Congress. In order to win the votes of Georgia and South Carolina, Jefferson's clause "reprobating enslaving the inhabitants of Africa," was struck out.

In that deleted clause Jefferson aimed directly at King George III:

> He has waged cruel war against human nature itself, violating its most sacred rights of life and liberty in the persons of a distant people who never offended him, captivating and carrying them into slavery in another hemisphere, or to incur miserable death in their transportation hither. This piratical opprobrium of [here, before striking the entire clause, Congress inserted the word "infidel"] powers, is the warfare of the ["Christian," as first inserted by Congress] king of Great Britain. Determined to keep open a market where [men, another insert] should be bought and sold, he has prostituted his negative for suppressing every legislative attempt to prohibit or to restrain this execrable commerce.*

Congress also struck out a section of the Declaration in which Jefferson railed against the practice begun by Virginia Governor John Murray, the Fourth Earl of Dunmore. In 1775, when it seemed obvious that war was coming, the governor raised "Dunmore's Ethiopians," troops of runaway slaves. The British had promised freedom to slaves but actually hoped to use them as a labor force, then quickly sell them to other British colonies in the West Indies. This would have had the effect of aiding the British while financially ruining American slave owners.

Jefferson wrote Richard Henry Lee, saying that Dunmore must be crushed "instantly," or he would "become the most formidable enemy America has." Initially Dunmore took in about one thousand slaves who had run away from their Virginia masters. By the end of

---

* As quoted by Jefferson in his *Autobiography.*

the Revolution more than five thousand slaves had left their American masters in favor of the British, who turned out to be just as bad, perhaps even worse. In fact, many British officers made fortunes by taking in runaway slaves, then selling them in other parts of the world. After all, the Americans learned from the British everything they knew about slavery.

Importantly few American radicals in 1776 considered slavery a permanent necessity, and, although some argued against including the issue in the Declaration, none "dared proclaim the evil [slavery] a good." Apparently, most of the Founding Fathers looked forward to seeing slavery end.

In a letter written July 3, 1776, one day *before* the Declaration of Independence was approved, John Adams wrote his wife Abigail that:

> Yesterday the greatest Question was decided, which ever was debated in America, and a greater perhaps, never was or will be decided among Men. A Resolution was passed without one dissenting Colony "that these united Colonies, are, and of right ought to be free and independent States, and as such, they have, and of Right ought to have full Power to make War, conclude Peace, establish Commerce, and to do all the other Acts and Things, which other states may rightfully do."

Adams referred to the day that Congress approved Richard Henry Lee's resolution to separate the colonies from Great Britain. More from John Adams's letter to Abigail:

> The Second Day of July 1776, will be the most memorable Epocha, in the History of America. I am apt to believe it will be celebrated, by succeeding Generations, as the great anniversary Festival. It ought to be commemorated, as the Day of Deliverance by solemn Acts of Devotion to God Almighty. It ought to be solemnized with Pomp and Parade, with Shews, Games, Sports, Guns, Bells, Bonfires and Illuminations from one End of this Continent to the other from this Time forward forever more.

Well, it almost happened that way. A nineteenth-century scholar felt this contradicted the growing American tradition of celebrating the Fourth of July, so he simply altered Adams's letter to conform. He changed July 3, 1776 (the date on which John wrote Abigail), to July 5, 1776, making it seem that John was writing about the fourth, the day the Declaration of Independence—the document, that is— was approved, not the day they voted to go it alone. The announcement, it seems, had already overshadowed the event.

On July 4, representatives of all thirteen colonies except New York, voted to adopt the Declaration of Independence; once New York approved the document, Congress ordered it printed and distributed to military units, to government officials, and to newspapers.

As for the Continental Congress, their big celebration came on July 8, with members taking part in a gala public demonstration outside the Pennsylvania State House. Guns were fired and soldiers paraded by; the Declaration was read to the public by Colonel John Nixon, the son of an Irish immigrant. People cheered and bells— including the one Philadelphians called the "Old One"—rang.

The Old One arrived in Philadelphia from England in 1752 and, during its initial test ring, it cracked. When the English manufacturers refused to repair the twelve-foot-wide bell—they claimed Americans didn't know the proper way to ring it—two local Philadelphians, John Pass and John Stow, took on the job. They broke it apart and recast it. The bell still didn't sound right, so Pass and Stow tried again, and this time the sound was better; and it was lifted to the belfry atop the Pennsylvania State House. It rang out on many occasions, including the time in 1765 when it tolled the arrival of ships bearing stamps ordered under the Stamp Act. When the Stamp Act was repealed, the Old One rang that out also. In 1771, when King George and Parliament pushed through the Tea Act, the bell was rung to call the Pennsylvania legislature into session to urge Parliament to repeal the act. When news reached Philadelphia of the Battles of Lexington and Concord, the Old One rang out the news.

When the British occupied Philadelphia over the winter of 1777 to 1778, residents were afraid the soldiers would melt down the city's church bells and use them for bullets, so they took the bells down and hid them in Allentown, Pennsylvania. The Old One lay hidden in the basement of the Zion High German Reformed Church until the British evacuated Philadelphia. Then the bell was returned to the State House, where it rang out on many occasions. In 1781, it pealed out the news that Washington and the Continental army had defeated Lord Cornwallis and the British troops at Yorktown.

In 1799, when Pennsylvania temporarily moved the state capital to Lancaster, the Old One went along with the legislature. That was the year George Washington died, and the bell tolled a funeral sound in his honor. It rang out to honor the Marquis de Lafayette when he visited Philadelphia in 1824, and it tolled to mourn his death ten years later.

By 1828, the former Pennsylvania State House was a museum run by painter Charles Wilson Peale. He moved out, and the state sold the Old One to a scrap dealer who wanted the bell but wanted the government to pay to have it removed. The two sides went to court, and the scrap dealer donated the bell to the city. It was about then that local residents began to realize the 2,080-pound bell was more than just a large gong show.

The eighty-three-year-old bell was tolling the death of United States Chief Justice John Marshall in 1835 when it cracked. The crack, however, was not enough to prevent its use. The Old One still had a few good, if somewhat sour, peals left in it, and it was rung during an antislavery demonstration in 1839. That's when the Old One got the name Liberty Bell.

The British bell makers had inscribed on it: "Proclaim Liberty throughout all the land unto all the inhabitants thereof," but the "Liberty" that gave it its name was the liberty—the freedom—from slavery; the Massachusetts Anti-Slavery Fair distributed a pamphlet entitled "The Liberty Bell, by Friends of Freedom." It was not in connection with the Declaration of Independence and freedom or liberty from England.

In 1846, as it rang in honor of George Washington's birthday, the Liberty Bell gonged its last gong. It cracked again.

When the Pennsylvania Assembly ordered it back in 1751, they said they wanted "a good bell." The Pennsylvanians—and Americans in general—got a bargain. The Liberty Bell cost only £60, about $81.

George Washington's troops first heard about the Declaration of Independence on July 9, when the document was read to them as they camped outside New York City. Slowly the news circulated around the colonies—rather, around the United States of America—for that is what the Declaration of Independence said we were. It wasn't until late August that King George III heard about it in London.

On August 10, 1776, a committee composed of Jefferson, Franklin, and Adams proposed a motto for the United States. It took a while, but Congress finally adopted the motto on June 20, 1782. It wasn't until 1796 that it began to appear on some U.S. coins.

The poet Virgil (Publius Vergilius Maro) had written something similar to it around 19 B.C., but the motto as we know it apparently first appeared in 1692 on the title page of the magazine *Gentleman's Journal,* something of a *Playboy* of its day in popularity.

E pluribus unum. Out of many, one.

CHAPTER THREE

Founding Fathers, Part Two:
Best Actors in Supporting Roles

Whatever praise is due for the task already performed, it is certain that much remains to be done. The Revolution is but half completed. Independence and government were the two objects contended for, and but one is yet obtained.
—Joel Barlow, address to the Hartford, Connecticut
Society of the Cincinnati, July 4, 1787

Ubi libertas ibi patria (Where liberty is, there is my country).
—James Otis, Motto

In November 1777, the Articles of Confederation and Perpetual Union, which had originally been submitted to the Continental Congress a week after the Declaration of Independence was adopted, were finally submitted to the states for ratification. It would be another three years before they were ratified.

At the time of the Boston Massacre, Henry Knox was a chubby, baby-faced, unknown bookseller who busied himself reading about war. A year later Henry Knox lost the third and fourth fingers of his left hand when a fowling piece burst during a hunting trip. From then on he usually held a handkerchief in his hand to hide the injury. He went on to serve as a volunteer at the Battle of Bunker Hill and in November 1775 was appointed colonel of the Continental Regiment of Artillery. Both the regiment and its artillery were virtually nonexistent. Knox became Washington's chief of artillery even though all the beefy bookseller knew of artillery was what he'd gathered from books. To paraphrase a twentieth-century TV commercial: Henry Knox wasn't an artillery expert, but he read about one in textbooks.

Following the Battle of Fort Ticonderoga, at which time several dozen British cannon were captured, Knox managed to drag the captured weapons from the fort to Boston, some three hundred miles, several mountains, and more than a few rivers away. Just how many cannon and mortars Knox managed to get to Dorchester Heights in January 1776 isn't certain, but it was somewhere between fifty and sixty. With the artillery looking down on Boston, the British realized they had to evacuate the city; and that ended the siege of Boston.

Knox later served as secretary of war under the Articles of Confederation and retained the position under George Washington after the Constitution went into effect.

Joseph Plumb Martin was a young man living around New Haven, Connecticut, where, as he later wrote:

> Time passed smoothly on with me till the year 1774 arrived. The smell of war began to be pretty strong, but I was determined to have no hand in it, happen when it might; I felt myself to be a real coward. What—venture my carcass where bullets fly! That will never do for me. Stay at home out of harm's way, thought I.

Then came Lexington and Concord. "Soldiers were at this time enlisting for a year's service," he wrote, adding, "I did not like that; it was too long a time for me at the first trial; I wished only to take a priming before I took upon me the whole coat of paint for a soldier." Joseph Plumb Martin took more than "the whole coat of paint." He took enough to paint a regiment. "Well, thought I, I may as well go through with the business now as not. So I wrote my name fairly upon the indentures. And now I was a soldier." It was July 6, 1776, two days after the Declaration of Independence was approved, but it's unlikely he'd heard about that just yet.

He became Private Joseph Plumb Martin, Samuel Peck's Third Company, William Douglas's Fifth Battalion, James Wadsworth, Jr.'s Brigade of new levies. He would remain in the army until 1784, long after the Yorktown victory, a year after the Treaty of Paris officially ended the Revolutionary War.

Martin's first duty as a soldier took him to New York City, "near the southwest angle of the city." And almost immediately he got into trouble, barely escaping the hangman. Not far away from his quarters was a wine cellar, and "by some means the soldiers had 'smelt it out.'" Seeing soldiers pour through his cellar door, the building owner tried to make the best of it by selling them the wine they were stealing. It didn't work. "While the owner was drawing [wine] for his purchasers on one side of the cellar, behind him on the other side another set of purchasers were drawing for themselves."

When General Israel Putnam heard about the wine theft, he "immediately repaired in person to the field of action," and began "haranguing the multitude, threatening to hang every mother's son of them." Luckily, Joseph escaped the gallows.

After the war he wrote down his experiences. They were first published anonymously in 1830, under the title *A Narrative of Some of the Adventures, Dangers and Sufferings of a Revolutionary Soldier, Interspersed with Anecdotes of Incidents That Occurred Within His Own Observation.* At the time Martin was seventy years old and lived in the small town of Prospect, Maine, apparently not far from Augusta.

Joseph Plumb Martin was not a George Washington or a Horatio Gates. You won't read about his storming Fort Ticonderoga with Ethan Allen and Benedict Arnold. He was the Revolutionary War real-life equivalent of the World War II cartoon characters Willie and Joe, and the Civil War's Johnny Reb and Billy Yank. In addition to the wine incident, Martin probably got into as much trouble as any other soldier in any other war. Just as likely, he probably neglected to pat himself on the back when it was needed. Martin suffered at Valley Forge with an army that "was now not only starved but naked." It was a warm autumn day when Joseph Plumb Martin marched through Williamsburg, Virginia, headed for Yorktown. "On the fifth of October," he wrote, "we began to put our plans into execution."

Before then Joseph Plumb Martin saw war from the aspect that many of his or any other generation did. He saw it from the ground up. While Washington and Lafayette rode by on shining stallions, Martin slogged through mud in half the colonies that would become the United States of America.

He was at Kip's Bay when British warships began discharging troops. The American army was poorly trained, poorly dug in, and poorly behaved. The British invasion led to a rout, with new American troops running away as fast as they could, and George Washington getting mad as hell.

It was on a Sunday morning, Martin wrote, "the day in which the British were always employed with their deviltry if possible, because, they said, they had the prayers of the church on that day." American troops crouched behind inadequate entrenchments, or, as Martin puts it, "nothing more than a ditch dug along the bank of the river with the dirt thrown towards the water."

British General Lord Howe had anticipated Washington's withdrawal from New York, and so set out to trap the American army with a flanking movement. The British fleet would bombard the city, and the army would cross over from the present site of Astoria, turn the Continental army's left flank, and then cut off Washington's communications. On September 13, Howe issued an order:

> An attack upon the enemy being shortly intended, the soldiers are reminded of their evident superiority on the 27th August [the Battle of Long Island], by charging the rebels with their bayonets even in woods where they had thought themselves invincible.
>
> The General therefore recommends to the troops an entire dependence upon their bayonets, with which they will ever command that success which their bravery so well deserves.

British commander Sir William Erskine issued a public proclamation ordering "all Committee men and others acting under the authority of the Rebels [to] cease and remain at their respective homes, that every man in arms lay them down forthwith and surrender themselves on pain of being treated as rebels." Within days, whole towns along Long Island petitioned Erskine for pardon and protection.

Most American troops on Long Island were untrained, untried militia. Only two hundred Continental troops were on the island, and they were commanded by twenty-six-year-old Lieutenant Colonel Henry Beekman Livingston. His situation was helpless, and on August 31, he wrote Washington saying he considered the British cavalry regiment "an insuperable obstacle" to independence.

"One evening," Joseph Martin wrote, "while lying here, we heard a heavy cannonade at the city, and before dark we saw four of the enemy's ships that had passed the town and were coming up the East River. They anchored just below us." Along the American line, sentinels passed the watchword, "All is well." Martin "heard the British on board their shipping answer, 'We will alter your tune before tomorrow night.' And they were as good as their word for once."

Howe had about four thousand men—British regulars and Hessian mercenaries—under him at the Battle of Kip's Bay. A British spy report claimed Washington had about five thousand men left in New York, but there weren't nearly that many around Kip's Bay.

The redcoats invaded on September 15, with General Henry Clinton in charge. Shortly before 11:00 A.M. British warships began landing troops near the American positions. The troops came ashore in eighty-four flatboats.

At first light Private Martin "saw their boats coming out of a creek or cove on the Long Island side of the water, filled with British soldiers." The Americans remained in their shallow ditches until the British "were almost leveled upon us, when our officers, seeing we could make no resistance and no orders [were] coming from any superior officer and that we must soon be entirely exposed to the rake of their guns, gave the order to leave the lines."

The American army shouted insults at the British troops, waved their guns at them, and urged them to try to come ashore. All the while English sailors continued loading and firing their cannon into the rebel lines. The wait grew to be too much for the militia troops; they grew more and more restless as more and more flatboats loaded with redcoats came into view.

Howe wanted to land in Harlem. He was talked out of that plan because it was too close to the tide rips of Hellgate. Kip's Bay, on the other hand, was a fairly deep indentation in the Manhattan shore—the modern-day location is about where Thirty-fourth Street reaches the East River—with a V-shaped meadow rising beyond it. Resisting the invasion would mean untrained American troops would be forced to fight well-trained British troops out in the open. Howe was certain it would be no contest. Major General Henry Clinton, on the other hand, wasn't so sure. That day he wrote in his diary:

My advice has ever been to avoid even the possibility of a check. We live by victory. Are we sure of it this day? J'en doute. [I doubt it.] These people are assembled in force. . . . I like it not. No diversion, no demonstration but what a child would see through, no prospect of victory without buying it dear.

It was now that Joseph Plumb Martin hid in "nothing more than a ditch dug along the bank of the river." At midmorning the English fleet began shelling the American positions, more than seventy large cannon bombarding the area for more than an hour. The young soldier was "demurely perusing" some old newspapers when the barrage began and "I thought my head would go with the sound." He "made a frog's leap for the ditch . . . and began to consider which part of my carcass was to go first."

While the bombardment went on, English and Hessian troops began heading for shore in large flatboats. Enemy troops, Martin said, "continued to augment their forces from the island until they appeared like a large clover field in full bloom." Henry Clinton was in the lead boat with Lord Rowdon, the young Irish nobleman who was his aide, beside him.

It was the first amphibious assault for many of the Hessian troops, and they were certain they were about to be slaughtered. They began singing hymns. The English weren't so religious and cursed their own officers, the Germans, and the American enemy equally.

The American commander in chief of the East River lines was sixty-two-year-old Major General Joseph Spencer of Connecticut. He was a veteran of the colonial wars who had been with militia troops during the siege of Boston. While some other officers thought it best to abandon New York, Spencer voted with Generals George Clinton and William Heath to defend the city.

Another Continental army general, Alexander McDougall, didn't think too highly of the trio of generals, saying Spencer, Clinton, and Heath were "a fool, a knave and an honest, obstinate man." McDougall himself may have been somewhat obstinate, certainly vocal in his opinions. He'd been thrown in jail in 1769 for writing a pamphlet called *A Son of Liberty to the Betrayed Inhabitants of the City and Colony of New York*. For this he was considered by many to be the first martyr in the patriot cause. In 1780, he succeeded Benedict Arnold as commander at West Point. In 1782, he was court-martialed for insubordination to General Heath. After the Revolution he organized and became the first president of the Bank of New York.

The "fool" in McDougall's trio was General Spencer. He'd apparently made no attempt to take charge of his troops at Kip's Bay and allowed individual commanders to operate at will against the advancing British and Hessian forces. Private Martin says he and his men "kept the lines till they [the enemy] were almost leveled upon us, when our officers, seeing we could make no resistance and no orders coming from any superior officer that we must be entirely exposed to the rake of their guns, gave the order to leave the lines." More than four thousand enemy troops were headed Martin's way.

Connecticut militiamen took one look at flatboats loaded with English and German troops coming out of the clouds of gunpowder, and they started running. By the time the first flatboat got close enough for troops to begin slogging through the mud, the only Americans left to defend the land were Colonel William Douglas and a handful of men.

Four New York regiments stationed near modern-day Sixteenth Street and five more regiments from Connecticut were near the vicinity of what is now Twenty-third Street. Instead of rushing to Douglas's aid, they dug deeper into their trenches. Not a shot was fired.

Henry Clinton couldn't believe it. He'd been doubtful about the assault, and now his men were swarming ashore unharmed and uncontested. Grenadiers marched forward with fixed bayonets, ready to skewer any American they faced, but there was no one to skewer. They'd all run away.

George Washington and his staff tried to rally the militiamen. It didn't work. When one regiment saw another of Douglas's regiment running away, they joined in the race. Seeing a small band of redcoats on a hill a quarter mile off sent them running even faster. Washington had ridden from Harlem to Kip's Bay when he heard the ships open fire. Seeing the untried Connecticut militiamen run off, he roared "Take the wall! Take the cornfield!" but the men hurried past him.

Joseph Martin told of an instance in which one trooper "was sitting by the highway side when the Commander in Chief passed by and asked him why he sat there." The man's answer, Martin wrote, was "that he had rather be killed or taken by the enemy than trodden to death by cowards."

As the militiamen rushed by, Washington went berserk. He threw his hat to the ground and cried out either "Good God, have I got such troops as these" or "Are these the men with which I am to defend America?" Whatever his exact words, Washington cursed and rode among the runaways, lashing out at anyone within reach of his riding crop, sometimes slapping them with the broadside of his sword. It didn't work, and Washington was left alone in a road littered by discarded muskets, bedrolls, and cartridge boxes. His aides quietly waited for their commander to do something.

Meanwhile, a group of equally bewildered English troops stood on the hillside, suspecting a trap. There was no trap; Washington's volcanic temper had drained him and left him unable to move. Finally one of his aides—possibly Joseph Reed—took the general's horse's bridle and led him up the road behind his panicked troops. Luckily, and thanks to gutsy General Israel Putnam, the remnants of the army to the south of the city escaped. Back and forth the man called "Old Put" rode, hurrying, cajoling, and threatening the raw American troops into something of an organized retreat.

Thanks, also, to a case of lethargy contracted by British General Howe, he could see no need for hurrying. After all, his Tory spies had misinformed him that the entire American force was north of Fifty-ninth Street. He rested his men. He regrouped his troops. The attacking troops slowly pushed inland.

Among the British troops were a group of sailors off HMS *Orpheus,* who had been sent with a barge to several of the flatboats then floating away. Rather than return to their ship, the sailors decided to collect souvenirs from among the gear the panicked Americans had left behind. Midshipman Bartholomew James was among the souvenir hunters and, as he wandered into a wooded area, he found himself faced with "two or three hundred Hessians, with flaming large brass caps on, and with charged [fixed] bayonets." The problem of allies who spoke different languages immediately became evident. James didn't understand the Germans, and they didn't understand him. Worst of all for the midshipman, they thought he was a rebel and began banging him about the head with their muskets. Midshipman James pointed to his uniform cuffs as proof that he was part of the British navy, but the Germans saw an American officer who lay dying nearby, his legs shot off by a cannonball. James's uniform was the same as the American's, and the Germans returned to banging the boy's head in. Finally a British officer who recognized James came riding up and ordered the Hessian troops to stop. In quintessentially English understatement, James later wrote that "they made a thousand ridiculous apologies for their treatment, and we returned to our ships, in need of both cook and doctor, and totally weary of our expedition."

Washington consolidated his men behind the fortified Harlem Heights, a triple line of entrenchments extending across Manhattan. The general ordered one group of three Virginia rifle companies to move to the enemy's rear, while another diverted the redcoats with a feigned frontal attack. Together they drove the enemy from a wooded area into a buckwheat field, the present site of Barnard College at 116th Street and Broadway. It wasn't much, but it *was* the first time in the New York campaign that the British retreated. The "victory" gave American soldiers a shred of confidence.

Guarding the approaches to the lower Hudson River were two American forts—Fort Washington, in what is now New York City's West 184th Street, and Fort Lee across the river in New Jersey. At the time the area was densely wooded. George Washington garrisoned the fort named after him with more than two thousand men. In mid-November the British attacked. First, however, they did what any well-bred, sophisticated army would do. They demanded the Americans surrender. When General Robert Magaw, the fort commander, refused, General Howe attacked from three directions and took the fort. Two days later Howe's troops rowed across the Hudson, scaled the Palisades, and took Fort Lee in twenty minutes.

Not only were nearly 3,000 American troops taken captive, but 146 cannon were taken as well, along with almost 3,000 muskets, 12,000 shot and shell, and 40,000 cartridges. And gunpowder and tents and picks and shovels and virtually everything else an army needs. The English and Hessian losses totaled less than 500 men.

Luckily for the American cause, British General Howe once again was in no hurry to pursue Washington's forces. He had an army of more than thirteen thousand under his command, but he moved very slowly to use it. It took Washington more than a full day to march his bedraggled army from Harlem Heights to White Plains, and all the time Howe left the Americans unmolested. It would be ten days before Howe moved against Washington, who then retreated through New Jersey and into Pennsylvania. Finally Howe controlled New Jersey and Pennsylvania, and Congress fled to Baltimore, abandoning Philadelphia.

General Howe gave residents of New Jersey a chance to quit the fight. Basically he declared the war over and offered a full pardon to any rebel who would pledge allegiance to the king. In two weeks three thousand people accepted the pardon, one of them a signer of the Declaration of Independence.

Private Joseph Plumb Martin was at the Battle of Monmouth, New Jersey, in June 1788. As his regiment reached the battlefield, "the left wing of the army, that part being under the command of General Lee, were retreating"—five thousand men and twelve cannon. The Battle of Monmouth was Lee's first test as a field commander, and he failed miserably; he never got around to drawing up a battle plan, so there's no way of knowing what, if anything, he actually planned to do. During the fighting Lee issued few orders. For instance, "Mad Anthony" Wayne never received any orders to attack; but then, he also never received any orders to retreat. Or to do anything else. Lee's confused troops soon began to withdraw. When Lafayette, who was with Lee (and who probably should have been given command of Lee's army) asked Lee why he wasn't following Washington's orders to attack, Lee said to him: "You don't know the British soldiers; we cannot stand against them."

Lafayette sent a message to Washington, who caught up with Lee's aides. Joseph Plumb Martin was sitting under a nearby tree and saw Washington cross the road "in a great passion." Martin heard Washington "ask our officers 'by whose order the troops were retreating,' and being answered, 'by General Lee's,' he [Washington] said 'd—n him.'" Washington rode up to Lee and, in a flaming rage, called the one-time English officer a "damned poltroon" and took command. All that Lee managed to say was "Sir! Sir!" Washington took it that Charles Lee didn't hear the question, and he asked it again. Lee took a while to answer and finally replied with complaints that he'd had faulty intelligence, that his orders had not been obeyed by his subordinates (meaning, it turned out, Anthony Wayne), and he finally offered that he believed the attack against British General Henry Clinton was not wise. Sending Lee to the rear of the army, Washington took control and restored order.

Hoping to stop the retreat, George Washington, along with Generals Wayne and Stirling, managed to form a strong line along a ridge. Clinton tried to push through, but by then the Americans, without Charles Lee to muddle up the works, had formed a strong defensive position near Monmouth Court House.

By early evening the British attack had failed. Washington tried to mount an attack, but his troops were as tired as the British. That night both sides lay on their arms, or at least the Americans did. When morning came, Washington found that Clinton and the British army had pulled back. The redcoats had rested until about ten at night, then, as he reported to Lord George Germain, Clinton "took advantage of the moon light" to remove his troops. The Americans didn't try to follow them. Clinton reached Sandy Hook, New Jersey, on June 30, where the navy picked them up and transported them back to New York City.

During the Battle of Monmouth, Clinton lost over three hundred men. Along the way fifty-nine others died from sunstroke (those heavy redcoat uniforms), and several hundred Hessian troops deserted. They'd been offered parcels of land beyond the Appalachian Mountains and decided to remain in America.*

Meanwhile, with the Battle of Monmouth, the war in the north began drawing to a close. General Sir Henry Clinton and the British

---

* See Chapter Ten.

army began ravaging the South—Savannah and Charleston, then headed north into North Carolina and Virginia.

Clinton rallied Loyalists around him and a bitter, almost interfamilial war broke out in Georgia and the Carolinas. When the British army took control of an area, Loyalists attacked those colonists they claimed were pro-Revolution. After the British left and American forces took over, rebels exacted equal or even greater punishment on Loyalists. It was some of the most intense fighting of the Revolution, with both sides killing, burning, and torturing people who once were their friends but who now were their enemies.

There has always been the smell of treachery around Charles Lee. Short of that, it likely was incompetency; it may have been both.

Charles Lee served the Continental army during the siege of Boston, where according to historian Douglas Southall Freeman, his "dirty habits and obscenity gave offense," but he was "endured for what he was supposed to know." New Hampshire patriot Jeremy Belknap described Lee as "a perfect original, a good scholar and soldier . . . but [with] little good manners; a great sloven, wretchedly profane, and a great admirer of dogs—of which he had two at dinner with, one of them a native of Pomerania, which I would have taken for a bear had I seen him in the woods."

Sent to Charleston, Charles Lee apparently concentrated on ruining what the previous commander, William Moultrie, had built. When Fort Sullivan was saved, despite his advice, he returned north to Philadelphia, where the Continental Congress advanced him $30,000 to pay for his Virginia (now West Virginia) property. He joined Washington's army at White Plains, New York, but left with some of the general's best men when the main army went south for the New Jersey campaign. In September, Lee wrote a letter to Washington's aide, Joseph Reed, but mistakenly Washington opened it himself. Reed had earlier written Lee after the fall of Fort Washington, a loss which, to Reed, Lee referred to as "a much greater disqualification than stupidity." The letter—when Washington returned it to Reed, he apologized profusely for opening it—showed the general that he'd have to be on the alert for the "fickle" Charles Lee.

Later, on December 13, Charles Lee wrote to General Horatio Gates, referring to George Washington, criticizing the general for his loss of Fort Washington:

> Entre nous, a certain great man is most damnably deficient. He has thrown me into a situation where I have my choice of difficulties. If I stay in this Province I risk myself and army, and if I do not stay the Province is lost for ever. I have neither guides Cavalry Medicines Money Shoes or Stockings. I must act with the greatest circumspection. Tories are in my front, rear and on my flanks. The mass of the people is strangely contaminated.
>
> In short unless something which I do not expect turns up we are lost.

Later the same morning Charles Lee wrote to Gates he was captured at his headquarters at Basking Ridge. A unit of the Queen's Light Dragoons was under a young subaltern. That officer was Banastre Tarleton, and he would go on to scourge the South in the campaigns of 1780 to 1781.

Tarleton was headed for Morristown when he learned that Charles Lee was at White's Tavern, not far away. The British caught two American sentries "without firing a shot." Threatened with death, the sentries told Tarleton where Lee was, about a mile and a half behind the lines. Lee had spent the morning arguing with officers of the Connecticut militia and ridiculing their old-fashioned wigs. About ten that morning Lee (who hadn't yet donned his own, presumably, more modern wig) went down to breakfast, still in his dressing gown. He literally was caught with his pants down. Looking out a window, an aide saw the British mounted-dragoons galloping down the driveway. Tarleton knew Lee was in the building, and "I fired twice through the door of the house and then addressed myself to this effect: 'I knew Genl. Lee was in the house, that if he would surrender himself, he and his attendants should be safe.'"

Initially the British believed it was a major coup to capture the Irish-born Charles Lee. George Washington, however, saw it as something less. It wasn't known until years later how right Washington was.

For all intents and purposes, Charles Lee collaborated with the enemy while being held prisoner in New York. Among other things, he submitted a plan to his captors on a way to end the war. It called for an offensive that would "unhinge the organization of the American resistance" by gaining control of the middle colonies—Pennsylvania, Maryland, and Virginia. The British, however, paid little attention to Lee.

He was exchanged a year later for British General Richard Prescott, who'd been captured during a raid on Newport, Rhode Island. Prescott and Lee were very much alike, ill-tempered and supercilious, so it probably didn't matter who was exchanged for whom.

It was then that Charles Lee became Washington's second in command in the Monmouth campaign, where he failed so miserably that he was later court-martialed. He argued that he'd hoped to cut the British rear guard off from the main body by attacking its flanks and rear. It was an argument that no one believed. During the trial Lee accused General von Steuben of being one of "the very distant spectators of the maneuver." The Prussian challenged him to a duel. The duel never came off after Lee explained that he meant no offense.

Following his court-martial Congress suspended Lee for a year. He tried to defend himself with a newspaper article in the *Pennsylvania Packet*, "Vindication," which didn't vindicate him at all but did manage to offend John Laurens. Like von Steuben, Laurens demanded satisfaction. This time the duel came off, and Laurens shot and slightly wounded Lee. The wound wasn't much; however, it *was* enough to keep him from accepting another challenge, this from "Mad Anthony" Wayne, whom Lee had also offended.

Finally, and perhaps not surprisingly, about the time when his year's suspension would have ended, Charles Lee learned that Congress intended to dismiss him. Lee wrote Congress a letter that was so offensive they *did* boot him out of the army. He died in 1782.

Even in death Charles Lee confounded Americans. For years it was believed the artist Rembrandt Peale had painted his portrait. It wasn't so. What was thought to be Lee's portrait was that of a man named Arthur O'Connor, and it was painted in 1803, long after Lee was dead, and misidentified by such publications as the *Cyclopedia of American Biography* and the *Magazine of American History*. There are several sketches apparently made of Lee. One was drawn by Polish engineer Tadeusz Kosciuszko. It shows the hook-nose Lee standing in a boot, possibly referring to England's Lord Bute. The drawing now hangs in New York's Metropolitan Museum of Art.

Dr. Thomas Young of Boston fought against the establishment for more than twenty years, battling everything from organized religion to royalty to the military. His favorite topic for argument was "we, the common people." Dutchess County, New York, officials once arrested him for calling Jesus Christ a knave and fool. During the Boston Massacre he stood in the crowd, "a sword in his hand."

Samuel Adams delegated him to be one of the principal organizers of the Boston Tea Party, and like Adams, he rejoiced at "the perfect crisis of American politics." Eventually he moved to Philadelphia, where he met other radicals in coffeehouses and taverns. Among them, Thomas Paine.

Paine was the son of a corsetmaker in Thetford, Norfolk County, England, and was born on January 29, 1737. His family name was Pain, without the "e," and he usually spelled it that way for the first half of his life; it was only after he emigrated to America in 1774 that he insisted on the extra letter. Tom Pain, as he was, attended the local grammar school, where he learned history, mathematics, and science. He had a bent for engineering, and in a later age he might have become a technician, perhaps, in the late twentieth century, a computer nerd. As it was, at age thirteen Tom was apprenticed to his father's corset trade. Over the next twenty or so years, Tom Pain lived what may be described as a mundane, often boring life—making corsets, collecting taxes, selling tobacco, being a schoolteacher and husband.

His early education was extremely ordinary for the time and place, but as he grew older he began educating himself, doing serious reading in the natural and political sciences. He had a father who couldn't decide if he was Church of England or Quaker and a mother Paine claimed could have been William Shakespeare's model for *The Taming of the Shrew.*

Thomas Pain had a poorly paying job as tax collector. He lost even that job after a little more than a year, when the government learned that like most other tax collectors, instead of going out collecting taxes, he stayed home and issued tax stamps without checking inventories or assets. Then his wife, Mary Lambert Pain, died in childbirth.

At age twenty-eight, he had to beg to get back his job. In London he joined with a group at the White Hart tavern, drinking, debating, and wrangling. He married again, this time to Elizabeth Ollive, his landlord's lovely blond daughter. She clearly worshiped him; he often said he pitied her.

As well as debating others at the White Hart tavern, Tom Pain began writing and produced a pamphlet, *The Case of the Salary of the Officers of Excise and Thoughts on the Corruption Arising from the Poverty of Excise Officers.* His idea was that low pay made tax men less zealous in conducting their duties and more susceptible to accepting bribes.

Hoping to make money out of his own complaint, Pain printed four thousand copies of his pamphlet and priced them at three shillings a copy. Instead of making money on the project, he went deeper into debt.

He sent a copy to Parliament, where it was greeted with outstanding indifference. It did, however, interest playwright Oliver Goldsmith, who was writing his comedy *She Stoops to Conquer* at the time, and he introduced Tom to his literary circle.

Meanwhile, Pain's wife, Elizabeth, began openly flirting with other men and finally left him. Later his enemies claimed Elizabeth had left Tom because he was impotent. There was, however, the death of Tom's first wife in childbirth, to somewhat discredit that claim. A eulogistic biography of Thomas Paine written in 1819 claims that Tom was not impotent but says his marriage to Elizabeth was never consummated.

In June 1774, Tom Pain was introduced to Benjamin Franklin. As a schoolboy Pain had read a book on the natural history of Virginia; now he said he wanted to see the western side of the Atlantic Ocean. It wasn't to Virginia that Pain went, however, but to Philadelphia. Franklin gave him a letter of introduction to his son-in-law, Richard Bache:

The bearer Mr. Thomas Pain . . . goes to Pennsylvania with a view of settling there. I request you give him your best advice and countenance, as he is quite a stranger there. If you can put him in a way of obtaining employment as a clerk, or assistant tutor in school . . . you will do well, and much oblige your affectionate father.

In Philadelphia, with the "e" added to his name, Paine's fortunes improved immediately. He was hired as the editor of the new *Pennsylvania Magazine*, and within four months the magazine's circulation more than doubled. In one of his early articles Tom argued for a plan to assist young people at the start of their careers and another to support them in their old age. Twenty years later he again wrote about the idea: Create a national fund to pay everybody a sum of £15 sterling when they reached age twenty-one, and, when they got to be fifty years old, to give them a pension of ten pounds a year, "to enable them to live in old age without wretchedness, and go decently out of the world." It would be a hundred years before pensions for the elderly came even close to being commonplace. It would not be until the twentieth century that the American government would institute a pension system for the elderly, and then it generally was used as a way to open jobs for younger people by turning the old out to pasture.

In Philadelphia, Thomas Paine got busy writing, editing, and fomenting trouble. In the November 24, 1775, issue of the *Pennsylvania Magazine,* in a letter appearing under the name "A Lover of Order," he attacked the colonial assembly. The Pennsylvania legislature had instructed its delegates to the new Continental Congress to "dissent from, and utterly reject, any propositions, should such be made, that may cause, or lead to, a Separation from Our Mother Country, or a change of the form of Government." Paine claimed the assembly had exceeded its powers. "The Delegates in Congress," he believed, "are not the Delegates of the Assembly but of the People—of the Body in Large."

When others objected to the plea made by "A Lover of Order," Paine wrote a defense under the pseudonym "A Continental

Farmer."* "I despise," he wrote, "the narrow idea of acting provincially, and reprobate the little unworthy principle, conveyed [as] 'In behalf of this colony, and the more so, because by a late resolve, all Colony distinctions are to be laid aside. 'Tis the American Cause, the American Congress, the American Army, &c, &c, Whom God preserve."

Tom Paine was only getting started. Less than a month later, on January 10, 1776, he published *Common Sense*. When he first offered it around, the pamphlet scared away publishers, but finally Dr. Benjamin Rush recommended a printer named "R. Bell" and even suggested to Paine the straightforward title for the pamphlet. It appeared as an anonymously written, two-shilling, forty-seven-page pamphlet, and it contained little original thinking. Its beauty and worth was that it put into words (and into print) the thoughts of many other Patriots.

It was not written by a lawyer such as John Dickinson or James Otis; it was not written in the language of a scholar, such as Jefferson. It was written by a common man in common words. In less than three months, more than 120,000 copies were sold in the colonies, and probably several hundreds, perhaps thousands, more were pirated to Britain. Eventually, at least half a million copies were sold. "Some writers," *Common Sense* begin, "have so confounded society with government as to leave little or no distinction between them; whereas they are not only different, but have different origins." He claimed he offered, "nothing more than simple facts, plain arguments, and common sense."

Tom Paine left no question as to what he believed: The time had come for America to declare its independence from Britain:

Everything that is right or reasonable pleads for separation. The blood of the slain, the weeping voice of nature cries, "'Tis time to part."

---

* Probably an allusion to John Dickinson, who opposed independence and who often wrote under the pseudonym "A Pennsylvania Farmer."

O! ye that love mankind! Ye that dare oppose not only tyranny but the tyrant, stand forth. Every spot of the Old World is overrun with oppression. Freedom has been haunted round the globe. Asia and Africa have long expelled her. Europe regards her like a stranger, and England has given her warning to depart. O! receive the fugitive and prepare in time an asylum for mankind.

King George III, needless to say, didn't like it. A political cartoon of the time shows George reading *Common Sense* and saying, "I say, Jenky, this Paine's book is All abuse! All Abuse! Flights of madness! Flights of madness!"

John Adams had mixed feelings about *Common Sense*. On February 18, he sent a copy to his wife, Abigail, and predicted that its arguments would become common faith among Americans. For a time many people believed John Adams himself had written *Common Sense*. Adams admitted: "I could not have written anything in so manly and striking a style." John was also somewhat jealous of the pamphlet's success; in fact, Abigail apparently liked *Common Sense* more than her husband did and later even used its words to spur on John to build up the army.

Thomas Paine had relied on the Bible's Old Testament as his authority—"In the early ages of the world, according to the Scripture chronology there were no kings; the consequence of which there were no wars." John Adams called this argument ridiculous, and he questioned Paine's sincerity. Adams wrote a pamphlet to refute Paine's argument, in which, among other things, Tom contended that the Jews had adopted the idea of monarchy from their heathen enemies.

That led to Thomas Paine going to see John Adams, who told the two-years-younger author that the plans for a new government Paine had included in *Common Sense* lacked both restraints and safeguards. As for Paine's idea about Jews getting the idea of monarchy from their enemies, Thomas Paine admitted he'd borrowed the concept from another author, John Milton.

Common Sense, as it was put at the time, "had made Independents of the majority of the country." As Paine himself wrote in a bit of backward logic, "To know whether it be the interest of this continent to be Independent, we need only ask this simple question: Is it the interest of a man to be a boy all his life?"

Common Sense greatly impressed George Washington, and after reading it, he urged Congress to notify Great Britain that "if nothing else could satisfy a tyrant and his diabolical ministry, we are determined to shake off all connections with a state so unjust and unnatural."

Thomas Jefferson received a copy of *Common Sense* from fellow Virginian Thomas Nelson, a member of the Continental Congress. Playing on the cost of the pamphlet, Nelson told Jefferson he was offering two-shillings' worth of common sense.

Tom Paine's writing may have ensured that the colonists would demand independence, but it didn't, as the saying goes, put bread on the table; it did not give military strength to the cause. By April, George Washington wrote, "I find *Common Sense* is working a powerful change in the minds of many men." Still, throughout almost all of 1776, Washington and his army were on the defensive, and soon after the Declaration of Independence was approved on July 4, Paine enlisted in the army.

He served as secretary to one general, then aide-de-camp to another and carried a rank of brigade-major. It was as an aide to General Nathanael Greene that Tom Paine met George Washington, and off and on for the next couple of years Paine served as an aide to Washington.

The winter of 1776 to 1777 was a miserable time for Washington's troops. The Continental army was down to less than five thousand men, and all of them suffered from a shortage of food, clothing, and munitions. It was during this time that Paine published a series of articles and pamphlets known collectively as *The Crisis*. The first was published in the *Pennsylvania Journal* on December 19, 1776. It contains one of the most stirring and now most familiar openings in all literature. Washington ordered it read to his troops.

These are the times that try men's souls. The summer soldier and the sunshine patriot will, in this crisis, shrink from the service of his country; but he that stands it now deserves the love and thanks of man and woman. Tyranny, like hell, is not easily conquered; yet we have this consolation with us—that the harder the conflict, the more glorious the triumph. What we obtain too cheap, we esteem too lightly: It is dearness only that gives everything its value. Heaven knows how to put a proper price upon its goods; and it would be strange indeed if so celestial an article as freedom should not be highly rated. . . .

And in his final paragraph of this first *Crisis* letter, Tom Paine attacked the German mercenaries fighting with the British redcoats, taking for granted a group that England's Edmund Burke had called "a rapacious and licentious soldiery."

By perseverance and fortitude we have the prospect of a glorious issue; by cowardice and submission, the sad choice of a variety of evils—a ravaged country—a depopulated city—habitations without safety and slavery without hope—our homes turned into barracks and bawdy houses for Hessians, and a future race to provide for, whose fathers we shall doubt of. Look on this picture and weep over it. And if there yet remains one thoughtless wretch who believes it not, let him suffer unlamented.

As a reward for writing *Common Sense,* and to give him a regular means of support, Congress appointed Thomas Paine secretary to the committee on foreign affairs, a position he held until January 1779, when he was forced to resign, at the urging of French ambassador to the United States, Conrad Alexandre Gérard. Paine had published an attack on America's emissary to France, Silas Deane. Gérard had become involved with Pierre Augustin Caron de Beaumarchais and a phony corporation (Hortalez & Cie.) Beaumarchais had set up in order to supply the Continental army with arms and material.

To understand the American Revolution, you need seating charts, as it were. It's often difficult keeping up with generations who insisted on calling each other by the same name, with several Johns in a single family, an equal number of Thomases in another.

For example, Thomas Nelson, Jr., of Virginia was not really a junior, not in the strictest sense; it was his grandfather who was Thomas Nelson, also known as "Scotch Tom," even though the town where he was born, Penrith, is now on the English side of the border. At the time of Scotch Tom's birth, Penrith *was* in Scotland, but border wars kept changing the site of the border, depending on that day's winner. Aaron Burr, who went on to become vice president of the United States, to become the winner of a duel with Alexander Hamilton, and an accused conspirator charged with trying to separate the western lands from the United States—yes, *that* Aaron Burr—was actually Aaron Burr, Jr. His father, Aaron Burr, Sr., was the second president of Princeton University, or New Jersey College, as it was then.

Patriot John Adams was the son of John Adams. James Otis was the son of James Otis. James junior's grandfather was named John, which doesn't help matters out too much. All fairly confusing.

An American "caucus" is "a private or preliminary meeting of members of a political party, to select candidates for office, or to concert measures for furthering party interests." In England a caucus is "a committee popularly elected for the purpose of securing concerted political action in a constituency." At least that's what *Oxford Universal Dictionary* says.

There's an early Algonkin Indian word, *cauccauasu,* that means "one who advises," and that may be where we first got the word. There is, however, a more likely story that it came from "caulkers," shipyard workers whose job it was to hammer caulk into spaces between a ship's planks. In Boston they formed the Caulkers Club. According to legend, when they wanted to gather, they'd walk down the streets, calling out "Caulkers, caulkers!" This evolved first into "corcas" and then into "caucus."

As early as 1724, a political cabal in Boston became known as the Caucus Club. It was founded by Deacon Samuel Adams of the Old South Meeting House. He was the father of the better-known Patriot Samuel Adams. The Caucus Club was made up of small shopkeepers and shipyard workers from the city's North End. For years it effectively set the agenda for Boston's town meetings and determined who would be appointed to what office.

By 1740, Massachusetts was in a deep economic depression, with many farmers and workers indebted to a few merchants. The worse economic conditions became, the less likely it was that merchants would accept paper money.* Deacon Adams and the Caucus Club joined in the fight. Needless to say, they sided with the farmers and small shopkeepers. Adams wanted to revitalize the economy by changing over to a land-banked system of floating currency backed by their real estate—farms or homes. Good for the farmers, bad for the merchants, who claimed it would promote inflation. The colony's conservatives demanded the present system of hard money, of gold and silver, be continued and paper money be declared illegal.

When the Land Bankers won control of the Massachusetts Assembly, the governor threatened to remove from office anyone who invested in the scheme and even had Deacon Adams ejected from his office as justice of the peace. The next election saw Land Bank supporters again win a majority of assembly seats, and it sent Deacon Adams to the colony's upper house, the Council. The governor, however, vetoed Adams's election.

Things got worse in 1741, when the British Parliament declared Adams's Land Bank illegal. At the last minute the colonial court stepped in, preventing the deacon from being charged with financial crimes, having his property seized, and ordering him sent to jail.

Deacon Adams, meanwhile, kept body and soul together by operating a malt business and selling his product to local brewers. Over the years he took his son into the family business, a point that apparently led a twentieth-century beer maker to use the younger Samuel Adams's name on a product he had nothing to do with. Tories mocked Adams as "Sammy the Malster."

---

* A long-accepted currency in America was the Spanish gold coin, the pillar. Often cut into eight pieces, the result became known as "pieces of eight." One piece of eight, a "bit," was worth about twelve and a half cents, thus today's quarter is known as "two bits," which brought about the old high school or college football cheer: "Two bits, four bits, six bits, a dollar; all for (insert your alma mater here), stand up and holler."

Deacon Adams paid Sammy the Malster's Harvard College tuition in molasses and flour, and the younger Adams graduated in the class of 1740. Samuel returned for a master's degree and didn't leave until 1743.

While at Harvard, Samuel came under the influence of George Whitefield, an evangelist from England who came to America in the Great Awakening. Like Patrick Henry to the south, the Great Awakening greatly affected Samuel Adams. In fact, Adams almost became a clergyman. He didn't, of course. Instead, he became perhaps America's first professional politician.

For a while he was confused. Reverend George Whitefield denounced the colony's rich and wealthy, powerful men whom he said lacked piety. Whitefield, however, also denounced the Land Bankers, which left Samuel in a quandary. So the young politician-to-be came down firmly on both sides of the issue; both the rich merchants and the poorer farmers were at fault, he claimed. In his final paper at Harvard, Samuel Adams argued that when the existence of a colony was at stake—and he believed it was in the case of the Land Bank question—it was lawful to resist even the highest civil authority.

Deacon Adams died in 1748, followed shortly by his wife. Their son was just twenty-six years old at the time, and he inherited the family malt company. Instead of riding the business into a successful position in Boston society, Samuel Adams let the business slide away. He and his wife lived on in Deacon Adams's deteriorating house on Purchase Street, where they quietly went broke.

Samuel not only inherited the malt company, he inherited his father's debts from the Land Bank. With his finances quickly going downhill, Sheriff Stephen Greenleaf almost confiscated Adams's house to sell at public auction. Samuel took out newspaper ads warning Greenleaf not to take such action. It was a technique he would use many times later in his political life. As he phrased it, always "put your adversary in the wrong. And keep him there." Sheriff Greenleaf backed down.

Samuel Adams and a group of friends began operating a newspaper, using it to attack the wealthy, the merchants, and the royal governor—anybody who was conservative. Conservatives themselves referred to Adams's newspaper as "the Whippingpost Club." Adams used its pages to tell Boston and the world of his passion for liberty and justice. Like all other money-making schemes Samuel Adams tried, the newspaper failed.

His wife also failed; she died after five pregnancies in six years. In 1763, he found himself, at age forty-one, unemployed, nearly broke, and a widower with a young son and daughter to support. A year later he remarried, this time to Elizabeth Welles. Twenty years younger than Samuel, and the daughter of one of Deacon Adams's closest friends, she was intelligent and amiable, a kindly stepmother who put up with her new husband's seeming lack of care for their financial upkeep. Apparently Elizabeth Welles Adams knew how to run a household on next to nothing, which was good, since that was her husband's annual income. Samuel Adams's first mother-in-law even tried to help out the couple by giving them a slave named Surry. Adams, however, immediately set her free, but Surry chose to stay on in the house as a servant.

That left Adams unable to support his new wife, two children, and a former slave. Destitute and besieged by creditors, they all lived in Adams's rundown birthplace, subsisting mainly on gifts and donations from friends and neighbors. By financial standards he was a failure. In other ways, however, he was a great success.

On Sundays, Samuel Adams sang in church, but for the rest of the week he used his voice in Boston's coffeehouses. He sat among those more wealthy than he, those with whom he had gone to college, and he wore the same red suit and cheap gray wig he'd owned for years. He roamed from coffeehouse to tavern, fraternal lodge to volunteer fire company (it was a time when, without a municipal fire department, volunteer and for-profit fire companies set up operations). Samuel Adams criticized aristocrats and asked shopkeepers their opinions. His belief was simple: The wealthy were evil; the poor were goodness.

Adams became a tax collector for the Crown, appointed not by the royal governor, but by the people. As it turned out, Samuel Adams didn't do much collecting of taxes. If times were bad for a home- or business owner, Adams deferred the taxes. He deferred them so often that his enemies accused Samuel Adams of skimming money from the royal coffers to support himself. Obviously they hadn't checked up on Adams. Same cheap red suit on his shoulders, cheap wig on his head. Samuel Adams walked mighty close to the debtors' prison door.

Early on he'd joined his father's Caucus Club, and it was as head of the club that Sam Adams became a leader of Revolutionary Boston. The Caucus Club regularly met at the Green Dragon Tavern on Union Street and, by the time war broke out, the tavern was being called the "headquarters of the Revolution."

When Samuel Adams joined the Continental Congress in Philadelphia, he took the Caucus Club with him and picked up as associates Virginia's George Wythe and Richard Henry Lee. Together they moved toward independence.

Perhaps the Founding Father most neglected by history is James Otis—politician, orator, and fifth-generation resident of Massachusetts. He was the mind of the fight to repeal the Stamp Act, while Samuel Adams was its mouth.

Otis and John Adams belonged to a small group of fellow lawyers who met regularly in Boston's South End. Adams thought Otis talked too much, and "takes up so much of our time and fills it with trash, obsceneness, profaneness, nonsense and distraction that we have no [time] left for rational amusement."

James Otis, Jr., was born in 1725, the first of thirteen children. He was described as "short-necked and eagle-eyed." Had it not been for a barroom brawl and a continuing mental illness, Otis likely would have been the leader of the American Revolution, could well have been the first president of the United States of America, and we might be celebrating his birthday instead of George Washington's. A Harvard graduate who turned to law, James Otis was admitted to the Massachusetts bar in 1748. Ten years later he was perhaps the most prominent lawyer in the colony, and he shared his father's dislike of Thomas Hutchinson.

In 1755, Parliament enacted the Writs of Assistance to combat frequent colonial evasion of the Navigation Acts. Writs gave customs officers the authority to demand that provincial officers aid them in searching private property for smuggled goods. They were general warrants which, as commonly interpreted, empowered customs officers under police protection arbitrarily to enter warehouses, stores, or homes to search for smuggled goods. The officers would not be required to present grounds for suspecting the presence of any illicit items. Such writs had been used in England since the time of King Charles II, but nothing like them had been tried in America.

British West Indies planters had pleaded for the Molasses Act, saying they were being outproduced and undersold by planters in the French and Dutch West Indies. In 1733, the Navigation Acts put a prohibitive tax on sugar and molasses imported into the colonies from non-British-owned lands. It was all tied to that infamous Triangular Trade and cut into New England's profitable wedge of the triangle. So New England–owned ships regularly smuggled molasses to ports in Massachusetts and Rhode Island. To stop the smuggling into Boston, the English Parliament enacted the Writs of Assistance, and nine years later they passed the first law specifically to raise money in the colonies, the Sugar Act. Boston shipowners wanted to have nothing to do with either the Molasses or Sugar Acts; they liked even less the Writs of Assistance used to enforce them.

James Otis had been the advocate general of the vice-admiralty court in Boston—that is, the prosecutor—but he resigned to argue against the Writs, even refusing to accept a fee for his services. Thomas Hutchinson, the colony's newly appointed lieutenant governor, and member of the Governor's Council, was the court's presiding judge.

The Writs of Assistance case involved Boston surveyor of customs, Charles Paxton. Sixty-three prominent Boston merchants joined to retain James Otis to represent them in the suit against Paxton.

Prosecuting the case was Jeremiah Gridley, and in his opening argument he said that general writs had been issued in England by the Court of Exchequer. For more than half a century, he said, the Superior Court had the authority to issue such writs.

It was February 24, 1761. Otis was described by a contemporary critic as "a plump, round-faced, smooth-skinned, short-necked, eagle-eyed politician." In a rousing speech before the Massachusetts Supreme Court, he questioned the legality of the Writs, adding, "an act against the Constitution is void; an act against natural equality is void."

In that speech Otis quoted famed English legal authority Sir Edward Coke. It was Coke's *Institutes of the Lawes of England* over which such would-be lawyers as Thomas Jefferson, John Adams, James Otis, and Patrick Henry all struggled while trying to learn their trade as lawyers.

In addressing the court, Otis argued:

A man's house is his castle; and while he is quiet, he is as well guarded as a prince in his castle. Custom-house officers may enter our houses when they please; we are commanded to permit their entry. Their menial servants may enter—may break locks, bars, everything in their way—and whether they break through malice or revenge, no man, no court may inquire. . . . I am determined to sacrifice estate, ease, health, applause and even life in opposition. . . .

The sum of his argument, Otis said, "is that civil government is of God." Good argument, but it didn't work. Britain not only continued the Writs of Assistance against Massachusetts, Parliament extended their use to other colonies.

John Adams wrote in his diary, "Otis was a flame of fire." The future president added that "with a profusion of legal authorities, a prophetic glance of his eye into futurity, and a torrent of impetuous eloquence, he hurried away before him. . . . Every man of a crowded audience appeared to me to go away, as I did, ready to take arms against the writs of assistance. . . ." More than fifty years later Adams remembered the speech and wrote, "Then and there the child Independence was born."

Otis went on for three hours, alarming parts of his audience, thrilling others. He denounced the writs as "destructive to English Liberty," saying they would give every petty customs official the right to invade any citizen's home on the mere suggestion of an informer. It didn't matter, he thundered, that Parliament had passed laws endorsing writs of assistance; they were void because they violated the English Constitution, that great unwritten charter of liberty.

"Right reason and the spirit of a free constitution," he declared, "require that the representation of the whole people should be as equal as possible." If such perfect equality was impossible, "no good reason however can be given in any country why every man of a sound mind should not have his vote in the election of a representative. If a man has but little property to protect and defend, yet his life and liberty are things of some importance." In this, his thinking was far in advance of most others in America. Eleven years before the Declaration of Independence, a year before Patrick Henry's Virginia Resolves, here was James Otis speaking out for liberty.

His speech must have been extraordinary; however, like all his other speeches, it gave future historians headaches. He never wrote out his speeches, but generally worked from no more than rough notes. History must rely on the note-taking of those who were there at the time.* For that reason, perhaps, and the fact that late in his life he destroyed almost all of his personal papers, James Otis has been neglected by history and historians.

John Adams was present when Otis spoke against the Writs of Assistance, and it was through his memory of that speech, sixty years later, that we read Otis's words. They are, however, Adams's memory of James Otis's speech, his version of what was said more than a half-century earlier. Adams's grandson and editor, Charles Francis Adams, even noted that his grandfather "insensibly infused into this work much of the learning and of the breadth of views belonging to himself."

Three months after the Writs of Assistance case, Otis was elected to the Massachusetts House of Representatives by an almost unanimous vote. At the same time, his father was reelected Speaker of the House.

According to John Adams, a week after the Otis family's election, Adams attended a dinner in Worcester at which Chief Justice Ruggles of the state Court of Common Pleas commented: "Out of this election will arise a d—d faction, which will shake this province to its foundation."

---

* In writing *The Life of James Otis of Massachusetts,* William Tudor, Jr., relied heavily on notes taken by witnesses to Otis's speeches, including those by John Adams. To a great extent, much of what we know about James Otis comes from William Tudor. In reconstructing Otis's speeches, Tudor did for him what William Wirt did for another Patriot, Patrick Henry.

In 1762, Otis wrote a pamphlet, *A Vindication of the Conduct of the House of Representatives,* and four years later he was the author of *The Rights of the British Colonies Asserted and Proved.* The British Constitution, he said, "is the most free one, and by far the best now existing on earth." With that in mind, he claimed:

> Every British subject born on the continent of America, or in any other of the British dominions, is by the law of God and nature, by the common law, and by act of Parliament . . . entitled to all the natural, essential, inherent, and inseparable rights of our fellow subjects in Great Britain. . . .
>
> [No] legislative, supreme or subordinate, has a right to make itself arbitrary. . . .To say the Parliament is absolute and arbitrary is a contradiction. . . .
>
> [No] man can take my property from me without my consent; if he does, he deprives me of my liberty and makes me a slave.

If that sounds as if he's saying "Taxation without representation is tyranny," no wonder; Otis is also credited with that line.

Like any other politician, Otis was not without his opponents. Customs officer Samuel Waterhouse was one, and he wrote a parody of the long-popular military marching song, *"Lillibullero,"** renaming it "Jemmibullero," after James, or Jemmy Otis.

> And Jemmy is a silly dog, and Jemmy is a tool;
> And Jemmy is a stupid curr, and Jemmy is a fool;
> And Jemmy is a madman, and Jemmy is an ass,
> And Jemmy has a leaden head, and forehead spread with
>   brass.

In another bit of popular music, *The Beggar's Opera,* the word *jemmy* is also used to designate a turncoat. Soon it was applied as an epithet to James Otis.

---

* See Chapter Seven.

So Jemmy rail'd at upper folks, while Jemmy's DAD was out,
But Jemmy's DAD has now a place, so Jemmy's turn'd about.

A few months after the parody appeared, Otis reportedly suffered "a Fit of Bleeding of the Nose which was Troublesome Some days." So Waterhouse added a verse to his song: "And Jemmy *pleads* his bloody nose when quarrels he would settle!"

Loyalist Martin Howard of Newport, Rhode Island, compared *"Lillibullero"* to Otis's contention of no taxation without representation. The song and the argument, he said, "made all the mischief in the colonies." Otis, meanwhile, predicted that everything from the laws passed by Parliament to life in general, was in jeopardy.

By 1769, James Otis was the "acknowledged political leader of his province." Except, that is, for Massachusetts's lieutenant governor, the family's old enemy, Thomas Hutchinson, who saw Otis as merely a thoughtful and well-intentioned man.

Comparing James Otis to Martin Luther, the father of Protestantism, John Adams said he was "rough, hasty and loved good cheer." At the same time Adams thought he was a bit unstable, and that proved to be true. The question is, what caused that instability?

That fall a Boston newspaper carried an ad paid for by James Otis, in which he assailed four of the colony's customs commissioners. Using only their first names, Otis asked Lord Hillsborough and the Board of Trade in London to

> pay no kind of regard to any of the abusive representations of me or my country that may be transmitted by the said Henry, Charles, William and John or their confederates; for they are no more worthy of credit than those of [Governor] Sir Francis Bernard . . . or any of his cabal.

In filing a defamation suit against Sir Francis, Otis referred to the other four men as "superlative blockheads." The "John" was John Robinson, and Otis said, "If Robinson misrepresents me, I have a natural right, if I can get no other satisfaction, to break his head." We assume he was being witty, but he also may have been serious enough to do something about it.

Learning that Robinson had purchased a heavy walking stick, Otis went to the same shop and bought one just like it. Stick in hand, Otis walked into the British Coffee House, a hangout for Boston Tories and British military officers, where he was roundly jeered.

When Robinson arrived, he saw that Otis wore no sword, so he removed his own, then turned to confront the man who had called him a blockhead. Instead of backing down, James Otis spoke out: "I demand satisfaction of you, sir."

Robinson asked what kind of satisfaction Otis wanted.

"A gentleman's satisfaction," Otis replied. Dueling with swords was against the law, so it would be a fistfight.

"I am ready to do it," Robinson said.

They walked toward the door, but before they could get outside, Robinson reached over and tweaked Otis's nose. Otis then tried to block Robinson's way, using his walking stick; Robinson threatened Otis with his own. For a while, onlookers said, it was something like dueling walking sticks. When their sticks were taken away, the two men began pummeling each other with their fists. Both men were about the same age, forty-five or so. Otis, however, was in enemy territory, and members of the Tory crowd began pushing him and holding his arms while Robinson beat him. John Gridley, Otis's nephew, happened by. Someone began yelling, "Kill him! Kill him!" so Gridley tried to break up the fight.

He grabbed one of the walking sticks and waded into the brawl. Several men were holding Otis while John Robinson beat him. Someone—perhaps Robinson, perhaps someone else—hit Otis in the head with a broadsword or cutlass, laying open his skull. Finally the fight ended, and Otis and his nephew were released. Otis left to have his wound dressed.

It seemed to be no more than a minor barroom brawl. Otis's wife even said that in a way, she was happy about it, because it kept her husband quiet and out of taverns. It led other Patriots to claim Otis was a martyr and was never quite right again because of the brawl.

Otis sued Robinson, charging him with "very unfair play." A month after the fight, Robinson married a merchant's daughter and sailed for England. Several years later, the courts ordered Robinson to pay Otis 2,000 pounds in costs.

116

By then it was too late for James Otis. Whatever the cause, and that blow to the head certainly didn't help any, Otis grew more and more unstable. "He now rambles and wanders like a ship without a helm," friends claimed.

In December 1771, it was obvious to his family that James Otis had been driven over the brink of madness. Occasionally he was violent, and he began drinking heavily. Sometimes, but not often, reason seemed to return to him. Finally a probate court declared him *non compos mentis,* and his younger brother Samuel was made his legal guardian.

James Otis followed a mysterious zigzag course that confused both his friends and enemies. So much so that occasionally the people of Boston didn't know whether he was a Tory or a Patriot, and it may be this more than anything else that has denied him his rightful place in American history.

There may be a valid reason for his inconsistency. James Otis may have been a manic-depressive. According to some medical authorities, a manic depressive may be sane enough to live a useful life but will go through cycles in which he is abnormally energetic, keyed up, ambitious, social, and talkative, then become abnormally quiet, moody, uncommunicative, unhappy, discouraged, and physically tired. James Otis often showed such wide mood swings, often was brilliant and often was morose.

Of manic depressives, textbooks say his or her brain will virtually seethe with ingenious ideas and possess a facile flow of thoughts and words. A manic-depressive individual believes whatever cause he has espoused is righteous and bound to succeed, and he may be unusually successful in persuading his friends to invest in something or to join them in some enterprise.

Today the disease is called a bipolar affective disorder. Those suffering from it are likely to be "live wires" but erratic and easily diverted. Because they are truly "bipolar," those who suffer from the disease switch rapidly from mania, where they are happy and social, to depression, where they are certain the world is out to get them.

There is little doubt that James Otis was often depressed. There is also little doubt that he just as often was manic. As the saying goes, Otis went where angels feared to tread. Walking into a tavern filled with his enemies is a good example of what a manic-depressive might do in the "up" phase of the disease.

There is little doubt that James Otis was the early intellectual voice of the Revolution, but that changed as his emotional instability grew. Modern medicine often uses chemicals such as lithium to control bipolar swings. In the eighteenth century the "cure" for any condition they referred to as "madness" often entailed nothing more than locking patients away in asylums, and it was about this time that America's first public mental hospital was built.

Often people suffering from bipolar disorders are able to convince others of their own delusional beliefs. Just as often, while we believe something is wrong with an individual, we're not quite certain just what it is. That apparently was the case with James Otis. If it wasn't the severe beating that brought about James Otis's collapse, then it's likely he was mentally disturbed all along. This disturbance was not understood then and not recognized by many modern-day historians now. Otis hated Thomas Hutchinson, but even that hatred wavered. Before the issue arose of whether James Otis, Sr., would become chief justice, both father and son were "friends to the government," and apparently were fond of Hutchinson. Later Otis said "I hate the L[ieutenant] G[overnor] should prevail in anything."

Thomas Hutchinson called him the "distracted demagogue of Boston." Often Otis became overwrought and sought out Hutchinson, to whom he tearfully apologized: "I meant well but am not convinced that I was mistaken. Cursed be the day I was born."

John Adams quoted Judge Peter Oliver as saying about Otis: "I have known him these 20 Years and I have no [good] opinion of his Head or his Heart. If Bedlamism* is a Talent he has it in Perfection." Otis himself once complained that government writers (that is, those who favored the British government) habitually used the term *madman* to describe their opponents, including him. It's a practice that continues today and, of course, goes beyond "government writers."

---

* Bedlam was a London hospital—officially, the Hospital of St. Mary of Bethlehem—used since 1547 as a hospital for the insane.

Speaking to the Massachusetts legislature, Otis remarked that it didn't matter what the kings of Europe were called, including Britain's George III. He said they might as well be referred to as "Tom, Dick, or Harry." In another of his mood swings, Otis called George III "the best and greatest Prince in the world." He had planned a series of essays, claiming "Liberty and [royal] prerogative [were] the same." However, Otis apparently never got around to writing the essays, and a month later resumed his opposition to both the king and Thomas Hutchinson.

Not everyone who fought in the Revolution was British or American. Some, like Lafayette, were from France. Tadeusz Kosciuszko and Casimir Pulaski were Polish, and John Paul Jones was Scottish.

Kazimierz (or, Casimir, as he more often wrote it) Pulaski's family was of the minor nobility. His father was a lawyer, actively engaged in politics, and according to a recent biography, "one of the Polish potentates."

Although ostensibly a free state, Poland was practically a Russian satellite. King Stanislaus Poniatowski had been one of Russian Empress Catherine II's many lovers but now was her puppet in Warsaw. With his brother Casimir helped their father in an anti-Russian and antiroyalty insurrection called the Bar Confederacy.

Partisan fighting served as a military school for Casimir Pulaski, and he learned well. At the Battle of Czestochowa, he defeated a Russian army heavily supported by Prussian artillery.

The confederation kidnapped King Stanislaus and hoped to force him to abdicate. However, the king escaped and public opinion turned against both the confederation and Casimir.

Eventually Russia repressed the Bar Confederacy. It was the first of many Polish insurrections against Russia and the first to lose. Casimir's father died in a prison in Turkey; one brother, Francis, was killed in battle, and another brother, Antoni, was taken prisoner by the Russians. Casimir went into exile, first in France, then in America.

In March 1777, Congress began recruiting and commissioning foreign-born officers. Among them were the Marquis de Lafayette, Baron Johan de Kalb, Tadeusz Kosciuszko, and Baron von Steuben. Not, however, Casimir Pulaski, who expected to be subordinate only to Washington or Lafayette. Congress refused, saying that "a compliance with those expectations would be as contrary to the prevailing sentiments in the several states as to the Constitution of our Army and therefore highly impolitic." With no commission from Congress, Pulaski served as a volunteer aide de camp to George Washington at the Battle of Brandywine Creek in Pennsylvania. It was early September.

The British high command were certain that wherever they *weren't*, the Loyalists *were*, just waiting to be delivered from the patriot curse. If not New York, they felt, then Pennsylvania, so they went there. General William Howe was certain the Pennsylvania countryside was just raging with anti-independence spirit. He was wrong.

Howe had decided not to march over land from New York but to go by ship, which may have taken less time, but it also greatly weakened his force—down the Atlantic, take a right at the Chesapeake, sail up to the Delaware River, then come ashore at Chadd's Ford, a point now on U.S. Route 1, southwest of Philadelphia. By the time they disembarked, many of Howe's troops and horses were sick.

The forty-eight-year-old general split his army into two columns, and at dawn on September 11, they moved out. Baron Wilhelm von Knyphausen (part of his regiment had been captured in the Battle of Trenton the previous December) took 5,000 men—the "Regiment Knyphausen," it was called—up one side of the creek, and General Cornwallis marched up the other with another 7,500. Cornwallis expected to turn Washington's right flank.

Howe himself expected to turn a quick victory, but it was touch-and-go, no thanks to George Washington's action that day. By all accounts Howe knew where Washington was, but Washington wasn't too sure about Howe.

The main problem seems to be that Washington didn't operate with his customary alertness. He also failed to use his cavalry, and that's where Casimir Pulaski came in.

They would eventually come to be known as "Pulaski's Legion," but at the time they were raw cavalrymen. Perhaps because they were raw, Washington didn't use the dragoons, but that was just one of the mistakes he made that day. Mainly Washington fought the Battle of Brandywine as if he were in a daze.

Perhaps the only thing that saved the American army was that an elderly local farmer named Joseph Brown warned Washington that, if he didn't move soon, he'd be surrounded. Washington's aides enlisted Brown to guide the army, although *enlisted* isn't the proper word. They told Brown that "if he did not instantly get on his horse and conduct the General by the nearest and best route to the place of action, he would run him through on the spot." When Brown slowed down, Washington himself urged him on: "Push along, old man. Push along, old man!"

That night Washington wrote John Hancock, president of the Continental Congress, about the first day's battle:

> Sir: I am sorry to inform you, that in this day's engagement, we have been obliged to leave the enemy masters of the field.
>
> Unfortunately the intelligence received of the enemy's advancing up the Brandywine, and crossing at the ford about six miles above us, was uncertain and contradictory, notwithstanding all my pains to get the best.

The Continental troops did well enough in the beginning, but as darkness fell, they began to wander off and run away. Finally their officers managed to regain control and go into camp near the village of Chester. It was from there that Washington wrote Hancock, adding: "Notwithstanding the misfortune of the day, I am happy to find the troops in good spirits; and I hope another time we shall compensate for the losses now sustained."

The Battle of Brandywine was a solid defeat for American forces. Of 11,000 Continental troops at Brandywine, somewhere between 1,000 and 1,300 were killed or wounded and another 400 were taken prisoner. In addition, the British took eleven American cannon. Of about 12,500 British and German troops under Howe, less than 600 were killed or wounded.

One of the American army wounded was the Marquis de Lafayette. He was shot in the left thigh. The *"Messieurs le anglais,"* Lafayette wrote his wife—"Dear Heart," he called her—had wounded him slightly in the leg. He added, "But it is nothing . . . for the ball did not touch bone or nerve." Some of Lafayette's critics said the wound was the best thing that happened to the Frenchman; it established Lafayette, you could say, as just one of the guys.

With Brandywine lost, and the British army only fifteen miles away, the Continental Congress again packed up its quill pens and evacuated the capital, fleeing first to Lancaster, Pennsylvania, then later in the month to York. On September 26, General Howe occupied Philadelphia.

Washington and the Continental army retreated, but in early October the two armies met again, this time at Germantown. Howe had swung his army northwest. Casimir Pulaski and his new dragoons galloped to meet the British. Pulaski made contact with Howe's Hessian Jägers and grenadiers, but before they could begin an all-out battle, they were hit by a sudden strong rainstorm. Their powder was soaked and the would-be battlefield became a quagmire. Hessian Major Baurmeister wrote that troops on both sides "sank to our calves."

Meanwhile Howe blundered into a little-known spot where General Anthony Wayne had stashed supplies—"3800 Barrels of Four, Soap and Candles, 25 Barrels of Horse Shoes, several thousand tomahawks and Kettles of Intrenching Tools and 20 Hogshead of Resin." It was called Valley Forge, and later, when Washington's army occupied the forge, Continental troops would have need of all those things that Howe's troops had stolen.

A few days later a British force surprised General Anthony Wayne at his camp near a spot called Paoli, south of the Schuylkill River. Major Samuel Hay of the Continental army wrote that "the annals of the age cannot produce such a scene of butchery. All was Confused." British forces attacked with fixed bayonets. After the raid the patriot cause cried "Massacre!" Major Hay wrote that "the scene was shocking—the poor men groaning under their wounds, which were all by stabs of bayonets and cuts of Light-Horsemen's swords."

Major John André, who would later play a major (and, to him, fatal) role in Benedict Arnold's treason, recorded in his journal that the British Light Infantry "rushed along the line putting the bayonet to all they came up with, and overtaking the main herd of the fugitives, stabbed great numbers. . . . Near 200 must have been killed, and a great number wounded. Seventy-one prisoners were brought off; forty of them badly wounded. . . ." Howe's troops suffered only six killed and twenty-two wounded.

The army court-martialed Anthony Wayne on charges he had failed to heed the "timely notice" of the attack. He was acquitted "with the highest honors." It did not, however, prevent American propagandists from declaring the Paoli skirmish a "massacre."

Germantown was a repeat of Brandywine, which had been a repeat of Kip's Bay: Initial confusion among Continental troops led to a rush to the rear. The confusion may have been due to the rain and fog (each side often mistaking its own men for the enemy and firing at them), but there were other causes as well. General John Sullivan's advance force lost its momentum and, when he paused, his troops turned and retreated. General Nathanael Greene didn't get his men in position in time, and—this is probably the main reason for the defeat—George Washington's battle plan was defective. He had eleven thousand troops, mostly amateurs, divided into four columns spread out over seven miles. Washington tried attacking at night, although he didn't know the roads, and he faced an army of professionals deployed over a smaller area, on relatively good terrain.

The battle, however, was going well for rebel forces until suddenly and inexplicably they panicked. "My Division," General Sullivan wrote, "finding themselves unsupported by any other troops, their cartridges all expended, the force of the enemy on the right collecting to the left to oppose them . . . retired with as much precipiation [sic] as they had before advances against every effort of their officers to rally them." Washington blamed the fog, which caused a lack of communication, which caused him to mistake his own troops for the enemy, although as a pro-Pulaski, anti-Washington writer puts it, "it must be said that the fog made for poor visibility for the British as well."

Pulaski's cavalry apparently tried to prevent the British from pursuing the retreating Continental troops, but they were also forced back. As they reached General Greene's troops, the Continentals mistook the dragoons for the enemy. That scattered the rebels and demoralized them even more.

One reason the Americans thought the dragoons were British was that the Battle of Germantown seems to have been the first appearance of a distinctive American mounted unit. Continental foot soldiers didn't even know they had a cavalry until they saw Pulaski's men riding toward them.

With Philadelphia won and the American army pushed beyond Germantown, British General Howe decided he'd done enough damage for one year and ordered his troops into winter quarters.

Halting a war for the winter was normal. The previous year, at Christmastime, it had allowed Washington to surprise Hessian troops at Trenton.

Without paved roads (even the so-called "corduroy roads," made by felling trees and laying them across the roadway) an army had trouble moving. Snow and rain often froze roadways and made travel difficult if not impossible. Worse was that it prevented the feeding of the horses and oxen that often carried troops or pulled wagons. Humans can go for days, weeks, or even months without food, as long as there's water, but horses and cattle cannot. When snow covered the grass, there was no food available for animals, and so the armies that relied on them for transportation generally called a halt to war until spring.

After the Battle of Brandywine Creek, but before getting rained out and fogged in at Germantown, Count Pulaski finally received his commission as brigadier general. He was also given the post "commander of the horse." When Washington's troops went into winter quarters at Valley Forge, Pulaski and Anthony Wayne went on foraging expeditions at Trenton and Flemington.

It was then that Pulaski was involved in some kind of trouble with another officer, Stephen Moylan. Before joining the Continental army, Moylan had hoped to be America's first ambassador to Spain, but he didn't get the appointment. Instead, Moylan raised a mounted unit for Washington's army. He became a colonel in the First Pennsylvania Regiment of Cavalry, assigned to General Pulaski's overall command, and it is likely that Moylan was disappointed that it was Pulaski and not he who'd been given command.

Moylan usually wore what was described as "a very remarkable uniform, consisting of a red waistcoat, buckskin breeches, bright green coat and bearskin hat." He also dressed his regiment in red coats. It was a point which, inasmuch as the British wore similar red coats, irked George Washington. The general ordered Moylan to dye his uniforms a different color, any color but red.

In October, Pulaski preferred court-martial charges against Moylan. Pulaski, who was anything *but* restrained, charged the flamboyant Irish-born Moylan with "disobedience to the orders of General Pulaski, a cowardly and ungentlemanly action in striking Mr. Zielinski, a gentleman and officer in the Polish service, when disarmed . . . and giving irritating language to General Pulaski." Moylan was acquitted of the charges and, perhaps in a fit of indignation, Pulaski resigned his commission the following March. As if to prove that Moylan, indeed, was innocent, Congress gave him temporary command of the Continental dragoons.

Like Pulaski, Tadeusz Andrzei Bonawentura Kosciuszko was the son of a member of Poland's minor gentry. He reached Philadelphia in August 1776, and joined the Continental army as colonel of engineers.

Fighting for freedom, it seems, was the second reason Tadeusz had come to America. The first reason was that he'd been unlucky in love. Kosciuszko apparently believed he'd won the heart of a young noblewoman named Ludvika Sosnowska. Problem was, he never got around to asking Ludvika's father for her hand before capturing the rest of her. Daddy Sosnowska sent his henchmen after Tadeusz, and they almost caught him in Paris. Kosciuszko solved the problem by sailing for America. Through an interpreter, since he neither spoke nor understood English, Kosciuszko told George Washington, "I have come to fight, a victim of love."

The Continental Congress first hired Tadeusz Kosciuszko to design defenses around Philadelphia, and he impressed George Washington so much that the general had Kosciuszko build fortifications along the Hudson River at West Point. It was there that Kosciuszko met Benedict Arnold.

If General Arthur St. Clair had taken Kosciuszko's advice to fortify Sugarloaf Hill (more commonly called Mount Defiance) at Fort Ticonderoga, the fort might not have fallen back into British hands. St. Clair, however, did not take that advice.

It was, of course, the same Fort Ticonderoga Ethan Allen and Benedict Arnold had captured earlier, when (at least according to legend) Allen claimed the fort was his "by the authority of the Great Jehovah and the Continental Congress!" Ethan Allen's authority must have lapsed, however, because later he was captured at Montreal and bundled off in irons to England and held prisoner for a year in Pendennis Castle. Benedict Arnold, or course, later turned traitor, and went to England of his own accord.

It was this same Fort Ticonderoga whose cannon and mortars Henry Knox had somehow managed to push and bully over the mountains and through the streams to the Heights of Dorchester overlooking Boston harbor. With those cannon aimed down at them, the British soon gave up Boston and sailed away.

It was this same situation—mountaintop cannon aimed at the enemy below—that led to the Americans losing Ticonderoga, and it was because an American general didn't listen to his Polish engineer.

In early 1777, Lieutenant-General John "Gentleman Johnny" Burgoyne persuaded Lord Germain, his boss back in London, that he could isolate New England from the rest of the rebelling colonies. It would take "not less than eight thousand regulars, rank and file," along with German mercenaries, Canadian, and Loyalist militia, to do the job. While Burgoyne pushed southward down Lake Champlain, General William Howe would move northward up the Hudson. They planned to meet at Albany, New York.

So, that June, Burgoyne and his army landed about three miles above Fort Ticonderoga on the eastern shore of Lake Champlain. It was an inauspicious beginning to an auspicious campaign for Burgoyne's army.

They began slogging their way down the lakeshore toward the American-held fort. *Slogging* is the appropriate word, because the area was filled with waterways too thick to swim through and too thin to walk on. Burgoyne's troops truly faced a forest primeval: deadfalls, windfalls, the air heavy with humidity. It was so hot and so humid that as they marched, the troops' legs would swell and their heavily whitewashed breeches would split. Their double-cuffed coats caught in bushes, their sabers, haversacks, and muskets banged against arms and legs and knees. And over it all hung a miasmatic cloud of mosquitoes. Welcome to America, boys.

The western side of the lake offered none of the problems the eastern side did, but Burgoyne didn't know that. He also didn't know that General St. Clair's defenses over there were extremely weak. So, slogging along, it took the army about a week to get within striking distance of Fort Ticonderoga.

The fort lay in two sections, one on either side of the lake, just about where Lake Champlain drains into Lake George. A floating bridge connected Ticonderoga with defensive works on nearby Mount Independence. The 750-foot-high Sugarloaf Hill lies a mile away and clearly commands the view of the fort. Seeing this, Kosciuszko recommended to General St. Clair that Sugarloaf Hill be fortified. St. Clair told the Polish officer not to worry, that it was impossible to drag cannon up the hill's steep, forested slope. It had never been fortified, St. Clair declared, and never would need to be defended against.

Burgoyne's expert on things mountainous was a young officer identified only as "a lieutenant Twiss." He agreed with Tadeusz. He and Kosciuszko were right and St. Clair was wrong. It took the British a couple of days, but they mounted cannon on top of Mount Defiance, and Fort Ticonderoga was as good as lost.

St. Clair's assistant adjutant, incidentally, was none other than General James Wilkinson, with whom Aaron Burr later would be involved in a scheme to divide up the new American nation. Wilkinson thought St. Clair should surrender Fort Ticonderoga, and in his memoirs he claimed that his commander, "lacked the resolution to give up the place, or in other words to sacrifice his character for the public good." With British cannon looking down on them, American forces didn't have much choice. As Wilkinson put it: "We must away from this place because our situation had become desperate."

In the twentieth century world of "What ifs?" we can ask: What if Arthur St. Clair had listened to Tadeusz Kosciuszko? What if he had fortified Sugarloaf Hill?

As it was, St. Clair did not fortify Mount Defiance, and American troops abandoned Fort Ticonderoga two years after Allen and Arnold captured it. St. Clair loaded his sick and infirm into bateaus (flat-bottomed boats with tapered ends) and sent them down to Skensboro, New York. Then, in the middle of the night, he marched the army over that floating bridge and headed southeast. He left behind supplies that the Continental army badly needed.

On the morning of July 6, British Brigadier General Simon Fraser* was at the head of a column advancing toward Fort Ticonderoga, when he learned that the American lines around the fort were deserted.

In saving his troops, St. Clair had partially made up for not listening to Kosciuszko and not fortifying Sugarloaf Hill. He made a second mistake, however, when he failed to destroy the floating bridge they'd escaped on. Fraser and his men used the bridge and took off after the Americans. They almost caught them.

That's when Burgoyne's troubles really began. He was all dressed up with enormous artillery and no place to use it. He had a baggage train that began large and full and ended small and empty. His troops had to cut their way through some of the heaviest forests in America. Rebel forces under Philip Schuyler didn't help. They felled trees in Burgoyne's path, destroyed crops, and drove cattle away from the oncoming British army.

Meanwhile Burgoyne was running out of just about everything, so he sent a force to seize stores at Bennington, Vermont. The American militia hit the detachment of seven hundred British dragoons under Lieutenant Colonel Friedrich Baum and turned them back. Baum's men were so sure of themselves that each dragoon carried an extra halter to use after they stole another horse.

From Burgoyne's perspective, things seemed to be going well. Baum sent back a few stray cattle he'd managed to pick up, but then came reports that the rebel militia was massing. Before Baum realized it, he'd pushed about twenty-five miles deep into enemy territory. He also didn't realize until it was too late that he was greatly

---

* Several men by the name of Simon Fraser fought with the British army during the American Revolution. This particular Simon Fraser was not the founder of the famed 78th Fraser Highlanders, and was not the son of Lord Lovat, who had been executed for high treason following the attempted Scottish uprising known as the '45.

outnumbered by General John Stark and some twenty-six hundred raw recruits.

Baum asked for more troops, and Burgoyne took this request as a sign that Baum simply wanted more men to steal more food and horses. Nevertheless, he sent along a German grenadier unit to help out. The Hessians, however, never reached the British-German force. In a downpour of rain, Baum's troops were being picked off by the rebel militia.

As the slow-moving German relief column trudged through the rain, the reinforcements themselves were hit. The Americans swarmed around them, and the Hessian troops panicked. Many surrendered, some retreated, and others slipped off into the woods, where they blended in with other Germanic inhabitants of the mountain area.

The British-German raiding party was beaten back. Lieutenant Colonel Baum was killed in action and buried in the middle of a road near Bennington. The part of his force not killed was taken prisoner, with many Tories being marched through Bennington, their hands tied together. All told, at least two hundred British and German troops were killed and about seven hundred were taken prisoner. Drums, broadswords, ammunition wagons, hundreds of muskets (and a few rifles), and four brass cannon were captured.

The tale of those cannon is one of frequent wars and trading back and forth, depending on the day's victor. French-made, they were first captured by General James Wolfe when the British took Quebec in 1759. American troops took them in 1777, and they would be surrendered to the British by General William Hull in 1812. American forces would take them again at Niagara in 1813.

The loss of men and equipment in what he'd predicted would be an easy campaign forced Gentleman Johnny to retreat to Saratoga, New York. Well, not retreat, because Burgoyne ordered that "this army must not retreat." It's just that the army was headed backward, which made it look like it was retreating.

Along the way they passed Bemis Heights, named for a man who ran a tavern on the road below. The cliffs rose two hundred to three hundred feet above thick stands of oak and pine. They'd been fortified under the direction of Tadeusz Kosciuszko—isn't it nice, when a plan comes together—using breastworks and the sharpened points of felled trees pointing outward, toward the expected enemy. Kosciuszko's fortifications ran from Bemis's tavern near the Hudson River, up the bluffs, to the top of the Heights, where he built three-sided breastworks about three-quarters of a mile long. About midway along each breastwork he dug an artillery redoubt. Inside the fortifications American troops waited.

Thanks to Kosciuszko's reinforcements atop Bemis Heights, Burgoyne's army could move only one way, to the north, toward Saratoga. And American militia and Continental troops hovered there like vultures.

American forces drove Burgoyne's scouts inside his lines, and that left the British army blind. As Gentleman Johnny put it, "Wherever the King's forces point, militia, to the amount of three or four thousand, assemble in twenty-four hours.

On September 19, three columns of Burgoyne's troops headed for the high ground on the American left, but before he got there he was met by American troops at a spot called Freeman's Farm. There, in a clearing about 350 yards long, the two sides met. It was cold and foggy when the fighting began, but Burgoyne's troops were cheerful. It was bright and clear by early afternoon and the English cheer was gone. Americans Daniel Morgan and Benedict Arnold were working on the invading troops.

Morgan's riflemen cut down any advancing redcoat venturing out of the woods. Many others stampeded to the rear. If Morgan's men charged the British troops but couldn't push through them, they bounced off and faded into the covering brush. In the best of backwoods (and later Hollywood) traditions, Morgan sounded a turkey-gobble call to summon his Virginians. The British may not have recognized the turkey call, but the Virginians did. They would reassemble and rock the enemy once more.

Back and forth across Freeman's Farm the two sides went, and by late afternoon the Americans were well positioned along the southern edge of the farm clearing. British bodies were stacked up among the drying corn stalks and in the nearby woods.

Burgoyne tried to counterattack, but the American forces held. On that day, the day called the First Battle of Saratoga, Burgoyne lost about six hundred men, while American loses totaled a little over half that figure.

For three weeks the two armies rested about a mile apart, nursed their wounds, and sent out patrols every now and then to snipe at the enemy. Each side hoped for reinforcements, and from New York, Henry Clinton sent a large contingent of his men up the Hudson River. They captured a group of small forts along the river but went no farther. Soon Burgoyne realized how bad his situation was. His men could not get past Tadeusz Kosciuszko's fortifications on Bemis Heights.

General Horatio Gates had victory in his grasp but for some unknown reason chose not to take the offensive. On October 7, Burgoyne sent columns of men toward the American positions back at Freeman's Farm. For several hours British and Hessian troops inched forward. At midafternoon they realized Daniel Morgan's Virginia riflemen were all around them. When Burgoyne sent a messenger with orders to pull back, the messenger was shot dead. In ten days Burgoyne had lost twelve hundred men, and now he found himself outnumbered three to one.

Benedict Arnold wanted to destroy the enemy, but his commander, General Gates, refused to commit reinforcements. Gates despised Arnold and relieved him of duty, which didn't stop Arnold. Recklessly Arnold rode back and forth in front of the troops on a huge black horse, looking "like the cocked hammer of a dueling pistol." When Arnold saw British General Simon Fraser rallying his men, Arnold said to Daniel Morgan, "That man on the gray horse is a host in himself and must be disposed of."

Tim Murphy was about to become a legend. The Pennsylvania native found a perch high in a nearby tree. With one shot he critically wounded Burgoyne's aide de camp, Sir Francis Clerke.

Murphy next aimed his rifle at General Simon Fraser. It was a three-hundred-yard shot, but Murphy fired and Fraser went down. The Baroness Riedesel (who, along with their three daughters, had accompanied her husband, Baron Friedrich Adolphus Riedesel, into battle) nursed Fraser through the night. It did no good, and he died the next morning. In accordance with his final request, Fraser was buried at sunset on the battlefield. Some, perhaps romantic, accounts claim that as his aides gathered to bury Fraser, American artillery opened fire. But when they realized what was happening, Continental troops stopped the shelling and even saluted "the noble Fraser" with guns from the Great Redoubt. Fraser's grave is still there.

Sir Francis Clerke, however, was still alive. According to an account written by General James Wilkinson (who by the time of the writing had become Gates's bitter enemy), the critically wounded Clerke was taken back to General Gates's tent. Gates tried to talk Clerke into joining the Americans in the Revolution. Clerke refused, and Gates stomped off, yelling, "Did you ever hear so impudent a son of a bitch?"

The Second Battle of Saratoga lasted fifty-two minutes. American losses totaled about 150 men. The British lost at least four times as many, along with almost a dozen cannon and thousands of prisoners.

On October 17, 1777, four years to the day before Washington and Cornwallis opened surrender talks at Yorktown, Burgoyne's troops lay down their arms in a "convention" rather than a formal surrender. Under the convention terms, the British, German, and Canadian troops pledged to go home, "not serving again in North America during the present contest." Congress, however, refused to honor Gates's convention and imprisoned Burgoyne's men for the rest of the war. They'd be known as the "Convention Army," and many were held in camps near Charlottesville, Virginia, then sent to Frederick, Maryland. The march to Virginia took twelve weeks in the dead of winter on starvation rations. As they straggled through Pennsylvania, many of the German troops slipped out of the columns and disappeared into the woods, where friendly residents hid them. Their guards had looked the other way. Of the nearly five thousand taken prisoner, only twenty-six hundred were alive at the end of the war, and some of those chose to remain in America.

General Gates did not permit American troops to watch the surrender ceremonies, apparently not wanting them to witness the British humiliation. As the captured troops marched off the Saratoga battlefield, however, an American band struck up "Yankee Doodle," which already had become something of an unofficial anthem of the Revolution.

The Saratoga victory had worldwide repercussions. In England it led to a request that Lord North resign. George III, however, refused to let him go. North realized his own incompetence but reluctantly agreed to stay on. Refusing to let North resign has been called "the most criminal [act] in the whole reign of George III" and "as criminal as any of those acts which led Charles I to the scaffold."

In America, General George Clinton replaced General Howe as the British commander, and the redcoat army headed south, where it was felt Loyalist sentiment was strongest. They hoped to cut the thirteen United States in half.

From London, Lord North dispatched a peace commission to America, empowered to negotiate with Congress if necessary for the withdrawal of British troops. Headed by Frederick Howard, Fifth Earl of Carlisle, the Carlisle Peace Commission, as it came to be known, was even authorized to recognize American independence. The brothers Howe—Lord Richard, the admiral, and Sir William, the general—were part of the commission.

Congress had earlier resolved that any man or group coming to terms with the commission was an enemy of the United States. It didn't sit too well, either, when commission members tried to bribe three congressmen. They also attempted to appeal to the American people over the head of Congress, offering general pardons for any past disloyalty.

When Congress learned that General Clinton was ready to evacuate Philadelphia, American lawmakers felt they had the upper hand. They turned down Carlisle's offer and the commission sailed back to England.

By offering peace and independence, Lord North's government had hoped to block American ratification of an alliance with France. Carlisle apparently felt one way to do this was to attack all things and all people French. He so offended Lafayette that the young marquis challenged Carlisle to a duel. Carlisle, however, refused, saying that he was answerable only to his country for his "public conduct and language."

A year and a half after Burgoyne's surrender at Saratoga, French King Louis XVI gave official diplomatic recognition to the United States and signed a treaty under which France would give them full military support. Saratoga and the French alliance marked the turning point in the Revolution.

Over the next several months Tadeusz Kosciuszko and General Horatio Gates became close friends. When Gates went south, he took Kosciuszko with him as chief engineer of the Continental army's southern department. The advice Kosciuszko had given St. Clair was good, but it wasn't taken. The advice he gave General Nathanael Greene was bad; regretfully it *was* taken.

It was the summer of 1781, at the Battle of Ninety-six, South Carolina,* Kosciuszko recommended that Greene attack the garrison's strongest point, the Star Redoubt. In retrospect, the Americans probably should have concentrated on the village's water supply.

Greene's artillery raked the Star Redoubt while Kosciuszko worked on extending his lines around the stockade. Inside, the defenders dug trenches and, in the words of novelist Kenneth Roberts, "went to living in holes like woodchucks, or lay huddled against the inside of the stockades." Despite the heat of a South Carolina summer, the men, women, and children inside the palisades managed to stay alive by sending slaves out at night with buckets to get water. They took it from the well Kosciuszko had recommended Greene not bother capturing. It was a major mistake that allowed the defenders of Ninety-six to hold out.

Lord Francis Rawdon-Hastings and his troops relieved the siege of Ninety-six, then chased Greene and his army into the Santee Hills along the Edisto River. Rawdon probably would have chased Greene even farther, but the weather was hot and his troops were running out of food and ammunition.

John Paul was born in Kirkcudbrightshire, just north of Solway Firth in Scotland's border country. He added the name Jones to escape two charges of murder. One centered around a 1770 incident in which Paul flogged his ship's carpenter, Mungo Maxwell. Mungo,

---

* Ninety-six was a stockaded village said to be ninety-six miles from the nearest frontier post at Fort Prince George. It was an important Loyalist post.

it seems, was not only incompetent, he was disobedient. During a voyage to Tobago, Mungo so got on John Paul's nerves that three times he had the carpenter tied to the ship's rigging and flogged with the cat-o'-nine-tails. In Tobago, Maxwell filed a complaint in the vice-admiralty court, exhibiting his scarred shoulders as evidence that John Paul had beaten him unjustly. The judge took one look at Mungo's torso and declared the stripes were "neither mortal nor dangerous," and dismissed the complaint.

Mungo shipped home on another vessel but, during the voyage, he was taken with a fever and died at sea. When Mungo Maxwell's father heard about his son's flogging and subsequent death, he accused John Paul of murder. When Paul's ship, the *John,* landed, he was met by the local sheriff and clapped into jail (the Scots called it the tolbooth) in Kirkcudbrightshire. When Paul was released on bail, he returned to the West Indies to obtain evidence of his innocence. He sent documents back to Scotland and cleared his record. Mungo's father, however, continued to claim Captain John Paul had murdered his poor son.

Back in the West Indies, Paul ran into trouble again. As captain of the ship *Betsy,* he refused to advance wages to his seamen, claiming he wanted to reinvest the money in another cargo and would pay them off back in England. The crew mutinied, demanding their pay then and there. When a man John Paul described as "the Ringleader"—a man apparently much larger than Jones*—tried to go ashore without leave, Paul stopped him. The Ringleader attempted to hit him with a bludgeon, probably a belaying pin, or kevel, used to secure ropes on a ship. John Paul ran him through with a sword. Paul tried to give himself up to authorities, but the local justice of the peace in Tobago said that wasn't necessary. Paul's unpaid and now-rebellious crew disagreed and threatened to kill him. On the advice of friends, Paul left Tobago for America, where he lived for a while with friends in Fredericksburg, Virginia. It was then that he changed his name to John Paul Jones.

---

* John Paul Jones was about five feet five inches tall and was referred to by John Hancock as "little Jones." Abigail Adams, whose husband wasn't all that tall, called him a "little man."

Why Jones? Good question. An early biographer suggests that Jones is a patronymic meaning the "son of John," which, of course, he was, since he was another of the Revolution's juniors, John Paul, Jr. Another story has it that John Paul selected the name Jones to honor Allen and Willie Jones of Halifax, North Carolina, whose family later claimed to have rescued John Paul after the captain left Tobago. Yet a third story says John Paul was on board the ship *Falmouth Packet*, when the ship's master, James Jones, fell ill of fever. This story has it that in order to clear the ship for landing, John Paul simulated the captain's signature. When the captain regained his health (and his ship) John Paul kept the "Jones" in order to escape prosecution for the earlier deaths of Mungo and "the Ringleader."

In any event, on December 7, 1775, the Scottish-born sea captain now called John Paul Jones was given a commission in the new U.S. Navy. By April 1778, he was master of the privateer *Ranger*, and for months he prowled the waters around the British Isles, looking for the spoils of war. John Paul Jones was a pirate, a legal one, of course, which officially made him a privateer, not that those he and his crew attacked cared what the title was.

On April 24, Jones captured the *Drake*. It was the first time an enemy warship had ever surrendered to a vessel sailed under the ownership of the new United States of America.

Capturing the *Drake* didn't mean much in England, but across the Irish Sea, it meant a lot. Someone, the Irish felt, was about to tweak Britain's nose, and they wanted in on it. Within weeks forty thousand men flocked to become Irish volunteers in the American Revolution.

John Paul Jones took his crew ashore in Whitehaven, England, where they spiked thirty-eight cannon at the local fort and then went on a rampage. A London newspaper carried the story: "Late last night or early this morning a number of armed men (to the amount of thirty) landed at this place by two boats from an American privateer." Jones's crew set fire to several English vessels and took others as prizes.

In a twenty-eight-day period, he captured seven such prize ships. He sailed most of them to France, which by now was ready to come out in support of the American cause, and which hailed as a conquering hero John Paul Jones, twice accused of murder and now a captain in the new U.S. Navy.

By the end of the summer the French had fitted out five ships for use by American privateers. One ship, the old and clumsy *Duras,* John Paul Jones named in honor of Benjamin Franklin's character, Poor Richard. In French this became the *Bonhomme Richard.*

Flying a flag that looked only superficially like today's Stars and Stripes—it probably was made up of alternating red, white, and blue stripes, with no stars—Paul Jones, as he called himself, sailed the *Bonhomme Richard* into battle against HMS *Serapis.* The battle lasted three hours, during which the rigging of the two ships became entangled. Lieutenant Richard Dale was on board the *Bonhomme Richard* and later wrote about the incident when the two ships were stuck together:

> We had remained in this situation but a few minutes when we were . . . hailed by the Serapis, "Has your ship struck [its flag]?" To which Captain Jones answered, "I have not yet begun to fight."

Midshipman Nathaniel Fanning also was on board the *Bonhomme Richard* at the time but remembered the incident slightly differently. He quoted John Paul Jones as saying he would strike his own colors, "when we can fight no longer, but we shall see [your colors] come down the first; for you must know that Yankees do not haul down their colours until they are fairly beaten."

Not quite as colorful, but it apparently worked out well for Jones, because it was Captain Pearson of the *Serapis* who surrendered. Jones boarded the English ship and, when it became obvious his own ship was sinking, transferred to the *Serapis.* The *Bonhomme Richard* sank two days later.

John Paul Jones became a hero, perhaps second in popularity only to George Washington. Congress voted to give him a medal—the only gold medal Congress ever awarded to an officer of the Continental navy. They balked, however, against promoting him to rear admiral over officers with more seniority.

One of the most amazing individuals who fought in the Revolution came to this country as a small boy but just where he came from, or who he actually was, isn't certain. On June 23, 1765, a four- or five-year-old boy was on board a ship when it docked at City Point (now Hopewell), Virginia. He spoke no English but apparently had come from a wealthy family; his obviously finely made clothing was dirty, but he wore silver buckles on his shoes. On the buckles the initials P. F. In the only words anyone could understand, he repeated: "Pedro Francisco." Since no one else knew what to do with him, a woman eventually took him to the Prince George County poorhouse.

A local judge, Anthony Winston (who was Patrick Henry's uncle) took the boy in and reared him, anglicizing the name the child had been repeating into "Peter Francisco." As they say in fairy tales, and this is no fairy tale, the young man grew and grew. In Peter's case he grew some more; as an adult he was six feet six inches tall and weighed two hundred sixty pounds.

When Judge Winston and Peter finally were able to communicate, the boy said that he had lived in a mansion near the ocean, that his mother spoke what he believed was French, but that his father spoke another language. Young Pedro was playing with his sister in the garden one day, when they were seized by a band of rough men. His sister got away, but Pedro was captured, tied up and blindfolded, gagged, and carried on board a ship, where he spent, it seemed to him, an awfully long time. Then he arrived at City Point.

In 1971, Virginia researcher John E. Manahan reported on studies he'd carried out regarding Pedro or Peter Francisco. There isn't much hard evidence, but apparently it worked out this way: The boy had been born on July 8, 1760, at Porto Judeo, on Terceira Island in the Portuguese-held Azores. Yes, he had been kidnapped, but apparently his noble Portuguese family had engineered it to protect the boy, who'd been ordered executed in reprisal for some political offense committed by his parents.

In March 1775, Peter went to Richmond with Judge Winston to a meeting of the new Virginia Convention. The boy, then about fifteen, stood outside St. John's Church as the judge's nephew, Patrick Henry, demanded, "Give me liberty or give me death!" Peter was ready to go to war right then, but the judge made him wait another year.

In 1776, Peter Francisco enlisted as a private in the Tenth Virginia Regiment. He served several months with the regiment in New Jersey and got his first taste of action in September 1777 at the Battle of Brandywine. For a crucial forty-five minutes Peter's regiment held the line at a narrow defile called Sandy Hollow Gap, allowing the rest of Washington's troops to withdraw and avoid an all-out rout. In this rear-guard action, Peter Francisco was injured, a gunshot wound to his leg. While he was being treated, he met another young man, who had also been slightly wounded that day: the Marquis de Lafayette. Despite the differences in background and rank, the two became friends.

By October, Peter was back in action at the Battle of Germantown. In mid-November he fought at Fort Mifflin, and in June 1778, at Monmouth, where he was wounded for the second time. A musket ball tore into his right thigh, leaving a wound that nagged him for the rest of his life.

In July 1779, at Stony Point north of New York City, his unit sustained so many casualties that only Francisco and three other men were able to reach their final objective. It was here, for the first time, that this giant of a man used a giant's weapon, a six-foot-long broadsword with a five-foot blade. George Washington had it made for Peter the giant. As the army moved by him, Peter Francisco received his third wound of the war, a nine-inch gash to the stomach.

He was back in action in August 1780, at Camden, South Carolina, and it was here (if it actually happened) that Peter Francisco performed something close to a miracle. The battle was one of the most disastrous defeats ever suffered by an American army. If it hadn't been for Francisco, it might have been worse. He was overtaken and surrounded by the enemy during the American retreat, but he speared one British cavalryman with his sword, then pulled the trooper from his horse, climbed on, and escaped through enemy lines by pretending to be a Tory sympathizer.

It was August 16, and Peter Francisco saw that the fleeing Continental troops had left behind two of its cannon. As the story has it, Francisco stooped beneath the gun and lifted the thousand-pound cannon off its carriage and onto his shoulder. Then he carried it off the field to keep it out of enemy hands.

After the Camden debacle, Francisco joined Colonel William Washington's guerrilla operations in North Carolina. A nineteenth-century book on the Revolution said that in one battle, Peter Francisco,

> a brave Virginian, cut down eleven men in succession with his broadsword. One of the guards pinned Francisco's leg to his horse with a bayonet. Forbearing to strike, he assisted the assailant to draw his bayonet forth, when, with terrible force, he brought down his broadsword and cleft the poor fellow's head to his shoulders!

Wound number four, and this time he almost died; in fact, nearly everybody thought he was dead. A Quaker named Robinson was checking the dead, when he found Peter still alive. He took him to his home and nursed the giant of a man back to health.

Still limping, Peter Francisco returned to Virginia. He'd been wounded at least four, possibly five times, but he was still willing to fight. When Colonel Banastre Tarleton and his horsemen raided Virginia, Francisco volunteered as a scout to observe the enemy troops. At a place called Ward's Tavern, nine of Tarleton's raiders surrounded Peter and tried to arrest him. When one horseman demanded Francisco hand over his silver shoe buckles, Peter, in effect, told the man to "take them yourself, if you can." When the cavalryman tried to do just that, Peter snatched the officer's saber and hit him in the head. The injured man shot Peter and wounded him in the side—wound five or six, but who's counting. He cut his way out of the circle of raiders and left two of the enemy dead.

Still, the war wasn't over for Peter Francisco. A few months later the man who had given Peter his broadsword asked him to be present on October 19. The man was George Washington, and the place was the surrender at Yorktown.

Later Francisco returned to Richmond with Lafayette. A story has it that as he and the marquis were strolling in front of St. John's Church, a young lady leaving the building tripped and Peter Francisco caught her. It was, the story continues, the first time Peter met Susannah Anderson, the woman he married in December 1784.

He became a blacksmith and a tavern owner. Judge Winston had reared him but never sent him to school. Now Peter began a program of self-education; within three years he was reading the classics.

With his marriage to the well-endowered Susannah, and with his own hard work, Peter Francisco became a member of the landed gentry, a country squire who dressed fastidiously—high hats, bright-colored waistcoats, and silk stockings. When Susannah died in 1790, Peter remarried, this time to Catherine Brooke; however, she died in 1821. Just as he seemed to survive wound after wound, he survived wife after wife, and he tried again—wife number three, Mary Grymes West, the widow of a Virginia planter. Together they moved to Richmond, where he became sergeant at arms in the Virginia House of Delegates. Lafayette was back in town in 1824, and Peter Francisco took his friend on a tour of the state.

Seven years later, on January 16, 1831, at the age of about seventy-one, Peter Francisco died, apparently of appendicitis. The House of Delegates adjourned that day in praise and sorrow. One hundred forty-four years later he was honored again, this time by the U.S. Postal Service, which issued a stamp in his honor. It shows this giant of a man carrying a thousand-pound cannon on his shoulder: "Peter Francisco—Fighter Extraordinary." It cost seventeen cents.

Perhaps the greatest myth of the Declaration of Independence is in the signing of the document. There's that famous painting by John Trumbull of Jefferson, Adams, Franklin, Livingston, and Roger Sherman, presenting the Declaration to John Hancock, the president of Congress. Around them are arrayed the other members of Congress, apparently ready to sign.

On the day the Declaration was passed, only two people signed the document—John Hancock and Charles Thomson, who was secretary of Congress. Most members of Congress didn't sign until August 2, and, according to some historians, at least one member didn't get around to affixing his name to the document until 1781, the year American and French troops defeated Cornwallis at Yorktown. That individual, Thomas McKean of Delaware, denied the charge. In fact, it was McKean who first challenged the popular belief that everybody involved signed the Declaration on July 4, 1776. The exact date of his signing is uncertain; McKean claimed it was in 1776, but it most likely was sometime after January 18, 1777—far before the 1781 date some opponents claimed.

Some of the fifty-six individuals designated by history as "signers," signed the document but never voted on the Declaration when it came up on July 4; some weren't even members of Congress when it came down to taking the yeas and nays. For instance, at first none of the New York delegation voted either for or against the Declaration; they'd been ordered by their colonial legislature in Albany *not* to vote either way—either on the issue of independence or the Declaration of Independence.

Before New York voted, the printed version of the Declaration read:

In CONGRESS, July 4, 1776, a DECLARATION by the REPRESENTATIVES of the UNITED STATES of AMERICA, in General Congress assembled.

After New York finally gave its delegates permission, they voted in favor of both, and Congress had the Declaration printed up, reading: "The unanimous Declaration of the thirteen United States of America."

Most of Congress—forty-nine of the members—signed on August 2, 1776. It wasn't until January 18, 1777, that Congress finally authorized the printing of the Declaration with all of the signers' names listed. There was the justifiable fear that the British would retaliate against those who autographed an open letter saying they wanted to have nothing more to do with Great Britain. It was, after all, an act of treason against the lawful government.

When those forty-nine signed the document, they forgot about some others, and late-coming signers had to crowd in their names at the bottom, men such as Elbridge Gerry of Massachusetts, who slipped his name in between Massachusetts and Rhode Island. Matthew Thornton refused to scrunch up his signature, and signed separate from his New Hampshire colleagues—down at the bottom of the first column on the right, at the end of the Connecticut delegates. George Wythe and Richard Henry Lee, however, found room above their fellow Virginians. Wythe was there at the voting but not there at the August 2 signing; he signed it in September. Lee, whose resolution it was that called for independence, had left town in June, and he wasn't there for the vote on either independence or the Declaration. He, too, later signed the document.

The Declaration they all signed, ended with these words:

> And for the support of this declaration, *with a firm reliance on the protection of divine providence,* *we mutually pledge to each other our lives, our fortunes, and our sacred honor.

They knew what could lie ahead of them, and for some, it did. Virginia's Carter Braxton had been one of the wealthiest men in the colonies prior to the Revolution. During the war he invested heavily in shipping, but the British captured most of his vessels and plundered several of his plantations. By the end of the war he was virtually ruined financially.

After winning the Battle of Brandywine, British troops advanced on Philadelphia, but they detoured enough to vandalize signer George Clymer's home in Chester County. Clymer's wife and children had to hide in nearby woods.

When British troops occupied Long Island, William Floyd's wife, son, and two daughters had to flee across the sound to Middletown, Connecticut. The redcoats, meanwhile, used the signer's home at Mastic for a barracks, and loyalists plundered his lands and belongings. Floyd's wife died in 1781 before she could return home, and when their children returned in 1783 they found their fields and timber stripped, fences destroyed, and their house greatly damaged.

British troops and Loyalist forces ravaged signer Lyman Hall's home in Georgia and confiscated his other property. In all, homes of fifteen of the signers were destroyed by British troops, Tories.

John Hart of New Jersey signed the Declaration in August 1776. That winter, redcoats invaded the state and wreaked havoc on Hart's farm and mills. After the American victories at Princeton and Trenton, Tories drove Hart into exile. Hart fled his farm at Hopewell and avoided capture by living in the snow-filled woods for several weeks.

---

* The italicized section was not written by Jefferson but is in the final version.

His wife wasn't so lucky and died of exposure. His family was scattered around the countryside, and Hart never fully recovered his health.

There were others.

William Hooper of North Carolina: Separated from his wife and family for nearly a year, he had to depend upon friends for food and shelter. Perhaps because of this, his health rapidly declined and he died in 1788 at age forty-six.

Lewis Morris of New York: When Britain invaded the colony, the redcoats ravaged his home, Morrisania, and forced the signer and his family to flee.

Several signers joined either their state's militia or the Continental army, and at least four of them were captured and held prisoner.

George Walton of Georgia was wounded and captured in the siege of Savannah in December 1778. The British held him for a year, finally exchanging him for a captured English navy captain.

Three signers from South Carolina were captured and held prisoner. Edward Rutledge was a militia captain captured by the British during the siege of Charleston in 1780. Held with him were Arthur Middleton (whose plantation outside Charleston was partially destroyed by the redcoats) and Thomas Heyward, Jr. The three men were held prisoner of war at St. Augustine, Florida, until July 1781. Just before he was released from prison, Heyward wrote new words to the British national anthem, "God Save the King," changing it to "God Save the Thirteen States."*

Yet another signer was captured by the British, and this is where the Declaration's clause "our sacred honor" comes into play. For years Americans proclaimed that "not one man of the fifty-six [signers] lost his 'sacred honor.'" That:

> Throughout the long ordeal of an often-floundering war, in a cause that at times seemed hopelessly lost, there was not among the fifty-six men a single defection—despite the reser-

---

* Another version of the story has a Dutch lady at the Hague rewriting the lyrics in 1779 in honor of American sailors there.

vations that some had had about independence at the beginning and despite the repeated sagging of popular support for the war.

Simply, that's not true. Many histories waffle on the subject, but one Declaration signer did recant his signature on that famous document: Richard Stockton.

He was born in 1730, the fourth generation of a wealthy and prominent New Jersey family; his father was a county judge. Richard graduated in 1754 from the College of New Jersey and studied law. Within a few years he was considered one of the outstanding lawyers in the province. When Britain enacted the Stamp Act, Stockton spoke out in opposition. Despite this, in early 1774, the royal governor of New Jersey, Benjamin Franklin's son, William, commissioned Stockton an associate justice of the New Jersey Supreme Court.

Toward the end of August 1776, Richard Stockton and signer George Clymer of Pennsylvania were named to a committee to inspect the northern Continental army, then being reorganized after failing to conquer Canada. Returning to his home, Stockton was surprised to learn that New Jersey had been invaded by the British. He managed to evacuate his family but was himself captured by a party of local Tories. Instead of being treated as a prisoner of war, even a political prisoner, Richard Stockton was treated like a criminal. Taken first to Perth Amboy, New Jersey, he was soon transferred to the infamous Provost Jail in New York City.*

Stockton's daughter was married to Dr. Benjamin Rush, another Declaration signer. With Stockton held by the British, Dr. Rush wrote Richard Henry Lee of Virginia, telling him that

> my much-honoured father-in-law [Stockton], who is now a prisoner with General Howe, suffers many indignities and hardships from the enemy, from which not only his rank, but

---

* See Chapter Ten.

his being a man, ought to exempt him. I wish you would propose to Congress to pass a resolution in his favour, similar to that they have passed in favour of General [Charles] Lee. They owe it to their own honour, as well as to a member of their body.

Congress, then as now, didn't like being called into question, so it resolved that George Washington should check into the report that Stockton was being held prisoner. If he was, the resolution declared, Washington should ask Britain's General Howe whether mistreatment of the signer "shall be the future role for treating all such, on both sides, as the fortune of war may place in the hands of either party." By mid-March 1777, Richard Stockton was back in Princeton, but apparently it wasn't due to anything that either Congress or Washington had done. Stockton had walked out of prison a free man by submitting to King George III, the man against whom he had forsworn allegiance six months earlier. Richard Stockton had recanted his signature on the Declaration of Independence.

The day Stockton was captured, Admiral Viscount Howe and his brother, General William Howe, issued a proclamation offering a free pardon to all American rebels who would return to their former allegiance within sixty days. That is, if the prisoner signed a loyalty oath.* Richard Stockton took the brothers Howe up on their offer of a pardon.

On February 8, 1777, fellow Congressman Abraham Clark wrote to John Hart, himself a Declaration signer and now speaker of the New Jersey assembly, regarding filling vacancies in New Jersey's congressional delegation:

> [Congressman] Sergeant talks of resigning and Mr. Stockton by his late procedure cannot Act. I wish their places may be Supplied by such as will be reputable to New Jersey, not only by their integrity but Abilities.

---

* In answer to the Howes' proclamation, George Washington made an offer of his own to those who would "acknowledge the UNITED STATES of AMERICA to be Free, Independent and Sovereign States. . . ."

Fellow congressman and fellow signer Reverend John Wither-spoon wrote his son David:

> I was at Princeton from Saturday . . . till Wednesday. . . . Judge Stockton is not very well in health and much spoken against for his conduct. He signed Howe's Declaration and also gave his Word of Honour that he would not meddle in the least in American affairs during the War.

British General Charles Cornwallis used Stockton's home at Princeton for his headquarters. After he left, Loyalists wrecked the house and made a bonfire out of Stockton's furniture and books. A Continental army sergeant wrote that when the British army evacuated Princeton, the town looked like

> a deserted village; you would think it had been desolated with the plague and an earthquake, as well as with the calamities of war; the college and church are heaps of ruin; all the inhabitants have been plundered; the whole of Mr. Stockton's furniture, apparel, and even valuable writings have been burnt; all his cattle, horses, and dogs, sheep, grain, and forage, have been carried away.

In December 1777, Richard Stockton took another oath. This time he swore allegiance to the United States, specifically to the state of New Jersey. His signed oath is now in the New Jersey State Archives. Apparently he signed the New Jersey oath after Congress called on those who had submitted to the brothers Howe to go to the nearest American general officer "and there deliver up such protections, certificates, and passports, and take the oath of allegiance to the United States of America." Not signing the American oath carried with it a threat. Any who refused should immediately "withdraw themselves and their families within enemy lines." Any who did not leave within thirty days would "be deemed adherents to the king of Great-Britain, and treated as common enemies of the United States."

Richard Stockton was a beaten man; his house had been severely damaged and his reputation ruined. He had signed the Declaration of Independence, signed an oath proclaiming allegiance to King George III, and signed another oath declaring his allegiance to the United States of America. Now his former friends shunned him.

In 1779, son-in-law Benjamin Rush wrote that Stockton "continues to mend. All his physicians agree now in pronouncing his recovery complete," which may not have been an accurate diagnosis, given later events. Richard Stockton's life never was the same again, and in fact didn't last long. He died of cancer in February 1781, at the age of fifty.

Eight months after Richard Stockton died, Cornwallis surrendered to Washington at Yorktown. Stockton's widow wrote a poem celebrating the victory and sent it to Washington, who replied with a letter of thanks. Later, while en route to New York for his inauguration as the nation's first president, George Washington stopped off in Princeton, where a group of young ladies threw flowers at the general and sang Mrs. Stockton's song: "Welcome, Mighty Chief, Once More!"

In 1954, one hundred seventy-eight years after Richard Stockton signed the Declaration of Independence, the only signer to recant that document was remembered in New Jersey. Morven, his once-ransacked home, was restored and became the official residence of New Jersey's governors.

Aaron Burr certainly ranks among those we should recognize as Founding Father stars in supporting roles, even though his support sometimes was doubtful.

Biographers say he was a bright, somewhat unruly, and attractive child—slight, with deep-set hazel eyes, a larger than normal head, and a wide mouth, which, come to think of it, may not have been so attractive after all. Aaron's parents died when he was young, his mother when he was an infant and his father (a former College of New Jersey president) when Aaron was a teenager; this seems to have sent Aaron Burr on a lifelong quest for affection, sometimes looking for it, as the saying goes, in all the wrong places. At five foot six inches, he was a somewhat short but notorious lover, and reportedly almost stole Dolley Paine Todd before James Madison won her over. It was not unusual for women to fall in love with Aaron Burr and, when he spurned them, they became devout Aaron Burr enemies. It didn't ameliorate their enmity that he refused to return their love letters.

When Aaron was just eleven (he looked nine) he applied to the college where his father had been president. The college rejected him, but two years later the school accepted Burr as a sophomore, and he graduated at the age of sixteen. He studied theology for a while, then decided to take up law.

That's when he eloped with a young lady named Dorothy Quincy, a fair-haired beauty of one of Boston's most famous families. The couple was caught trying to catch a ferry to cross a river. When they found the loving couple, Dorothy's brothers dunked Aaron in the river as discouragement, which apparently didn't work on either Dorothy or Aaron. After that, though they saw each other occasionally, they were never allowed to be alone.

Over the winter of 1775 to 1776, Burr joined the Continental army's march to Quebec, serving as captain on Benedict Arnold's staff during America's ill-fated expedition north. Dorothy Quincy apparently hadn't gotten over him yet, and when Burr headed out, she wrote him, saying, "You will die, I know you will die."

After Arnold extolled Burr's virtues to General Richard Montgomery, Aaron was transferred to the general's staff, where he trained a unit of fifty men to climb ladders and storm the fortress walls at Quebec. "To the storming we must come at last," Montgomery shouted as they tried to take the city, and then he was shot in the heart. Burr tried to drag him away, but the hefty general was too heavy for the little captain to lug very far. Montgomery cheered his men: "We shall be in the fort in two minutes," but he died before that could happen. His rattled troops fled.

Burr wintered with Washington at Valley Forge, and the two men rapidly grew to dislike each other. As his mentor Benedict Arnold later felt, Aaron Burr believed he didn't advance fast enough under George Washington. During General Charles Lee's Monmouth debacle, Burr sided with Lee but managed to avoid becoming part of the "Conway cabal" that tried to remove Washington as commander in chief of the Continental army.

In March 1779, Aaron Burr claimed ill health and resigned his commission. A year later he resumed his study of law. By 1783, Burr was living in New York City, where he was among the most sought after attorneys in town.

Burr was elected U.S. senator from New York in 1791 but was not reelected the next time around. Back on the state level, he used the St. Tammany's Society to capture the state legislature.

It's uncertain whether the name Tammany means "affable" or "deserving." At any rate, Tammany Hall was formed in 1789, partly as a fraternal society for mechanics and shopkeepers, partly to oppose immigrants. Ironically enough, it was named after a legendary Delaware Indian chief, but the group's first constitution provided that only whites were eligible for the exalted office of "sachem."

Society founder William Mooney was an upholsterer and wallpaper dealer who may or may not have served in the Revolution as he sometimes claimed. Mainly William Mooney served William Mooney and all the little Mooneys. For two years he was superintendent of the New York almshouse, during which time he cut provisions meant for inmates and used the funds for his own family. This was the first of many scandals to hit the society, and "trifles for Mrs. Mooney" became a byword among anti-Tammany men.

By Aaron Burr's time, Tammany Hall had turned to politics, but it still opposed nonwhites and foreigners. Not until the 1840s, and the increasing flood of immigrants, was Tammany Hall opened to the Irish. Over the years Tammany Hall became a political machine, trading jobs for votes.

In the election of 1800 to 1801, Thomas Jefferson chose Burr to be his vice president. The Constitution called for the two offices—president and vice president—to be voted on together in the electoral college, which even then nobody understood. Theoretically they ran as a team, if not yet a political party, against another paired team. The individual with the largest number of votes would be president, the one coming in second would be vice president. This system, of course, works only if every candidate is out to do only his or her best for the country, with winner and almost-winner working together for a glorious future, which seemed never to be exactly as promised.

When the votes were counted on February 11, 1801, Jefferson and Burr had each received 73 of the 276 electoral votes from the then-existing sixteen states. The remaining 130 votes went to other candidates: John Adams, who would be the outgoing president, got sixty-five votes; Charles Cotesworth Pinckney of South Carolina received sixty-four; and John Jay got one of Rhode Island's vote; a Maryland elector, perhaps thinking None of the above, chose not to vote for anybody.

It was the only time in American history that the electoral college has had a tie vote. That sent the election to the House of Representatives, where Jefferson was elected on the thirty-sixth ballot—ten states for Jefferson and six for Burr.

That election was one of the few times Alexander Hamilton sided with Thomas Jefferson. He threw his weight behind Jefferson in order to beat John Adams, and that turned Aaron Burr into Hamilton's bitter enemy. When Burr was nominated for New York governor in 1804, Hamilton again spoke against him, and again Aaron Burr lost. Their animosity ended, literally, in a fight to the finish.

What caused the duel between Burr and Hamilton still isn't certain. Perhaps the most salacious story is that Hamilton accused Burr of having sexual relations with his own daughter, Theodosia Burr. Neither Burr nor his daughter ever acknowledged the accusations. Theodosia Burr Alston, who truly was a loving daughter, died at sea in 1813 while trying to reach her father.

In any event, and for whatever reason, on the morning of July 11, 1804, Alexander Hamilton and Aaron Burr met at ten paces on the heights of Weehawken, New Jersey. They fired at the same time. Hamilton missed. Burr did not.

Aaron Burr was still vice president at the time, and, even though he was under indictment for murder, he continued presiding over the U.S. Senate, reportedly doing an even-handed job.* He frequently sided with the anti-Jefferson Federalist Party, which didn't sit well with the president. In the election of 1804 to 1805, Jefferson dumped Burr and took as his vice-president George Clinton of New

---

* Burr was indicted for murder by a New York grand jury even though New York had no jurisdiction over the events in New Jersey, where the duel took place.

York, who, incidentally, had saved Aaron Burr's career when he made him state attorney general back in 1789.

Even while he was in office, Aaron Burr frequently extolled a scheme to separate the western territory from the United States. The summer of his duel with Hamilton, Burr met frequently in Philadelphia with General James Wilkinson, and they would continue to meet. Burr, Wilkinson, and Benedict Arnold had all been on that mission to Quebec in 1776—"an interesting collection of scoundrels," historian Mark Boatner calls them.

General Wilkinson and Burr met again in 1805, when Wilkinson was governor of the Territory of Orleans (Lower Louisiana), part of the land recently bought from France. Burr reportedly asked for Wilkinson's aid in separating the western lands from the Union. He hoped that Great Britain would come into the scheme with financial aid.

As far as the United States was concerned, Burr's plot could have been the worst thing possible. Chopping off the area west of the Appalachian Mountains could have been fatal to the new nation.

Joe Daviess, the U.S. attorney for Kentucky at the time of the Burr scheme, wrote President Jefferson, warning of a widespread western plot. Initially, however, he didn't mention Aaron Burr. Who is involved? Jefferson asked, and Daviess sent the president a list of ten suspects. They included everyone from U.S. Attorney General John Breckinridge to the governor of the Indiana Territory, William Henry Harrison. Add to that two judges, two senators, and Henry Clay. Oh, Wilkinson and Burr as well. Thomas Jefferson was, at the least, disinclined to believe Daviess, who, after all, was a Federalist and a brother-in-law to John Marshall, one of Jefferson's growing list of enemies.

Burr's western land scheme never materialized: Wilkinson, his fellow conspirator, defected; many of the frontiersmen who might have been involved in the plan decided they'd rather remain in the United States; and there was no international aid on the horizon. Taken into custody and brought to Richmond, Virginia, for trial, a grand jury charged Aaron Burr with treason and misdemeanor. He was tossed into jail, a prison Burr himself described as a "mansion"—

three rooms on the third floor with a polite jailer. He received visitors, messages, and gifts—"oranges, lemons, pineapples, raspberries, apricots, cream, butter, ice, and some ordinary articles," he wrote. Those around him referred to Aaron Burr as the "emperor of the penitentiary."

U.S. Supreme Court Chief Justice Marshall presided over the trial, and in a presidential first, Thomas Jefferson was subpoenaed to appear as a witness. The next sitting U.S. president to be subpoenaed by a court was also a Jefferson, William Jefferson Clinton, in 1998.

The subpoena obviously was a political move, Marshall the Federalist (egged on by Jefferson's former vice president, now turned adversary, Aaron Burr) versus Thomas Jefferson the Democrat-in-Republican's clothing. Instead of appearing as ordered, Jefferson agreed to supply information, which seemed to satisfy Marshall. The justice went on to hand down a narrow construction of the treason law based on Article III, section 3 of the Constitution—that treason consisted "only of waging war" against the United States or "adhering" to the nation's enemies, and must consist of "an overt act" testified to by two witnesses. Based on this ruling, on September 1, 1807, the jury acquitted Aaron Burr.

There was still the misdemeanor charge against Burr, and Jefferson urged that he be tried on that count; he was and again Burr was acquitted. The following year Aaron Burr sailed for England. This time he tried to raise support for a revolution in Mexico. England ordered him out of the country, so he moved on to Sweden, then Denmark, and Germany, and finally to France, where he approached Napoleon about his Mexico scheme. Napoleon also turned him down, which meant he had no place left to turn, so he tried coming home. Even that didn't go smoothly. His ship was captured by the British in a sidelight of the coming War of 1812. The English (who had kicked him out of the country not too much earlier) now held him prisoner. Finally Burr was released. He returned to New York, where he practiced law and operated a private water works.

Until the early 1800s there were no municipal water supplies in the United States. There were, however, private waterworks, and

Aaron Burr's Manhattan company dominated New York's water for a half-century. In 1801 the first sizable public waterworks in the United States was designed by the official U.S. surveyor, Benjamin Strobe. It brought in water from the Schuylkill River to Philadelphia and provided water to the capital. Until major fires or cholera epidemics hit their cities, many Americans refused to buy water, saying it was as absurd as paying for air to breathe.

CHAPTER FOUR

Benedict the Bold:
Arnold the Traitor

We are not afraid to follow truth wherever it may lead, nor to tolerate any error so long as reason is left free to combat it.
—Thomas Jefferson to William Roscoe*

My sentiments respecting the war were well known....I disclaimed any idea of independence or a separation from Great Britain.
—Benedict Arnold

Bermuda, Ireland, and Canada were almost part of the United States, perhaps the fourteenth, fifteenth, and sixteenth colonies. Some residents of the West Indies made sympathetic noises favoring alignment with the rebels, but Bermuda island leaders realized they would be ruined by the type of economic sanctions put into effect in the mainland colonies. Then, too, the British navy's strong presence on the island was enough to keep them in the royal court.

Ireland had been England's first and most oppressed colony. Volunteers flocked to the American Revolution, but most of them fought for the king.

Canada was the subject of much wishful thinking among American rebels. The area had been settled primarily by French trappers, and it wasn't until the Treaty of Paris ending the French and Indian War that Britain had much say in Canadian affairs.

It remained, of course, the "thirteen colonies."

---

* Roscoe was an English historian, pamphleteer, writer, and liberal. He and Jefferson frequently corresponded as the former president worked to complete establishment of what came to be known as "Mr. Jefferson's school"—the University of Virginia.

• • •

Benedict Arnold was born in Norwich, Connecticut, in 1741, a grandson of a Rhode Island governor. He almost became a druggist, and was apprenticed at age fourteen to the local pharmacist. Instead of learning to fabricate medications and sell nostrums, he ran away to join the army, enlisting in the New York militia in 1758. His mother, however, had Benedict brought back home; she was a domineering, austere, and pious woman who did not want her son off with some military riffraff. Dr. Benjamin Rush quoted Arnold as saying that "his courage was acquired, and that he was a coward till he was 15 years of age."

Two years after his mother had him brought home, Benedict ran off again. After his parents' death Arnold sold the family property and went with his sister to New Haven, where he opened what seems like something that would fit well in a twentieth-century shopping mall, a combination pharmacy and bookstore. It, and therefore Benedict Arnold, was a success.

With the French and Indian War at an end, Arnold turned his one store into a successful shipping company, sailing his own ships to Canada and the West Indies. While in Canada he traveled and traded in Montreal and Quebec, probably doing a bit of smuggling along the way. At age twenty-six he married Margaret Mansfield; in five years they had three children, all boys.

When it became obvious the American colonies would go to war with the mother country, and the Continental Congress began naming generals to lead the war, Arnold expected to be among them. After all, he'd fought in the French and Indian War, he'd run a successful business, and, thanks to an inheritance, he owned thousands of acres of land in New York's Mohawk and Hudson valleys. It wasn't Arnold that the Congress named, however. It was another New Yorker, Philip Schuyler. Arnold decided to volunteer, and it was as an elected captain of the militia that he marched to Cambridge, Massachusetts, in December 1774 with a company of volunteers.

Benedict Arnold was taller than average for the time, standing about five feet nine inches. He was said to be unusually strong, with great stamina. Ice-gray eyes, black hair, and a swarthy complexion. He may (there's no confirmed portrait of the man) have had a beak nose and a heavy, jutting jaw.

Almost as soon as Arnold arrived at the American lines outside Boston, he turned around and left. He'd talked the authorities into allowing him to take part in the seizure of Fort Ticonderoga with Ethan Allen. After taking the fort, Arnold went on to capture St. Johns, Quebec.

He was convinced he could do just as good a job on Quebec City. Congress was also convinced, more or less. Arnold sailed with a group of about a thousand volunteers to the mouth of the Kennebec River in what is now Maine but then was still part of Massachusetts. With him were Daniel Morgan, who would play a decisive role at Saratoga, and a young man who would play a decisive role in several other events, Aaron Burr. Arnold loaded his men and material onto bateaus and headed off; those who couldn't fit in the bateaus marched along the riverside. He promised it would take only twenty days. It took forty-five. Small matter: He believed it was only 150 miles when it really was more like 350.

Arnold and his men left Cambridge, Massachusetts, on September 13. Eleven days later they reached the rapids above what is now Augusta, Maine.

One of the volunteers who went with Benedict Arnold was twenty-two-year-old Abner Stocking, a private. "Zealous in the cause," Stocking wrote, "and not knowing the hardships and distresses we were to encounter, we as usual began our march very early. . . . Many pretty girls stood upon the shore, I suppose weeping for the departure of their sweethearts." Private Stocking kept a journal, recording the ordeal of the march and the lack of food along the way. On September 27, they "carried our batteaus and baggage round the Ticonnick Falls." Two days later they had to portage around Skowhegan Falls: "It occasioned much delay and great fatigue. We had to ascend a ragged rock, near on 100 feet in height and almost perpendicular."

Arnold's boats leaked, and he lost much of his food supply; but the men fished and caught as many as ten dozen an hour. The twelve-mile portage called the Great Carrying Place left the men tired and worn out; each bateau weighed four hundred pounds. When Arnold and his men reached the Dead River, it was anything but dead. It was alive with violent currents and snags and rapids. Sometimes it stopped the army's progress completely. By the time they had covered thirty miles and reached the watershed between the Kennebec and Chaundière rivers it was the end of October and snow had already fallen. Arnold hoped to cross Lake Megantic, then sail up the Chaundière to the St. Lawrence River.

Snow, half-frozen rivers and lakes, a great need of supplies, food, clothing, and shoes. They all worked against Arnold.

On October 28, according to Dr. Isaac Senter, who, like Abner, was just twenty-two, the men divided up the food they had, and "the provisions [were] five pints per man. Pork, though the only meat, was not properly divisible, as the whole amount would not have been an ounce per man."

By the time they reached the St. Lawrence River, more than three hundred of them had turned back and many others had been left sick or dead along the way. An argument had broken out among the men who stayed with Arnold and those who went back; each side thought the other had received too large a share of the supplies. Arnold was left with only 675 men still able to march.

In a letter written November 27, an egotistic Arnold said that "in about eight weeks we completed a march of near six hundred miles, not to be paralleled in history." Along the way, much of the army's ammunition was ruined—"inserviceable and not ten rounds each for the men, who were almost naked, bare footed and much fatigued." He proposed to attack the town immediately "and make no doubt in a few days to bring Gov. Carlton to terms." It would be the end of December before Arnold reached Quebec.

On December 3, Montgomery and three hundred men arrived at Quebec City after a relatively easy victory at Montreal. Their combined assault on the citadel ended at dawn on December 31 when Montgomery was killed instantly by a cannon shot. A musket ball broke Arnold's knee.

John Henry was a private in Arnold's expedition and later dictated his account:

> Now we saw Colonel Arnold returning, wounded in the leg and supported by two men. . . . Arnold called to the troops in a cheering voice as we passed, urging us forward, yet was observable among the soldiery, with whom it was my misfortune to be now placed, that the colonel's retiring dampened their spirits. . . .

At this time it was discovered that our guns were useless, because of the dampness. The snow, which lodged in our fleecy coats, was melted by the warmth of our bodies. Thence came that disaster.

The attack on Quebec disintegrated. The Americans lost about sixty killed and another four hundred were taken prisoner, including Daniel Morgan, who had taken command when Arnold was wounded. The British defenders lost only eighteen killed or wounded. As Arnold withdrew he fell from his horse, further injuring his leg.

He refused to retreat, however, hanging on to the hope that reinforcements would arrive and that the American expedition to Canada would be successful. Some rebel reinforcements *did* arrive, but almost as many who joined the army died of disease. Smallpox had been prevalent among the troops and now reached epidemic proportion.

When the ice started breaking up in the St. Lawrence, and the British fleet sailed all the way up the St. Lawrence River to Quebec, it became obvious the American attack on the Canadian capital had failed. Arnold insisted on being the last to be evacuated.

In a gesture of admiration Congress elevated Benedict Arnold to brigadier general. They expected big things from the one-time apothecary's apprentice.

In the spring of 1774, Governor Dunmore dissolved the Virginia House of Burgesses, and radical members of that body reconstituted themselves as the Virginia Convention. It became the colony's de facto government, with the Committee of Safety, in effect, the executive branch.

In March 1775, the convention met in St. John's Church in Richmond—an armed British warship stationed in the James River had delegates afraid to meet in the capitol at Williamsburg. Patrick Henry declared that Virginia should be put "in a posture of defense."

Resolved, That a well regulated Militia, composed of Gentlemen and Yeomen, is the natural Strength, and only Security, of a free Government. . . .

That the Establishment of such a Militia is at this Time particularly necessary. . . .

"There is no longer any room for hope," Henry exclaimed. In as ringing a speech as any ever made anywhere, Patrick Henry declared:

They tell us, sir, that we are weak—unable to cope with so formidable an adversary. But when shall we be stronger? . . . There is no retreat but in submission and slavery! Our chains are forged. Their clanking may be heard on the plains of Boston! The war is inevitable—and let it come! I repeat it, sir, let it come!

It is in vain, sir, to extenuate the matter. Gentlemen may cry, "Peace! peace!"—but there is no peace. The war is actually begun! The next gale that sweeps from the north will bring to our ears the clash of resounding arms! Our brethren are already in the field! Why stand we here idle? What is it that gentlemen wish? What would they have? Is life so dear, or peace so sweet, as to be purchased at the price of chains and slavery? Forbid it, Almighty God! I know not what course others may take, but as for me, give me liberty or give me death!

At the time, Thomas Jefferson remarked, Henry "left us all far behind."

On April 19, 1775, British troops marched on Lexington and Concord, Massachusetts, to confiscate gunpowder the colonists had been storing. Not waiting for Virginia rebels to squirrel away gunpowder the way their northern brethren had done, on April 20, Governor Dunmore beat them to the punch. In something more than a coincidence, sounding like a plan concerted in London, he ordered British marines to remove the gunpowder stored in the magazine on Duke of Gloucester Street, and placed it on board an armed schooner anchored in the nearby James River. He claimed it was due to the convention's resolution to form a militia.

The public was incensed. Those same militia troops Dunmore had not wanted trained were mustered, and Patrick Henry, as titular commander of military forces, led a group of volunteers in a march on the Governor's Palace, where he demanded either the return of the powder or payment for it.

The governor warned the crowd that if the militia didn't disperse, he'd free the slaves and burn Williamsburg to the ground. Then Dunmore seemed to back down. He agreed to pay £300 for the powder, double its worth. Henry and his militia bought the idea, never realizing that if they'd held out, Dunmore might have backed down and returned the gunpowder. As it was, they'd have to buy more, and there was no place in America where they could purchase gunpowder; the colonies didn't make it in great quantities.

To top this, after the rebel militia had dispersed, Governor Dunmore declared Henry an outlaw. He then turned tail, and with his wife and family sought safe quarters on a British man-of-war, HMS *Fowey,* off Yorktown.

Thinking Dunmore had backed down and paid for the powder, the rebels disbanded and an uneasy quiet prevailed in Virginia until word reached them a few days later of the skirmishes at Lexington and Concord. A broadside carrying the news in Williamsburg read: "The Sword is now drawn, and God knows when it will be sheathed."

In September, forty-three-year-old Governor Dunmore confiscated a printing press from John H. Holt's *Norfolk Intelligencer.* Dunmore took the press on board a British warship and in November issued a proclamation declaring martial law in Virginia, calling on every loyal citizen to support the Crown. He also offered freedom to all slaves belonging to those who were in rebellion against the king if they would join him in fighting their masters. It was just what Southern plantation owners were afraid of: a black insurrection. There were upward of a quarter million slaves in Virginia; in the capital city of Williamsburg about half the population was made up of slaves. However, when Dunmore left Williamsburg on June 8, he made no attempt to free his own fifty-seven slaves.

One Virginia slave who ran off was Eva, who worked in a spinning house for Peyton Randolph, the first president of the Continental Congress. In 1776, Eva was appraised at one hundred dollars, an indication that she was a skilled adult worker. She joined hundreds of

Virginia slaves who heeded Governor Dunmore's proclamation. In the summer of 1780, for whatever reason—and it may have been that she was captured—Eva returned to Williamsburg. Apparently Mrs. Randolph—husband Peyton had died in 1775 of what was called "apoplexy"—didn't want to have Eva around slaves who had not run away. "Eva's bad behavior laid me under the necessity of selling her," Betty Randolph wrote. Part of the money from the sale of Eva went to buying another female slave.

In a strange piece of logic, some delegates to the Virginia Convention proclaimed that the British king had "forced the Slave Trade on us for several Years," then "ordered his Governor Lord Dunmore to arm our Slaves against us." In reply to Dunmore's proclamation, the Virginia Convention said that all slaves returning to their masters within ten days would be pardoned.

When George Washington heard about Dunmore's proclamation, he wrote Richard Henry Lee: "If . . . that man is not crushed before spring, he will become the most formidable enemy America has; his strength will increase as a snow ball, by rolling; and faster, if some expedient cannot be hit upon to convince the slaves and servants of the impotency of his designs."

It wasn't easy escaping from their masters. They had to move in small numbers, because it was against the law for more than six blacks to assemble at one time, except under the direction of their masters. They had to be wary of patrols looking for runaways. Still, as many as three hundred slaves not only ran away, many of them gathered together in the Dismal Swamp into a force known as Lord Dunmore's Royal Ethiopian Regiment. They wore white sashes across their chests, emblazoned with the words "Liberty to Slaves," and were drilled by officers of the British Royal Marines.

After spending the summer of 1775 gathering a fleet of ships, in October Lord Dunmore set up headquarters at the Gosport Navy Yard, in present-day Portsmouth. By mid-November he had seized more than seventy rebel cannon. The militia and British forces took aim at each other. They met at the Great Bridge in the first fight between English troops and American militiamen since the Battle of Bunker Hill.

The bridge that gave the battle (and later a town) its name was a forty-yard-long wooden affair that crossed the swampy southern branch of the Elizabeth River. It's about eight miles southeast of Portsmouth. The Virginians arrived at the southern end of a causeway approaching the bridge, and Dunmore's troops were stationed on the northern end, where they'd removed some of the bridge's wooden planking and were building defense works the rebels called "the Hog Pen."

Dunmore had about 150 regulars and 300 members of the Royal Ethiopian Regiment. His plan was for two units of black troops to circle behind the militiamen before daylight and to force them out at sunrise. After the Ethiopian troops would draw the militia's fire, troops from the redcoat garrison in the Hog Pen would then storm across the bridge.

Among those on the Patriot side was William Flora, a free black from Portsmouth. As the redcoats charged across the Great Bridge, Flora "kept firing at the attacking British when all his comrades had retired to their breastwork."

Captain Charles Fordyce spearheaded the British attack with his force of about two hundred regulars, including sixty grenadiers. Legend has it that Fordyce waved his hat over his head and shouted, "The day is ours!" and rushed forward. He was shot dead. In addition to Fordyce, twelve others from the British side died and forty-nine more were wounded. The only American wounded was a militiaman who hurt his finger.

The first battle of the Revolution in Virginia lasted less than half an hour. Over the next three days British troops and Tory sympathizers, including many Scottish merchants, evacuated Norfolk. On New Year's Eve, Dunmore, who was on board a ship in Norfolk harbor, was told that Patriot troops were parading in the city, "hats fixed on their bayonets." Dunmore saw this more as impertinence than exuberance and ordered the city to be bombarded. It was 4:00 A.M. when the ships opened fire. Annoyed by snipers from waterfront buildings, Dunmore sent ashore landing parties of Royal Marines to set fire to a nearby warehouse. Norfolk was then Virginia's largest city—about six thousand people—and it went up in flames. "The detested town of Norfolk is no more!" wrote a midshipman aboard HMS *Otter.* "Our boats now landed, and set fire to the town in several places," the midshipman added. "It burned fiercely all night, and the next day."

The *Pennsylvania Evening Post* reported the next day that "the Houses being chiefly of wood, took fire immediately, and the fire spread with amazing rapidity. It is now become general, and the whole town will probably be consumed in a day or two." About nine hundred houses, more than two-thirds of the buildings in Norfolk, were destroyed. Those that were not left in ashes by Lord Dunmore and the British navy were destroyed by the Virginia militia when they evacuated the town in February.

During the bombing of Norfolk, a nine-pound cannonball fired by rebels on shore tore through the cabin of Dunmore's flagship, slightly wounding him in the leg. He sailed off to Gwynn Island at the mouth of the Piankatank River in Chesapeake Bay, where he tried to set up a new base; militia forces drove him off the island in early July. Dunmore later conducted a minor raid up the Potomac, in which he may have tried to kidnap Martha Washington and destroy Mount Vernon. The raid failed when a heavy storm hit.

Lord Dunmore sailed off for the West Indies, taking with him almost a thousand slaves who had run to him when he promised them freedom. He sold them to sugar plantations, pocketed the cash, and set off for New York. In late 1776, John Murray, the Fourth Earl of Dunmore, left America for England. He sat for eleven years as a Scottish peer in Parliament, and in 1787, he became the governor of the Bahamas, not a bad second chance for the man who lost Virginia. Apparently the Bahamians liked their new governor. They named a city on Eleuthera after him, and it's still there: Dunmore Town.

The Battle of Great Bridge came three weeks before Montgomery and Arnold's disastrous attack on Quebec. It would be more than three years until the war again came to Virginia. There would be several raids beginning in 1779, but the next major battle in Virginia came at the hands of the American hero at the Battle of Quebec. It was in December 1780, and by then Benedict Arnold had turned traitor and was on the other side.

Cowboys bring to mind America's Wild West. The word *cowboy* itself, however, goes back much further and even to a different country. In the Gaelic language of Ireland, it was *buachaill bó*, literally "boys who herded cows." Until the twentieth century, whenever troops were engaged in or just training for war, they herded hogs and cattle with them. Those who herded the cattle often weren't soldiers but were hired for that sole purpose and were called cowboys. Our modern definition of cowboy didn't come until 1877, when it was first used in print.

Cowboy had a far less bovine meaning during the Revolution. A different place too: Westchester County, New York. It was in the so-called "neutral ground" near New York City, where in 1775, Loyalists became noted for their barbarous treatment of opponents. They operated off and on throughout the war, stealing cattle and selling them to the British, and generally rousting out anyone who objected to English rule. In time that version of the word *cowboy* was applied to just about any lawless individual.

Loyalists, of course, didn't have the game to themselves. While Cowboys were on the British side, on the Patriot side were a group known as the "Skinners."

This latter group was named for General Courtlandt Skinner, who raised a brigade of Loyalist troops in New Jersey. Originally they fought for and alongside the British. Later, however, they switched sides, becoming Patriots and doing to the Loyalists just what the Cowboys were doing to Patriots. This brought about frequent skirmishes between the Cowboys and the Skinners.

One incident began simply enough but evolved into one of the biggest scandals of the Revolution. It concerned a man traveling as John Anderson.

Dressed in civilian clothing, he was riding south on the east side of the Hudson River toward Tarrytown, when he came across three men—"bushmen," a Continental army lieutenant called them—loitering by a stream, playing cards. Bands of Skinners and Cowboys had been roaming the countryside in something of a no-man's-land between the two armies, robbing anyone who wasn't on their side—Patriot or Loyalist.

One of the men who stopped Anderson wore a British army coat, and the traveler assumed they were Loyalists. According to Lieutenant Joshua King, Anderson said to the men, "I hope, gentlemen, you belong to the Lower [Tory] party."

"'We do,' says one.

"'So do I,' says [Anderson], 'and by the token of this ring and key you will let me pass. I am a British officer on business of importance, and must not be detained.'

"One of them took his watch from him and ordered him to dismount. The moment this was done, he said he found he was mistaken and he must shift his tone. He says, 'I am happy, gentlemen, to find that I am mistaken. You belong to the Upper [patriot] Party, and so do I. A man must make use of any shift to get along, and to convince you of it, here is General Arnold's pass,' handing it to them, 'and I am at your service.'

"'Damn Arnold's pass,' says they."

The three "bushmen"—John Paulding, Isaac Van Wart, and David Williams—not only were Skinners, they were extortionists. "You said you was a British officer," Lieutenant King quoted them. "Where is your money?"

When Anderson claimed he had no money, the boys decided, "Let's search him." When they could find no money in Anderson's pockets, the three Skinners decided, "Let's search his boots."

Anderson tried to buy them off by bribing them into escorting him to a bridge at the southern end of this no-man's-land: "Name your sum." Agreeing on a price—Lieutenant King says, "I cannot recollect whether it was five hundred or a thousand guineas, the latter, I think"—the four men set out.

Either Paulding, Van Wart, or Williams decided that the risk was too great, and they might be seized by the British. Either that, or they realized that a thousand pounds was too great a sum for a traveler such as Anderson appeared to be able to pay.

Whatever, that's how the three Skinners captured John Anderson, whose real name was Major John André, Sir Henry Clinton's adjutant general, one-time Philadelphia dancing partner of beautiful Peggy Shippen,* who, not too long before the incident alongside the

---

* Her cousin, William Shippen, married Alice Lee, sister of Richard Henry, Francis Lightfoot, William, and Arthur Lee of Virginia. Which, in a convoluted way, made Peggy Shippen Arnold Civil War General Robert E. Lee's aunt by marriage.

road, had married the widower Benedict Arnold. None of this, of course, sounds like coincidence, and it probably wasn't.

Peggy Shippen had made a play for half of Washington's generals while he was in Philadelphia, or at least she played the beautiful and coquettish young darling. She had been just as beautiful and just as coquettish with General Howe's officers when the British controlled the city. Among the British officers with whom Peggy flirted, and with whom she grew close and often danced, was the handsome Major John André, a.k.a. John Anderson.

"The females who stayed in the city [Philadelphia] cut a curious figure," a returning Patriot wrote, "I cannot learn whether the cork rumps (sort of like bustles) have been introduced here, but some artificial rumps or other are necessary to counter-balance the extraordinary weight which some of the ladies carry before them." Apparently society women of Philadelphia wore an eighteenth-century version of a padded bra.

To honor Sir William Howe, Major John André arranged a grand party known as a Mischianza to mark the general's departure. The extravaganza included a regatta with decorated barges, a mock tournament, a banquet, and a dance. Young Peggy Shippen had rehearsed a part in the Mischianza, but at the last minute her father put his foot down and forbade her participation. Instead of Peggy Shippen, John André took as his partner for the event Shippen's friend, Peggy Chew, from whom we'll hear later.

Obviously André and Peggy Shippen were well acquainted. A pencil drawing of the socialite by the young major now hangs in the Yale University Art Gallery. It shows an attractive young lady wearing the typical bosom-baring dress of the day; her hair is either piled high and partially covered with a bonnet, or maybe she's wearing a wig; it's hard to tell from the drawing. Such wigs were rarely taken off, even at night, and women were known to set mouse- or louse traps in their wigs to snare vermin attracted to the wheat flour often used as white powder.

When General Howe marched out of Philadelphia, leaving it to the Americans, many Loyalists went with him. Peggy Shippen did not. This teenage "reigning belle" of Philadelphia society stayed on, with no one apparently realizing she was a spy. Marching in with

Washington was the man who would be the military governor of the city, Benedict Arnold, and the thirty-eight-year-old, swarthy, and hook-nose general was smitten with Shippen.

Arnold was recovering from his second leg wound of the war, this one received at Bemis Heights outside Saratoga. Unlike Major André, Arnold couldn't dance much, but he could write. However, the words he used in writing to Peggy were recycled from an earlier romance:

> Twenty times have I taken up my pen to write to you, and as often my trembling hand refused to obey the dictates of my heart. . . . My passion is not found on personal charms only; that sweetness of disposition and goodness of heart, that sentiment and sensibility which so strongly mark the character of the lovely Miss P. Shippen, renders her amiable beyond expression and will ever retain the heart she has once captivated.

Within a year Arnold and Peggy were married. An aide supported Arnold during the wedding ceremony at her father's home, and at the reception the bridegroom sat with his leg on a camp stool. A month later he took the first step toward treason and defection.

Now, it's difficult to say who was responsible for Arnold's decision to sell out to the British, Benedict or Peggy; somewhere there's a desire for money and fame. Arnold's prewar wealth would not have allowed it, but he and Peggy soon bought a mansion—Mount Pleasance—on the Schuylkill River, where they enjoyed the good life, complete with liveried servants and a coach and four. Recuperating in their newly acquired mansion, Benedict Arnold brooded over not being promoted as rapidly as he had hoped.

Peggy-the-society-belle was used to money, but as a Continental army general, Benedict apparently didn't have enough of it. The Arnolds entertained lavishly with fine china and plate—silver plated utensils at a time when knives and spoons generally were made of wood or base metal. This should have caused Benedict's fellow officers to raise an eyebrow or two, since he was always hard up for money. More than an eyebrow should have been raised when the Arnolds' friends seemed to be more Tory than Patriot.

From the beginning Peggy was aware of Arnold's conspiracy. She would send letters to her friend (and André's date at the Mischianza) Peggy Chew on the British side of the war, interlining her letters with messages in invisible ink. Openly the letters talked of that infamous mock tournament she never got to participate in, but the invisible messages had other meanings.

With Peggy Chew as an intermediary, Peggy Shippen Arnold and John André resumed their acquaintance. With that, as detective Sherlock Holmes would say, the game was afoot.

Benedict Arnold's fellow officers may not have given much thought to his new lifestyle, but a group of civilian busybodies known as the Continental Congress did. They began asking questions, including why General Arnold was so free in giving passes for the round trip between British-held New York and American-held Philadelphia. Congress also wanted to know why Arnold had used public transportation (e.g., military wagons) for private ends. And was it true that he had used his office to buy goods cheaply and then resell them to the public at a high profit? These and other such questions began cropping up. What did not crop up was the fact that Benedict Arnold had already sold out. Benedict the bold of Quebec and Saratoga had become Arnold the traitor of West Point.

Previously an unfortified point along the Hudson River, West Point was in George Washington's words, the "key to America," and the Continental army began garrisoning it with men and equipment. It had high cliffs out of reach of ships' cannon in the river and could control traffic along the Hudson and, thus, south to New York City and north to Lake Champlain. Three thousand American forces were garrisoned at West Point, along with artillery and stores.

Sometime in June 1779, British General Henry Clinton, possibly using the correspondence between Peggy Arnold and John André, proposed that Benedict Arnold join the British army and accept a command. Arnold agreed, but he wanted money, £10,000 no matter what happened, and £20,000 "if I point out a plan of cooperation by which Sir Henry shall possess himself of West Point, the garrison, &c., &c." It took five weeks for word to get back to Arnold that Clinton would pay if West Point fell but would not pay if it did not.

Meanwhile Arnold sent the British bits and pieces of information, relaying them through his wife's invisible-ink letters.

Benedict Arnold didn't know it, but George Washington and his French counterpart, Jean Baptiste Donatien de Vimeur, Comte de Rochambeau, were working out plans for a joint operation against the British in which Arnold was to have commanded a wing. The joint operation became the Battle of Yorktown, but by then Arnold was on the other side.

On August 3, 1780, Arnold was given command of West Point, just what he'd been pestering George Washington for. In September, André sailed up the Hudson on HMS *Vulture,* and met with Arnold at Loyalist William Smith's house not far from West Point. André wore a blue caped cloak over his British officer's red coat. For £6,000— all that André had been authorized to pay—Benedict Arnold turned over to André the plans to West Point. He would also be given an "ample stipend."

André was to have returned to the *Vulture* following their meeting, but the ship had been fired upon and had to drop downstream. The English officer, now in civilian clothing, would have to make his way back overland, through difficult country, that no-man's-land between American and British lines. Arnold gave him a pass that read: "Permit Mr. John Anderson to pass the guards to the White Plains, or below, if he chooses; he being on public business by my direction." It was near Tarrytown that he was caught and searched.

Back to those three Skinners. When they forced John Anderson to strip, they found in his boot confidential papers from Benedict Arnold. They hustled their captive to a nearby American post and the officer in charge sent the papers on to Alexander Hamilton, who gave them to General Washington, who exclaimed, "My God! Arnold has gone over to the British."

By this time Anderson had admitted he was André but claimed that he wasn't really traveling as a spy and that his had been a mission of peace, which was marred by his being forced against his will to use a false name. On hearing that Anderson/André had been captured, Benedict Arnold deserted and made his way to the *Vulture.*

Before Arnold left he went to see Peggy and told her he'd have to leave the country. Peggy Arnold "fell into a swoon at this declaration," Lieutenant King testified at André's trial, "and he left her in it, to consult his own safety, till the servants, alarmed by her cries, came to her relief."

André was quickly tried for treason, the board hearing his case presided over by six major-generals. As a spy André's sentence was automatic: death by hanging. However, he wrote to General Washington:

Sir:

Buoyed above the terror of death by the consciousness of a life devoted to honorable pursuits, and stained with no action that can give remorse, I trust that the request I make to your Excellency at this serious period, and which is to soften my last moments, will not be rejected.

Sympathy towards a soldier will surely induce your Excellency and a military tribunal to adept the mode of death to the feelings of a man of honor.

Washington refused to change the board's order; however, he told the British he would exchange John André for Benedict Arnold. The British refused, and the next day André was hanged.

John André was a spy. Benedict Arnold was a traitor. He was not, however, the only American officer approached by the British. Generals John Sullivan, Daniel Morgan, Philip Schuyler, and even Israel Putnam had all been sounded out. Unlike Benedict Arnold, they had rejected the overtures. Even the man who rowed Arnold out to the *Vulture* the night he learned of André's capture would not go. Arnold asked Corporal James Larvey if he would go with him. "No, Sir!" Larvey replied. "One coat is enough for me to wear at a time."

CHAPTER FIVE

G. Washington:
The Myth Who Would Be Man

"George," said his father, "do you know who killed that beautiful little cherry tree yonder in the garden?"
"I can't tell a lie, Pa, you know I can't tell a lie; I did cut it with my hatchet."
—Mason Locke Weems, 1800

[Washington's] mind was great and powerful, without being of the first order ... and as far as he saw, no judgement was ever sounder. It was slow in operation, being little aided by invention, but sure in conclusion. ... His integrity was pure, his justice the most inflexible I have ever known, no motives or interest or consanguinity, of friendship or hatred, being able to bias his decision.
Thomas Jefferson, 1814

The average American soldier in the American Revolution stood slightly less than five feet six inches tall. By the Civil War the average had shot up to five feet eight and a half inches tall. In World War II, it was just about the same, five eight, 144 pounds. In other words, after an increase of about two inches, nothing much changed until after World War II. The change in this century came about with better nutrition. More of us are taking more vitamins, for instance, than at any other time in history.

At an even five feet, Martha Washington wasn't really all that short for her time, but when she stood next to her husband, the man she referred to as "the general," she must have looked like one of the Wizard of Oz's little people. When George met Martha Dandridge Custis she was just barely a widow, her husband only recently dead. Daniel Parke Custis had been twenty years older than Martha and left her with two children, Martha Parke Custis and John (Jacky) Parke Custis. At age twenty-six Martha was about nine months older than George.

George was, according to his friend George Mercer, "straight as an Indian." Mercer added that Washington's "bones and joints are large, as are his hands and feet."

Washington's adopted son—actually, Martha's grandson; the boy's father was Martha's boy, Jacky—George Washington Parke Custis was eighteen when the general died. In his book, *Recollections and Private Memoirs of Washington by His Adopted Son, George Washington Parke Custis,* he wrote: "General Washington, in his prime of life, stood six feet two inches, and measured precisely six feet when attired for his grave." Custis added that

> Washington's powers were chiefly in his limbs; they were long, very large and sinewy. . . . His frame showed an extraordinary development of bone and muscle; his joints were large, as were his feet; and could a cast have been preserved of his hand, to be exhibited in these degenerate days, it would be said to have belonged to being of a fabulous age.

Custis quotes Lafayette as saying, during a visit to Mount Vernon in 1824, "I never saw so large a hand on any human being, as the general's."

There were other oddities about Washington's appearance and, together, they form a physiological description that may have special meaning. George Washington appears to have had what's called XYY syndrome, a chromosomal abnormality that in some can lead to criminal behavior and in others leads to sterility.

XYY syndrome includes dental disorders, everything from "shovel-shaped" teeth to premature tooth loss. Washington's problems with his teeth and difficulties with dentures are the stuff of legend and they're true. Again, to quote Washington's friend George Mercer: "His mouth is large and generally firmly closed, but which from time to time discloses some defective teeth." At the time of Mercer's comment, George was twenty-two years old. For the rest of his life he suffered dental problems, aching teeth, and swollen and inflamed gums. He used every modern convenience of the day, which of course weren't too modern: toothbrushes made of sponges, tinctures of myrrh, and false teeth. By 1789, the year Washington became president, he had only one natural tooth left in his head. And then that one was gone. He tried just about every type of false teeth available, from wooden (true, but he didn't wear those more than once or twice), human (it was an age when some poverty-stricken individuals sold their teeth for food, which is sort of a "Gift of the Magi"–type event), and hippopotamus ivory attached by gold rivets. The famous Gilbert Stuart portrait of George Washington—for generations, copies of it were virtually mandatory in schoolrooms—shows Washington with his mouth obviously distended, pursed as if he were about ready to whistle. In the unfinished portrait George obviously is uncomfortable. The story goes that Washington and Stuart didn't get along well, and that Stuart made no attempt to play down the president's enlarged lips.

Another report says that by the time Stuart got around to painting Washington, the president's dentures were so ill fitting that the artist tried to restore George's original facial expression by stuffing the man's mouth with cotton padding. But Washington didn't like Stuart; he liked even less being touched (perhaps Martha was the exception here). It's not likely, then, that Washington would allow Stuart to degrade him this way.

XYY syndrome includes prominent, raised glabella regions of the head, that portion of the face where the forehead and nose bridge meet. Again, artist Gilbert Stuart:

> There were features in his face totally different from what I had observed in any other human being. The sockets of the eye, for instance, were larger than what I ever met with before, and the upper part of the nose broader.

XYY syndrome also includes frequent outbreaks of teenage acne, and Washington's face in adulthood was severely scarred. True, in 1751, at age nineteen, he contracted smallpox, while traveling with his brother in Barbados, and it's likely most of the scars were the result of the disease not the syndrome; however, that can't be ruled out.

Men with XYY syndrome also, according to some experts, often exhibit behavioral disturbances bordering on the criminal, a lack of emotional control, an excessive number of temper tantrums, and a poor sense of self. There is little doubt that George Washington was insecure; he longed all of his life to be accepted, appearing day after day before the Continental Congress in his Virginia militia uniform, hoping to be chosen as the Continental army's commander in chief. On many occasions he lost his temper—at the Battle of Kip's Bay, for example, when he took the broadside of his sword to his panicking men. And after being rejected by the French emissaries in 1753 at Fort Le Beouf, Washington chose not to return home slowly with his small force (which included some far more experienced backwoodsmen) but virtually to go it alone. Trekking about in the snow up to his knees, falling off a hurriedly built raft, and pressing his way back to Virginia as fast as possible—this may indicate Washington was emotionally out of control. Certainly he didn't have to worry about the French beating him back to Virginia; they were snowed in up in northwestern Pennsylvania. And when fighting with General Braddock he charged the enemy again and again—saying in a letter to his mother: "I luckily escape'd with't a wound, tho' I had four Bullets through My Coat, and two Horses shot under me."

Obviously no one can check it out today, but Washington appears to have had XYY syndrome, and while there are these other traits associated with XYY syndrome, perhaps the most significant one is sterility. Martha, through her first marriage, gave birth four times, with two of the children living past infancy. George Washington, however—the Father of His Country—so far as is known, never fathered anyone.

George Washington's complexion was sallow, his face pockmarked from his teenage contraction of smallpox. He had reddish hair as a young man, but by the time he was president, that had turned to gray, which he usually wore powdered. Washington normally did not wear a wig. His eyes were blue-gray.

It was Washington's adopted son who first tried to debunk the Washington-throwing-a-dollar-across-the-Potomac myth. Apparently Maryland-born Mason Locke Weems started the tale of the dollar and the companion I-cannot-tell-a-lie story of a young George chopping down his father's cherry tree.

He identified himself as Parson Weems, "Formerly Rector of Mount Vernon Parish," even though no such parish ever existed; yet, he was an ordained deacon of the Anglican Church, and served several parishes in Maryland. Primarily Weems was a writer and book dealer whose chief accomplishment in his life came in 1800 with his book *Life and Memorable Actions of George Washington.* The book went on to more than seventy editions and changed often. The cherry tree story, for example, came in the fifth edition in 1806. It's probable that most people got their information about George Washington from this sometime minister, sometime bookseller, sometime storyteller. Apparently he never let facts get in the way of a good story.

Back to the dollar-across-the-Potomac business: George Washington Parke Custis wrote:

> The power of Washington's arm was displayed in several memorable instances; in his throwing a stone from the bed of the stream to the top of Natural Bridge [Virginia]; another over the Palisades into the Hudson, and yet another across the Rappahannock [River], at Fredericksburg.
>
> Of the article with which he spanned this bold and navigable stream, there are various accounts. We are assured that it was a piece of slate, fashioned to about the size and shape of a dollar, and which, sent by an arm so strong, not only spanned the river, but took the ground at least thirty yards on the other side.

There's a big difference between tossing anything—coin or slab or slate—across the Rappahannock, which is about 250 feet across, and the Potomac, which at Mount Vernon is about two and a half miles across.

George Washington Parke Custis's natural father, Jacky Custis, died in 1781; he caught a fever while at the Battle of Yorktown with General George. That's how Jacky's son, already named after the great man, came to be adopted by Washington.

Psychologically George Washington was insecure and longed to be accepted. A lot of his emotional problems may have come from his mother, Mary Ball Washington, a rather domineering woman who, even when it seemed obvious George was on the road to success, complained that he was neglecting her in favor of his country.

Mary Ball was Augustine Washington's second wife, and throughout his life George's mother never let him forget that fact. Augustine died when George was eleven, and George's elder half brother,

Lawrence, inherited their father's estate, including the plantation along the Potomac River. His formal education ended three years later, when he was fourteen.

A trick question that comes up every now and then is "Who was the first president of the United States?" to which nearly everybody answers, "George Washington." George Washington, however, once wrote a man named John Hanson, addressing Hanson as "President of the United States." The trick, of course, is that Washington was the first president of the United States under the Constitution.

In 1781, the Maryland legislature became the last colony to approve the Articles of Confederation. Then came into being a loose thirteen-colony nation. The Marylander who signed his state's acceptance of the confederation was John Hanson, who also was president of the Continental Congress at the time. A few months later, after Washington's victory over Cornwallis at the Battle of Yorktown, Hanson wrote the general, congratulating him on beating the British. Washington wrote back, addressing his letter to Hanson: to the "President of the United States."

George Washington was sworn in under the Constitution on Thursday, April 30, 1789, the ceremony held on the balcony of the senate chamber of New York City's Federal Hall. From the beginning Washington tried to play down any flamboyance and wore a plain brown broadcloth suit made specially for the occasion, along with white silk stockings. His sword hung at his side. He was fifty-seven years sixty-seven days old at the time Robert Livingston administered the oath of office.

Officially when Washington took the oath of office he became president of only eleven states; two states—North Carolina and Rhode Island—were late in ratifying the Constitution. The Rhode Island legislature had refused even to consider a ratification convention.

In a way North Carolina made up for Rhode Island by holding two conventions. The first was so heavily anti-Federalist that even though it was known that ten state conventions had already approved the Constitution—enough to put the new document in effect—the North Carolina convention refused to ratify. They rejected it by a substantial margin of 184 to 83. North Carolina held a second ratifying convention in Fayetteville in November 1789, seven months after George Washington was sworn in. This time the Federalists were in power in North Carolina. They were satisfied by the September 25 submission to the states of a Bill of Rights to go along with the Constitution and voted 194 to 77 in favor of ratification.

It would be another seven months before Rhode Island ratified the Constitution, finally voting on May 29, 1790—more than a full year after George Washington took office. Even then, it was close— 34 to 32.

On April 21, 1789, nine days before George Washington was sworn in as president, John Adams took the oath of office as vice president.

As Robert Livingston finished administering the Constitution-prescribed oath to Washington, the new president added something of his own, something not written into the Constitution. He said, "So help me, God" and kissed the Bible Livingston had held. From then on every president has added those unwritten words.

With the first oath of office taken, then came the first-ever presidential inaugural address. George Washington spoke to his "Fellow Citizens of the Senate and of the House of Representatives." He did not, as most would later, address himself to "My fellow Americans." Washington had, of course, not really been elected by the people. Under the Constitution, technically speaking, no American president has been; it's the electoral college that actually votes for the office holder. In theory, we the people elect the electors.

Standing before a joint session of Congress, Washington delivered this first inaugural address, just 1,428 words, apparently written by Washington's young friend from Virginia, James Madison. In it he offered to serve as president without pay, to "renounce every pecuniary compensation." Just as he had offered during the Revolutionary War, he said he would serve without pay if Congress would pay his expenses—"such actual expenditures as the public good may be thought to require." The Continental Congress had agreed during the war, and it cost them more in expenses than his pay could ever have been. This time the Congress under the Constitution refused.

Washington ended his address, "resorting," he said, to the "benign Parent of the Human Race in humble supplication," the same "benign Parent" that had given the American people "opportunities for deliberating in perfect tranquillity."

By the time of his second inaugural on March 4, 1793, the temporary capital had been moved from New York to Pennsylvania. This time Washington stood in the senate chamber of Philadelphia's Congress Hall. By then he'd been criticized for "elitism," and he addressed himself to his "Fellow Citizens." "I am," he said, "again called upon by the voice of my country to execute the functions of its chief magistrate." Washington's second inaugural address was short, just 133 words. He closed the address by reminding the Congress

> that if it shall be found during my administration of the government I have in any instance violated willingly or knowingly the injunctions thereof, I may (besides incurring constitutional punishment) be subjected to the upbraidings of all who are now witnesses of the present solemn ceremony.

Washington may have been the only president (or anybody else, for that matter) ever to be sincere when he reminded Congress that if he broke the law, he should be punished. In years to come, other presidents would, in fact, claim they were above the law in many ways.

Before Washington was sworn in as the first president under the Constitution, Congress was already on the job, busy at work, looking out for their fellow Americans. The first law they passed was a tax.

Victory in the American Revolution was never a foregone conclusion; almost at any point the British could have won. The difference was that Patriots had a philosophy, and they were more cohesive in their thoughts. Loyalists, on the other hand, had no real philosophy other than the status quo—let's leave things as they are. It was easier to be for something (independence) than against something (the retention of the British king as an authority). After all, members of the Patriot army voluntarily gave up their way of life to fight for something they wanted—liberty.

CHAPTER SIX

Founding Mothers:
Hear Them Roar

*To the Printer: sir, I am just now nineteen and, without vanity believe as well quali-
fied for a husband as any of my neighbors.... [However,] the men are grown so
stupid nowadays that I believe they expect the women to court them....*
P.S. Pray, Mr. Printer, please take in the letters that come for me.
> —*The Virginia Gazette,* Diana Languish, February 2, 1767

We want bread and roses too.
> —Slogan of women strikers, Lawrence, Massachusetts, 1912

By the time of the Revolution most of the white inhabitants of the
American colonies were native born. Black immigrants, forcibly removed from their homelands, continued to be brought in throughout the century.

Still, there was a steady stream of white immigrants—mainly from
England, Scotland, Ireland, and the European continent—and most
were men. The earliest settlers had been male, and while the number of women increased, they were in the minority. Consequently
there were, to be blunt, never enough women to go around. Men
"left out in the marital game of musical chairs," as one historian puts
it, "were constantly on the lookout for wives." Only seldom did a girl
get beyond her teens before she was married. Sometime between the
1690s and the 1700s for whites, between the 1720s and 1730s for
blacks, the number of women grew large enough for what historian
Allan Kulikofe calls "generational replacement."

Over the next hundred years, as more women became "available,"
the females' age at first marriage increased dramatically. In the mid-
seventeenth century the average age when women married was under seventeen. A hundred years later, as the Revolution began, first-
marriage age for women had increased to twenty-two years.

William Byrd II, whose family was among the wealthiest in colonial Virginia life, once wrote a friend in England that his daughter Evelyn was "one of the most antick [antique] Virgins" he knew. At the time Evelyn Byrd was twenty.

Sometimes these "antick Virgins" were more independent than you might believe. Take the time when Dr. James Blair, the founder of Virginia's College of William and Mary, married Sarah Harrison. Her family would include a signer of the Declaration of Independence and a couple of presidents, and when it came time for the minister, a Mr. Smith, to recite the wedding vows, Sarah showed she had a mind of her own. Mr. Smith got to the "love, honor, and obey" part. Sarah Harrison stopped the proceedings and said, "No obey." Mr. Smith, according to a still preserved account, tried again: "love, honor, and obey." Once again Sarah said, "No obey." A third runthrough by the minister, and a third "No obey." Finally Mr. Smith went on with the ceremony. We have no idea whether Sarah Harrison Blair ever did obey.

The Maryland colony had a rather curious reputation, a "particularly happy hunting ground for women who wished to find husbands," one historian puts it. It seems a larger percentage of women married in Maryland than in the other thirteen original colonies. An English visitor to Maryland, Nicholas Cresswell, called Maryland "a paradise on Earth for women . . . That great curiosity, an Old Maid, is seldom seen in this country. They generally marry before they are twenty-two, often before they are sixteen."

George Alsop was an eighteenth-century indentured servant who eventually became a successful planter. According to him, "The Women that go over into this Province as Servants, have the best luck as in any place of the world . . . for they are no sooner on shoar [*sic*], but they are courted into a Copulative Matrimony." Alsop claimed that many women who were "so ill-favored that they would have had a hard time finding husbands anywhere else" met, courted, and married rather quickly. Or as he bluntly put it: "Some of them (for aught I know) had they not come to such a Market with their virginity, might have kept it . . . until it had been mouldy. . . ."

• • •

As soon as colonial men formed themselves into the "Sons of Liberty," colonial women grouped themselves into the "Daughters of Liberty." They pledged not to buy clothing that came from England and formed spinning societies to make their own yarn and linen. Considering that even the best of American society wasn't all that far from the time when nearly all clothing was home-grown and home-made, it wasn't that much of a change.

Deborah Franklin was Ben Franklin's common-law wife, and a most forgiving soul she had to be. Leaving Deborah home alone, Franklin strayed into the arms of several other young ladies, one of whom he impregnated. He did, however, do the right thing, more or less. He took the little bastard home to live with him. And Deborah. The long-suffering common-law wife, by all accounts, did the job happily. Of course, she had help. Ben Franklin also took to his household as a housemaid his illegitimate son's mother.

It was at the Battle of Monmouth that Mary Ludwig Hays earned the nickname "Molly Pitcher." It sounds like something out of the Parson Weems school of writing, but apparently it was more or less true. The "more" means that there likely were several "Molly Pitchers," and that it was a nickname given to various women who carried water to their husband/father/son/friend during the heat of battle. As for Mary Hays, she seems to have been the best known of the Molly Pitchers.

Mary (or Molly, as she was known from an early age) Ludwig married John Hays, a barber, and when war broke out, John joined the army as a private. Molly went right along with him. It was at the Battle of Monmouth Court House that she became famous. With the temperature hovering at one hundred degrees, Mary was taking water to her husband, when he was shot dead. She'd watched him swab the cannon's bore so often, she knew his job as well as he had, so she picked up where hubby left off and grabbed a rammer to keep John's cannon firing through the end of the battle.

Private Joseph Plumb Martin was also at Monmouth and witnessed Molly in action.

One little incident happened during the heat of the cannonade, which I was eyewitness to, and which I think would be unpardonable not to mention. A woman whose husband belonged to the artillery and who was then attached to a piece in the engagement, attended with her husband at the piece the whole time. While in the act of reaching a cartridge and having one of her feet as far before the other as she could step, a cannon shot from the enemy passed directly between her legs without doing any other damage than carrying away all the lower part of her petticoat. Looking at it with apparent unconcern, she observed that it was lucky it did not pass a little higher, for in that case it might have carried away something else, and continued her occupation.

Molly, according to Martin, smoked, chewed tobacco, and "swore like a trooper."

One version of the story has Mary being presented to George Washington after the battle was over, and he praised her for her courage, even making her a noncommissioned officer: Sergeant Molly. It's the kind of story that if it isn't true it should be. For years a toast offered by army artillerymen went:

> Drunk in a beverage richer,
> And stronger than was poured that day
> From Molly Pitcher's pitcher.

Another contestant for the Molly Pitcher title was Margaret Cochran Corbin of Pennsylvania. Her husband, John, was manning a cannon during the British attack on Fort Washington when he was killed. Margaret took over his duties until she was severely wounded, shot three times by musket fire and grapeshot; one arm was almost severed. After the battle she was taken along with the other wounded to Philadelphia. In 1779, she became the first woman to receive a military pension from the Continental Congress—thirty dollars for her immediate needs, half pay for life, and "one complete suit of cloaths." She was finally mustered out of the army in April 1883, settling in Westchester County, New York, where she was known as "Captain Molly." Philadelphia society women heard about Captain Molly and made plans to erect a monument to her. But when they heard how she'd died a hard-drinking, impoverished veteran at the age of forty-eight, society matrons canceled the monument. Margaret "Captain Molly" Corbin is buried in the West Point cemetery.

Throughout the Revolution hundreds of women followed their loved ones to war. Camp followers, they became known as, but in many cases that is too derogatory a phrase for them. They looked after their men, shared their lives and their danger. They were washerwomen and cooks, they sewed for the men and nursed them when they were sick or wounded. Some, of course, were prostitutes. Often, as with the two Molly Pitchers, women fought alongside men.

When the Continental army marched, the women (and sometimes children) camp followers were at the end of the train, some marching, some riding in wagons. Often they were listed simply as "baggage." It was, however, not unusual to see women in combat.

Deborah Sampson even masqueraded as a man. At five feet eight, she was taller than the average Revolutionary soldier. In October 1778, Deborah enlisted under the name Robert Shurtleffe. She served for three years and was wounded twice.

Apparently Deborah wasn't exactly pretty and was known as "smock face," and while her fellow soldiers still believed she was a he, because her face was whiskerless they jokingly called her "Molly." At a skirmish at Tappan Zee, New York, Deborah suffered a musket wound to the knee and was taken to an aid station. Realizing she'd be found out, she limped off, allowing the wound to heal itself.

She was injured a second time, a bullet wound to her shoulder. It wasn't until she came down with a fever that an army doctor named Birney discovered that Robert was Deborah. But instead of exposing her secret, the doctor had her taken to his own house in Philadelphia. While helping to take care of "Robert," the doctor's niece fell in love with the young soldier. Then word got out that he was really Deborah, and the game was up. Deborah was about to be booted out of the army unceremoniously when General Washington stepped in and Robert Shurtleffe was honorably discharged.

After the Revolution, and back as a woman, Deborah Sampson married a Sharon, Massachusetts, farmer, Benjamin Gannett. First the Massachusetts Assembly, then Congress, awarded her a pension, four dollars a month as an invalided soldier; they doubled that in 1818.

Early in the nineteenth century, Deborah Sampson Gannett took to the lecture circuit to capitalize on her fame as a soldier. She appeared, usually in uniform, in several New England states.

George Washington realized that the women were necessary to the army, but he called on his officers to "permit no more [women] than are absolutely necessary, and such as are actually useful," to follow the army. The general, however, allowed them to draw the same rations as soldiers.

Not only isn't much in the Declaration of Independence about slaves, there's not much there for women either. It may be likely that when Thomas Jefferson wrote "all men are created equal" he emotionally included women, but the words aren't there. Not that women weren't demanding their rights.

Abigail Adams, for instance, handed back to her husband, John, the arguments of equality and representation for all that he'd made and heard in Congress. "[In] the new Code of Laws which I suppose it will be necessary for you to make," she wrote John, "I desire you would Remember the Ladies, and be more generous and favorable to them than your ancestors."

> Do not put such unlimited power into the hands of the Husbands. Remember, all Men would be tyrants if they could. If perticuliar care and attention is not paid to the Ladies, we are determined to forment a Rebellion, and will not hold ourselves bound by any Laws in which we have no voice, or Representation.
>
> That your Sex are Naturally Tyrannical is a Truth so thoroughly established as to admit of no dispute, but such of you as wish to be happy willingly give up the harsh title of Master for the more tender and endearing one of Friend. Why then,

not put it out of the power of the vicious and the Lawless to use us with cruelty and indignity with impunity. Men of Sense in all Ages abhor those customs which treat us only as the vassals of your Sex. Regard us then as Beings placed by providence under the protection and in immitation of the Supreem Being make use of that power only for our happiness.

In replying to his wife's wondering when the Declaration of Independence would be completed, he told her to be patient. It would come soon. And her other "suggestions":

As to your extraordinary Code of Laws, I cannot but laugh. We have been told that our Struggle has loosened the bands of Government every where. That Children and Apprentices were disobedient—that schools and Colledges were grown turbulent—that Indians slighted their Guardians and Negroes grew insolent to their Masters. But your Letter was the first Intimation that another Tribe more numerous and powerful than all the rest were grown discontented.—This is rather too coarse a Compliment but you are so saucy, I wont blot it out.

Depend upon it. We know better than to repeal our Masculine systems. Altho they are in full Force, you know they are little more than Theory. We dare not exert our Power in its full Latitude. We are obliged to go fair, and softly, and in Practice you know We are the subjects. We have only the Name of Masters, and rather than give up this, which would compleatly subject Us to the Despotism of the Peticoat, I hope General Washington, and all our brave Heroes would fight.

In May, Abigail commented that "many are the solitary hours I spend, ruminating upon the past, and anticipating the future, whilst you overwhelmed with the cares of State, have but few moments you can devote to any individual." It was a soft opening for her hardening sell for women's rights:

I can not say that I think you very generous to the Ladies, for whilst you are proclaiming peace and good well to Men,

Emancipating all Nations, you insist upon retaining an absolute power over Wives. But you must remember that Arbitrary power is like most other things which are very hard, very liable to be broken—and notwithstanding all your wise Laws and Maxims we have it in our power not only to free ourselves but to subdue our Masters, and without violence throw both your natural and legal authority at our feet. . . .

The relationship between John and Abigail Adams, even two hundred years later, is a wonder, their letters to each other, marvelous to read. They openly show John and Abigail's great mutual affection. "My dear Nabby," he calls her. "My much Loved Friend," she refers to him. "My dearest Friend," they call each other.

In late 1775, while John was off in Philadelphia trying to persuade the Continental Congress to come to grips with the problems existing between England and America, Abigail remained in Braintree (now Quincy), Massachusetts, taking care of the perhaps more mundane aspects of life. "We have nothing to expect but the whole Wrath and Force of G. Britain," John wrote. In the same letter, he added:

It may amuse you to hear a Story. A few days ago, in Company with Dr. Zubly, somebody said, there was nobody on our side but the Almighty. The Dr. who is a Native of Switzerland, and speaks but broken English, quickly replied "Dat is enough. Dat is enough," and turning to me, says he, it puts me in mind of a fellow who once said, The Catholicks have on their side the Pope, and the K. of France and the K. of Spain, and the K. of Sardinia, and the K. of Poland and the Emperor of Germany &c. &c. &c. But as to them poor Devils the Protestants, they have nothing on their side but God Almighty.

Abigail told John that she had been "confined with the Jaundice, Rhumatism and a most violent cold; I yesterday took a puke which has relieved me. . . ." It was cold; they'd had "great and incessant rains . . . and a flight of snow, which I hope will purify the air of some of the noxious vapours." Despite frequent letters from John, in which he at least hinted at items being discussed in Congress, this was not enough for an obviously intelligent, obviously concerned, and just as obviously distressed Abigail:

> I wish I knew what mighty things were fabricating. If a form of Government is to be established here what one will be assumed? Will it be left to our assemblies to chuse one? and will not many men have many minds? and shall we not run into Dissentions among ourselves?
>
> I am more and more convinced that Man is a dangerous creature, and that power whether vested in many or a few is ever grasping, and like the grave cries, give. The great fish swallow up the small, and he who is most strenuous for the Rights of the People, when vested with power, is as eager after the prerogatives of Government.

He sent her a pamphlet entitled *Common Sense, Written in Vindication of Doctrines which there is Reason to expect that further Encroachments of Tyranny and Depredations of Oppression, will soon make the common Faith.* And he closed the letter: "Write me as often as you can—tell me all the News. Desire the Children to write to me, and believe me to be theirs and yours."

"I must bid you good night," Abigail wrote:

> Tis late for one who am much of an invalid [it was that "jaundice and rhumatism"]. I was disappointed last week in receiving a packet by the post, and upon unsealing it found only four news papers. I think you are more cautious than you need be. All letters I believe have come safe to hand. I have Sixteen from you, and wish I had as many more. Adieu. Yours.

Still in Braintree in March 1777, Abigail told John about the weather—"About the middle of Febry. came a snow of a foot and a half deep," but worried more whether the three letters she had written him since he left home had reached John. "We know not what is passing with you," she wrote, adding, "any more than if we lived with the Antipodes. I want a Bird of passage."

"My Mind is again Anxious," John wrote in July, "and my Heart is Pain for my dearest Friend. . . ."

> Three Times have I felt the most distressing Sympathy with my Partner, without being able to afford her any Kind of Solace or Assistance.
> When the Family was sick of the Dissentery, and so many of our Friends died of it.
> When you all had the small Pox.
> And now I think I feel as anxious as ever.—Oh that I could be near to say a few kind Words, or shew a few Kind Looks, or do a few kind Actions. Oh that I could take from my dearest, a share of her Distress, or relieve her of the whole.

Abigail was about to give birth to their daughter. The child was stillborn on July 10.

Theirs was more than a love story. It was a story of a mutual affection and appreciation. It was a happy and enduring partnership.

She repeatedly pestered her husband on equal rights for women, and while the cause of women's rights made no overt gains in the Revolution, this did not stop Abigail Adams from pushing for them. She found her role as wife and mother satisfying, but she wanted more. It is not too far-fetched to imagine Abigail Adams in the twentieth century. She would have marched for voting rights in the twenties, strengthened her family as it rode out the dust bowl years. In the 1940s she would have been Rosie the Riveter, who, with the war over, refused to give up her job. She would have been a nurse, a physician, an astronaut, or an economics specialist in the eighties, taking a seat in Congress in the nineties or taking the lead in industry.

The term hadn't yet been invented, but in 1797, when John Adams became president, Abigail Adams became the nation's second First Lady. Abigail Adams was the first First Lady to occupy the executive mansion. It wasn't yet called the White House, and Abigail herself referred to it as "a castle of a house."

She was the only woman to have been both the wife and the mother of a president—John Adams and John Quincy Adams. John

Quincy Adams and his wife, incidentally, tried raising silkworms in the White House. It didn't work.

When Patience Lovell was born in 1725, a book by London author Thomas Tryon was popular on both sides of the Atlantic: *Wisdom's Dictates, or, Aphorisms and Rules, Physical, Moral and Divine, for Preserving the Health of the body and the Peace of Mind . . . To which is added a Bill of Fare of Seventy-five Noble Dishes of Excellent Food.* In succinct and numbered passages Tryon laid out his precepts on diet, cleanliness, and clothing, telling how the masses should live. He threw in dozens of recipes for good measure.

Tryon's most widely read book, however, was titled *Ways to Health, Long Life and Happiness, or, A Discourse of Temperance and the particular Nature of all things requisite for the Life of Man. . . .* In it he condemned war as "the Whole-sale Murthering Art" and religious bigotry, which he traced to those who think like "some bloody, sottish, Belly-cod, devilish Priest." *Way to Health* was studied by a young Boston printer's apprentice, who in later years used the work as a basis for his own "way to wealth" as part of *Poor Richard's Almanack.*

Patience Lovell's father, John, adhered to Tryon's *Way to Health.* He never ate meat and wore only all-white clothing. Even his long hair and beard were white. In the Lovell household Thomas Tryon's writings were as influential as the Bible. "Females," Tryon also wrote in *A New Method of Educating Children,* "are of a quick, penetrating Fancy, apt to comprehend anything that is fine or curious, as the Art of Housewifery, Needle-work, Painting, Musick, Writing &c. In these things no man can exceed them."

Patience Lovell was born the fifth of nine girls; her parents also had a boy, who may have felt left out of life. When she was twenty years old Patience took Thomas Tryon's words of independence and equality to heart. She "got herself privately removed to [Philadelphia] which . . . was the Queen of all the Cities in America." That is, she ran away from home. For more than a year Patience lived in eighteenth-century sin with her cousin Robert Feke. Three years later she married Joseph Wright, the son of a large landowner across the Delaware River in Burlington, New Jersey. When he died a few years later, he left Patience with five children and very little income.

As a child growing up in a Quaker community, Patience Lovell Wright had done a most un-Quakerish thing; she made, as they say, graven images. Patience learned to sculpt clay. As a widow, Patience turned to making wax images for a living, and her childhood hobby became an adult career as she set up what could be considered a wax museum in New York.

However, it burned to the ground, and Patience Lovell Wright sailed for London. Once there, her fame as a sculptor grew. Even King George III and his wife Charlotte posed for Patience Wright.

She met Benjamin Franklin in London, and her wax statue of him went into her new waxworks along with those of the king and William Pitt. Her wax statue of Pitt, made in 1779 after he became the Earl of Chatham, is her only work surviving in its original form. It's in Westminster Abbey.

In addition to being a sculptor, Patience Wright was a spy who used her friendship with George III to learn what the British army was up to. She even tried to convince Benjamin Franklin to help launch a rebellion in Britain.

Over the months leading up to the Revolution, Patience wrote old friends in America, passing on to them news and information she gained at her waxworks. While undoubtedly intelligent, her spelling left much to be desired:

> Mansfld (the earl of Mansfield, chief justice) and Bute (the earl of Bute, former British Prime Minister) and Hilsbrah (the earl of Hillsborough, successor to Lord Townshend as Secretary of State for the Colonies) is determined to Drive you into the Sea by the new Canady Bill (the Quebec Act). Take cear of decception and Prviden will work all for good. . . .
>
> The Parlement meet soon and then some New act of Regulation to be Past that will be more dredful than you Can Imagine.

In 1775, she warned John Dickinson that "the Ministry is determined to Cary thir Point and Bring the Coloneys into a Compliance by force." A month later she wrote Dickinson again, warning that "the fleat is any moment to sail and a new Constructed Cannon, lite,

Portable on horse Back, 32 Inches Long, wide muzzel to fire at the Inhabitants and kill many at a shot."

When news of Concord and Lexington reached London, Patience Wright spoke out to the king himself. It was his war, she said, and he was being ill advised. With that in mind she could no longer consider him a "worthy" monarch. Taking the king to task was too much for New York businessman William Dunlop, who was in London at the time. Mrs. Wright's manners, Dunlop remarked, "were not those of a courtier." He added that Patience "once had the ear and favour of George the Third, but lost it by scolding him for sanctioning the American war."

Her friendship with Franklin (who had returned to America after the Hutchinson letters) also caused her problems. Any friend of Franklin's, it seems, was an enemy of the king's. Besides, she may have seen Ben as more than just a friend. She signed a letter written to Franklin in March 1779; "I am Honord Sir yr old Friend P. Wright." To this she added, complete with her own quotation marks:

> "I long to see you and love you more than Ever if I dont write to you it is not for want of good will bor for fear of being troubelson—would to god you would sind for me—my services are worthy of the Pleneypotentorey of america. For my gardien Spirit The great Philosopher and american Agent."

When Franklin became America's agent in France, Patience traveled across the English Channel to see him. The American colonies were not the only ones needing revolution, she believed. And she asked Franklin to aid her in fomenting rebellion in Britain. In fact, she envisioned Franklin coming to London with an army at his back. There is no word, however, on Franklin's reaction to Patience Wright's proposal. He, of course, did not lead any army into Britain.

Patience Lovell Wright once said that "women are always usful [*sic*] in grand Events." She died in Charing Cross, London, on February 25, 1786. Her obituary was carried by many newspapers but most stopped at calling her "the celebrated modeller in wax." An item possibly written by her son Joseph said her death was "occasioned by a fall in returning from a visit to our ambassador, Mr. Adams—America has lost in her a warm and sincere friend."

Another American Quaker who did a bit of spying was Lydia Darragh of Philadelphia. When General Howe occupied the city, he tried to confiscate her house at 177 South Second Street but was talked out of it. He agreed to use only the downstairs area for staff meetings, allowing Lydia and her husband, William, to remain at home.

Lydia convinced British forces that she wanted nothing to do with the war. After she was considered harmless, she went to work gathering information. It was December 2, 1777, and General Howe was preparing to attack Washington's army.

Downstairs Lydia pressed her ear to the closed door, listening to Howe and his staff: They would march out of town on the fourth with a force large enough to end the American Revolution once and for all. The next day, as she'd done often before, Lydia set out to walk the five miles to a flour mill northwest of the city, on Frankford Creek. She'd used the visit to the flour mill only as a ruse, and she took off cross country, toward the Rising Sun Tavern, a local rebel hangout on Nice Town Lane—it was owned by the Widow Nice. There Lydia met Colonel Elias Boudinot. Ostensibly commissioner of prisoners, Colonel Boudinot was Washington's chief of intelligence, an early CIA, if you will.

In a journal he wrote of his exploits, Boudinot told of meeting a Quaker woman at the tavern, who handed him "a dirty old needlework with various small pockets in it." Inside he found a piece of paper rolled "into the form of a pipe shank." Lydia had spelled out what she'd heard at Howe's staff meeting: An army of six thousand would march out of the city the next day with thirteen cannon, baggage wagons, and eleven boats on wheels to be used in an amphibious landing. At once Colonel Boudinot set off for Washington's headquarters.

At three the following morning Howe's artillery opened fire on Washington's front lines. But the Continental troops were ready. Thanks to reports from Lydia and others, Washington had strengthened their fortifications, and the British surprise attack failed. With that Howe withdrew into winter quarters, and Washington's army was saved.

• • •

From September 11 to 13, 1782, settlers inside Fort Henry (named after Patrick Henry) at Wheeling, Virginia,* were besieged by a band of Indians and Tories under a renegade terrorist named Simon Girty. Girty, along with his brothers James and George, lived with and fought alongside Shawnee and Delaware Indians. Simon and his brothers operated out of modern day Saint Marys, Ohio, known then as "Girty's Town."

The villagers had enough warning to take refuge in the fort, but in early skirmishes twenty-three of the garrison's forty-two men were either killed or captured by the Girtys and their Indian allies. When those left in the fort refused to surrender, Girty led a six-hour battle. After that only a handful of defenders were left. A few days more, and the few remaining defenders were running out of gunpowder.

Ebenezer Zane had stored a keg of powder in his cabin, but his cabin was a good sixty yards outside the fort. To get to it, defenders would have to cross open ground, and no man in his right mind was about to try that. A woman did.

Ebenezer's twenty-three-year-old sister, Elizabeth, figured that the attackers would be so shocked at seeing a woman strolling across the no-man's-land that they wouldn't shoot her. She casually walked out the fort's gate, sauntered the sixty yards to the cabin, opened the door, and walked inside. The Indians and Tories were so busy gawking that nobody shot at her.

Elizabeth dumped gunpowder onto a spread-out blanket and walked out the cabin door. Only then did the attackers realize what was happening. She was halfway to the fort before they began shooting at her. A nineteenth-century historian wrote that Elizabeth "sped with the fleetness of a fawn" and reached the fort unharmed.

After the Revolution, Elizabeth and Ebenezer built a road from Wheeling to Limestone (now, Mayville), Kentucky, a road that became known as "Zane's Trace." Elizabeth married twice and lived to be eighty-eight, long enough to pass along her pioneering spirit to a descendant, western writer Zane Grey.

---

* During the Civil War the westernmost counties of Virginia seceded to form West Virginia.

• • •

Mercy Otis Warren was James Otis's sister and the wife of Dr. James Warren. In 1805, she published a three-volume history of the American Revolution: *The Rise, Progress and Termination of the American Revolution*. It was the earliest account of the era written by an American. It is a provocative and astute telling of the Revolution; however, it is singularly biased and anti-Federalist. She's particularly unfavorable to her brother's friend, John Adams. The *Dictionary of American Biography* calls Mercy Otis Warren an "historical apologist for the patriot cause." On the other hand, historian Page Smith calls Mercy Otis Warren "a delightful letter writer, a mediocre poet, and a skillful if contentious historian."

Betsy Ross was none of those things, and we probably would never have heard about her if it weren't for her grandson, William J. Canby. He first brought up the Betsy Ross story in 1870, when he was eighty-four years old. According to Canby, George Washington asked Betsy to sew America's first Stars and Stripes flag.

Grandma Betsy was born Elizabeth Griscom, one of seventeen children of a Philadelphia Quaker family. Her father, in fact, was a workman who helped build what we now call Independence Hall. They apparently were a loving family until Betsy married non-Quaker John Ross. Then the elders kicked her out of the Quaker fellowship.

Betsy, it seemed, had nothing but bad luck. John Ross died when the gunpowder he was manufacturing exploded. She married again, this time to Joseph Ashburn, who quickly signed on as a crew member on a privateer, and that's the last Betsy ever saw of him. A British ship captured Ashburn, threw him into prison, leaving him to die of malnutrition and disease.

Twice married and twice widowed, Betsy Griscom Ross Ashburn tried earning a living as a seamstress. Grandson William claimed that George Washington, Robert Morris, and George Ross (apparently no kin to Betsy's first husband, John) came to her with an order to sew the first official American flag, complete with thirteen six-pointed stars. Bad idea, Canby claimed Grandma Betsy told the boys; five-pointed stars would be better. With that, as generations of schoolchildren have been taught, Betsy Ross showed Washington and company how to fold a piece of paper just so, and you had a five-pointed star. This happened, Grandson Canby said, in June 1776.

One problem, however, is that it wasn't until a year later, June 14, 1777, that the Marine Committee of the Second Continental Congress passed a law regarding a national flag. It read: "Resolved, That the Flag of the Union be thirteen stripes, alternate red and white; that the union be thirteen stars, white in a blue field, representing a new constellation."

When the new states of Vermont and Kentucky were admitted to the Union, two new stars and two new stripes where added to the flag. It became obvious that pretty soon the U.S. flag would be too unwieldy with rows and rows of stripes. So in 1818, Congress ordered that only thirteen stripes, symbolizing the first thirteen states, would be used, but that each time a new state was admitted, another star would be added to the flag. There still is no law stating exactly how the stars, up to fifty as of 1960, should be arranged permanently.

Betsy Ross likely did sew several flags, at least one of them a thirteen-star flag, possibly in the circle pattern we associate with her name. It's unlikely, however, that she made the first Stars and Stripes, and it's unlikely we'll ever know who did.

George III, America's last king. He found it hard to understand why Americans called him a tyrant. Because he favored the country-side rather than London, he was known as "Farmer George." (The Royal Collection, H.M. Queen Elizabeth II.)

A British cartoon depicted Boston Liberty Boys tarring and feathering a tax collector. Cartoon in mez-zotint, published by Sayer and Ben-nett, London, 1774. (National Archives.)

Patrick Henry by an unknown painter in the early 1800s. Unlike more famous paintings of Henry, the words from Henry's "Give me liberty or give me death" speech make it obvi-ous who this is. (Shelburne Museum, Shelburne, Vermont.)

Paul Revere's engraving of the Boston Massacre as it appeared in a broadside, three weeks after the events of March 5, 1768. The account of the massacre was reprinted from the Boston *Gazette* of March 12. Both the picture and the text are highly inaccurate. (National Archives.)

The attack on Bunker Hill and the burning of Charlestown, Massachusetts, June 17, 1775. (Engraving by Lodge from a drawing by Miller. National Archives.)

John Adams, Thomas Jefferson, Benjamin Franklin, and the other members of their committee present their draft of the Declaration of Independence to John Hancock and other members of the Continental Congress. On the wall are British regimental standards captured in the American invasion of Canada. (Painting by John Trumbull. Yale University Art Gallery/National Archives.)

Patriots in New York City pulled down a gilded lead statue of George III. It was melted down for bullets and was set up on a spike near the Blue Bell Tavern, near modern 181st Street and Broadway. Later, Loyalists stole the head and, it was sent to England "to convince them at home of the Infamous Disposition of the Ungrateful people of this distressed Country." (From a painting by William Walcutt, Yale University Art Gallery/National Archives.)

Major John André, Benedict Arnold's contact in the British army, made this sketch of himself on the day George Washington signed the execution order. The following day André was hanged. (Culver Services/Metropolitan Museum of Art, New York.)

The execution of Major John André. George Washington called him a "man of first abilities." The American government tried to exchange him for Benedict Arnold, but the British refused to surrender Arnold. On October 2, 1780, he was hanged. (Engraving by John Goldar, 1783. The Mary Evans Picture Library.)

When the British burned New York City, American spy Nathan Hale was trapped inside the city, leading some to believe he may have participated in setting the fire. He was unceremoniously hanged and, for a while, forgotten by both sides. (An anonymous painting of 1820, Culver Pictures.)

John Paul Jones capturing the *Serapis*. (Engraving from a painting by Alonzo Chappel, National Archives.)

British caricature of John Paul Jones as a pirate. (Full-length engraving published by A. Park, London. The Mariners Museum/National Archives.)

Colonel Daniel Morgan wearing what he called his "battle uniform." At six feet, two hundred pounds, Morgan led three companies of riflemen in the American attack on British-held Quebec. A first cousin of Daniel Boone, Morgan beat Britain's Banister Tarleton at the Battle of Cowpens in January 1781. (New York Public Library/National Archives.)

Molly Hays, one of at least two who were dubbed "Molly Pitcher," at the Battle of Monmouth, New Jersey. When her husband fell, Molly took over his cannon. (Engraving by J. C. Armytage from a painting by Alonzo Chappel. National Archives.)

Taddeus Kosciuszko, a Polish-born military engineer, designed the defenses that brought about the American victory of Saratoga. After the American Revolution, Kosciuszko attempted to lead a similar revolt in his native land but was crushed by Russia. (Engraving from a bust by George E. Perine. National Archives.)

Mercy Otis Warren, the sister of James Otis, Jr., and the wife of James Warren. Poet and playwright, she also wrote a three-volume history of the Revolution. (Museum of Fine Arts, Boston.)

Baronness von Riedesel. Captured in 1777, at Saratoga along with her husband, Baron Friedrich Aldolphus Riedesel, the Baronness and their three children became part of the "Convention Army." The surrender agreement called for the British and Hessian prisoners to lay down their arms, march to Boston, and be returned to England or Germany. Instead, the prisoners and camp followers such as the Baronness von Riedesel, marched through several states before ending up in Virginia. One of the Riedesel's children died during the 12-week trek. (Painting by Tischbein. National Archives.)

The British prison ship *Jersey*, moored off Wallabout, Long Island. The *Jersey* was the most infamous prison of its time. Eight thousand captive Patriots died of disease and starvation while on board the ship. (John Trumbull drawing c. 1780. Fordham University.)

CHAPTER SEVEN

Rag-Tag and Bob-Tail*:
If It Moves, Salute It

Whoever looks upon them as an irregular mob will find themselves much mistaken. . . . You may depend upon it, that as the rebels have now had time to prepare, they are determined to go through with it.
—Lieutenant General Hugh Percy, 5th Fusiliers

I rejoice that America has resisted. Three millions of people, so dead to all the feelings of liberty, as voluntarily to submit to be slaves, would have been fit instruments to make slaves of the rest.
—William Pitt, Earl of Chatham, Speech to the House of Commons, January 14, 1766

John Peter Gabriel Muhlenberg was the son of a Lutheran missionary. Born in 1746, and sent back to Germany to be educated, Peter, as he was called, became a minister. In 1774, he not only was pastor of a church in Woodstook, Virginia, he was elected to the House of Burgesses, where he became associated with several of the colony's Revolutionary leaders.

The story goes that one Sunday in 1775, Reverend Muhlenberg took as his scripture of the day, Ecclesiastes 3:1—"To every thing there is a season, and a time to every purpose under the heaven." Reverend Muhlenberg was also a colonel in the militia, and he added, "There is time for all things, a time to preach and a time to pray; but there is also a time to fight and that time has now come." He tossed aside his robes and revealed his militia uniform.

Leaving the pulpit, Reverend, now Colonel, Peter Muhlenberg walked to the church door, where he had a drummer boy waiting. He ordered him to beat the call for recruits, and almost three hundred members of his congregation joined up to become the 8th Virginia, better known as the "German Regiment."

---

* A common phrase from the seventeenth through the nineteenth centuries, meaning either "the whole lot" or, simply, "rabble."

Muhlenberg fought in the Battles of Charleston and Brandywine Creek. A brigadier general, he was at Monmouth Court House and, when Benedict Arnold invaded Virginia, the fighting parson was there.

After the war he returned briefly to Woodstock, Virginia, then moved to Pennsylvania, where he was instrumental in having the state approve the Constitution. Twice Muhlenberg was elected to the new House of Representatives and, in 1801, became a U.S. senator, resigning to become supervisor of revenue in Philadelphia.

John Peter Gabriel Muhlenberg was tall, courtly, and strikingly handsome. Today his likeness stands in the Statuary Hall in Washington, D.C.

"A time to love, and a time to hate; a time of war, and a time of peace."

Whenever the British army wanted men, it contracted with some distinguished citizen to recruit a regiment, giving him what were termed "beating orders," orders to have a drummer stand in a town square and beat a call. It was hoped the sound of the drum would bring out anyone likely to join up. It would be this distinguished citizen, not any recruit, who would receive a bounty for those who signed up, and he'd sell commissions. The government paid the salary and expenses of the regiment's colonel, who, in turn, was expected to pay the troops and provide them with clothing.

With enlistments generally lifelong arrangements, the army wasn't exactly popular. It was so unpopular that only twenty thousand British troops were available at the outbreak of the American Revolution.

Their pay was miserable—eight pence per day for privates—and their living conditions were worse. Noncommissioned officers were brutal, and they took much of a soldier's wages to pay for expenses.

Nathan Hale was a schoolteacher before he turned spy. It's what he is famous for, but Hale probably said nothing about regretting to have only one life to give to his country. The phrase apparently came from poet Joseph Addison, who lived from 1672 to 1710: "What pity it is/That we can die but once to serve our country!" Since Hale was a Yale-educated schoolteacher, Addison's words could have come to him just before the British draped a noose around his neck and hanged him. A British officer who witnessed the hanging claimed the American spy—and Hale never denied he was a spy—wrote in his diary that his last words were: "It is the duty of every good officer to obey any orders given him by his commander-in-chief."

Music was a large part of eighteenth-century life in America and a large part of the Revolution. "I can neither sing . . . nor raise a single note of any instrument," George Washington once told Francis Hopkinson. But that didn't stop him from trying or from being concerned about the quality of music in the army. On June 4, 1777, an order came out of the Continental army camp "Head Quarters, Middle-Brook" Massachusetts:

> The music of the army being in general very bad, it is expected that the drum and fife Majors exert themselves to improve it, or they will be reduced and their extraordinary pay taken from them. Stated hours to be assigned, for all the drums and fifes, of each regiment, to attend them and practice—nothing is more agreeable, and ornamental, than good music; every officer, for the credit of the corps, should take care to provide it.

One song that has been around for years is "Johnny Has Gone for a Soldier:"

> I'll sell my clock, I'll sell my reel;
> Likewise, I'll sell my spinning wheel
> To buy my love a sword of steel;
> Johnny has gone for a soldier.

Another song, by an anonymous writer, was first heard in 1775, "What a Court Hath Old England":

> There's no knowing where this oppression will stop;
> Some say there's no cure but a capital chop,
> And that I believe's each American's wish,

Than to drench them with tea and deprive them of fish.
Derry down, down, down, derry down.

"Yankee Doodle" originally was an English drinking song and derided the colonists. Quickly it became popular with the rebels. It may have been in Andrew Barton's opera, *The Disappointment.* Another version of the story says it was written in the 1740s or 1750s by a British surgeon named Dr. Richard Shuckberg. However it was, it goes like this:

Yankee Doodle came to town,
For to buy a firelock,
We will tar and feather him,
And so we will John Hancock.

(CHORUS)

Yankee Doodle keep it up,
Yankee Doodle dandy.
Mind the music and the step,
And with the girls be handy.

American rebels apparently liked the song so much that any derogatory meaning was quickly lost. Of course, they changed the lyrics, and when Burgoyne surrendered at Saratoga, a Continental army band played "Yankee Doodle."

Father and I went down to camp
Along with Captain Gooding,
And there we see the men and boys,
As thick as hasty pudding.

(CHORUS)

And then the feathers on his hat
They looked so 'tarnal finey,
I wanted peskily to get,
To give to my Jemimy.

(CHORUS)

There came General Washington,
Upon a snow white charger,
He looked as big as all outdoors,
And thought that he was larger.

(CHORUS)

Yankee Doodle keep it up,
Yankee Doodle dandy,
Mind the music and the step,
And with the girls be handy.

The song played by the British as they surrendered at Yorktown four years later was "The World Turned Upside Down." While the title sounds ironic, it was simply just an old English drinking song. Another well-known drinking song at the time was "The Anacreontic Song." Later we slowed it down and added new words to make it the American national anthem, the "Star-Spangled Banner."

Life in the seventeenth and eighteenth centuries moved unbelievably slowly compared to ours. Take the popularity of *Lillibullero*, or *Lillibulero*. It was written in 1688 by Britain's Lord Warton. Part of the refrain ridicules the Irish. It hinted that the Irish were about to invade England along with the French, and it claimed that Catholics (papists, as they were often referred to at the time) were planning a general massacre of Protestants. It implied that nothing was safe, that no one could be trusted; everybody and everything were in jeopardy. Seventy-five years after it was first sung, *Lillibullero* still had an impact, not only in England but in the American colonies as well. In the 1760s, Patriot leader James Otis claimed that when the song was first written, it had "sung a king out of three kingdoms." During the American Revolution, *Lillibullero* was still a popular song in colonial taverns, and those of the patriot persuasion likely were hoping it would "sing out" another king.

About twenty miles west and a little north of Philadelphia, where the Schuylkill River is joined by Valley Creek, was an old forge on a ravinelike estuary; travelers called it the Valley Forge. In December 1777, George Washington and his army marched (more likely, dragged themselves) from their camp at Whitemarsh. It was at Whitemarsh that General Howe had tried to deliver the coup de grâce, a knockout punch, if you will, to the Continental army. Thanks to information given Washington by spies, Continental fortifications were too strong, and Howe decided to end the fighting and go into winter quarters.

As they trudged to Valley Forge, the American army showed just how close it was to giving it all up and going home. The thirteen-odd miles between camps were marked by baggage wagons going astray, soldiers drifting off, stopping and starting. It took the remnants of Washington's army more than a week to cover the thirteen miles. Roads first were soggy, then it snowed and the dirt froze, then it thawed, then the troops were hit by stinging rain, and they trampled on dug-up, boggy roads stiffened into knife-sharp ridges. Washington's troops were virtually shoeless, and the ice-hardened roads cut into their rag-bound feet. The general said that "you might have tracked the army . . . to Valley Forge by the blood of their feet."

The broken, beaten columns reached the plateau above the Schuylkill River on the afternoon of December 19. What food they had came from their haversacks; the commissary hadn't caught up with them. When they tried to warm themselves with fires, the few men who had shoes found that the heat dried the leather, then cracked it and split it; they joined their comrades in wrapping their feet in rags. Those who already wore foot wrappings had to worry about them drying out, catching fire, and scorching bruised and bleeding feet.

There was neither village nor plain nor valley at Valley Forge, but the west side of the Schuylkill would be home to Washington's ragtag and bob-tail army for six months. The good points about the site was that it was close to Philadelphia yet sat between the enemy and Congress, which had evacuated to York, Pennsylvania. Defensively it also was a good location, heavily wooded (which would provide building materials), and close to an abundant supply of water.

When Private Joseph Plumb Martin arrived at Valley Forge, however, water *was* a problem. "It was dark [when he arrived on December 18, 1777]; there was no water to be found and I was perishing with thirst." Some other troops "had some water in their canteens which they told me they found a good distance off, but could not direct me to the place as it was very dark." They refused to give Martin a drink of water; however, "at length I persuaded them to sell me a drink for three pence, Pennsylvania currency, which was every cent of property I could then call my own."

As soon as possible, Washington's troops began building huts. The standard floor plan was about fourteen by fifteen feet, six and a half feet high at the eaves, with wooden bunks, a fireplace at one end, and a door at the other. Roofs were covered with boards or slabs of wood, then thatched with straw, sometimes crudely shingled. Notched logs were chinked with clay. Apparently there were no windows, and often the single chimney would not draw well, leaving the men to choke on smoke or to freeze outside. It would be mid-January before many of the men were able to move inside. Until then, they lived in tents, in "miserable conditions," Private Martin remembered, telling about going "into the wild woods and [building] us habitations to stay (not to live) in, in such a weak, starved and naked condition, [it] was appalling in the highest degree."

Surgeon Albigence Waldo of the Connecticut Line wrote on December 21: "Provisions scarce . . . My skin and eyes are almost spoiled with continual smoke. A general cry thro' the damp this evening among the soldiers, 'No meat! No meat'" Many of the troops were left with "nothing but fire cake (flour and water baked in thin cakes on hot stones) and water," for dinner, Waldo recorded.

"These are the times that try men's souls," Thomas Paine wrote two days after Waldo's journal entry. "The summer soldier and the sunshine patriot will, in this crisis, shrink from the services of their country. . . ."*

A complete breakdown in the supply system left close to four thousand men so destitute of clothing that they couldn't leave their huts. Conditions wouldn't improve until Nathanael Greene assumed the duties of quartermaster general in late March.

---

* *The American Crisis*, No.1, December 23, 1776.

During the darkest days at Valley Forge, when Congress could not or would not send supplies needed by Washington's starving troops, the general would fly into a rage. In letter after letter he called on Congress to send supplies, sometimes suggesting the government was not worthy of the patriotic efforts being waged on its behalf. Two days before Christmas, George Washington wrote to the president of Congress:

> Full as I was in my representation of matters in the Commys. departmt. [the commissary] yesterday, fresh, and more powerful reasons oblige me to add, that I am now convinced, beyond doubt that unless some great and capital change suddenly takes place . . . this Army must inevitably be reduced to one of three things. Starve, dissolve, or disperse . . .

"What have you got for breakfast, lads?" Surgeon Waldo asked, and the answer was the same he'd received from them at dinnertime the night before: "Fire cake and water, Sir." But then he asked himself: "Why do I talk of hunger and hard usage, when so many in the world have not even fire cake and water to eat?"

Somehow the army held together despite the often-heard chant "No pay, no clothes, no provisions, no rum." The Marquis de Lafayette recalled seeing "a miserable being . . . flitting from one hut to another, his nakedness . . . only covered by a dirty blanket." At one time, Lafayette wrote, "nearly three thousand men were [listed] unfit for duty from the want of clothing." He added that "it cannot be deemed strange that sickness and mortality were the consequence of such privations in the midst of an inclement season."

Yet, even while enlisted men suffered at Valley Forge, General Washington continued to lead the good life of wine, women, and song.

Wine: Enlisted men lived in hand-hewn huts, but General Washington commandeered the two-story stone Isaac Potts house, keeping with him his slave, Billy. Washington often invited his staff to dine with them, supplying claret wine, which his officers generally couldn't afford.

Women: Martha moved in with the general in February, and when things got crowded, she had a separate dining room (actually, a dining cabin) built onto the house. Washington forbade most other women from coming into the camp at Valley Forge because he was afraid they would spy on the Continental army. The order was meant, of course, not to keep out the wives of his officers but to prevent women from Philadelphia from plying whatever trade they might among the troops.

And song: Martha frequently presided over social events in the Potts house during which officers and their ladies sang lustily and played whatever musical instrument was at hand. Frenchman Étienne Duponceau, who only recently had arrived in America, wrote of seeing George Washington at one such Valley Forge social event:

> I could not keep my eyes from that imposing countenance; grave, yet not severe; affable, without familiarity. Its predominant expression was calm dignity, through which you could trace the strong feelings of the patriot, and discern the father, as well as the commander of his soldiers. I have never seen a picture that represents him to me as I saw him at Valley Forge, and during the campaigns in which I had honor to follow him.

Another French officer, however, remembered attending dinner parties among the troops to which no one with a whole pair of trousers was admitted.

Traditional history tells of suffering, starvation, and death at Valley Forge, as many as twenty-five hundred deaths. Nontraditional history tells a somewhat different story. In the 1970s, archaeologists and historians carried out surveys on behalf of the National Park Service. Their report claimed that nobody starved at Valley Forge, that nobody froze to death, and that morale was high. There was, the report claimed, even enough food during the December 1777 to February 1778 period. Each month the ten-thousand-man army received a million pounds of flour and a million pounds of meat and fish, which, broken down, meant that each soldier received more than three pounds of flour along with three pounds of fish or meat per *day!* Researcher Barbara MacDonald Powell says that the shortages of food and clothing at Valley Forge "were not much worse than during other periods of the war, and none of the privations suffered were any more severe than those of preceding or succeeding winters."

The following winter of 1779 to 1780, at Morristown, New Jersey, after the Battles of Trenton and Princeton, may have been worse. Once again, the Continental army's commissariat broke down, leaving from ten thousand to twelve thousand troops facing cold and starvation. In fact, a modern brochure for Morristown notes: "We suffered more."

As for troops at Valley Forge having so little clothing that they often went naked—"flitting from one hut to another [in their] nakedness," Lafayette recorded—we may be misreading the statement. *Naked* in the way eighteenth-century writers used the word is not the way twentieth-century readers interpret it. In other words, we likely misunderstand and misinterpret the word. *Naked* during the period of Valley Forge did not mean being without clothing, but being without *proper* clothing, which, to Lafayette, simply could have meant the man in question had no coat under his blanket.

A private in a state militia was entitled to $36 per month in 1775 (said by at least one authority to equal $150 in 1924, but it's uncertain what this would amount to in 1999). His counterpart in the Continental army was supposed to draw $6.67. But then, neither actually got paid very often, so it didn't matter.

On March 18, 1775, in one of its first acts, the Continental Congress ordered American soldiers to drink beer. They ordered a ration of one pint of beer a day per soldier. Like every other ration for American soldiers, they didn't always get their beer.

CHAPTER EIGHT

Tea Parties and Rude Bridges: Little Things That Mean a Lot

Yesterday, being St. Patrick's Day ... was observed ... with the usual solemnity. [The] natives [of Ireland] adorned their Hatts with Sham rogs.
—*Boston Weekly News-Letter,* March 18, 1752

The Tumults in America I expected would have produced in Europe an unfavorable opinion of our political state. But it has not.
—Thomas Jefferson, 1787

When the argument with the mother country began, many American colonists realized their biggest weakness was their lack of a central government. Individual colonies had long traditions of local government but no tradition of central management and jurisdiction. In the summer of 1754, at the request of British authorities, delegates from seven colonies met in Albany, New York, ostensibly to work out a single treaty with the Iroquois, whose allegiance at the time was shifting from the traditional favoritism of the British to that of France.

In 1764, Massachusetts denounced "taxation without representation," and called on its fellow colonies to pledge not to import many items into America—a nonimportation agreement aimed at overturning the Grenville Acts, which included the Stamp Act, the Currency Act, and the Sugar Act. Almost all the colonies except New York (which began a practice of either not taking part or of voting "present" instead of yes or no) agreed. It worried British merchants and manufacturers so much that Parliament repealed the Grenville Acts.

The Townshend Revenue Act in 1767 brought another colonial call for another nonimportation agreement, and once again it worked. Together the colonies reduced their importation of English goods by nearly 40 percent in two years. Just as it had earlier, Parliament reacted by annulling the Townshend Acts. More or less.

"Champagne Charlie" Townshend didn't care; he died in September 1767, even before the acts named for him went in place. He left to his successors the question of how to raise money in the colonies. And Townshend's successors left in place part of the acts, the tax on tea.

At the time, however, it was virtually ignored. The Townshend Acts had levied a duty of threepence on every pound of tea imported into America. The duty was all on this side of the Atlantic, since the tax on tea imported into England was removed. One reason George III insisted on retaining the tea tax was as proof that he had the right to levy taxes on Americans. What it did was to increase the amount of tea smuggled into the colonies. Included among the smugglers was that erstwhile Founding Father, John Hancock.

The East India Company was second only to the Bank of England in its wealth. Thomas Hutchinson of Massachusetts, for example, had heavily invested in the company, some four thousand British pounds, which represented almost all of his ready capital. It looked to be a good investment. After all, in America alone the three million or so colonists drank more than a million pounds of tea each year, 60 percent of it smuggled in. By 1771, however, thanks to massive mismanagement and corruption within its ranks, the East India Company was nearly bankrupt. Its stock on the London exchange had dropped from £280 to £160.

For the large American drinking population, the company raised its price from two shillings to three shillings a pound. In Europe the price remained at two shillings a pound, which meant that American-based smugglers such as Hancock had a product easy to sail around customs agents and one that would bring in a high profit for them.

For years, the East India Company wasn't alone in trading in the commodity; tea was sold at public auction, with traders bidding on it and then shipping the leaves to America in their own vessels. Then, too, there were the smugglers, who generally bought tea on the European continent, where it was cheaper than at auction.

In order to save the floundering East India Company, the English government gave the company a monopoly in the American market; there would be no public auction and no middleman. The price

Americans would pay for tea would actually go down. Parliament authorized the East India Company to ship half a million pounds of tea to America with the nominal threepence-a-pound tax.

This would do several things. It would save the company. It would undercut the price John Hancock and other smugglers charged for tea they brought in from Europe, mainly Holland. And it reminded everybody that King George and Parliament could still tax Americans.

First consignments of this taxed tea were headed for New York, Charleston, Philadelphia, and Boston. In October 1773, Philadelphia consignees of the tea were forced to resign. They weren't alone.

In New York the friendly neighborhood Sons of Liberty branded the consignees enemies of America, passing out handbills telling merchants just what dangers they would encounter if they tried to peddle the taxed tea. The ship *Nancy* was on its way to New York, but so was that courier of all couriers, Paul Revere, who cantered down the Post Road from Boston to New York, crying "The tea is coming! The tea is coming!" New Yorkers got the idea and dumped it into the East River.

On December 2, Charleston, South Carolina, tea consignees were forced to resign and the tea was impounded after a proscribed twenty-day waiting period. They tossed most of it into the Cooper River but kept the remainder until the outbreak of hostilities, when they sold it at public auction with the proceeds going into the South Carolina war chest.

In Massachusetts, however, the consignees would not resign, and that brought about the Boston Tea Party, which brought about the closing of the Port of Boston, which brought about the hoarding of weapons and gunpowder by the colonists, which brought about a raid by British regulars to seize the weapons and gunpowder, which brought about Paul Revere and William Dawes and others riding out into the Massachusetts countryside announcing the pending arrival of the British, which brought about the Battles of Lexington and Concord, which brought about the minutemen following the redcoats' retreat and taking potshots at them, which brought about Lord Percy's mission to reinforce the regulars, which stopped the minutemen's target practice around Cambridge and led to the burning of several farms by the disgruntled, unhappy, and in general enraged and ticked-off British soldiers. Out of all of this came the American Revolution.

The Tea Party happened this way.

In a letter to Mercy Otis Warren, Abigail Adams referred to the tea as a "weed of slavery." To her husband John, Abigail wrote, "The flame is kindled, and like lightning it catches from soul to soul."

On November 28, 1773, the *Dartmouth* arrived in America. It was the first of the ships sailing to Boston harbor with the now-taxed (and presumably now-hated) tea. Once the tea was in the customshouse, the shipowner had twenty days to pay the tax. If it hadn't been paid by then, the tea was liable to seizure. The *Dartmouth* was owned by a young merchant named Francis Rotch, and he wanted the ship unloaded.

After all, not only did he have hundreds of cases of tea to get rid of, he had a load of whale oil waiting to be sent to England. Governor Hutchinson also wanted the tea brought ashore. He knew that if the tea was not unloaded within that twenty-day period, it could be seized and stored. Hutchinson hoped to force the issue. It was the law; all he had to do was wait until the twenty-day waiting period was up on December 16.

Samuel Adams knew this and realized the Sons of Liberty couldn't sit idly by, so on November 29, he organized a mass meeting at the Old South Meeting House. More than five thousand people were on hand to hear the radicals put it simply: The tea had to go back to England. On the 30th, Adams held another, equally large meeting at Old South.

They weren't legal town meetings, but they passed resolutions anyway, demanding the tea be sent back. The resolutions went to those designated "enemies of the people," who were to take consignment of the tea. Those "enemies," however, had already taken refuge in Castle William out in Boston harbor.

The Sons of Liberty put a guard on the *Dartmouth* to make certain the crew didn't reposition the ship and unload it somewhere else. The deadline for payment of duties was only three days off, and by then two other ships, the *Eleanor* and the *Beaver,* had arrived loaded with East India Company tea.

On December 14, another large crowd gathered and demanded Rotch ask for clearance to ship the tea back to London. On the 15th, however, Governor Hutchinson refused to approve the clearance, and Rotch returned to Old South to say his request (actually, the mob's demand) had been refused. Samuel Adams announced that there was nothing more the people of Boston could do.

On the evening of December 16, Josiah Quincy, who along with John Adams had defended British soldiers involved in the earlier Boston Massacre, spoke to another meeting in the Old South Meeting House. "It is not," he said,

the spirit that vapors within these walls that must stand us in stead. The exertions this day will call forth events which will make a very different spirit necessary for our salvation. Whoever supposes that shouts and hosannas will terminate the trials of the day entertains a childish fancy. We must be grossly ignorant of the importance and value of the prize for which we contend; we must be equally ignorant of the power of those who have combined against us; we must be blind to that malice, inveterace and insatiable revenge which actuate our enemies, public and private, abroad and in our bosom, to hope that we shall end this controversy without the sharpest conflicts, to flatter ourselves that popular resolves, popular harangues, popular acclamations and popular vapor will vanquish our foes.

It was one day before the deadline, and that night between two hundred and seven thousand men—obviously estimates vary greatly—all thinly disguised as Mohawk Indians took to the streets. They even had a rallying song:

Rally, Mohawks! bring out your axes,
And tell King George we'll pay no taxes
On his foreign tea;
His threats are vain, and vain to think
To force our girls and wives to drink

His vil Bohea!
Then rally, boys, and hasten on
To meet our chiefs at the Green Dragon.

Our Warren's there and bold Revere,
With hands to do, and words to cheer,
For liberty and laws;
Our country's "braves" and firm defenders
Shall ne'er be left by North-Enders
Fighting Freedom's cause!
Then rally, boys, and hasten on
To meet our chiefs at the Green Dragon.

A man named George Hewes later claimed that he was one of the "Mohawk Indians" who took part in the Boston Tea Party. Of course, it was in 1834 when he admitted it.

It was now evening, and I immediately dressed myself in the costume of an Indian, equipped with a small hatchet, which I and my associates denominated the tomahawk, with which, and a club, and after having painted my face and hands with coal dust in the shop of a blacksmith, I repaired to Griffin's wharf, where the ships lay that contained the tea. When I first appeared in the street being thus disguised, I fell in with many who were dressed, equipped and painted as I was, and who fell in with me and marched in order to the place of our destination.

When we arrived at the wharf, there were three of our number who assumed an authority to direct our operations, to which we readily submitted. They divided us into three parties, for the purpose of boarding the three ships which contained the tea at the same time.

They tossed all 342 chests into Boston harbor—90,000 pounds of tea, valued at about £10,000. Within minutes the water in Boston harbor was filled with chests of tea. By the next morning some of the chests had floated as far as Dorchester Neck.

The next day John Adams wrote in his diary: "3 Cargoes of Bohea Tea were emptied into the Sea. . . . This is the most magnificent Movement of all. . . . I cant but consider it as an Epocha in History."

The "Indians" had been careful not to damage any of the ships. A padlock was broken, but the next day an unidentified man replaced it. They had even been careful that no one took home any of the tea, not even as a sample by which they could remember the night.

Just who, besides George Hewes, took part in the Boston Tea Party isn't certain. Probably Samuel Adams's Sons of Liberty, probably a fairly broad spectrum of the population, probably farmers from nearby villages. Probably everybody but Adams, who would *really* have been in trouble if he'd gone along and been caught.

John Andrews was a Boston selectman. He wrote a relative and told him about the world's most famous tea party:

> [Before] nine o'clock in the evening, every chest from on board the three vessels was knocked to pieces and flung over the sides. They say the actors were Indians from Narragansett. Whether they were or not, to a transient observer they appeared as such, being clothed in Blankets with the heads muffled, and copper colored countenances, being each armed with a hatchet or ax, and pair of pistols, nor was their dialect different from what I conceive these geniuses to speak, as their jargon was unintelligible to all but themselves.

They stripped the ship's captain of his clothing and "gave him a coat of mud, with a severe bruising into the bargain; and nothing but their utter aversion to make any disturbance prevented his being tarred and feathered."

Governor Hutchinson's official report reached London on January 27, 1774. The king's ministers were outraged, loudly referring to the tea party-goers as "rabble." And they closed the port of Boston.

The Boston Port Bill went into effect on June 1, 1774, prohibiting the loading or unloading of goods in Boston harbor until the tea was paid for. Benjamin Franklin and some others wanted to pay the East India Company; Boston radicals, however, refused.

The only items that could be brought into Massachusetts were military stores, food, and fuel for the regular army, and these came in through Salem or Marblehead. Even a short-run ferry across Boston harbor was shut down, and nothing got into or out of Boston except across the narrow neck of land that linked it to the mainland. Boston was closed, and revolution moved another step closer.

The East India Company continued to operate, and in the mid-1800s virtually ran the government of India with what Winston Churchill called "only a moderate degree of supervision from London." The company still exists today as Davidson Newman & Co., Ltd. It even exports tea to modern Boston, where sales are reported to be "very satisfactory."

The Boston Port Bill was part of a series of measures called the Coercive Acts. Americans dubbed them the Intolerable Acts, and they shook the colonies as nothing before them had ever done. Parliament had targeted Boston, but soon it wasn't just residents of Massachusetts who felt the Intolerable Acts.

The charter of Massachusetts had virtually been canceled. The governor's council would be appointed by the Crown and responsible only to the Crown. The provincial attorney general, the judges, sheriffs, and even juries would be selected by the Crown or a Crown appointee. Town meetings could be held only with the written consent of the governor, and then he had to give prior approval of the meetings' agenda.

On the heels of the Intolerable Acts came the Quebec Act, and that, perhaps, alarmed the colonists as much as shutting down the port of Boston. The Quebec Act was well intentioned and in part, by today's standards, was a good thing. It confirmed for French Canadians their ancient rights and customs and allowed the Roman Catholic Church to operate without government interference. Protecting Catholicism was a sore point for many in America, however, and many in the colonies saw it as another union of Church and state.

By one reckoning at least, there were two different types of colonies or states in America, referred to as three-sided and four-sided colonies. The three-sided settlements had sea-to-sea charters.

The four-sided, or land-locked, colonies weren't so lucky—New Hampshire, Rhode Island, New Jersey, Delaware, Pennsylvania, and Maryland. Four-sided colonies believed Congress should have power to establish the boundaries of all colonies. Virginia and Massachusetts believed their charters gave them land from the Atlantic to the Pacific oceans, from sea to sea. The three- versus four-sided argument carried with it animosity and held up ratification of the Articles of Confederation for four years.

Congress wrote the Articles in 1776, approved them in 1777, but they weren't ratified until 1781. They declared that "Canada, acceding to this confederation, shall be admitted into . . . the union, but no other colony shall be admitted [unless] by nine states."

Which didn't stop American rebels from trying to force Canadians into joining the Revolution. Congress decided that if General Philip Schuyler "finds it practicable and that it will not be disagreeable to the Canadians, he shall immediately take possession of St. Johns, Montreal, and any other parts of the country." Schuyler did find it practicable; however, when he fell sick, his command passed to Colonel Richard Montgomery.

Benedict Arnold held a grudge against Philip Schuyler, and he went to General Washington with his own plan to invade Canada. Unlike others, Benedict Arnold believed that Canadians "have little love for Britain; they will welcome our forces of liberation."

Part two of the Quebec Act extended Canada's southern boundaries to the Ohio River, which means much of the modern-day state of Ohio would be a Canadian province. It cut into territories claimed by Connecticut, Massachusetts, and Virginia, held, these colonies said, by virtue of ancient grants.

The act further forbade emigration west of the Allegheny Mountains, despite the fact that many colonies had promised large parcels of land there to veterans of the French and Indian War.

So the port of Boston was closed, and that drew American colonies closer together and led to the First Continental Congress. The Quebec Act, by forbidding emigration beyond the Allegheny Mountains, prevented colonies from expanding beyond their current boundaries, and that stopped them from living up to the promises they'd made to veteran soldiers.

• • •

With the closing of the port of Boston, a strange, and to the British government unexpected, thing happened. Other colonies came to Boston's rescue. After galloping down to New York, Paul Revere rode on to Philadelphia. Coming home, he brought with him the news that Pennsylvanians had promised their full support. New York guaranteed Boston a ten-year supply of food and sent a herd of more than one hundred sheep up from Long Island meadows.

Connecticut sent more sheep, one hundred twenty-five of them, driven by a veteran of the French and Indian War, Israel Putnam, formerly of Rogers Rangers. Captured by the French in August 1758, the then Major Putnam was rescued just as he was about to be burned at the stake. In 1775, it was "Old Put" who recommended the colonists dig trenches for the Battle of Bunker Hill. "The Americans are not at all afraid of their heads," he's said to have commented, "though very much afraid of their legs; if you cover these, they will fight forever."

Charleston, South Carolina, which had its own tea problems, sent cash to buy meat and fish. From the low-country also went a large quantity of rice, in case the Bostonians wanted a carbohydrate to go along with the protein.

On learning of the Boston Tea Party, William Lee, a London alderman, wrote his brother, Richard Henry Lee, about the Boston Port Bill:

> The intention of this act is totally to annihilate the town of Boston, which will effectively be done, if the people there permit it to be carried into execution. . . . [The] king with his usual obstinacy and tyrannical disposition is determined, if it be possible, to enslave you all. . . . Neither king nor Minister [Lord North] ever do anything wrong, because Parliament is very ready to sanctify what the king or Minister determines to be right.

In Williamsburg, on May 16, 1774, the Virginia House of Burgesses passed a resolution protesting the sealing of the port of Boston:

This House, being deeply impressed with Apprehension of the great Dangers, to be derived to British America, from the hostile Invasion of the City of Boston, in our Sister Colony of Massachusetts Bay, whose Commerce and Harbour are, on the first Day of June next, to be stopped by an armed Force, deem it highly necessary that the said first Day of June be set apart, by the Members of this House, as a Day of Fasting, Humiliation, and Prayer, devoutly to implore the Divine Interposition, for averting the heavy Calamity which threatens Destruction to our Civil Rights, and the Evils of civil War. . . .

Among the burgesses who attended Bruton Parish Church on the day of fasting was a member from northern Virginia, George Washington. "Went to Church," he wrote in his diary, "and fasted all Day."

Washington had introduced a measure framed by George Mason that asserted the sole right to tax Virginians lay with the governor and the burgesses.

The following day Governor Botetourt dissolved the assembly. It didn't stop the radicals, however, and they quickly adjourned to the Raleigh Tavern, where eighty-nine of them entered into a general association against the East India Company:

We are further clearly of Opinion, that an attack, made on one of our sister Colonies, to compel Submission to arbitrary Taxes, is an Attack made on all British America, and threatens Ruin to the Rights of all, unless the united Wisdom of the Whole be applied.

The burgesses then appointed a Committee of Correspondence, recommending "that they communicate with their several corresponding Committees, on the Expedience of appointing Deputies from several colonies of British America, to meet in general Congress."

Individual colonies would no longer have to work by themselves. Rhode Island and Pennsylvania and New York all called for a gathering of representatives from the several colonies. In June the Massachusetts House of Representatives proposed that a congress be held in Philadelphia; by August 25, all thirteen colonies except Georgia had named delegates. As with the Stamp Act Congress, Governor Sir James Wright remained too powerful for Georgians to comply.

The First Continental Congress met in Philadelphia's Carpenter's Hall (the State House had too many signs of royal authority and control to suit the business at hand) with fifty-six delegates from twelve colonies. On September 5, they elected Peyton Randolph of Virginia as president.

John Adams was a delegate to the First Continental Congress, as was Patrick Henry of Virginia. According to Adams's notes, Henry rose and said:

> Government is dissolved. Fleets and armies and the present state of things show that government is dissolved. Where are your landmarks, your boundaries of colonies? We are in a state of nature, sir. I did propose that a scale should be laid down; that part of North America which was once Massachusetts Bay, and that part which was once Virginia, ought to be considered as having a weight. Will not people complain? Ten thousand Virginians have not outweighed one thousand others.
>
> I will submit, however; I am determined to submit if I am overruled.
>
> A worthy gentleman (ego) near me seemed to admit the necessity of obtaining a more adequate representation.
>
> I hope future ages will quote our proceedings with applause. It is one of the great duties of the democratical part of the constitution to keep itself pure. It is known in my Province that some other Colonies are not so numerous or rich as they are. I am for giving all the satisfaction in my power.
>
> The distinctions between Virginians, Pennsylvanians, New Yorkers and New Englanders are no more. I am not a Virginian, but an American.

Henry wanted the vote to be on a basis of population, and with Virginia having the largest population, that colony would have wielded the most power. Finally a measure recommended by John Jay of New York was approved: Each colony had but one vote.

On September 9, at a convention in Suffolk County, Massachusetts, delegates heard a series of resolves drafted by Dr. Joseph Warren: "Whereas the power but not the justice, the vengeance but not the wisdom of Great-Britain, which of old persecuted, scourged, and exiled our fugitive parents from their native shores, now pursues us, their guiltless children, with unrelenting severity. . . ."

They declared the Coercive Acts unconstitutional and therefore Massachusetts would not obey them. Massachusetts citizens would form a government of their own, not obligated to the king. They would collect taxes but withhold them from royal authorities until the Coercive/Intolerable Acts were repealed. As for the Quebec Act: "The late act of parliament for establishing the Roman Catholic religion and the French laws in that extensive country, now called Canada, is dangerous to an extreme degree . . . and, therefore, as men and Protestant Christians we are indispensably obliged to take all proper measures for our security." They advised local towns and villages to gather arms and to form their own militia. In effect, the Suffolk Resolves urged the colonists to perform what in the twentieth century would be called "acts of civil disobedience."

On September 17, President Randolph read the Suffolk Resolves to Congress. Carpenter's Hall broke out in cheers, and the delegates endorsed the resolves without changing a word in them. Even conservatives among the representatives opposed the Coercive Acts.

Those same conservatives, however, tried under Joseph Galloway to solve the growing problems with England by setting a union of colonies in which each province had home rule but were members of something like a dominion. The Galloway Plan of Union would see a royally appointed president-general serve at the king's pleasure over this dominion, with authority to veto acts of a grand council, whose members would be chosen by each colony. The commonwealth would remain inferior to Great Britain but would have authority to regulate commercial, civil, criminal, and police affairs when more than one colony was involved.

Galloway sent a copy of his proposed Plan of Union to Benjamin Franklin who was still in London, and Franklin showed it to several of the king's ministers. About the only thing Franklin would say was that "when I consider the extreme corruption prevalent among all orders of men in this rotten State, and the glorious public virtue so predominant in our rising country, I cannot but apprehend more mischief than benefits from a closer union." Such a union, he believed, would "drag us after them in all the plundering wars which their desperate circumstances, injustice and rapacity may prompt them to undertake; and their wide-wasting prodigality and profusion is a gulf that will swallow up every aid we may distress ourselves to afford them."

Instead, Congress appointed a committee to, as committee member John Adams wrote in his autobiography thirty years later, "prepare a bill or rights, as it was called, or a declaration of the rights of the Colonies." The declaration and resolves of the First Congress were adopted on October 14, 1774, and in them "the inhabitants of the English Colonies in North America, by the immutable laws of nature, the principles of the English constitution, and the several charters or compacts, have the following Rights . . .

1. That they are entitled to life, liberty, and property, and they have never ceded to any sovereign power whatever, a right to dispose of either with or without their consent.

2. That our ancestors, who first settled these colonies, were at the time of their emigration from the mother country, entitled to all the rights, liberties, and immunities of free and natural-born subjects within the realm of England. . . .

The colonists had the right to assemble peaceably; that "the foundation of English liberty . . . is a right in the people to participate in their legislative council"; that standing armies should not be kept in the colonies without the consent of the legislature of those colonies. Only colonial assemblies had the right to tax their population. In all, the declaration and resolves declared illegal some thirteen acts of Parliament. Further, economic sanctions—that is, nonimportation—would be applied until Parliament itself repealed those acts. As of December 1, 1774, all imports from England were to cease.

In mid-November 1774, King George III wrote a letter to his prime minister, Lord North. North remained as prime minister for twelve years, among the most eventful dozen years in English history, re-signing only after the news of Cornwallis's surrender in 1781. Lord North had few admirers and many enemies. Among his friends, how-ever, was George III, who of course could have demanded his resig-nation anytime he wanted to, but who wouldn't accept it when offered.

The King to Lord North.

Queens House Novr. 18th, 1774

I am sorry that the line of conduct seems now chalked out, which the enclosed dispatches thoroughly justify; the New Eng-land governments are in a state of rebellion, blows must decide whether they are to be subject to this country or independent.

Late on the night of April 18, 1775, twenty-one companies of picked British soldiers marched out of Boston. They went looking for American guns and ammunition. General Thomas Gage knew that rebels were collecting weapons and ammunition in the town of Concord. The rebels knew that he knew. About the only thing secret was when the redcoats would go after the stores and how they would get there: ferried across the river to Charlestown and then inland—a sixteen-mile "sea" and land route, or a twenty-one-mile hike over the narrow spit connecting the city to the mainland—Boston Neck—and on into the countryside. Since the Boston Port Bill had shut down all nonmilitary shipping into the city, all commerce with the city had relied on the Neck to survive.

Gage had already confiscated military stores in Boston, Cam-bridge, and Charlestown. To General Gage it was simple; armies without ammunition were powerless, so he would take the muskets and gunpowder from the Patriots before they could even become an army. On April 14, Gage received instructions from Lord Dart-mouth in London to do what he had to do—get control of the guns. He summoned to his office in Boston Colonel Francis Smith of the 10th Infantry. "Sir," Gage said to Smith:

You will march with the Corps of Grenadiers and Light In-fantry put under your command with the utmost expedition and secrecy to Concord, where you will seize and destroy all the Artillery and Ammunition, provisions, Tents & all other military stores you can find.

Patriot leaders knew that sooner or later the redcoats would try to confiscate the cache at Concord. Most of the rebel leaders were already out of town, staying away from the British as much as possible. Sam Adams and John Hancock, for instance, were in the Lexington parsonage of the Reverend Jonas Clarke, the same parsonage where Hancock had grown up. Adams and Hancock were about to leave for Philadelphia to take their seats as delegates to the Second Continental Congress.

Dr. Joseph Warren, however, remained in town. He was in charge of rebel spies and couriers in Boston. Paul Revere, for instance, later said that he was only "one of upwards of thirty, chiefly mechanics, who formed ourselves into a committee for the purpose of watching the movements of the British soldiers." They had a well-organized grapevine. A British officer let slip word to a Boston gunsmith, who told a member of the Committee of Safety, who told Dr. Warren, who sent word to the countryside that the British are coming.

William Dawes was a twenty-three-year-old shoemaker who'd previously smuggled a cannon out of Boston under the British army's nose. He, too, spread the word that night, but thanks to Henry Wadsworth Longfellow's poem, *Paul Revere's Ride*, it was Revere, not Dawes, who is remembered.

About 10:00 P.M. Dr. Warren had Paul Revere rousted out of his house on North Square. Revere still didn't know which way the redcoats were coming, so he arranged with a friend, John Pulling, to place a signal in the tower of the Old North Church (the present-day tourist mecca known as Christ Church). It would be, as Longfellow's poem later declared, "one if by land, and two if by sea." Friends sculled Revere across the Charles River.*

---

* There's a story that the men needed a cloth to muffle the sound of their oars, so one of them gave a whistle beneath his sweetheart's window, and she threw down her petticoat. They wrapped the petticoat—still warm from the young lady—around the oars and silently rowed across the river.

On the near shore Colonel William Conant of the Charlestown Committee of Safety handed Revere the reins of a fast horse and told him he'd seen two signal lanterns; the redcoats were to be ferried across the river. With that the silversmith-turned-courier set off. "We rid [rode] down towards Lexington, a pretty smart pace." His trip took him through Charlestown, past Breed's and Bunker Hills, along the Mystic River to Medford, then west to Menotomy (now Arlington) and northwest to Lexington.

William Dawes went the long way round—by way of Boston Neck to Roxbury and Brookline, over Cambridge Bridge and through the little town, northwest to Menotomy and on to Lexington. At Lexington both Dawes and Revere raised the alarm.

Dr. Samuel Prescott, a young Concord physician, was in Lexington that night, courting his girl, Lydia Mulliken. Lydia's brother, Nathaniel, was a Lexington minuteman and he told Dr. Prescott about the British coming their way. Prescott—"a high son of Liberty," Revere later testified—jumped on his horse and headed for Concord, overtaking Revere and Dawes along the way. They joined forces, but halfway to Concord the three riders were stopped by a British patrol. Revere was captured, but Dawes got away and returned to Lexington.

Prescott also escaped the British patrol. "The doctor jumped his horse over a low stone wall," Revere said, "and got to Concord." It was Dr. Prescott, not Revere or Dawes, who carried the warning to those farther along the way.

Meanwhile Revere convinced the British that he'd already warned the countryside and that five hundred militiamen were waiting for them at Lexington. Apparently they believed him and let him go, keeping his borrowed horse so that he couldn't alert yet another five hundred militiamen. Revere returned to Lexington and he convinced Hancock and Adams to get out of town before the redcoats arrived. The two rebel leaders hopped into Hancock's carriage (Sam Adams disliked riding a horse) and together headed to safety.

Lexington was a town of 755 people, including five slaves. As many as 400 cattle often grazed on the town commons.

Captain John Parker of the Lexington minutemen had been alerted, and he in turn alerted his teenage drummer boy, William

Diamond. About one o'clock in the morning Parker ordered Diamond to beat the call for assembly. Depending on whom you believe, anywhere from forty to seventy-seven men eventually gathered on Lexington green that April morning. They ranged in age from the sixteen-year-old drummer to a sixty-three-year-old veteran of the Battle for Louisbourg in 1758. Two others were also in their sixties, four were in their fifties, eight in their forties. It was a decidedly older group, with fifty-five of the militiamen at Lexington over age thirty and more than twenty of them veterans of the French and Indian War. There were several father-son teams. At least a quarter of the men were related either to Parker or his wife. Everybody either knew someone or was related to someone. Twenty-nine of the men had come from just six families.

In the democratic way of New England militiamen, when they gathered, they discussed the issue and decided what to do. In this case, Captain Parker remembered, it was "not to be discovered, nor meddle or make with said Regular Troops." Most of the minutemen then spent the evening at Buckman's Tavern, near the town green.

Just as the sun was coming up, British troops under Major John Pitcairn arrived. Parker ordered his men to stand fast. Years later Captain Parker's grandson Theodore remembered him saying "Don't fire unless fired upon! But if they want a war, let it begin here," which is glorious and patriotic and all of that, but it's not what Parker said. At least not according to him. "I immediately ordered our Militia to disperse and not to fire," Parker testified at a hearing on April 25.

Meanwhile the British truly were coming. Two platoons of the 10th Infantry had formed a battle line about forty yards from the militiamen. "Disperse, ye rebels!" Major Pitcairn ordered. "Lay down your arms!"

"Immediately," Captain Parker claimed, "said Troops made their appearance and rushed furiously, fired upon us and killed eight of our party, without receiving any provocation therefor from us." By most accounts, the Americans began to disperse when a single shot was fired, but who fired it isn't known. It could have been a militiaman, but they were leaving, so it's not likely. It could have been one of the British, but the British were well-trained, so it's less likely some

Redcoat did it. Perhaps somebody tripped and fell and a musket discharged. Perhaps some onlooker not otherwise involved with the event fired a shot. Whoever fired that first shot, two or three other shots followed. A British officer ordered "Fire!" And the war was on.

From their carriage where Sam Adams and John Hancock were escaping into the dawn, Adams heard the gunfire and exclaimed: "Oh, what a glorious morning is this!"

The battle was over in a matter of minutes. Eight Americans were dead and ten more were wounded. The only British wound was to Major Pitcairn's horse, which had two small scratches. Pitcairn himself would die two months later at the Battle of Bunker Hill.

In the best New England tradition, the road from Lexington to Concord was the Concord road if that's the way you were going. It was the Lexington road if you were heading the other way. Samuel Prescott reached Concord between 1:00 and 2:00 A.M. Alarm bells were rung and the Concord militia gathered at Wright's Tavern. They arranged for a signal to reassemble on the approach of the British and then dispersed to help townspeople hide as much of the remaining stores as they could.

Concord had about twice Lexington's population, and about 250 armed militiamen gathered. Again, in a democratic fashion, they decided to march down the road to Lexington, their drums beating and fifes playing. They were marching down the Lexington road, going "to meet the British," who, of course, were on the Concord road, headed their way. Seven hundred fifty trained British regulars against 250 untrained if eager minutemen.

The two forces were within five hundred yards of each other when the Americans turned around and marched back toward Concord, drum and fife still playing. It was about eight in the morning when the British arrived at Concord. They had been rousted out of their bunks about nine the night before. They'd marched, fought a small skirmish, and marched some more; it had taken them eleven hours to come seventeen miles.

As the British entered Concord they found themselves on less satisfying terrain than a few hours earlier. Lexington was a flat, open green, and the Americans had lined up across the open space. Concord was a town of hills, and as the regulars marched in, the minutemen stood looking down from a series of ridges.

The militiamen, again in democratic fashion, debated what to do: "If we die, let us die here." "Let us stand our ground." "Let us go and meet them." "No, it will not do for us to begin the war." Reverend William Emerson, the local pastor and grandfather of poet Ralph Waldo Emerson, reported that the more prudent among the minutemen won out, and they retreated "till our strength should be equal to the enemy's."

Redcoated infantrymen searched the town for gunpowder, arms, and any hoarded food. Grenadiers hacked down the town's liberty pole and set it on fire. At Wright's Tavern, some of the officers ordered breakfasts of meat and potatoes. Before they could eat, however, there was word of trouble at the North Bridge. By midmorning, militiamen had gathered about a mile out of town, on Punkastasset Hill, overlooking the North Bridge. From there they saw smoke coming from the town and assumed the British had set torches to their homes. Actually there were only a few fires—the liberty pole, a gun carriage, flour, and a couple of wagons—and the British soldiers put those out.

At midmorning the militia started moving down the ridge toward the North Bridge; only about thirty-five regulars faced 400 minutemen. Again the American drums and fifes played. This time the minutemen halted momentarily on the last ridge overlooking the bridge, that "rude bridge that arched the flood," Ralph Waldo Emerson wrote. British troops began to tear up planks at their end of the bridge.

The commander of the American soldiers, Major John Buttrick, called out to the British to stop the destruction. They did not, and Buttrick cried, "Fire, fellow soldiers, for God's sake, fire!" They did, and that was "the shot heard round the world."

Later, British Captain Walter Laurie of the 43rd Regiment said that "I imagine myself that a man of my company . . . did fire his piece." Another officer, however, claimed that it was an American who fired first.

Not that it matters much. Both sides fired, and North Bridge became the emotional heart of the Revolution. In a three-minute exchange, three British soldiers were killed and eight others wounded. Two Americans died and another three were wounded.

The British retreated, but at first the Americans made no effort to follow them. A teenage American boy ran across the bridge following the skirmish and, for some reason, hit a wounded British soldier in the head with an ax or hatchet. Later General Gage claimed that Americans were guilty of atrocities, that the soldier had been "scalped, his Head much mangled and his ears cut off" while he was still alive.

Back in Lexington, young William Diamond beat his drum to assemble the minutemen. It had been only six hours since the first assembly, and a third of those who had gathered on the common had died. Now Captain Parker's men reassembled, and this time they marched to Concord. As Billy Diamond beat his drum, Jonathan Harrington played "The White Cockade" on his fife. Earlier in the day Harrington's cousin had been among those killed on the Lexington common.

By noon the news of the skirmish at Lexington had traveled scores of miles in every direction, and hundreds of minutemen dropped what they were doing. They lined up on village greens, then marched off to war. As the British withdrew back to Boston, upward of five thousand militiamen converged on them. At least that's how many the British felt they were facing. The militia closed in on the retreating columns of redcoats. Minutemen fired from behind trees and stone walls, from houses and woodpiles. As General Gage would later report, his troops "were attacked from all quarters where any cover was to be found, from whence it was practicable to annoy them; and they [his men] were so fatigued with their march that it was with difficulty they could keep out their flanking partys to remove the enemy at a distance."

Along the Lexington road, minutemen ran out of ammunition and ran home for more. The British could not run home. It was, an officer said, "a Veritable Furnass of Musquetry."

British losses were at least 19 officers and 250 men killed and wounded out of 1,800 who had left Boston. It might have been worse, but Lord Hugh Percy arrived with reinforcements from the Boston garrison, and with them were two small cannon. The retreat resumed, and militiamen continued to hound and harass the British troops, halting only now and then when a cannonball came their way. The hit-and-run sniping continued until the redcoats reached Bunker Hill.

By one reckoning, 3,763 Americans took part in the Battles of Lexington and Concord. The war of words was over.

On June 17, 1775, the Battle of Bunker Hill was fought on Breed's Hill, which has since been renamed Bunker Hill. The colonists had intended to fortify Bunker Hill, but it was night and apparently they got lost. The original Bunker Hill is now so crowded with homes, there's no place for tourists. Almost immediately after the battle, the Boston Committee on Safety began claiming they had intended to fortify Breed's Hill all along. If they had used the real Bunker Hill, by most estimates the British never could have pushed them off.

Soldiers in the British army spent less time on tactics than they did keeping their red coats clean and their white pants sparkling. When the regular troops marched up Breed's Hill (both the colonists and British thinking it was Bunker Hill), it's a wonder any of them made it to the top. Not just that the colonists were shooting down at them, but you have to consider everything the average soldier had to wear and carry with him.

British regular uniforms were modeled after the German-style outfit, not the least reason being that King George III had a lot more German ancestors than he had English. Those uniforms were as ornamental as they could be, and it was all the men could do not to stagger in line. The uniforms were noted for their brilliant scarlet woolen coats (thus, the nicknames "redcoats" and "lobsterbacks"), which made them perfect targets for any rifleman not totally blind. Inside the coat was a heavy lining, outside, colored facings with piping, lace, and brass or pewter buttons. Generally soldiers wore either red or white waistcoats, what Americans refer to as "vests." Further restricting the soldier's movement was the coat's stiff collar. A heavy leather stock necktie he wore almost cut off his breath.

Beneath this the poor soldier wore heavily whitewashed white knee breeches; he used the same type of whitewash Mark Twain's

Tom Sawyer would later employ on a Missouri fence. The soldier's breeches were so tight that they seemed to have been designed to cut off the man's circulation at the knees. Below that our redcoated infantryman wore long, buttoned gaiters that rose higher than his knees (perhaps so as not to show off any unsightly break between stockings and breeches). Then came heavy boots. At the time, and continuing halfway through America's Civil War, there was no such thing as a left or right shoe. All boots and shoes were made straight on, and they became left or right only with their wearing. Ideally the wearer would switch them back and forth to extend the shoes' wear (much like modern car owners rotate tires), but in practice this didn't happen all that often.

Around his bright red coat our British regular soldier wore a tight-as-could-be wide white belt (another job for the whitewash bucket) from which hung a bayonet. His hair usually was worn in a queue or club, which had been stiffened with grease and coated with white powder, frequently the same white powder that had gone into making the whitewash he'd used on his breeches and belt. At the front of his head and around his ears he had tight curls.

One could not, of course, go on parade or into battle without a hat, and in the case of our British soldier that article sometimes was a heavy bearskin hat. If he was a grenadier, he wore an even taller helmet that was extremely awkward but made him even more imposing.

When General Howe sent his troops up Bunker/Breed's Hill, they marched off as if going on an expedition. That is, they carried their bedrolls as well as cooking and eating implements. Fully equipped (and highly restricted), our British soldier carried a weight totaling about 125 pounds. All of this when he might not weigh much more than that himself.

The American colonists at Bunker Hill had no such uniform problem, mainly because they had no uniforms. They weren't yet an army and wore whatever clothes they happened to have on at the time. At least they didn't have to pay for them. The British army deducted from the regulars' pay the cost of uniforms, replacing them as they wore out. That is, if the supply sergeant had uniforms on hand and got around to issuing them.

As it was, the British lost more than 1,000 of the 2,500 regulars who climbed up the hill and fought. American forces probably were never more than 3,000, with no more than half of them being there at any one time. The patriots probably lost a total of 140 killed and 301 wounded; thirty of the wounded were captured. Bunker Hill was a costly "victory" for General Gage, so costly that London replaced him with General William Howe.

CHAPTER NINE

Who, What, and Where:
Big, Bigger, and Not So Big

I always consider the settlement of America with reverence and wonder, as the opening of a grand scene and design in providence, for the illumination of the ignorant and the emancipation of the slavish part of mankind all over the earth.
— John Adams, 1765

Then join hand in hand, brave Americans all!
By uniting we stand, by dividing we fall.
— John Dickinson, *The Liberty Song*, 1768

Essentially the American colonies were rural. In the North, towns were surrounded by small farms within walking distance of a common green. It was not unusual for a family to live in the center of Boston, New York, or Philadelphia and the father and sons walk to the outskirts of town and tend their farm.

As the Revolution began, Philadelphia was the second largest city in the British Empire, with a population of about 40,000. London's population was about 750,000, while Bristol, England, had about 36,000, and Edinburgh and Dublin were slightly larger. Boston, 15,000; New York, 22,000; and Charleston had about 12,000. Britain's population at the time was about 8,000,000.

Rivers were America's highways of commerce, at least so far as they ran from the Atlantic Ocean inland. Going north to south, they were commerce's major obstacle. Getting from one side to the other always, to some extent, posed a problem. There was, after all, not a single major bridge over a major river. There were, however, ferrymen who operated boats across most rivers.

We have a mixed picture of poverty and wealth in Revolutionary America, and it may be that writers saw what they wanted to see. Take Benjamin Franklin. In 1772, he wrote, "I thought often of the happiness of New England, where every man is a freeholder, has a vote in public affairs, lives in a tidy, warm house, has plenty of good food and fewel [*sic*], with whole cloaths from head to foot, the manufacture perhaps of his own family. . . ." This was, of course, Franklin's memory, as he sat on the other side of the Atlantic Ocean in a luxurious home in London.

Gottlieb Mittelberger of Philadelphia would have agreed. In 1758, he wrote that "even in the humblest or poorest houses, no meals are served without a meat course." However, not everyone was as lucky as Franklin's everyman freeholder or Mittelberger's humblest or poorest.

There's also the testimony of a Quaker named John Smith, who wrote in his diary; "It is remarkable what an Increase of the number of Beggars there is about this town in winter." About the same time, the spring of 1776, visitors to the Philadelphia almshouse reported that of the 147 men, 178 women, and 85 children living there, "most of them naked, helpless, and emaciated with Poverty and Disease to such a Degree, that some have died in a few Days after their Admission." The almshouse was only a few blocks from Independence Hall, where delegates debated breaking with England. And less than two decades earlier, the Boston Overseers of the Poor reported that "the Poor supported either wholly or in part by the Town in the Almshouse and out of it will amount to the Number of about 1000. . . ." Boston's population was only 15,000. Poor relief, city officials claimed, was double that of any town of similar size "upon the face of the whole Earth."

So, as the colonies began to revolt, they faced two prospects: tidy, warm houses and no meals served without meat, or an increasing number of beggars and almshouses full of naked, helpless individuals. It would take a team of sociologists to figure this one out.

Meanwhile, hundreds of thousands of people continued to immigrate to America every year. Even during the Revolutionary War they didn't stop. For example, between the years 1763 and 1775, over twenty thousand Scottish Highlanders left their homes to seek a better life in the forests of America. America was an inviting asylum for those whose lives were less than livable. In the case of the Scots, they fought on both sides of the Revolution.

"The practical liberty of America," wrote historian George Flower, "is found in its great space and small population." He added that "good land, dog-cheap everywhere, and for nothing, if you go for it, gives as much elbow room to every man as he chooses to take."

Comparatively speaking, the eighteenth century saw immigration explode at a rate as large as any other time in American history. From less than 300,000 at the beginning of the century, by 1760, the total population for the thirteen colonies was 1,685,000. By 1775, it had grown to between 2,418,000 and 2,803,000, excluding Indians but counting slaves.

During the Revolution one out of six Americans was black, and 99 percent of blacks in America were slaves. Blacks were held as slaves in all thirteen colonies. There were black slaves at Lexington when British regulars met American minutemen on the town common.

At Yorktown, when Cornwallis's trapped men ran short of food, they sent back across the lines many of the runaway slaves they had taken in, forcing them to fend for themselves. They were part of the estimated 20,000 slaves who had run away to join the British army as it rampaged through the Carolinas and Virginia. German Captain Johann von Ewald said the British army had so many blacks attached to it that it resembled "a migrating . . . Tartar horde."

The Continental army also enlisted blacks. In 1777, Rhode Island fielded a 125-man black regiment. As would be the case all the way through the Civil War, however, white officers were in command. Massachusetts planned to create an all-black regiment, but eventually mixed black recruits into white regiments. In 1779, Henry Laurens of South Carolina urged Congress to raise up to 3,000 black soldiers by offering them freedom and compensating their owners at the rate of $1,000 per man. Delegates from South Carolina and Georgia rejected the plan, afraid to arm that many blacks.

During America's Civil War, President Abraham Lincoln did not authorize enlistment of blacks until August 1862. From the beginning of the Revolution, however, blacks served in the ranks. Originally they fought under a substitute system, which permitted a man to send his slave rather than go himself. Later Congress not only approved their enlistment, but, over the objection of South Carolina delegates, called for the *reenlistment* of blacks. On average there were fifty blacks per Continental battalion. By 1779, 15 percent of the Continental army was black, usually as service troops building defenses, but often as line soldiers. By the end of the Revolution, several states had abolished slavery and others gradually voted to emancipate their slaves.

One of the best-known blacks in Revolutionary America was Paul Cuffe. Later his name would be used as a derogatory expression: "Cuffee" became as pejorative as "Sambo." By 1780, when he was barely twenty-one, Paul Cuffe was captain of his own ships, built in his own shipyards. Twice, he petitioned local and Massachusetts state assemblies, asking that blacks be relieved from paying taxes, since they had "no voice or influence in the election of those who tax us." Sort of handing back to the legislators the "no taxation without representation" argument they'd used themselves. His petitions were rejected, and he became convinced that only by getting out of America could black people achieve a decent existence. In 1815, Cuffe began transporting groups of free American blacks to Sierra Leone in Africa.

CHAPTER TEN

Revolutionary Potpourri:
Bits of This and That

On Tuesday last was married at May Fair Chapel, Henry Merriton of Chelsea, aged near Ninety, to Miss Alice Gray, a young lady under twelve Years of Age, with all the Accomplishments that can be expected from one of her Age to render the married State happy.

—*Boston Weekly News-Letter,* July 27, 1752

The American Revolution was not a common event. Its effects and consequences have already been awful over a great part of the globe. And when and where are they to cease?

—John Adams, 1818

British forces captured more than 4,000 American prisoners in New York in 1776. When Charleston fell, another 5,000 Americans surrendered. Five thousand British, Germans, and Canadians were taken prisoner after the Battle of Saratoga, and when Cornwallis surrendered at Yorktown in 1781, more than 8,000 British and Germans became prisoners of war. We don't know how many prisoners were taken, but we do know the numbers were about the same on each side.

We also know that neither side was either prepared for the numbers taken prisoner or, for the most part, intentionally mistreated them. While the British had firm holds on New York, Quebec, and Halifax, the American army was constantly on the move and didn't want to take prisoners along with them. Generally the Americans used whatever was available—local jails, warehouses, churches, or underground mines to house captives. The abandoned Simsbury, Connecticut, copper mines, about ten miles northwest of Hartford, were particularly horrendous. Prisoners were forced to climb down ladders into the mine, then food and water were lowered down or often just thrown down to them, and they were left to languish in the cold and damp pits. Luckily for the prisoners, it apparently wasn't too difficult to escape from the prison mines.

Surgeon Albigence Waldo, who'd been with Washington at Valley Forge, was later taken prisoner. In his journal he recorded how American prisoners in Philadelphia, "in their last agonies of hunger, scraped mortar and rotten wood from the walls and greedily ate it for the temporary sensation of nourishment which it gave."

The English kept many of their prisoners in ships in New York harbor, and a lot of them died—poor conditions, poor food, brackish water. As many as 11,500 Americans died while in British prison ships, perhaps more rebels than died in fighting. The most notorious prison ship was the HMS *Jersey*. It was a sixty-four-gun ship that was declared unfit for service and partially dismantled. It held more than 1,000 prisoners crowded into the ship's hold.

To keep from going crazy, and to keep up their spirits, the American prisoners sang patriotic songs—"For America and all her sons forever will shine" was one refrain—and this infuriated their jailers. Rhode Island farmboy Christopher Hawkins was held on board the *Jersey* and recalled how prisoners "were often set at defiance" of their guards, and sometimes shouted, "We dare you to fire upon us." Killing them, they told the guards, would be easy—"only half work, for many of the prisoners are now half dead from extreme sufferings."

As Private Joseph Plumb Martin put it, "Inhuman treatment was often shown to our people when prisoners by the British."

William Slade of Connecticut was captured at Fort Washington in November 1776. He was first marched to a barn in Harlem, later taken under guard to a church, then confined on the ship *Grovner* in the North River. "There was now 500 men on board," he wrote, adding, "this made much confusion." From Slade's diary he kept during the time he was held prisoner:

Saturday, 7th. We drawed 4 lb of bisd [biscuit] at noon, a piece of meat and rice. . . . This day the ships crew weighed anchor and fell down the river below Govnors Island and sailed up the east river to Turcle Bay [Turtle Bay, at the foot of 23rd Street], and cast anchor for winter months.

Sunday, 8th. . . . We spent the day reading and in meditation, hopeing for good news. . . .

Friday, 13th of Decr. 1776. We drawed bisd and butter. A little water broth. We now see nothing but the mercy of God to intercede for us. Sorrowful times, all faces look pale, discouraged, discouraged. . . .

Tuesday, 17th. No fire. Suffer with cold and hunger. We are treated worse than cattle and hogs. . . .

Friday, 27th. Three men of our battalion died last night. The most melancholyest night I ever saw. Small pox increases fast. This day I was blooded. Drawed bsd and butter. Stomach all gone. At noon, burgo. Basset is verry sick. Not like to live I think.

Saturday, 28th. Drawed bisd. This morning about 10 o'clock Josiah Basset died.

A prisoner's chances of surviving on the *Jersey* were less than one out of five. "The dysentery, fever, phrenzy, and despair prevailed," one who did survive wrote, "and filled the place with filth, disgust, and horror." Dead bodies were heaved over the side, and at low tide they lay exposed in the nearby mud banks. After the war the bones of thousands of dead prisoners were recovered and buried.

After the Battle of Saratoga the so-called "Convention Army" of prisoners was marched to a camp in the mountains of Virginia near Charlottesville. "We passed through a picturesque portion of the country," the Baroness Riedesel* wrote, which, "by reason of its wildness, inspired us with terror. Often we were in danger of our lives while going along these break-neck roads; and more than all this we suffered from cold and, what was still worse, from a lack of provisions." Unlike the rank-and-file prisoner, however, the Riedesels "had built for us a large house, with a great drawing-room in the centre, and upon each side two rooms, which cost my husband one hundred guineas." It was, the baroness wrote, "exceedingly pretty."

Like the baroness, many of those captured at Saratoga were Germans. American forces didn't have the means to hold on to them,

---

* Wife of Baron Friedrich Adolphus Riedesel, she and her husband, along with their three daughters, were taken captive at Saratoga in October 1777. All five were held prisoner until they were exchanged three years later in 1780.

so many of those they captured simply wandered off; a lot of the Hessians were allowed to "escape," since it was well known they probably would peacefully remain in America and not return to the British who had paid the German authorities for their services. Of about 30,000 German mercenaries, about 5,000 deserted and another 8,000 or so were killed or died of disease while fighting for a cause they had no part in.

In 1780, Congress sent Henry Laurens to Holland to arrange a ten-million-dollar loan. When the British captured his ship, Laurens tried to destroy his official papers by throwing them overboard. It didn't work. The English retrieved the documents and used one paper as a pretext for declaring war on the Dutch. In London they told the captured Laurens, "You are to be sent to the Tower of London, not to a prison; you must have no idea of a prison." Laurens remained in the Tower for fifteen months under conditions so severe that his health was seriously impaired. The British offered to release him if he would agree to serve the king. Laurens refused but twice petitioned Parliament for his release, trying to justify his role in the Revolution.

The British released Laurens on bond after the Battle of Yorktown, finally exchanging him for Lord Cornwallis. He sailed to France to join the other peace commissioners, where one of his chief contributions to the treaty was his insistence that upon evacuating American ports, British troops should not carry off Negroes who had defected to the losing side.

Back in America, Henry Laurens retired to his plantation, Mepkin, on the Cooper River about thirty miles from Charleston. His time in the Tower of London had been hard on him, and Henry Laurens died in 1792, at the then ripe old age of sixty-eight. In one of the first instances of the practice in America, Henry Laurens stipulated in his will that he be cremated.

At the Battle of Bunker Hill, General Israel Putnam reportedly ordered his men, "Don't fire until you see the whites of their eyes!" He may or may not have done just that, although if it did happen, it more likely was Colonel William Prescott who shouted the command. In other battles soldiers were told, "Don't fire until you can see their buttons." The key here is that most of the light weapons used in the war weren't accurate beyond the distance where you could see the attackers' eyes and/or buttons, certainly not past fifty yards. The weapon of choice for both sides of the Revolution was a version of the famous Brown Bess, a .75-caliber flintlock musket. John Churchill, the Duke of Marlborough (and ancestor of Britain's Winston Churchill) introduced the Brown Bess more than fifty years earlier, during the reign of Queen Anne. It was the standard infantry weapon for over a century.

The Brown Bess got its nickname in any of three ways, take your pick. Tradition has it that it took its name from the artificial oxidation of the barrel in the process that basically pickled the metal; the barrel was brown, so the weapon became the Brown Bess. A second version, however, says the Brown came not from the shade of the barrel, but from the color of the wooden stock, and "Bess" may have been the British soldier's humorous attempt to change the name of the previous musket, the brownbill, into a feminine equivalent. Just to confuse matters, a third possibility has the "Brown" coming from either the pickled barrel or the wooden stock, with "Bess" being a corruption of "buss," as in "blunderbuss," an earlier form of wide-barreled musket.

However it got its name, the original Brown Bess had a barrel about forty-six inches long, but by the time of the Revolution, that was down to thirty-nine inches. Then there was the stock, which made it another foot and a half longer, a total of about four and a half feet, something like a foot shorter than the average soldier. Complete with bayonet, the Brown Bess of the Revolution weighed fourteen pounds. By the Civil War the standard infantry weapon was the Springfield musket, which fired a .58-caliber Minié bullet. By World War II, American troops had the M1 Garand, a .30-caliber, gas-operated, semiautomatic weapon that weighed 9.6 pounds loaded with an eight-round clip.

The Revolution's .75-caliber lead ball itself weighed about one ounce, which, if you were hit, could put, as they said, quite a hole in your person. "As to firing at a man at 200 yards with a common musket," a British expert observed, "you may just as well fire at the moon and have the same hopes of hitting your object."

Loading and firing a musket was, at best, a time-consuming operation. During a battle there just wasn't time to load a musket from scratch, so to speak, so between skirmishes, while sitting around the campfire, troops prepackaged cartridges. To do this, first a soldier had to fill a pan with lead, then melt it and pour the molten metal into a bullet mold. The resulting bullet was about three-quarters of an inch in diameter.

While the molded bullets cooled, the soldier took a six-inch hollow dowel and used it to form a cartridge. After cutting down the molded bullet to proper size (the holes in the bullet mold produced an excess amount of lead called sprue, named after the holes through which the molten lead was poured), the soldier rolled wrapping paper around the cooled and pared-down bullet and dowel. One end of this wrapped paper was twisted and tied off with twine and the dowel was removed. Gunpowder (with just a little extra to be used as a primer) was poured into the rolled cartridge, and the top of the paper was twisted in place. The ready-made cartridge was now ready to go, carried in boxes over the soldier's shoulder (usually the man's right shoulder, since the average soldier was right-handed). Like just about everything else during the Revolution, there was no set number of cartridges carried, but a leather, wood, and linen box generally carried between twenty and thirty cartridges.

Loading a musket was a twelve-step system. The first order was to pull back the cock (that's the part that holds a piece of flint) into a half-cocked position—it's where we get the phrase "to go off half-cocked." So, "Half-cock your firelock!" then: "Handle your cartridge," in which the soldier grabbed a cartridge out of his box, took it by the non–bullet-holding end, and bit off the twist of paper, pouring a bit of powder into the musket pan. "Prime!"

Biting off the cartridge end always caused a bit of black powder to be smeared around the soldier's mouth and over his face. After a battle you could easily tell which soldiers had actually fired their weapons; they were the ones with dirty faces.

Okay. You've primed your weapon. Step four is to close the pan, or as the order went "Shut your pans!" Step five is to charge your musket with that cartridge you spent all your spare campfire time preparing: "Charge with cartridge!" That left the cartridge somewhere at the business end of the musket, not nearly where it should be to shoot, so the sixth order was to "Draw your rammers!" an order not nearly as interesting as it sounds. When not in use the ramrod (in earlier times, it was known as a scouring stick, because it also was used to clean out the musket barrel) was fitted by loose brackets to the musket barrel. Order seven: "Ram down your charge!" or the cartridge. Number eight: "Return your rammers!"—replace them in their brackets on the barrel, then immediately bring your musket into a sort of port arms position. This was followed by step number nine, "Shoulder your firelocks!" For step number ten you were ordered to "Poise your firelock," then eleven, "Cock your firelock!" Finally, step twelve: "Fire!"

And this was just the American system. The British army had an even more elaborate procedure.

What may seem like a missing all-important step ("Aim") often as not wasn't given. Simply, most of the time soldiers didn't aim. Not only was there no attempt made to aim, British regulars were taught to look the other way, so as not to have the musket flash blind them. At times the whole line would fire a volley at an angle, say the left, reload, and fire a volley at the right angle. Accuracy was superfluous; mass speed firing was the key.

The standard rate of fire with a musket was three or four rounds per minute, somewhat better than they were taught: "load and fire fifteen times in three minutes and three-quarters" was how they were trained. At one shot every fifteen seconds, that meant about two effective shots during an average enemy charge. With a few notable exceptions—Lexington, Concord, Cowpens, and Kings Mountain— the popular myth that foolish British troops formed perfect formations to march across an open field, while wily Americans took pot shots from behind trees and stone walls, is just that, a myth. Generally Americans fought in this same silly fashion. During the winter of Valley Forge, General von Steuben did a lot to train American troops in the ways of war, but one thing he did *not* do was to train the troops in what might be termed "backwoods" warfare. That is, in fighting from behind cover. American troops harassing the redcoats out of Concord did that, but for the most part Continental forces fought the way their British and Hessian enemies did: formed up in order and marched head-on into the next bunch. Firing in volley—that is, the whole line shooting at once—was the usual method of warfare.

In fact, this same technique of self-annihilation carried over into the Napoleonic Wars and into America's Civil War. The tactic was to line two or three ranks up shoulder to shoulder, with the next file as close behind as possible, about six feet. Now, the reality of having the second file so close had to be rather daunting to those in the first file; as the man in front died, the next man stepped over him and took his place. The third moved up, and so on. With bayonets fixed, the whole line moved forward. Watching this had to get kind of scary. Hundreds of men, shoulder to shoulder, marching forward, with either the enemy lined up behind, say, a wall, or marching shoulder to shoulder toward you. Each side tried to hold its fire until they were no more than fifty feet apart. And wait for the other side to fire first. Hordes of troops would march with shotgunlike muskets loaded with a three-quarter-inch bullet—a full ounce of lead—until they were near the enemy, then open fire. If one side was lucky enough to have, say, a stone fence to hide behind, more likely than not that was the side who won. Madness prevailed, but it was the ordinary soldier, carrying a Brown Bess musket and a bayonet, who won the war.

"It became," historian Hoffman Nickerson points out, "the *ne plus ultra* of the art to take, not to give, the first fire; to stand the losses and to put in your own volley so close that every shot went home." So, "Don't fire until you see the white of their eyes" wasn't all that unusual.

The twelve-step program of loading and firing was just for your run-of-the-mill soldier who used a smooth-bore musket and had prepackaged his cartridge back there at the campfire. For riflemen it was different, and most carried the makings, so to speak, not prepared cartridges: a hunting bag with lead balls and flints, a horn full of powder (often with a tip end of the horn attached to a chain or strap and used to measure the amount of charge for the pan), and greased patches in a compartment cut into the stock of the rifle and covered with a brass plate.

To load your rifle you primed your pan with powder, measured an exact charge, and poured it into the rifle barrel. You'd then take a greased patch from the patch box in your rifle stock and place it over the center of the barrel (once again, the business end of the barrel), and with your ramrod in hand place a preformed musket ball in the patch. Ram home the patch and ball. Since a rifleman generally was someone special, chances are no one bothered to order that twelfth step, and on his own he "Fired!" If for some reason the rifleman forgot to load in a bullet but simply rammed home his powder and patch, when he took a shot, it likely didn't amount to much. Except, that is, to add another phrase to our lexicon. One who fired without first loading a bullet, would "shoot his wad," a very telling phrase.

Rifled weapons, of course, were far superior in accuracy. They were reliable up to about three hundred yards, but they also were slower. It simply took more time to load a rifle than a musket. Apparently prior to the Revolution no one seriously considered using a rifle in wartime. It was a hunting weapon only, mainly because of the length of time it took to load and fire. When the English first faced American riflemen, they were surprised. Not only could the American rifleman load faster than the British military believed, he could do it on the run.

Up until about 1775 rifles were virtually unknown in New England. They were brought to the American frontier by German immigrants, where the weapons were unreasonably given the name "Kentucky" or "Pennsylvania" rifles. American gunsmiths perfected the weapon and made it so accurate that British soldiers referred to them as "widow makers" or "orphan makers." Any redcoat hanging around 250 to 300 yards away from a rifleman stood a good chance, as the saying went, of being perforated.

That said, we should note that rifles and riflemen did not play all that great a role in the Revolution: (1) There weren't that many rifles; George Washington, for one, didn't like rifles and wanted more muskets. (2) Rifles were more awkward to handle and riflemen could deliver far fewer rounds per minute than could musketeers. (3) You could not attach a bayonet to a rifle because it would have been much too long and unwieldy to carry. If you no longer had time to load a rifle, and the enemy was charging you, your bayonetless rifle became something akin to an early baseball bat, with a redcoat analogous to a high fast ball coming out of the dappled sunlight on a September's day at Wrigley Field.

Sometimes riflemen weren't even wanted. The Maryland legislature once offered to send a rifle company to join the Continental army at Philadelphia. They were more or less refused. The secretary of the Continental Congress said the men would be welcome, but "if muskets were given them instead of rifles the service would be more benefitted, as there is a superabundance of riflemen in the Army." If Congress could, the secretary added, it would replace all the rifles with muskets, "as they are more easily kept in order, can be fired oftener and have the advantage of Bayonets."

There was, however, a mystique about the riflemen. Generally they were from the backwoods areas of the colonies, often coming from beyond the mountains (and then returning once the individual battle that concerned them was over) to fight in the Patriot cause. A rifleman often wore a fringed hunting shirt described as a "white frock"; George Washington apparently tried to have Congress adopt the hunting shirt as the official uniform of the Continental army. "No dress can be cheaper," Washington wrote, "nor more convenient, as the wearer may be cool in warm weather and warm in cool weather by putting on undercloaths which will not change the outward dress, Winter or Summer—Besides which it is a dress justly supposed to carry no small terror to the enemy, who think every such person is a complete marksman." Apparently George wanted them to look like riflemen even if he didn't want rifles. The shirts were made from the same general pattern—four pieces of deer leather or homespun linen, plus a double collar (large, so as to be of use in foul weather), and with fringes that allowed water to drip off the shirt faster. This kept the wearer from feeling wet quite so long and may have provided the world's first "fringe benefits." All of this would be sewed together with strips of cloth. Cloth shirts could be dyed just about any color available at the time, but often were left undyed and unbleached. They were cheap, efficient, and without too much difficulty most soldiers, given the necessity, could sew them themselves.

• • •

Perhaps as much as anything else, the bayonet was the thing that greatly contributed to the British army's equipment superiority. When the British finally drove the Americans off Bunker Hill, it may have been because of the Americans' lack of bayonets as much as their shortage of ammunition.

Each colony required its militiamen to furnish themselves not only with a flintlock musket but with a bayonet as well. Most, however, did not. There were several styles of bayonets prevalent in the Revolution; regretfully for the American side, redcoats generally carried them, Continentals frequently did not. The standard British bayonet was a triangular blade about sixteen inches long. It was square at the base, with a reinforcing band and zigzag notch that fit over a stud on the musket barrel, locking it in place. Toward the middle of the Revolution, the Continentals began receiving French-made muskets and therefore French-made bayonets. These were shorter, about fourteen to fourteen and a half inches long, also triangular. They, too, had zigzag slots in the base and, later on, had bands of reinforcing steel around the base.

Both officers and men sometimes preferred bayonets to bullets, especially during a sneak attack or during foul weather. As historian George Trevelyan puts it, a good rain "put military science four centuries back." A downpour reduced "good musketeers to the condition of indifferent spearmen; and the Americans were in worse case still, because some of their regiments were not even provided with bayonets." In fact, "British soldiers prayed for rain so they could attack with bayonets without fear of enemy fire."

Often as not, when troops went into battle they marched with bayonets fixed to unloaded muskets. During a surprise attack (such as at Trenton or Yorktown), officers simply didn't trust their men to carry loaded weapons; somebody certainly would panic and start firing. It was harder to make a mistake with a bayonet.

Paul Revere is primarily known as both a silversmith and a courier who took that midnight ride to Lexington. But he was also a dentist. Revere once ran an ad in the *Boston Gazette:*

Artificial Teeth—Paul Revere
Takes this method of returning his most Sincere Thanks to the Gentlemen and Ladies who have employed him in the care of their Teeth and he would now inform them and all others, who are so unfortunate as to lose their Teeth by accident & otherways, that he still continues the Business of a Dentist, and flatters himself that from the Experience he has had in fixing some Hundreds of Teeth, that he can fix them as well as any Surgeon-Dentist who ever came from London.

In late May 1775, Revere made false teeth for Patriot leader Dr. Joseph Warren. Later it would be Warren who sent Paul Revere out on his midnight ride to warn of the coming British. Now it was Revere the dentist who joined two artificial teeth together with silver wires for Joseph Warren.

It was the same Joseph Warren of whom Abigail Adams said, "We want him in the Senate; we want him in his profession; we want him in the field." The same Joseph Warren that Loyalist Ann Hulton referred to as "a rascally patriot and apothecary of this town." Which shows you can't please everybody.

Joseph Warren had been appointed major general of the Massachusetts militia but had not yet been given a commission; therefore, he had no military command and, officially, no title. So, during the Battle of Bunker Hill he was just another volunteer with a musket, and General Israel Putnam assigned him to a redoubt at Breed's Hill.

After that it's unclear what happened. He reportedly was seen "up to his knees in British blood," but it seemed that was the last time he was heard from. The battle was on a Saturday, but as late as Monday the 19th, his body had not been recovered. The Provincial Congress met at 3:00 P.M. to elect a replacement for Warren, who was "supposed to be killed in the late battle at Bunker's Hill." By Tuesday, still no word, and stories began making the rounds of his last words: "I am a dead man, fight on, my brave fellows, for the salvation of your country." As historian Richard Ketchum points out, however, it would have been a difficult statement for a man to make after being shot in the head. That, apparently, is what happened.

Toward the end of the battle, as the redcoats finally broke through a hastily built barrier, Joseph Warren was shot in the face and died. Now, days after the battle, dozens of men reported seeing him fall.

The retreating Patriots tried to remove their casualties, but they weren't able to get to all of them, and the body of Dr. Joseph Warren was left behind with several other dead. One story has it that General Howe was awakened the night of the battle, told that Dr. Warren had been killed, then buried; that John Burgoyne had come to see the body, and it was dug up, then reburied. Captain Walter Sloan Laurie, who had commanded the British detachment at Concord's North Bridge, and had been badly beaten in that fight, was in charge of a burial detail at Bunker Hill. He found Warren's body and, as he said, "stuffed the scoundrell with another Rebel into one hole and there he and his seditious principles may remain."

The two bodies, one "a person with a frock on," were buried in an unmarked grave. Nine months later, with the redcoats gone, the bodies were recovered. They found the two bodies. One was apparently a farmer wearing a farmer's frock. The other appeared to be Dr. Warren.

That's when Paul Revere used his records of Warren's teeth to identify the physician's body. It was the first known use of dental records to identify a corpse.

Before the British buried Joseph Warren, they went through his pockets and came up with some letters from James Lovell, and Warren's indiscretion of taking those letters into battle almost cost Lovell his life. In them Lovell had given Warren information about British troop strength and their disposition around Boston. Until then the redcoats hadn't known Lovell was a spy.

They recalled that Lovell's sisters had been spending a lot of time with the British colonel of artillery, Samuel Cleaveland. Obviously, Cleaveland had leaked information to the sisters, who leaked it to James, who leaked it to Warren. Two weeks after the Battle of Bunker Hill, the British tossed James Lovell into Boston Gaol, where he remained until the redcoats evacuated the town nine months later. They didn't release him but took him to Halifax, where he was visited in prison by his father, John Lovell.

John was a Loyalist master of the Boston Latin School until April 19, 1775, the day of the Battles at Lexington and Concord. Hearing of the two skirmishes, John Lovell dismissed classes and hung a sign on the door: WAR'S BEGUN—SCHOOL'S DONE. John Lovell went with the British when they evacuated Boston. It was there that the Tory father visited his Patriot son in prison. John Lovell was so shaken by events that he died brokenhearted two years later.

After taking James Lovell on to London, the British finally exchanged him for Colonel Philip Skene in November 1776. Back in America, James Lovell eventually was elected to Congress, then became receiver of continental taxes and collector of the port of Boston.

In the summer of 1775, a Yale College student began working on an invention he believed could put a quick end to the Revolution. David Bushnell left college and journeyed to Boston, where he would decide if he should quit school and join the American army. From a hill overlooking the port city, Bushnell looked down on the British army occupying the city and, especially, the British navy clogging the harbor. He realized that one supported the other, that without the navy the army could not exist long—food, arms, men, everything came to the army from outside Boston, and it was the navy who hauled everything and everyone.

What, he wondered, would happen if suddenly the British ships riding so peacefully at anchor were to be blown out of the water? Placing cannon on the heights was a good idea (and, indeed, this is what eventually happened), and that would send both army and navy scurrying away. But what if someone could sneak up *under* the ships, attack them *under*water? Great idea, he thought, and he returned to Saybrook, Connecticut, where he invented the submarine.

By the end of the year he had the outer hull completed, a vessel he christened the *Turtle.* David Bushnell shaped six-inch-thick oak timbers into something that looked like a child's top. Or, as Bushnell thought of it, a turtle, "two upper tortoise shells of equal size, joined together; the place of entrance into the vessel being represented by the opening made by the swell of the shells at the head of the animal." He bound the timbers with iron bands and coated the exterior of the vessel with tar to make it watertight.

He used a transverse beam as a seat and reinforced the sides against the pressure of the water. A brass hatch cover was hinged to an iron band, which itself strengthened the hull; the hatch could be screwed down until the *Turtle* was waterproof. Around the collar of the hatch were six small glass portholes, each about an inch in diameter. He hoped the portholes would give him enough light to see to navigate; he had a compass but no periscope. His depth gauge and compass were illuminated with a phosphorescent weed called foxfire.

Bushnell equipped the *Turtle* with pedal-powered screw propellers—the horizontal propeller was fitted to a shaft in front of the vessel; the smaller vertical propeller was twelve inches long and four inches broad, and was worked by a hand crank. It took a strong arm and a lot of energy to propel the craft. Bushnell added a hand-operated drill, hoping that once the submarine operator found a victim ship, he could bore through its hull and attach a bomb.

For stability David Bushnell built into the base seven hundred pounds of lead, about two hundred pounds of it detachable for instant surfacing if the *Turtle* got into trouble. For regular surfacing the vessel's bilge tanks would be pumped out. The *Turtle* carried enough air for the one-man crew to remain underwater about a half hour.

Bushnell's brother, Ezra, was a sergeant in the Continental army, and he received permission from George Washington to go to Connecticut with David and test the invention in the Connecticut River. David was too frail to operate the submarine, so the huskier Ezra became the crew. It was a secret project, but in October 1775, one Samuel Osgood wrote to Congressman John Adams from New York: "The famous water machine from Connecticut is every Day expected in Camp; it must unavoidably be a clumsy Business, as its Weight is about a Tun. People say it will take a year to put it into action against the enemy."

Secrets of war seldom are as secret as they're hoped to be, and the existence of the *Turtle* was no different. The Bushnell brothers told a friend, Dr. Benjamin Gale of Killingworth, Connecticut, what they were doing. Gale told a friend, Congressman Silas Deane, who was in Philadelphia, describing the submarine in detail, outlining the difficulties the brothers were having getting parts, and even told of what the Bushnells hoped to accomplish.

In the Revolution your local tavern keeper was also your local postman, with letters being kept behind the bar until the designated recipient showed up and asked for them. In this case, the local tavern keeper in Killingworth was a Loyalist. When he saw a letter addressed to a member of the Continental Congress, he opened it up and read it. Realizing what he had discovered, the tavern keeper copied the letter and forwarded it to Governor William Tryon, formerly of North Carolina, but now in New York. Fortunately for the *Turtle*, Governor Tryon didn't take the information seriously. He wrote the commander in chief of the British navy squadron in North America, Vice Admiral Molyneux Shuldham: "The great news of the day with us is now to Destroy the Navy, a certain Mister Bushnell has completed his Machine. . . . You may expect to see the Ships in smoke." Apparently Admiral Shuldham thought so little of the information that he didn't even reply to Tryon.

So, early in the new year, David and Ezra Bushnell took the world's first submarine out into Long Island Sound, assuming conditions there would be similar to those in Boston harbor. From the deck of their sloop they lowered the *Turtle* into the water; Ezra climbed in, screwed tight the hatch, and slowly submerged to the bottom of the Sound. Then he rose and circled the sloop. Less than ten minutes later Ezra surfaced. It was a success, and the brothers shook hands. Now they had to find a way to attach an explosive device to a ship's hull.

At Yale David Bushnell had surprised some of his teachers who believed gunpowder would not explode underwater. As a freshman he said he'd "accidentally discovered" that it could be accomplished. "Once I knew this hitherto undiscovered fact," he wrote, "it became a controlling force in my life. Somehow, I knew that I was destined to put this to awesome use."

Bushnell met with George Washington, explaining the plan to attach a device to a British ship in Boston harbor. The general was skeptical but gave the brothers money and half a dozen assistants.

Just about the time the brothers were set for their first attack, Ezra came down with what was called the "camp disorder"—most likely typhus. Doctors believed it would be weeks before he'd be strong enough to work the gears, crank the propellers, and guide his way through Boston's murky waters. Through General Samuel Parsons, Bushnell came across twenty-seven-year-old Sergeant Ezra Lee of the Connecticut Line. He was General Parsons's brother-in-law.

Back in Saybrook, David Bushnell trained Sergeant Lee, and when it looked as if this second Ezra was ready, they traveled to New York, where the Continental army was in disarray. It was early September and Washington estimated his strength to be twenty thousand effective troops; General Howe had at least five thousand more. It was likely to get worse, with many in the militia set to go home. General Israel Putnam suggested that the American army abandon New York, burning the town as it left.

Bushnell went to General Parsons, urging an immediate attack on Admiral Howe's flagship. Parsons agreed.

It was September 6, 1776. The *Turtle* was hidden on board a sloop at the South Ferry landing. Bushnell decided to attack that night. The *Turtle* was slowly lowered into the water. Sergeant Lee squeezed through the hatch, then screwed it shut. The tanks were flooded, and the submarine began sinking. Lee pumped out the water, and the vessel rose. Everything was ready. Two whaleboats took Ezra Lee and the submarine in tow, heading out into the harbor for its first combat mission. Despite the darkness they couldn't get too near the British fleet; however, as Lee put it, they came "as nigh the ships as they dared and cast me off."

Almost immediately Lee was in trouble; apparently no one had bothered to check the tide, and it was going out, taking the *Turtle* with it. First Ezra Lee was swept past the *Eagle*, then for two and a half hours he had to paddle and crank just to keep from being washed out to sea. Finally "the tide slacked," he said, "so that I could get along side of the man-of-war which lay above the transports."

Lee had the hatch open, his head sticking out just above water. He could "see the men on deck and hear them talk." Once he reached the *Eagle*'s stern, Sergeant Lee "shut down all the doors, sunk down and came under the bottom of the ship. Up with the screw against the bottom." But the drill "would not enter." He tried again, cranking and cranking the drill. Still, it wouldn't bite into the ship's hull. Each time he tried, the *Turtle* floated away from the target. British ships were being coated with copper sheathing at the time, and Lee thought that was the problem. It wasn't. David Bushnell had planned on that, and the drill could have cut through. What he didn't plan on was Sergeant Lee aiming at the iron bar connecting the rudder hinge with the stern. "Had he moved a few inches," Bushnell believed, "which he might have done without rowing, I have no doubt he would have found wood where he might have fixed the screw."

Trying to find a soft spot on the *Eagle*'s hull, Lee accidentally released some of the submarine's ballast, and the *Turtle* shot to the surface. It was almost dawn, and he didn't want to be seen, so Lee turned a valve, letting water in. He "sunk again like a porpoise."

Realizing that at any time the British fleet would awaken and begin sending boats across the harbor, Lee believed that "the best generalship was to retreat as fast as I could." He began paddling away. It was a four-mile trip that passed by the British-held Governor's Island. But Lee was unfamiliar with New York harbor, and his compass did him only so much good. He was "obliged to rise up every few minutes to see that I sailed in the right direction."

Once more the tide worked against him, this time sweeping him toward Governor's Island. Rising to the surface once more, he saw "3 or 400 men . . . upon the parapet [observing] me." Quickly the British launched a twelve-oared boat with a load of troops to see what this strange sight was. As the English neared, Sergeant Lee released the waterproof bomb he had been paddling around New York harbor all night; the clock and gunlock mechanism automatically began ticking away.

Lee later said he hoped "that if they should take me they would likewise pick up the [explosive] magazine, and then we should all be blown up together." But when the British saw the magazine, instead of being curious enough to fish it out of the water, they began rowing for shore as fast as they could. Just about then, time ran out on the clock-gunlock. The magazine exploded, "throwing up large bodies of water to an immense height."

The blast shook up the town, reportedly knocking people out of their beds. Nobody on either side, however, was hurt in the world's first submarine attack. About all that Sergeant Lee had done was to waste 150 pounds of badly needed gunpowder.

But it encouraged both David Bushnell and the American military. General Putnam was so cheered, he vowed that the Connecticut genius, as he called the young inventor, would have the full cooperation of the American army.

A year or so later Bushnell tried again, this time attacking the British frigate *Cerberus* off New London, Connecticut. When *Cerberus* (named after the dog which, in Greek mythology, guarded the gates of Hell) reached Boston in May 1775, it was immortalized with the following bit of doggerel:

> Behold the Cerberus the Atlantic plough,
> Her precious cargo, Burgoyne, Clinton, Howe.
> Bow, wow, wow!

To avoid the earlier mistake of not being able to drill into the target ship's hull, Bushnell told Sergeant Lee to attach the bomb—he called it a torpedo—near the ship's waterline. This time, just as Lee was about to release his torpedo, he was spotted by a British sailor and was forced to dive.

Underwater, the *Turtle*'s depth gauge malfunctioned. Not really a gauge, it was a cork that bobbed up and down, giving the pilot an idea of how deep the submarine was. With his cork not floating properly, Lee took the vessel to the river bottom. Once again he found himself being swept out to sea and had to spend hours paddling to safety.

By then the English navy had tired of the idea of someone or something diving beneath it and trying to attach a bomb to its ships' hulls. They decided to sweep the Hudson River of any and all floating or sunken American weapons. Besides the *Turtle*'s attack, several ships and barges had been set on fire and sent sailing against the English fleet. British frigates set out to attack anything on the river larger than a rowboat. Among the American vessels they assaulted was the galley *Crane*, mother ship to the *Turtle*. The *Crane* was sunk and with it the *Turtle*. It was the last time a submarine would be tried until the Civil War, when Confederate forces sent several undersea boats against the enemy, an enemy who this time would be American.

The *Turtle* may have been less than a total success, but the army recognized Bushnell's explosive abilities. The next time he put those abilities to use was after the British had won control of the Delaware River in the campaign for Philadelphia. Working under Bushnell's directions blacksmiths and gunsmiths built twenty heavy oak barrels, banding them with iron. Bushnell described his coming assault on the Royal Navy:

> I fixed several kegs under water, charged with powder to explode upon touching anything as they floated with the tide. I set them afloat in the river, above the English shipping at Philadelphia, to fall with the ebb [tide] upon the shipping.

The weather—it was midwinter—worked against Bushnell and his barrels. Ice was forming on the river as the kegs were set afloat. Because of the ice it was morning before they reached their intended targets. Seeing the kegs floating nearby, British seamen tried hauling them on board ship. At least one of the kegs exploded, and as David Bushnell put it, "Several persons who imprudently handled it too freely were killed or injured."

The English navy wasn't certain what the kegs were, but they knew they didn't like them; so marksmen began shooting at any object floating by. Only days later did the British realize that what they had been firing at were kegs full of gunpowder.

Once again David Bushnell's plan to attack the British fleet had failed. The New Jersey *Gazette* reported the incident:

> Yesterday . . . several kegs . . . made their appearance. An alarm was immediately spread through the city. Various reports prevailed, filling the city and the royal troops with consternation. Some reported that the kegs were filled with armed rebels who were to issue forth in the dead of night and take the city by surprise, just as the Grecians of old did from their wooden horse at the siege of Troy. . . .

[The] battle began, and it was surprising to behold the incessant blaze that was kept up against the enemy, the kegs. . . .

The action began about sunrise, and would have been completed with great success by noon, had not an old market woman, coming down the river with provisions, let a small keg of butter fall overboard, which . . . floated down to the scene of action. At the sight of this unexpected reinforcement of the enemy, the battle was renewed with fresh fury, and the firing was incessant 'til the evening closed the affair.

Writer Francis Hopkinson, a signer of the Declaration of Independence, made the best of it, writing the poem "The Battle of the Kegs." It later was set to music.

> The cannon roar from shore to shore,
> The small arms make a rattle,
> Since wars began I'm sure no man
> Ere saw so strange a battle.
>
> These kegs, 'tis said, though strongly made
> Of rebel staves and hoops, sir,
> Could not oppose their powerful foes,
> The conquering British troops, sir!
>
> Such feats did they perform that day
> Against those wicked kegs, sir,
> That years to come if they get home,
> They'll make their boasts and brag, sir.

Much of the way American troops drilled—the way they marched, the way they loaded their weapons—may have been due to Frederick William Augustus, Baron von Steuben. He talked George Washington into issuing his famous "Regulations for the Order and Discipline of the Troops of the United States." It became a manual for U.S. Army drill sergeants for the next thirty-three years, known as the "blue book."

Von Steuben was about Washington's age at the time of Valley

Forge, forty-seven or so, and although he spoke no English, he did speak with authority. Von Steuben had met both Silas Deane and Benjamin Franklin in Europe, and it was through them that he came to America. Unlike some others, however, he didn't demand to be a general; instead, he volunteered to serve without rank or pay. In fact, he didn't want to command troops in battle. He wanted to drill them.

In ways that even modern troops would recognize, he trained America's first army. He got them up at three in the morning. He marched them around camp. He taught them how to handle their rusty muskets in something like a professional manner. To get his orders across, he'd first issue them in broken French to an aide, Captain Benjamin Walker, who'd then reissue them in America's version of His Majesty's language.

It may have been the picture that did the job. A short, powerfully built, chubby, graying officer standing in front of a shivering, ill-clad, underfed band of awkward boys and old men. "*Viens*, Walker, *mon ami*," he'd say to Captain Walker, "God dam de *gaucheries* of *des badauts. Je ne puis plus.*" Which roughly translates as "Now, my friend Walker, let's get these goddamn bums moving."

He seems to have loved the rebel soldiers, who often laughed at him, and he treated them with kindness. They usually returned that kindness, but still their lack of training often got the best of von Steuben. "*Sacre* Godamn!" he once called out to Captain Walker. "These fellows won't do what I tell them! Come swear for me!"

Von Steuben had to adapt in other ways as well. As he wrote to a friend back in Europe, with Prussians or Austrians, "You say to your soldier, 'Do this,' and he does it, but I am obliged to say [to Americans], 'This is the reason you ought to do that.' And then he does it."

Depending upon which source you choose to believe, von Steuben was either a genius whose "general staff training and service has not been appreciated," or his "considerable services have commonly been overpraised." In any event, when von Steuben presented himself to Deane and Franklin, claiming he was "a Lieutenant General in the service of the King of Prussia," he wasn't telling the truth. In the first place, the name he'd been baptized under was Fredrich Wilhelm Ludolf Gerhard Augustin von Steuben; taking into consideration the American way with words, he shortened his name somewhat. And he wasn't a lieutenant general but a half-pay captain; he'd been discharged from Frederick the Great's army in 1763. Later von Steuben became a chamberlain in the court of Hohenzollern-Hechingen, where he attained the title *Frieherr,* or baron.

By 1775, after a trip to France, von Steuben was in Germany and in debt. He tried to catch on with several foreign armies—France, Austria, and Baden—but nobody seems to have wanted him. Until Deane and Franklin and the American cause came along. With the financial aid of France's Beaumarchais, who advanced von Steuben funds from that phony Hortalez & Cie. outfit, the captain-who-would-be-general was on his way.

Some critics claim the American army wasn't really a rabble in arms when von Steuben joined the forces and by far not a perfect fighting machine when they marched out of camp in June. Yet he instilled in the army a sense that they were something other than a rag-tag and bob-tail bunch who would run away at the first sign of a British redcoat. He established a model company—100 hand-picked men—then spread his instructions throughout the army.

A lot of what he drummed into the heads of Continental soldiers was elementary sanitation. Animal carcasses should not be left to rot above ground. Latrines should not be built close to kitchen areas, and, for God's sake, use the latrines, don't just relieve yourself wherever you stand. Wash your face and hands at least once a day, and bathe whenever the creek is high enough. Under von Steuben, American officers began inspecting the troops' tents and huts and making certain the men used clean straw for bedding.

Von Steuben was at the Battle of Monmouth Court House, when Charles Lee seemed unable to move. He challenged Lee to a duel when Lee said von Steuben was a "very distant spectator" at the battle, but he withdrew the challenge when Lee claimed he meant no offense. When Nathanael Greene took control of the Continental army in the south, he also took von Steuben with him. In Virginia he was with Washington at the siege of Yorktown. Now he was a real general and fought with distinction.

By 1783, by an act of, first, the Pennsylvania legislature, and later the New York Assembly, von Steuben became an American citizen. As a volunteer for most of the Revolution, von Steuben went heavily into debt; he hoped Congress would pay him the $60,000 he believed his service had been worth. After the Treaty of Paris, Congress did give Steuben a financial award, a pension of about $2,500 a year. The State of New York chipped in with a gift of 16,000 acres of overgrown and virtually worthless, wild land.

Finally Alexander Hamilton arranged funds for von Steuben by setting up a mortgage on the general's acreage. It would be years later that the aging bachelor straightened out his finances.

He spent winters in New York City and summers on his property in the Mohawk Valley. When he died in 1794, he willed his property to his old friend and translator, Benjamin Walker: *Viens,* Walker, *mon ami.* God dam de *gaucheries* of *des badauts. Je ne puis plus.*

CHAPTER ELEVEN

Rituals of Life:
History with the Bark on

What is the first part of politics? Education. The second? Education. And the third?
Education.

—Jules Michelet, Le Peuple

I cannot live without books.

—Thomas Jefferson

Pre-Revolution America wasn't known for its schools, either the readin', writin', and 'rithmetic variety or colleges. At the time, the colonies could boast of less than a dozen colleges: Harvard, William and Mary, Yale, the University of Pennsylvania (originally, the College, Academy, and Charitable School of Philadelphia), Moravian State University in Pennsylvania, the College of New Jersey (now Princeton University), today's Washington and Lee University, Columbia University (then King's College), Rhode Island's Brown University, Rutgers (Queen's College it was called then), and the College of Charleston, South Carolina.

By the end of the seventeenth century most colonies had newspapers whose print shops frequently were also bookstores—some imported books, others published right there in the shop. Massachusetts Bay was the first colony to have a printing press. It was operated in Cambridge beginning in 1640, only three years after the founding of Harvard. Perhaps the first important book to be published in the colonies came out of that printing shop: *The Whole Book of Psalms* edited by Richard Mather.

Early on, the Mathers realized that they could propagate their brand of Christianity through books of their choice. Together Richard's son Increase and Increase's son Cotton published more

259

than four hundred titles aimed at disseminating and propagating the religious and secular ideas of Puritanism. They supplied peddlers with religious tracts and printed sermons, and even sent them to South Carolina to keep residents of the southern colony from falling into the heresy of Anglicanism.

Over the years many wealthy colonials built up large private libraries. Both Cotton Mather of Boston and William Byrd II of Virginia counted more than 3,600 volumes in their private libraries, and if ever there were two beings of the same species less alike, it was Mather and Byrd.

Libraries were opened in Boston and Philadelphia, the Library Company of Philadelphia formed by Benjamin Franklin in March 1732 with fifty members investing. Franklin ordered 45 books (at a cost of £100) from London bookseller James Logan. By 1734, the company had over 250 books as well as 25 periodicals in its collection, and by 1741, it counted nearly 400 volumes and over 70 members.

Newport, Rhode Island, had its Society for the Promotion of Knowledge and Virtue by a Free Conversation beginning in 1730, and, after a local benefactor saw what was going on with Franklin's library, the society added its own set of books. Charlestown, Massachusetts, began its Library Society in 1748, and Boston got its first circulating library in 1756, with twelve hundred volumes. Its members paid annual dues of £1.8.

A decade after founding the Philadelphia library, Franklin was at it again, this time establishing the American Philosophical Society.

John Adams believed he lacked the education (and probably the smarts) to be president, yet today some say he was our most underrated president. Thomas Jefferson, the man many of those same critics say was our most *over*rated president, still is seen as the nation's early intellect of record. Adams was a Harvard man, as they say, while Jefferson attended the College of William and Mary and later "read" law in Williamsburg. James Madison left his native Virginia to attend the College of New Jersey, where he stayed for an extra year after graduating, possibly unable to quit those wild and crazy Princeton parties. George Washington never went to college, and, in fact, had no formal education after about age fourteen. He did, however, have "a commission from the President and Masters of the College [of

William and Mary] appointing him surveyor of that county." Interestingly he received his commission *after* he'd worked for a while as a surveyor. Washington wasn't the only surveyor to become president of the United States, just the first. For a while Abraham Lincoln also was a surveyor.

Life in colonial America was sometimes rich, occasionally rewarding, often deadly, and periodically perverted. Sometimes our ancestors were burdened with sins we can only imagine today. To cope with this problem, they invented a variety of interesting ways to punish "sinners," everything from forcing unwed mothers to wear a "scarlet letter" on their clothing to nailing a "criminal's" ear to the jailhouse door and even drilling holes in thieves' tongues.

At the turn of the eighteenth century the average lifespan for a male in Andover, Massachusetts, was sixty-five years; for a female it was sixty-two. In Middlesex, Virginia, however, a man could expect to live only to age forty-nine and women only to age forty. One child in five lived to age twenty.

An individual nearing age sixty undoubtedly thought of himself as growing old. Those, according to Puritan Increase Mather, "who have attained to threescore [sixty years] are everywhere accounted as old men." Only about 5 percent of the population lived beyond sixty, and for them their final years often were filled with misery.

For many of those to whom we refer today as "senior citizens," the highest rank of society was accorded; their longevity, after all, was a sign from God of chosen status. "If a man is favored with long life," Mather rationalized, "it is God that has lengthened his days."

As in just about everything else, however, people often did not practice what their preachers preached. If a man could no longer farm his land, his son or sons likely would take over the property and virtually leave him out in the cold. If a man died and left a widow, and if he had not prepared a will specifying her rights, the widow, too, might be left out in the cold.

Stephen Hopkins was sixty-nine and afflicted with palsy when he signed the Declaration of Independence. "My hand," he said, "trembles, but my heart does not!" Edward Rutledge, on the other hand, was less than half Hopkins's age and, at age twenty-six, was the youngest signer. Benjamin Franklin, of course, at age seventy, was the oldest signer.

Thomas Jefferson was a young thirty-three when he took quill pen in hand to write the Declaration, while Paul Revere was a comparatively old man at age forty when he took that midnight ride. George Washington was just forty-four when he fathered a country (if not a child) in 1776, and John Adams was forty-one when he wrote Abigail that he was "Yours, yours, yours." By the time John Paul Jones was twenty-nine he had beaten a murder charge, been commissioned an officer in the fledgling U.S. Navy, and become involved with several mistresses older than he.

Plainly, during the Revolution experiences varied from person to person, and age was not necessarily either a drawback from action or a precursor to heroics. Some individuals accumulated both influence and authority at a young age. Just as they did with wealth, they carried power throughout their lives. Others—the retired, the childless, the widowed, and the poor—often "found themselves segregated from society in their last years."

While Increase Mather suggested that the elderly were favored by God, evangelist John Wesley suggested younger individuals ignore parental teachings. Wesley was one of the new lights of the Great Awakening and preached against the young allowing the elderly to control their lives. One of the founders of the Methodist movement, Wesley had this advice for young women:

> Your mother or your husband's mother may live with you, and you will do well to show her all possible respect. But let her on no account have the least share in the management of your children. She will undo all that you have done; she will give them their own will in all things. She would humor them to the destruction of their souls if not their bodies.

Before 1750, the Philadelphia Almshouse had never admitted more than fifty paupers a year. But beginning in that year they enrolled nearly five hundred annually. About a third of the group cited old age as the primary cause of their destitution. Clearly something was changing. Town records began listing the destitute aged not just by their names but by the derogatory prefix "old." As the Revolution came and went, "Old Tom" and "Old Sarah" and "Old Josiah" had passed beyond the realm of individuals and become simply overaged and poor.

Which is to say, in its treatment of the elderly, society hasn't changed much over the past two hundred years.

America's Founding Fathers were not especially devout church-goers, certainly not to the extent some modern-day religious politi-cians claim. Not Washington, who attended church only on special occasions; not Jefferson, who at various times was called anti-Chris-tian, an infidel, and "a Virginia Voltaire" (he finally became known as a deist, acknowledging the existence of God on reason but re-jecting religion as such); neither Franklin, John Adams, nor Hamil-ton could be listed as ardent churchgoers. When the Continental Congress decreed a day of fasting and prayer in 1776 "to confess and bewail our manifold sins . . . through the merits and mediation of Jesus Christ," Washington omitted the reference to Christ when he read the decree to his troops.

Franklin professed a belief in God but said there might be more than one God. He did, however, strongly believe in an afterlife. In 1756, when his brother John died, Benjamin Franklin suggested to mourners, "Why should you and I be grieved at this, since we are soon to follow, and know where to find him?" In his *Autobiography* Franklin wrote; "I soon became a thorough Deist." Thomas Paine was not only a deist, but was vocally aggressive about it.

When asked about a rising missionary zeal in 1816, John Adams asked: "Would it not be better, to apply these pious subscriptions, to purify Christendom from the corruptions of Christianity, rather than to propagate these corruptions in Europe, Asia, Africa, and America?"

Alexander Hamilton apparently was religious early in life, be-came something of a backslider in middle life, and then, in either a stroke of precognition or good luck, returned to religion just in time to be gunned down by Aaron Burr. A college roommate re-membered Hamilton "praying upon his knees both night and morning." During the Revolution and while secretary of state,

Alexander Hamilton's actions, certainly, and possibly his beliefs in God, declined. Hamilton at best was indifferent to religion, but later he bemoaned the religious beliefs of his enemy Jefferson. But when his political career began to decline, he once more became intensely religious.

James Madison studied religion while at the College of New Jersey at Princeton, and there was talk of him becoming a minister. An ancestor, also named James Madison, had been president of the College of William and Mary and first bishop of the Protestant Episcopal Church in Virginia. Madison-the-president-to-be later sponsored a measure in the Virginia House of Delegates that amounted to the disestablishment of the Anglican Church. Later he (along with Jefferson corresponding from France) wrote the Virginia Statute on Religious Liberty. In pushing for the statute, in a letter to Jefferson, Madison wrote: "Who does not see that the same authority which can establish Christianity, in exclusion of all other Religions, may establish with the same ease any particular sect of Christians, in exclusion of all other sects?"

Fifty years before the Revolution, religious revivals swept the colonies, dramatically transforming the social situation of the colonies and setting up a dichotomy between the haves and have-nots. The Great Awakening, as it was called, was a response to the growing prosperity of the American colonies. It was the nation-to-be's first big religious revival, and it came (as other revivals would later) with tent meetings, converts, and speaking in tongues. It was a religious revival that called for a return to Spartan piety, even to giving up more colorful and fashionable clothes and return to the black, gray, and white style of New England's seventeenth-century Puritans. It was a time when the colonies were described as one of "the most unchurched regions in all of Christendom."

The Great Awakening stimulated a new attitude in the relationship between men and the state; religious ideas could not be separated from daily life. It showed a growing religious diversity in the colonies and challenged the strict Puritan concepts prevalent in New England and widespread in the other colonies.

Among the Great Awakening's proponents there was a strong belief in the tortures of hell awaiting sinners. They only hinted that God was reasonable and would likely react favorably to those who, while not perfect, had good intentions.

By 1775, colonists had a new belief—they had the right to rebel from England.

It is often difficult to read Revolutionary War newspapers. There's the obvious age of the paper, which sometimes causes letters and words to fade beyond recognition. Sometimes microfilm and microfiche are out of focus. And there's that bewildering habit of using ſ in place of an s in the middle of words, as in Williamſburg or Engliſh. They would also use a strange f for s at the beginning or end of a word, as in syſtem of almoſt. More often, however, there is the plain difference in language.

From the very first in America, the English language was spoken differently from the way it was in England. We are truly two nations divided by a common language.

In physically isolated areas such as Tangier Island, Virginia, you still can hear colonial-era English being spoken. Ask a Tangier waterman (they're the ones who make a living hauling in crabs) not to go away, and he'll answer something like "I'll here be waiting." Suggest he might want a beer on a hot summer day and he'll say, "Don't have to worrysome about that none," which means, of course, Yes, I'd love to have one, thank you. Until recent years the area around Nags Head, North Carolina, was noted for its natives who spoke almost pure Elizabethan English; thanks (?) to radio and television and an influx of tourists, the locals now sound about like the rest of us. In New England, of course, natives continue to add or subtract the letter "r" at their own choosing.

Revolutionary-era diaries and journals often use different words. Take "pretty," as in a "pretty young man." It has nothing to do with the young man's beauty or lack of same; in the eighteenth century "pretty" meant "brave" or "gallant." Strangely enough, often when the Scots said "pretty" they meant "stout." An eighteenth-century "mechanic" would be any skilled laborer, not necessarily a person who, for example, works on auto engines. During the Revolution, soldiers from one side might "amuse" their enemies, meaning they would "divert the attention" of the enemy, that is, mislead them. If a general was "sensible" of the enemy, he was, in our terms, "aware." It was during the time that writers began adding "er" to an object, making one who works with a dress a "dresser"; one who works with armor became an "armorer."

Words fascinated Thomas Jefferson. He invented words, used new words, and twisted words. An argument between Thomas Jefferson and John Adams during the writing of the Declaration of Independence is frequently repeated and sworn to and argued over by grammarians. Jefferson insisted that "all men are created equal; that they are endowed by their Creator with Certain *in*alienable rights. . . ." Adams claimed the word was *un*alienable and won the argument by getting to the printer and having his way before the Declaration was published.

"There are so many differences between us and England," Jefferson wrote, adding, "*Judicious neology* can alone give strength and copiousness to language, and enable it to be the vehicle of new ideas." "Neology," by the way, means "the use of new words," something of which Jefferson greatly approved. His British critics, however, didn't always approve. For instance, the word *belittle*. When he took to using the word, it was ridiculed in London.

Benjamin Franklin taught himself to read by copying essays from London's *The Spectator* and became a printer by trade; his tombstone bears that simple legend: BENJAMIN FRANKLIN, PRINTER. Marvelous understatement.

It was Franklin who really started America on something of a language of its own, certainly its own spelling. In 1768, he wrote *A Scheme for a New Alphabet and a Reformed Mode of Spelling*. "Honour" would become "honor." "Theatre" would be "theater," "plough" would be simplified to "plow," and "curb" instead of "kerb."

In the early 1780s, the Marquis de Chastellux, a French officer and writer who was with Washington at Yorktown, wrote that some Americans "propose introducing a new language; and some persons were desirous, for the convenience of the public, that the *Hebrew* should be substituted for English."

Several members of Congress, who were obviously angry at the former mother country, argued that the new United States of America should adopt as its official language, French. Or German. A few even suggested we adopt the Greek language, a proposal that was rejected, however, on the grounds "it would be more convenient for us to keep the language as it was, and make the English speak Greek."

In 1782, the citizens of the rebelling colonies were proudly christened "Americans." And in 1802, the U.S. Congress first recorded use of the phrase "the American language."

Noah Webster solved the problem. Born in West Hartford, Connecticut, in 1758, he graduated from Yale and then studied law. Later turning to teaching, he became dissatisfied with the texts then available, so he wrote his own—a speller, a grammar, and a reader—that were later collected as *A Grammatical Institute of the English Language.* It was an immediate and immense success. Americans not only wanted to rebel against England for taxation and representation purposes, they carried it into the spoken and written word. In 1789, Webster wrote *Dissertations on the English Language.*

His *American Speller* even taught students how to sound out words: a-d becomes *ad;* m-i becomes *my;* r-a *ra* for "admira." T-i-o-n was sounded out as *shun,* and it became "admiration." It was an entirely new system.

Webster earned one cent royalty per copy of the *American Speller,* and it sold over eighty million copies in his lifetime. It was second only to the Bible, which Webster's salesmen often also sold as they traveled the country.

"Our American honor," Webster wrote, "requires us to have a system of our own, in language as well as government." In 1828, he wrote *An American Dictionary of the English Language.* It is what today we refer to simply as *Webster's.*

"Waggon" became wagon. "Fibre" was fiber. It is the American defense, not the English "defence." And Americans use tires, not "tyres." Webster changed our spelling, which in turn changed our speech, which in turn even changed the way we look. Articulating words certain ways forces us to hold our mouths, therefore our entire faces, in certain positions. Americans neither sound nor look like the English or the French or the Irish.

American Loyalists were driven into exile, partly by mob violence and partly to protect their investments. Some went to England, some to the West Indies, but a majority went to Canada, where they compromised between British and American spelling. It brought about something of language schizophrenia. Canada is a country where "chesterfield" is used for sofa and "eh" is almost universal. *Canajan, eh?* Where else would people live with such a compromise as "tire centre"?

CHAPTER TWELVE

And the Winner Is?:
The Trenches of Yorktown

Soon after landing we marched to Williamsburg, where we joined General Lafayette, and very soon after, our whole army arriving, we prepared to move down and pay our old acquaintance, the British, at Yorktown, a visit.
　　　　　　　　　　　—Pvt. Joseph Plumb Martin, Continental Army

The late affair has almost broke my heart.
　　　　　　　　—General Lord Charles Cornwallis, January 21, 1781

Because of his own bout with smallpox, George Washington insisted on his troops being inoculated against the disease. "I took that delectable disease, the itch," Private Joseph Martin wrote. He added: "We had no opportunity, or, at least, we had nothing to cure ourselves with during the whole season." They asked their officers "for assistance to clear ourselves from it, but all we could get was, 'Bear it as patiently as you can.'"

Riding a series of fast horses over bad roads, it took Paul Revere six days to ride from Boston to Philadelphia, carrying news that Britain had closed the port. It typically took eight days for a letter to travel from New York City to Yorktown, Virginia. It may be this lack of easily traveled roads that allowed the Continental and French armies to beat the British/German coalition at Yorktown.

In the summer of 1775, London authorities had developed plans for a military expedition to the South. Virginia, Georgia, and North and South Carolina had already driven their royal governors out of office. In early 1776, believing the British might attack Charleston, Congress authorized South Carolina to increase the number of Continental army regiments from twelve to fourteen.

When Washington learned in January 1776 that the British were mounting a seaborne operation against New York, he ordered General Charles Lee to take command of Fort Lee, across the Hudson River in New Jersey. Congress, however, ordered Lee to take command of troops in Charleston. On June 1, Lee reported that the British fleet had appeared off Charleston but then had put back to sea. Three weeks later they were back.

Colonel William Moultrie (whose brother John was a Tory) tried to improve the fort, but he'd been forced to use inferior materials: parallel walls made of palmetto logs with a sixteen-foot space between filled with sand. By the time the British attack began, Moultrie had managed to finish only the wall facing the ocean. The side walls had been raised only seven feet high and the northern tip of the island, Long Island (now the Isle of Palms), was open and undefended. When Lee reached Sullivan's Island he took one look at the fort and said it would be impossible to defend. It was "absolutely necessary," he said, "to have a bridge of boats for a retreat." So Lee devised a floating bridge across the mile-wide cove, but it was abandoned when it was learned the bridge wouldn't support troops. Lee's next bit of advice? Since there was "no way to retreat," abandon Fort Sullivan. Otherwise, as Colonel Moultrie remembered him saying, "the garrison would be sacrificed; nay, he called it a 'slaughter pen.'" Neither Moultrie nor South Carolina Governor John Rutledge agreed, believing the fort could be defended. They were right and Lee was wrong.

Moultrie later wrote that "Capt. Lamperer, a brave and experienced seaman" pointed to the British men-of-war off the island and said, "'when those ships . . . come to lay along side your fort, they will knock it down in half an hour.'" Moultrie replied, "Then . . . we will lay behind the ruins and prevent their men from landing."

It helped that three British ships went aground on the shoals off the island and that the British army's landing on nearby Long Island didn't work out. Oh, General Clinton landed on the island, but when he tried to cross over to the fort, he made only a halfhearted attempt at an amphibious assault and abandoned the plan. If Clinton had really tried, it would have been easy to cross over, as the general himself later discovered. Water in the channel separating Long Island from Sullivan's Island was only eighteen inches deep, not the minimum of seven feet that he'd been told.

On June 28, the British fleet opened fire on Fort Sullivan. The bombardment began about ten in the morning and continued past eight at night. At least nine English ships were in the attack and mounted more than 240 cannon. Often, balls from three or four English warships hit at the same time.

Meanwhile, in the distance, Colonel Moultrie saw General Lee approaching the fort he said would be a slaughter pen. As Moultrie wrote, "Gen. Lee paid us a visit through a heavy line of fire and pointed two or three guns himself; then he said to me, 'Colonel, I see you are doing very well here. You have no occasion for me. I will go up to town again,' and left us."

As it turned out, Moultrie's local construction materials worked very well, thank you. The palmetto logs were soggy and didn't shatter the way other wood might have. And, as anyone who has walked the soft sands of Sullivan's Island beaches can imagine, the impact of a cannonball is cushioned. Only shots fired through parapet openings, the embrasures, caused injury to the American troops.

Lee later wrote that

the behaviour of the garrison, both men and officers, with Colonel Moultrie at their head, I confess astonished me. It was brave to the last degree. I had no idea that so much coolness and intrepidity could be displayed by a collection of raw recruits.

There were, of course, wounded among the defending troops—men losing an arm or leg to a cannonball. "Fight on, my brave boys," one sergeant is quoted as saying, "don't let liberty expire with me today." In a letter to his wife, Major Barnard Elliott told of the most famous incidents of the Battle of Fort Sullivan:

My old grenadier, Serj. [William] Jasper, upon the shot carrying away the flag-staff, called out to Col. Moultrie: "Colonel, don't let us fight without our flag!"

"What can you do?" replied the Colonel. "The staff is broke."

"Then, sir," said he, "I'll fix it to a halberd and place it on the merlon [a section of the parapet] of the bastion next to the enemy," which he did, through the thickest fire.

It was more than simple bravado. Without a flag both the enemy and the thousands of Americans might believe that the fort had surrendered. When Governor Rutledge later gave Jasper a sword and tried to commission him an officer, the sergeant took the sword but turned down the commission on grounds of being "ignorant." Jasper later became a roving scout under Moultrie and Generals Francis Marion and Benjamin Lincoln. During the assault on Savannah in October 1779, Jasper once again tried to save the colors. This time, however, he was killed. One of the redoubts at Fort Sullivan (now Fort Moultrie) was named the "Jasper Battery."

By midnight the British ships were gone with the tide, leaving only the abandoned *Actaeon,* which had been damaged, then set on fire by her crew.

The first Battle of Charleston was over, with only ten Americans killed and twenty-two wounded. The British losses were heavier: More than 225 were killed and upward of 130 were wounded. One of the wounded was former South Carolina royal governor Lord William Campbell. He'd joined Clinton's forces and volunteered to man the guns aboard the HMS *Bristol.* Campbell was wounded in the arm, from which he died two years later.

In 1780, the British attacked again. This time General Clinton was successful, capturing not only Charleston but taking captive the 5,400-man American garrison at Forts Sullivan and Johnson.

With Charleston claimed again for the Crown, General Clinton left Lord Cornwallis with about 8,000 men to maintain and, if possible, extend British control of the South. It was a bloody running battle that saw guerrilla bands led by Andrew Pickins, Francis Marion, and Thomas Sumter keeping the British from consolidating their strength until General Gates could lead a contingent of the Continental army southward.

Dan Morgan likely was born either in Bucks County, Pennsylvania, or across the river in Hunterdon County, New Jersey (records are either missing or mixed up). Youth in the eighteenth century apparently were not much different from youth in our own time, and when he was seventeen years old, Dan Morgan got into an argument with his father and left home. Two years later he joined Braddock's expedition as a teamster. With Braddock fatally wounded, Morgan escaped and helped evacuate the injured troops. During this time the young mule skinner got to know George Washington.

For a year or so Morgan hauled supplies to British and colonial troops along the frontier, but then he got into an argument with an officer. The officer slapped Morgan with the flat of his sword and, rather than take the injury and insult, Morgan struck back. The mule skinner was sentenced to 500 lashes. Later Morgan bragged that he owed the British army one stripe; the drummer, he claimed, had miscounted and Morgan received only 499 lashes with the whip.

In 1775, Dan Morgan was commissioned a captain in a Virginia rifle company, and a month later he marched his company 600 miles to join the growing American lines outside Boston. Dan Morgan's company was among the leaders in Benedict Arnold's march on Quebec in the fall of 1775, and when Arnold was wounded on New Year's Eve, Morgan took command.

He was taken prisoner but was paroled by the English in the fall of '76. The following spring he joined his old friend George Washington and served in the New Jersey operations in what Washington referred to as a "Corps of Rangers, newly formed." Later Dan Morgan and his riflemen fought with Horatio Gates in the Battles of Saratoga. When Gates began trying to undermine Washington's command, Morgan refused to join in the cabal.

Daniel Morgan resigned his commission in July 1779, ostensibly for health reasons. In reality it was because he wasn't given command of the 1st Infantry Brigade in Anthony Wayne's army. Congress tried to order Morgan to report to Gates's army, but Morgan refused. It wasn't until he learned of the disaster at Camden, South Carolina, that he rejoined the army.

British General Cornwallis, with a much smaller army than General Gates had under his command, had attacked the Continentals in one of the fiercest fights of the Revolution. An outstanding leader, Cornwallis was backed by some of the finest and most experienced

British troops in America. Of Gates's forces, only about one-third were regulars, with the remaining two thousand or so made up of militia.

Seeing which way the wind was blowing at Camden and the direction the British bayonets were pointed, Horatio Gates hopped on his horse and didn't stop until he'd galloped to Charlotte, North Carolina, sixty miles away. The defeat finished Gates's career and scattered the remainder of his nearly three thousand troops to the nearby woods and swamps.

When Morgan heard about the disaster at Camden, the one-time mule skinner put aside his personal grievances and rushed back to join Gates at Hillsboro in late September. Gates gave Morgan command of a corps of light troops and, in mid-October, Congress appointed Morgan brigadier general. When Nathanael Greene succeeded Horatio Gates as the army's commander, he confirmed Morgan's appointment. Thanks to his days as a mule skinner twenty-five years earlier, Morgan's troops called him the "Old Wagoner."

Banastre Tarleton had already earned the nickname "Bloody Ban," and the phrase "Tarleton's Quarter" had entered the American lexicon before the May 29, 1780, Battle of Waxhaws, South Carolina. British troops circled the American flank and charged for the colors that had been posted in the center of the Continental army. As an ensign was raising a white flag to surrender, Tarleton rode up and cut the young man down with his sword. Tarleton's horse was shot from under him and, before he could find another, word went out, in Tarleton's own words, "amongst the calvary that they had lost their commanding officer. [This] stimulated the soldiers to a vindictive asperity not easily restrained." Tarleton once said that the conditions suffered (and surmounted) by both sides in the southern campaign would "appear insuperable in theory, and almost incredible in the relations." The area of North and South Carolina, he said, was the most difficult of all provinces in America to attack. Material assistance, he claimed, must be obtained from the inhabitants, and thus far he hadn't been able to do that.

On January 17, 1781, Daniel Morgan led Tarleton into a trap in the high rolling ground of northwestern South Carolina, where a group of young men, known locally as "cowboys," herded cattle together for local owners. The area was, and is, known as the Cowpens.

As a leader of cavalry, Tarleton was unmatched for alertness, dash, and daring. As a human, however, he was coldhearted, ruthless, and vindictive. And at Cowpens he was thoroughly beaten by Daniel Morgan.

The battle is either one of the greatest scenes of triumph or the greatest example of luck in the Revolution. Morgan's victory at Cowpens is often compared to Hannibal's defeat of the Romans in 216 B.C. at the Battle of Cannae. Then again, it may have just been that Morgan found himself in a bad spot and made the best of it.

The night before the battle, General Morgan went from campfire to campfire explaining his plan, not just to the officers, but to the men who would be on the line at first light. He told members of the North Carolina regiment that he'd heard they were the best marksmen in the bunch. Now, he said, was their chance to prove their marksmanship. It was a challenge the Carolinians (as well as the other troops) took up.

Morgan realized that individual American troops reacted better when they knew the plan of attack. So, the night before the Battle of Cowpens, we have American Dan Morgan walking among his troops, telling them what he wants, and Britain's Ban Tarleton giving only his officers the battle plan. Different attitudes entirely.

Morgan put a group of 150 Georgia and North Carolina riflemen in the first line; they would wait until the British were about fifty yards off, then fire two shots, picking off officers and sergeants. In the first assault about 40 percent of the British killed were officers.

After their first two shots, line one would fall back to join the second line. As they ran to join their comrades, they would reload, something that astonished British and European war "experts," who still believed riflemen had to stand erect, shoot, reload, and then stand out in the open for another shot.

That second line of about 300 North and South Carolina militiamen would be along a crest, about 150 yards behind the first. As the first line withdrew, the second line would also fire two shots and fall back, at just about the time British troops were within range of a bayonet charge. But instead of lines one and two falling back onto the third line, and probably causing a lot of confusion and disorganization, groups one and two would be led around their own flank by Colonel Andrew Pickens. They would reassemble.

Back yet another 150 yards was the main battle line, approximately 400 yards long. The third line consisted of about 450 Maryland and Delaware Continental troops along with Virginia and Georgia militia who had seen some service in the Continental army. Line three, then, was made up of Morgan's most experienced men.

Morgan saw that his men were fed and rested the night before the battle. The British under Tarleton had camped about eight miles away, so the first thing they had to do was march to the site Morgan had selected, pot shots from American marksmen peppering the redcoats all the way, not enough to do much harm, but enough to heckle and harass them. Tarleton had more than one thousand men, almost all of them either well-trained British regulars or experienced Loyalists; he had no doubt they would do as he commanded; and he had no doubt he would drive the rebelling Americans off the field, sending them headlong to the north.

As he rode forward, Tarleton saw the first American line, possibly the second behind them, and he sent his Loyalist British Legion cavalry forward to disperse them. As planned, the Georgia and North Carolina riflemen knelt or stood behind trees, and they calmly followed Dan Morgan's plan, the plan they knew all about. Actually they did more damage than Morgan had believed they would (perhaps because of his challenge of their marksmanship), and the Loyalist legion cavalry quickly fell back behind their own infantry.

When Tarleton saw that the American rabble had turned back his trained British troops, he became infuriated. His next move was straight out of the book, a book the American troops probably not only had never heard of but probably couldn't have read if someone showed it to them. Tarleton had his infantry in the center with the Seventy-first Highland Regiment held in reserve when the beaten-off legion cavalry retreated.

Believing the Americans had panicked and run away, the redcoats surged forward and, in eagerness, some broke ranks. The third American line fired away, a volley that shocked the well-trained, disciplined British regulars.

Off to Tarleton's right, some of his dragoons had pursued Pickens's men of the first and second American lines. Morgan was prepared for this, and cavalry under Colonel William Washington, a kinsman of the man who would be president, quickly chased the British dragoons off the field.

British troops, meanwhile, were having to struggle up a hill and right into fire from the American third line. Tarleton sent in his regiment of Highlanders. Pipes skirling, about two hundred kilted Highlanders started forward. It was just then that the American line moved backward to face the new attack. It almost cost them the day.

The Continental line believed that someone had ordered a general withdrawal. Still, they were veterans and didn't panic; they pulled back calmly and in good order.

Just then General Morgan appeared. Back behind a hill, out of sight of the British, Morgan and Colonel Pickens had reformed the militia units. They charged around the other side of the American line, ready for another go at the redcoats. Tarleton hadn't expected anything like this; it hadn't been in any of his textbooks.

When the British line came within fifty yards of the apparently retreating Continentals, Colonel John Howard ordered the Americans to fire. Swinging about, the militia fired from the hip, then with bayonets fixed they charged straight for Tarleton's men.

The British and Loyalist troops were totally unprepared for the charge. As they turned around, they were hit again by Pickens's men on their left flank and by Washington's cavalry on their right. Soon only the Highlanders continued to fight, but finally they, too, were overwhelmed.

Colonel Banastre Tarleton escaped with several members of his Loyalist British Legion. Washington followed in hot pursuit.

Suddenly Tarleton and two of his officers turned back for a dramatic finale, and the two groups collided. Washington slashed away with his saber at the officer on Tarleton's right, breaking his own weapon near the handguard. Just as Washington's intended victim began slashing away himself, a fourteen-year-old bugler shot the British officer in the shoulder. As another officer slashed away at Washington, a dragoon sergeant parried the saber.

Tarleton charged Washington, who now had nothing to defend himself with but a broken saber. Snatching a pistol, Tarleton fired. He missed Washington but hit the American's horse. It was the final shot of the Battle of Cowpens.

When Tarleton and his dragoons straggled back to the rear area where they had left their baggage, they found a group of their Tory guides looting the luggage and trying to steal horses the British had left in their keeping. The dragoons drove them off.

Finally Tarleton rounded up what was left of his dragoons and rode back to the main British camp, dejected and defeated.

The Battle of Cowpens lasted only about one hour. In that time 100 British were killed, 229 more were wounded, and another 600 were captured, including the first battalion of the Seventy-first Regiment. American losses included only twelve dead and sixty wounded. The Americans captured horses, muskets, wagons, and—important for the Continentals' morale—the Seventy-first's colors. Worst for the Highlanders, the Continentals even captured the battalion's bagpipes.

In a single stroke nearly one-third of Cornwallis's field army was wiped out. Perhaps more important, Daniel Morgan had found a way to use the American militia—don't just line them up and let them fire away, expecting all along they probably would run off at the first sight of a bayonet. He didn't expect them to do too much but carefully planned and just as carefully explained to his men what he hoped they could accomplish. Instead of marching into battle like a line of troops on parade, he had them use whatever cover was available—trees and rocks—and he told them to wait. Just as at Bunker Hill, to wait until they saw the whites of their enemy's eyes. By pretending to run off, Morgan's inexperienced troops had fooled the far more experienced British regulars and Loyalists. And Lieutenant Colonel Banastre Tarleton.

All things considered, the Battle of Cowpens wasn't nearly as much a victory as Daniel Morgan and the Continentals claimed. But they believed it, and in this case believing really made it so.

In August 1881, Joseph Plumb Martin's Continental army regiment was in the highlands of New York. When orders came to move out, he expected to be sent to New York City, to attack British forces holding the city. Instead, he found himself on a ship in Philadelphia, heading south. To deceive the enemy, Washington pretended to attack New York, but instead, he joined with French forces in attacking General Cornwallis at Yorktown, Virginia.

Martin's regiment passed by the French fleet anchored off Chesapeake Bay, "two or three fifty-gun ships . . . lying in Lynnhaven Bay." The lineup of ships' masts so many, he thought, looked like "a swamp of dry pine trees."

The Americans had traveled some 450 miles in a well-planned, well-coordinated move. Landing near Williamsburg, Virginia, Martin's regiment was joined by General Lafayette, who'd been harassing General Cornwallis through the Carolinas and into Virginia. Together they "prepared to move down and pay our old acquaintance, the British, at Yorktown, a visit." Washington had ordered any troops who might run across the British, to shoot once, "then decide the conflict with the bayonet." The American commander in chief was trying to conserve his powder and ball for the battle he knew would come soon.

During the following siege of Yorktown they often heard their officers call out "Your Excellency!" George Washington rode among his troops, often exposing himself to danger. "I do not remember, exactly, the number of days we were employed before we got our batteries in readiness to open upon the enemy," Martin wrote, "but think it was not more than two or three." Finally, on October 10, American and French artillery began pounding the British.

The story goes that new Virginia Governor Thomas Nelson (who'd been held in Yorktown but released under a flag of truce) was with American forces that day. Lafayette invited Nelson to be present when Captain Thomas Machin's battery first opened fire, as both a compliment and knowing Nelson lived in Yorktown and would know the localities in the riverport area. "To what particular spot," Lafayette reportedly asked Nelson, "would your Excellency direct that we should point the cannon." Nelson replied, "There, to that house. It is mine, and . . . it is the best one in the town. There you will be almost certain to find Lord Cornwallis and the British headquarters." Nelson was right; Cornwallis was using his house.

"A simultaneous discharge of all the guns in the line," Joseph Martin wrote, was "followed [by] French troops accompanying it with 'Huzza for the Americans.'" Sounding much like the Nelson legend, Martin's account added that "the first shell sent from our batteries entered an elegant house formerly owned or occupied by the Secretary of State under the British,* and burned directly over a table surrounded by a large party of British officers at dinner, killing and wounding a number of them." It was, Martin remembered, "a warm day to the British." The Nelson house is still standing with cannonballs embedded in its east wall.

Joseph Plumb Martin was part of a detachment that charged the British trenches. Their password was "Rochambeau," the name of the commander of the French forces. Pronounced *Ro-sham-bow*, the Americans changed it to "Rush on boys."

It was October 14 when the allies made simultaneous assaults— the French and Americans using about 400 men each—on British redoubts number 9 and number 10. It was dark, and the troops carried unloaded muskets with fixed bayonets. The French took number 9 but incurred heavy casualties. American troops, under Lieutenant Colonel Alexander Hamilton and Lafayette's aide Jean-Joseph Soubader de Gimat, were equally as successful and less harmed. In swarming over the defenders at redoubt number 10, only nine Americans were killed and twenty-five wounded.

Number 9 was larger and more heavily defended (about 150 Hessians and British) than number 10 (only about fifty men), and each redoubt faced overwhelming allied numbers. The night attacks were a combination of terror and romance. Perhaps the biggest difference between the French and American charges was the way the two armies attacked the enemy. The formally trained French soldiers waited for ax men to clear gaps in the abatis (obstacles formed of trees felled toward the enemy) British and Hessian troops had built around the redoubt. The less-trained Americans simply scrambled through the abatis, down and up the berm (the ditch), through the fraises (palisades made from pointed trees, either pointed horizon-

---

* Thomas Nelson earlier was secretary of the Virginia Council.

tally toward the direction of attack or slanted up and down) surrounding the redoubt, then charging the defenders.

On the morning of October 17, General Cornwallis tried to ferry his troops across the north side of the York River to Gloucester, also controlled by the British. But he couldn't find enough boats and those he did find were driven back to Yorktown by heavy rain. Next morning, between nine and ten, a redcoated British drummer boy appeared on the parapet of the horn work. He was beating a signal indicating General Cornwallis wanted to talk. A British officer appeared with a white handkerchief. Two days later the British army marched out to surrender. Truly, as the band played, it was a "world turned upside down."

> If ponies rode men and if grass ate cows,
> And cats should be chased into holes by the mouse. . . .

About half of Cornwallis's men marched in the surrender. The rest were wounded and remained in Yorktown. Lord Cornwallis himself claimed "an indisposition" and stayed behind his lines. He sent his second in command, General Charles O'Hara, to surrender for him. O'Hara tried to offer his sword to General Rochambeau, but Rochambeau refused, saying he and his French troops were subordinate to the Americans. "General Washington," Rochambeau said, "will give you your orders." O'Hara then tried to present his sword to Washington, but the general motioned for him to hand it to *his* second in command, General Benjamin Lincoln, who'd been denied the honors of war at the defeat of Charleston.

Many of the British troops seemed drunk as they marched out of Yorktown; some cried, and some bit their lips to keep from crying. When they were ordered to give up their arms, some tried to damage them and hurled them down. And the band played on:

> If summer were spring and the other way round,
> Then all the world would be upside down.

Two weeks later the surrendered troops were marched to camps in Maryland and Virginia.

Admiral De Grasse sailed the French fleet back to the West Indies.

George Washington was concerned with his stepson, Jack Custis, who was ill but had insisted on being at Yorktown for the surrender. Soon afterward Jack died, and Washington's concern turned to Custis's young widow and his mother, the general's wife, Martha. Leaving Yorktown, Washington spent a week at Mount Vernon. He still considered America at war, and technically he was correct. The American army marched back to their old post outside New York.

Congress learned of the British surrender on October 22, when Washington aide Tench Tilgman reached Philadelphia.

The bad news arrived in London on Sunday, November 25. Reportedly when Lord North was given the message, he said, "Oh, God! It is over."

George III's popularity was so low that he even wrote a letter of abdication. "At last," he said, "the fatal day has come."

> His Majesty is convinced that the sudden change of Sentiments of one Branch of the Legislature has totally incapacitated Him from either conducting the War with effect, or from obtaining any Peace but on conditions which would prove to be destructive to the Commerce as well as essential Rights of the British Nation.

He never submitted his abdication and ruled until 1820.

In March 1782, a new British cabinet met and recognized the independence of the United States of America. That November a preliminary peace treaty was signed in Paris. It would take several months for the treaty to be sent back to America, argued over and agreed upon, and returned to Paris for final signing.

Almost two years after the Yorktown surrender American negotiators met to sign the treaty. Today there's a nondescript plaque on an outer wall of a modest four-story building at 56 Rue Jacob. The plaque is well above eye level and is seldom noticed. An inscription loosely translates as:

And the Winner Is?

In this building, formerly the York Hotel, on Sept. 3, 1783, David Hartley, in the name of the King of England, Benjamin Franklin, John Jay and John Adams, in the name of the United States of America, signed the definitive peace treaty recognizing the independence of the United States.

Now, as Jefferson had written in the Declaration of Independence, the United States of America could "assume among the powers of the earth, the separate and equal station to which the Laws of Nature and of Nature's God" entitled it.

CHAPTER THIRTEEN

The Constitution:
"We the People"

'Tis done. We have become a nation.
—Dr. Benjamin Rush, Constitutional Convention delegate

I consent, Sir, to this Constitution because I expect no better, and because I am not sure, that it is not the best.
—Benjamin Franklin, September 17, 1787

Casualties of war don't always tell the whole story, and in some cases they virtually lie to us. Take, for instance, the casualties of two Revolutionary War battles compared with two Civil War battles. Factor in the general population of the country at the time of the events.

In 1790, the first census of the United States of America showed a total population of 3,929,000. Following the Revolution, immigration soared. By 1860, just prior to the start of the Civil War, the count was 31,443,321, almost exactly eight times the earlier figure.

Two of the most important battles of the American Revolution were the First and Second Battles of Saratoga, New York, in September and October 1777. First Saratoga saw 319 American casualties; that is—killed, wounded, captured, and missing. Second Saratoga (which led to British General Burgoyne's surrender ten days later) totaled 150 American casualties. So, total Americans killed, wounded, or captured at Saratoga was 469. British casualties for each engagement numbered about 600, for a total of 1,200 lost.

The total American force under General Horatio Gates was about 7,000. The exact number under Burgoyne is uncertain, but it was about 5,600. The British, of course, lost everybody, since they surrendered and the survivors marched off to prisoner-of-war facilities, where many died and some ran away. But in pure numbers—

casualty versus casualty—it came down to Americans, 469; British, 1,200. Burgoyne's casualties amounted to 21.5 percent of his force, while Gates's were just over 6.5 percent. No wonder Burgoyne gave up.

But then, eighty-five years later, Union and Confederate forces combined at the Battle of Gettysburg, lost 51,112! That was more than 32 percent of the 157,289 participants in the three-day battle. At the two-day Battle of Chickamauga two months later, Union and Confederate forces lost 34,624, almost 28 percent.

At the Battle of Yorktown in 1781, the combined American-French force of just under 19,000 lost 378 men killed and wounded, or 2 percent. Despite winning the battle, about 250 Americans deserted during the fighting and later were transported to New York. Britain's Lord Cornwallis had approximately 9,725 army and navy personnel under his command at Yorktown. They suffered about 6 percent casualties, or 596.

Certainly the casualties at the Battle of Yorktown were nothing like those suffered by combined Union and Confederate troops in most Civil War battles. In fact, the Revolutionary War casualty rate was far below most other wars we've fought. Still, the figures are both mind-boggling and mind-numbing.

- The American Revolution saw an estimated 250,000 individuals fight, with deaths totaling 4,435, or a .0177 mortality rate.
- In America's Civil War, about 3,712,582 fought (2,213,582 Union and about 1,500,000 Confederate); 498,323 American troops were casualties in the Civil War (364,512 Federal and 133,811 Rebel), a .24356 mortality rate.
- During World War I, 4,743,826 Americans fought, with 116,708 dying, a rate of .02464.
- World War II saw more than 16,353,659 Americans serve and 407,316 killed, for a .0249 mortality rate.
- In the three years of the Korean War, 5,764,143 served and 36,916 died, a mortality rate of .0064, much smaller than either Vietnam or the Civil War, but still too high for those involved.
- The Vietnam War saw more than 8,752,000 serve and counted at least 58,193 deaths, a death rate of .00664.

•The Gulf War of 1991, which lasted about one hundred days, including air strikes, and about one hundred hours for land forces, saw 467,539 Americans serve with 299 losing their lives, a rate of .0006389.

In the American Revolution less than 2 percent (.01174) of the population were casualties of war. In the Civil War the figure was much higher, .028762 of the population in 1860.

Bluntly, the American Revolution was a bargain in casualties. After all, we got a whole new country out of it, and it all led to the Constitution.

Under a grant from King Charles I of England, George Calvert settled in what was then Virginia but would soon become Maryland. Calvert had converted to Catholicism, which meant he could not take the Oath of Supremacy, pledging himself to the king. Because of their friendship, the king made Calvert an Irish peer, Baron of Baltimore, giving him both a large Irish estate and the American grant.

Early in 1634, Calvert and two ships loaded with Catholic would-be colonists headed for Virginia. First, however, they stopped in the West Indies, where some of their colonists decided to remain with a group that had been ousted by the Jamestown colonists, "Irishmen . . . expelled by the English of Virginia on account of their profession of the Catholic faith."

Then Baltimore sailed the ships *Ark* and *Dove* up the Atlantic and into Chesapeake Bay, through Hampton Roads, and up the James River to Jamestown, where they were met with something less than good cheer and open arms. The colony had already tossed out that West Indies group of Catholic colonists and would have done the same with Calvert's crowd if it hadn't been for Virginia Governor John Harvey. The governor, it seems, wanted to impress the king, and, instead of ordering Baltimore to leave, Harvey provided an escort to the mouth of the Potomac River.

George Calvert, Lord Baltimore, bought a large tract of land from the local Indians and began a town he named for the Virgin Mary; St. Mary's he called it. The colony became Mary's Land, or Maryland. Governor Harvey continued to aid Baltimore by sending him cattle and tools and even ordering a group of Virginians to vacate several islands, where they had begun plantations.

One old planter who did not approve of the order was Captain Samuel Mathews. When he learned what was going on, Mathews threw his hat to the ground, stamped on it, and cried, "A pox on Maryland!"

More than 150 years later, Virginians were still saying "A pox on Maryland," still arguing over water rights. In 1786, the long-standing dispute led to the Annapolis Convention, at which delegates from five states met to try to work out an agreement. They failed, and the argument continues to this day, with occasional armed battles taking place between Virginia and Maryland watermen fighting over fishing, oystering, and crabbing rights.

Delegates to the Annapolis Convention decided to meet again, this time in Philadelphia, and this time the issues would concern more than crabs and oysters. They would meet the following summer to alter the Articles of Confederation. Congress had, more or less, given its sanction. Meeting in New York the previous February, Congress said the Philadelphia Convention was "for the sole and express purpose of revising the Articles of Confederation." It's doubtful, however, whether many of the delegates even considered merely revising the Articles; they very likely knew what they were about to do.

In May 1787, for four months during a long, hot summer, fifty-five delegates from twelve states met in long, grueling secret sessions. Only Rhode Island did not send a delegation.

On June 6, James Madison wrote his friend and mentor Thomas Jefferson, who was in Paris and could not (perhaps would not if he'd been able to) attend the convention. "The names of the members," Madison wrote, "will satisfy you that the States have been serious in this business." In addition to Madison, there was George Washington, Alexander Hamilton, Benjamin Franklin, John Rutledge and the two Pinckneys from South Carolina, the two Morrises of New York—Robert and Gouverneur, John Dickinson of Delaware (he had moved from Pennsylvania), George Wythe, George Mason, and John Blair of Virginia, Roger Sherman of Connecticut, Rufus King and Elbridge Gerry of Massachusetts. As historian Catherine Drinker

Bowen writes, "The roster reads like a Fourth of July oration, a patriot hymn." It was, Jefferson declared, "an assembly of demi-gods."

They ranged in age from twenty-nine-year-old Charles Pinckney to eighty-one-year-old Benjamin Franklin. On average, though, they were a young group. James Madison was only thirty-six. They all, however, were, as Richard Henry Lee of Virginia wrote, "gentlemen of competent years." They were experienced in local, state, and national government; nearly three-fourths had been members of the Continental Congress, and many had served in state legislatures, even helping (as Madison had) to write their state constitutions. Eight of those present in Philadelphia in 1787 had been there earlier and had signed the Declaration of Independence. Almost half had fought in the Revolution.

Patrick Henry was elected as delegate to the Philadelphia Convention, but he declined to attend, saying he "smelt a rat."

James Madison stood only five feet four inches tall and weighed under 100 pounds. Historian Catherine Drinker Bowen says he had "a calm expression, a penetrating blue eye—and looked like a thinking man." He was commissioned a colonel in the Orange County, Virginia, militia, but the extent of his military service amounted to marching and drilling; he saw no active duty. Rather, he turned to politics and was elected to the Virginia House of Delegates in October 1776. He was defeated the following April because he wouldn't go along with the tradition and furnish rum in exchange for votes. That fall he began serving on the Virginia Council of State for Governors Patrick Henry and Thomas Jefferson. Two years later, in 1779, he was elected to the Second Continental Congress, the youngest member ever of the Congress. In 1787, he became the architect of a new form of government.

Delegates to the Philadelphia Convention looked for a solution to the imperfections as set up in 1776 by the Whigs—the Continental Congress Patriots. They proposed, argued, changed, and deleted. What emerged in September were not changes in the Articles of Confederation; it was a totally different new form of government. They sent their plan to the states, hoping they would accept what the delegates called the Constitution of the United States of America.

Under the Articles of Confederation, government was sovereign. Under the Constitution, the people were sovereign. Not everybody agreed.

When the Constitution was complete, Patrick Henry objected to, among many other things, the heading: "We the People of the United States. . . ." Henry believed that the Union, as described in the Constitution, meant the states, not the people, and he didn't like that idea. He claimed bitterly that the phrase would permit the "national government to ride roughshod over the states and their rights."

Although Patrick Henry and some others in the new nation objected to the phrase, in Europe it served "as an inspiration, a flag of defiance against absolutist kings."

Writing the Constitution in 1787 was very much a part of the Revolution, the end product, if you will. In essence the Revolution began with the Stamp Act, which revealed to many on both sides of the Atlantic Ocean that colonial Americans no longer were willing to be subordinate to and dependent on the mother country. The Revolutionary War proved that Americans no longer were powerless. All of it—from Stamp Act to Boston Massacre, Lexington and Concord to Bunker Hill, the Battle of Great Bridge to Charleston and Savannah, from Cowpens to Yorktown—concluded with the writing of the Constitution.

The American Revolution was more than a war. It became a way of life for a people. We're still fighting for and enjoying that way of life. In many ways, however, the government determined by the Constitution was based on the very system we fought to overthrow. The executive, the president, was the king. The king's council was the president's Cabinet. The House of Lords was the U.S. Senate, and the House of Commons became the U.S. House of Representatives. The difference, of course, is that when we don't like the president, we usually don't kill him off or overthrow the government the way the French and English did.

The convention gave final approval to the Constitution on September 17. Benjamin Franklin suggested that every member of the convention sign it. Thirty-nine did, but three did not. Edmund Randolph said he wanted "to keep himself free to be governed by duty, as it should be proscribed by his future judgment." George Mason thought the Constitution was too aristocratic, and he didn't sign. Elbridge Gerry believed that, as Madison put it, "a civil war may result from the present crisis of the United States." He declined to sign the document.

Two other delegates, Robert Yates and Robert Lansing, both of New York, had objected early and left early.

While the last members of the convention were signing the Constitution, Benjamin Franklin sat with tears streaming down his face. According to Madison, Franklin looked "towards the president's chair, at the back of which a rising sun happened to be painted." Franklin, he wrote,

> observed to a few members near him, that Painters had found it difficult to distinguish in their art, a rising from a setting sun. "I have," said he, "often and often, in the course of the Session, . . . looked at that behind the President without being able to tell whether it was rising or setting: But now at length I have the happiness to know that it is a rising and not a setting sun."

When it was all said and done, the U.S. Constitution was written by a gentleman named Jacob Shallus. Literally. Shallus was a calligrapher, and the Constitutional Convention paid him $30 to copy out the Constitution. "We the People of the United States . . ." It is one of the most beautiful and famous works of any calligrapher. Shallus was thirty-seven years old when he "wrote" the Constitution.

The Constitution is both a beautifully written document and a beautifully copied one. As a freelance calligrapher, however, Jacob Shallus made something of a major error, especially considering his day job at the time as a Pennsylvania General Assembly clerk. He wrote "Pensylvania."

CHAPTER FOURTEEN

The Sting of Death:
Final Acts, Final Honors

Revolution is like Saturn—it eats its own children.
—George Büchner, Danton's Death, 1835

Death be not proud.

—John Donne, *Holy Sonnets,* No. 10, 1

The French Revolution began in 1789, and unlike the American Revolution, it would be a bloody one for the average citizen. The crew of HMS *Bounty* mutinied in 1789, and in 1789, the U.S. Post Office was established. That same year George Washington was inaugurated as first president of the United States.

Sam Adams pushed America toward separation from Great Britain, and when he signed the Declaration of Independence in 1776, he effectively signed his resignation from Revolutionary leadership. He remained in Congress for five more years but, as biographer John Miller writes, "His career . . . was marred by factiousness, intrigue and broils." Part of that intrigue, according to John Hancock, was being part of the Conway Cabal to get rid of George Washington. When Hancock stepped down from Congress to return to Massachusetts, Adams even backed an attempt to prevent the legislature from offering a vote of thanks. Sam had argued that a man need not be thanked for simply doing his duty.

Sam Adams returned to Massachusetts seven months before Yorktown, even poorer than when he'd gone away. During the British occupation of Boston, the redcoats had badly damaged Adams's house. His furniture had been confiscated. The Massachusetts government rented him a house formerly owned by a ports commissioner.

By then, his influence was minor. During the peace talks in Paris, Sam Adams vowed to oppose any settlement that did not protect New England's fishing rights. His new cry became "No peace without the fisheries!"

He became a state senator and ran against John Hancock for governor, finishing a distant second, but became lieutenant governor. When Hancock died in 1793, Samuel Adams took over and was later elected on his own.

Sam Adams first opposed the Constitution, saying it advocated a centralized government. Assured by the Bill of Rights, he finally gave it his support.

"His face," his grandson and biographer William Wells wrote, had a "benignant but careworn expression, blended with a native dignity." Sam Adams was of medium height, with dark blue eyes and heavy eyebrows, a clear and virtually unwrinkled forehead, Wells wrote, even at age seventy. He died in 1803, still professing, "I love the people of Boston."

Sam's second cousin, John Adams, in 1796, beat out Thomas Jefferson by three electoral votes to become America's second president. He served only one term and lost to Jefferson by eight votes in 1800. They once were friends (and would be again), but when Jefferson was inaugurated, John Adams refused to attend the ceremonies.

At four o'clock on the morning of March 4, 1801, Tom Jefferson was still at Conrad and McMunn's boardinghouse. John Adams packed up his belongings in the President's house (not yet the White House) and left Washington City (as it was called then) to return to his home in Quincy, Massachusetts.

In 1798, President Adams signed an amended naturalization act, changing the period of residence required for full citizenship from five to fourteen years (it was changed back to five years under Jefferson). It became the first of four laws known as the Alien and Sedition Acts. Another of the acts called for fining and imprisoning anyone—citizen or alien—who spoke out or wrote "with the intent to defame" or "to bring [them] into contempt or dispute" through false or malicious statements, the president, Congress, or the government in general. Many anti-Federalist writers were European refugees, and even Washington had approved of their prosecution, calling it necessary to prevent "a disunion of the States."

When the Sedition Act was approved, many wondered whether the Adams administration would tolerate an opposition party strong enough to win the presidency. Their passage was like an ink blot on the Bill of Rights and shows just how frail America's liberties were.

Adams went to England as America's first minister plenipotentiary to the Court of St. James's, and on June 1, 1785, he presented his credentials to the man he'd helped oust as king of America, George III. While he was in England, the U.S. Constitution was written, and Adams wrote a three-volume *Defense of the Constitutions of Government of the United States of America.* It offended many back home because of its aristocratic overtones. America, he said, should have a senate composed of "the rich, the well-born and the able." He drew pictures of a majority of the poor attacking the rich, abolishing all debts and dividing all property among them. "Property," John Adams wrote, "is surely a right of mankind as real as liberty." He clearly believed in liberty but abhorred equality and the very thought of the "leveling" of society. When there was talk of Massachusetts extending the vote to non–property holders, he warned that "new claims will arise; women will demand a vote; lads from twelve to twenty-one will think their rights not closely enough attended to; and every man who has not a farthing will demand an equal voice with any other, in all acts of state."

In retirement John Adams wrote a history of the Revolution he had helped create. However, it was flawed by his own notoriously bad memory. He lived to see his son, John Quincy Adams, inaugurated as president in 1824. By then, however, John was a widower. His "Dear Friend," Abigail, died in 1818.

John Adams's own death eight years later is perhaps one of the most written-about of all the Founding Fathers', because it came on the fiftieth anniversary of the document he had fought so hard to have approved, the document Thomas Jefferson had written at Adams's insistence, the Declaration of Independence.

John Adams's last words were said to be "Jefferson survives," but he was wrong. Thomas Jefferson had died a few hours earlier.

• • •

On July 4, 1826, President John Quincy Adams rode with Vice President John Calhoun in a parade down Pennsylvania Avenue in Washington. A Revolutionary War veteran read the Declaration and the crowd heard a plea to subscribe money to keep Monticello from being put up for sale. The Sage of Monticello, as Jefferson was often called, was broke.

During gatherings at the presidential mansion, Jefferson's predecessors had stood silently while guests bowed to them. Jefferson changed all that. He shook hands with White House guests, as many as one hundred in one day.

Under Jefferson's orders, Secretary of State James Madison withheld one of Adams's "midnight appointments" of 1801, William Marbury, who took Madison to court. *Marbury v. Madison* was dismissed, but in writing the opinion, the high court declared part of the Judiciary Act of 1789 unconstitutional. It was the first time the court held an act of Congress invalid.

In 1800, the United States physically ended at the Mississippi River, and many in America—Thomas Jefferson among them—believed that left them vulnerable regarding whatever foreign nations owned the western lands. First, in the Treaty of Paris ending the French and Indian/Seven Years' War, France ceded the Louisiana Territory to Spain. Now, Spain, under pressure from Napoleon, was about to cede the land back to France. Many in Jefferson's Democratic-Republican Party looked on the land west of the Mississippi as "Republican country." Americans were already moving into the territory.

The thought of having France on America's western frontier was enough for Jefferson to consider an alliance with, of all people, the English. Warning that "the day that France takes possession of N. Orleans" is "the moment we must marry ourselves to the British fleet and nation," Jefferson sent Robert Livingston and James Monroe to Paris. They would offer to buy New Orleans for ten million dollars. At the very least they would negotiate advantages for American traders on the Mississippi.

The story goes that the deal was struck while Napoleon lay soaking in a bathtub. Preferring that a weak but friendly United States own the Mississippi, rather than a strong America backed by Great

Britain, between scrubbing his back and soaking in the suds Napoleon offered to sell the whole thing. For about fifteen million dollars Jefferson doubled the size of the United States. It was one of the greatest land deals in history, approximately four cents an acre. To make the deal, however, Jefferson had to work with the Alexander Hamilton–backed Bank of the United States. Jefferson thought the bank was unconstitutional (which would have meant his four-cents-an-acre land deal was unconstitutional), but in an exceedingly nonstrict constructionist conclusion Jefferson decided it was the best for the country.

It was also during Jefferson's presidency that United States Marines, as the song says, went to the "shores of Tripoli." In 1785, Spain concluded a peace treaty with Algiers and lifted its blockade of the Strait of Gibraltar. That permitted some rather aggressive pirates to sortie out into the Atlantic. The schooner *Maria*, out of Boston, was seized and its captain and crew taken prisoner. Soon the other Barbary States—Morocco, Tunis, and Tripoli—joined in this pirate business. By 1801, one-fifth of America's annual revenue went to pay tribute to the Barbary States, either to ransom prisoners or for permission for American merchant ships to sail the Mediterranean Sea.

The bashaw of Tripoli thought he wasn't getting enough money from America and declared war on the United States. It wasn't much of a war, but it dribbled on for three years until the U.S. Navy sent a task force to bombard Tripoli. One of the ships, however, the frigate *Philadelphia*, went aground on a reef. The enemy floated it free and imprisoned the *Philadelphia*'s crew.

By then the American consul at Tunis, William Eaton, had had enough and developed a deep disgust for the pirate prince of Tripoli. He was certain bombarding and blockading the country would never work, so he gathered up a force of sixteen members of the U.S. Navy and Marine Corps, along with about forty Greeks and a handful of Arabs, a hundred or so nondescript individuals, and a fleet of camels. Eaton marched this motley collection across the Libyan desert to Derna, more than five hundred miles away, and captured the city. The result was a favorable treaty with Tripoli.

After retiring from the presidency, Thomas Jefferson rarely

strayed more than a few miles from Monticello. He supervised the farming of his estates and designed a plow that revolutionized agriculture. Rebuilding and rebuilding again his mountaintop home was a major venture and major financial drain on Jefferson.

His problems were due to the usual combination of too much outgo and too little income. He had less property than he'd had fifteen years before; he'd made gifts to his daughters and their husbands of much of his land. His farmland wasn't as profitable as it had been in earlier years. To top this all off, he still bore the burden of pre-Revolutionary debts to British firms. During his eight years of the presidency, he'd incurred an additional $11,000 debt. His income was roughly $2,500 a year. In all, Thomas Jefferson's financial life was a mess.

In addition to the constant rebuilding of Monticello, Jefferson continued his love of books. His slave Isaac observed that

> Old Master had abundance of books; sometimes would have twenty of 'em down on the floor at once—read fust one, then tother. Isaac has often wondered how Old Master came to have such a mighty head; read so many of them books; and when they go to him to ax him anything, he go right straight to a book and tell you all about it.

At one point Jefferson's library consisted of more than ten thousand books and took up, he figured, precisely 855.39 square feet of wall space, occupying 676 cubic feet altogether. During the time right after his wife Martha's death, Tom found solace in arranging his library. In 1815, after the British burned much of Washington City, Jefferson sold 6,487 of his books to the Library of Congress for a price of $23,950. Members of the Federalist Party objected to the government paying so much for Jefferson's books, claiming the price was too high. The library, according to the *National Intelligencer,* was "for its selection, rarity and intrinsic value, . . . beyond all price." Funds from the sale relieved his financial burden somewhat, but he was still in debt, and soon began purchasing more books.

In 1819, he received legislative permission to dispose of some of his property by the then-common method of a lottery. It was yet another lottery, one to save Monticello, that was underway on July 4,

1826. The plan was for Jefferson's friends to buy the lottery tickets and, on July 4, to destroy them; Monticello would be saved and Jefferson would go on living on his mountaintop. The plan was never carried out. No lottery tickets were ever destroyed because none had ever been sold.

In the summer of 1825, Thomas Jefferson jokingly wrote a friend that he had one foot in the grave and the other was ready to follow it. On June 24, 1826, he wrote Roger C. Weightman, the chairman of a proposed Independence Day celebration in Washington. It is Jefferson's last extant letter. Weightman had asked Jefferson to attend the ceremonies, but Jefferson declined. He regretted, he said, "that ill health forbids me the gratification of an acceptance."

The illness that took Jefferson's life began in late June 1826. He called for his physician, Dr. Robley Dunglison, a professor at the school Jefferson had founded in Charlottesville, the University of Virginia. Jefferson told Dr. Dunglison that he was troubled so much with diarrhea that his strength was being depleted. He never recovered his strength and his condition worsened.

Shortly before midnight on July 3, he asked Nicholas Trist, who was with him at Monticello, "This is the Fourth?" Trist later wrote his brother, "He has been dying since yesterday morning, and till twelve o'clock last night, we were in momentary fear that he would not live, as he desired, to see his own glorious Fourth."

When Dr. Dunglison tried to give Jefferson another dose of medicine, Jefferson refused to swallow it, "Oh God!" he said, and then, "No! nothing more." Jefferson was eighty-three. A few hours after Thomas Jefferson's death, John Adams also died.

Sally Hemings died in 1835 at age sixty-two. Her two sons, Madison and Eston, who had been freed under Jefferson's will, moved to Ohio. One of her grandsons, Thomas Eston Hemings, fought in the Civil War as a Union soldier. He was captured and died in the infamous Andersonville prison.

Before Thomas Jefferson died, he was so deeply in debt—partially due to his constant rebuilding of Monticello and partially due to the hospitality and generosity he extended to anyone who stopped by— he tried to auction off the mountaintop home he loved so much. There were no takers.

• • •

Only one other signer of the Declaration was still alive, Charles Carroll of Carrollton, in Maryland. A Roman Catholic who had been educated by Jesuits in France, Charles Carroll first objected to British law concerning taxes and the Church of England. The law used public tax money to support the Church of England and forbade Catholics from having their own schools. It also denied them the vote.

Carroll was one of Maryland's first two U.S. senators under the Constitution. In 1804, he retired from public life and concentrated on managing his landholdings—some eighty thousand acres in four states—and on building the Baltimore and Ohio Railroad. On November 14, 1832, after six years as the nation's only surviving signer of the Declaration, Charles Carroll died at the age of ninety-five.

In 1806, George Wythe's sister's grandson, George Wythe Sweeney, poisoned the eighty-year-old signer of the Declaration of Independence. Wythe had left a legacy to a longtime slave, and Sweeney objected to it. Sweeney laced a pot of coffee with arsenic, apparently trying to kill the slave in order to inherit everything. Instead, he killed his grand-uncle. George Wythe, however, lived long enough to disinherit Sweeney.

A black cook was to be the principal witness during Sweeney's murder trial, but under Virginia law at the time a black could not testify against a white, and Sweeney was acquitted. Wythe was among many Revolutionary-era Virginians who personally, if belatedly, opposed slavery, and in his will he freed his slaves.

Former General Tadeusz Kosciuszko was involved in Jefferson's financial problems. With Kosciuszko in Paris, Jefferson had power of attorney over Kosciuszko's American investments, including $4,500 in investments with a Washington bank. When the notes were about to be retired, and the money to go to Kosciuszko, it was proposed that the fund be lent to Jefferson at the same 8 percent the bank had been paying. Jefferson would, he said, repay Kosciuszko in five or six years. It took longer, however, and the funds came out of Jefferson's sale of books to Congress.

The Sting of Death

• • •

The only book Benjamin Franklin ever wrote, his *Autobiography*, was never finished and covers only up to 1757. "The older I grow," he once commented, "the more apt I am to doubt my own judgement." The same year the Revolution began, 1775, he wrote an old friend in London:

> You are a member of Parliament, and one of that majority which has doomed my country to destruction.—You have begun to burn our towns, and murder our people.—Look upon your hands: They are stained with the blood of your relations!—You and I were long friends:—You are now my enemy,—and I am
> Yours, B. Franklin

In February 1790, Ben Franklin retired from public life after more than fifty years of service. Two years earlier he'd fallen on his garden steps and never quite recovered; for a while he took opiates to relieve the pain. During the night of April 17, 1790, Benjamin Franklin died. He was eighty-four years and three months old.

Four days later, at one of the greatest gatherings of the time, the coffin that bore his body was carried "by citizens" to the Christ Church burial ground in Philadelphia. He was laid to rest next to his wife, Deborah.

British spy John André's life was short after he was, so to speak, unmasked. Traitor Benedict Arnold lived long after his comrade in crime was hanged. Arnold failed to deliver West Point, but the British made good on their promise. They commissioned Benedict Arnold, a brigadier general, and compensated him for the loss of his property in Philadelphia, £6,315. Peggy Arnold and their children received government pensions.

General Arnold was given a command, and he tried to raise a legion of fellow deserters and Tories, even offering a bounty of three gold guineas. There were not many takers, and less than a third of the number he needed signed up. In December 1780, Arnold sailed south from New York, planning to destroy military stores in Virginia and rally Loyalist support.

If Benedict Arnold had been tough and tenacious as an American soldier, as a British officer he was equally rough, perhaps more audacious, and certainly graceless. He burned his way through Virginia, which violently angered Thomas Jefferson, who wanted Arnold kidnapped. Jefferson even offered a five-thousand-dollar reward if the traitor were taken alive. The gentle, peace-loving man from Monticello wanted Arnold hauled around the country and exhibited as a public display of infamy. Jefferson said that Benedict Arnold's left leg, which had been wounded at Quebec and Saratoga, was the only patriotic part of his body, that when the traitor was captured, his leg should be cut off and buried with full honors. The rest of him he'd hang.

It didn't happen, of course, and after the Revolution, Benedict and Peggy Arnold moved to England, where he was occasionally consulted on American affairs. The British army never did offer him a field command, and just as with the Continental army, Benedict Arnold felt snubbed.

Toward the end of 1785, Benedict Arnold reentered the West Indies trade and established himself as a merchant-shipper in St. Johns, New Brunswick. He fathered an illegitimate son named John Sage, although he tried to claim the boy had been born before he met Peggy Shippen. In his will Arnold left money for the boy.

Apparently Arnold's Canadian neighbors liked him no better than did many Americans. They burned down his warehouses and accused him of setting the fire for the insurance money.

During a debate in the British House of Lords, the Earl of Lauderdale called Benedict Arnold a traitor, which, of course, he was. Arnold challenged Lauderdale to a duel. Arnold shot but missed. Lauderdale held his fire.

Benedict Arnold died in June 1801, a bitter, broken man. He left his family a heritage of debts, lawsuits, and a name that continues as synonymous with traitor.

Thomas Paine harangued thousands of people into fighting for American independence, and then he left the country, moving on to other projects, including the design of iron bridges. When the city of Philadelphia decided to replace the ferry across the Schuylkill River with a four-hundred-foot wooden bridge, Tom Paine designed one using crisscrossed iron girders. Philadelphia bought neither the bridge nor Paine's idea, and he took them elsewhere. He built a thirteen-foot model bridge and showed it to the French Academy of Sciences, which declared it "ingeniously imagined." Nobody, however, was willing to build one across the Seine or any other river in France. So Paine took his idea to England, where he had a 110-foot model built. It is, he wrote Thomas Jefferson, "a favorite hobbyhorse with all who have seen it." Still, he couldn't get a full-sized bridge built.

In 1791, Paine published part one of *The Rights of Man*, the basic points of which he had argued with John Adams back in 1776. In it he vindicated events in the French Revolution and critiqued the British form of government—"Can anything be more limited," he wrote, "and at the same time more capricious, than what the qualifications [for suffrage] are in England?" The "idea of hereditary legislators is as inconsistent as that of hereditary judges, or hereditary juries, and as absurd as an hereditary mathematician, or an hereditary wise man." Paine was outraged by England's Edmund Burke, who sympathized with the French royal family. France, meanwhile, declared Thomas Paine a French citizen. They even elected him to the French legislature, the *Convention*, even though Thomas Paine couldn't speak French.

Not speaking the language stifled his social life and later almost cost Paine his life itself. He was in France when revolutionaries captured the French royal family and brought them back to Paris. Paine was a spectator as the royals were carted through town. He was mistaken for an aristocrat and threatened with hanging. He had not, it seems, adorned himself with the cockade worn by all revolutionary-thinking people. He was saved only when an English-speaking Frenchman recognized and rescued him.

When the Gironde Party, to which he'd attached himself, fell out of power, Tom Paine wound up in prison in Luxembourg Palace, now held by the Jacobin revolutionary regime. He remained there for ten months, constantly under threat of execution. When he was released, he withdrew from politics and left Paris.

John Adams had once praised what he called Paine's "democratical" philosophy. Later Adams ridiculed the spread of egalitarian ideas on both sides of the Atlantic as "Paine's yellow fever."

In 1795, he wrote a long, reproachful letter to George Washington. James Monroe convinced him not to send it, and it didn't appear in print until some eighteen months later, and then as an appendix to his *Memorial Addressed to James Monroe*. *The Rights of Man* had been dedicated to George Washington. Now he attacked Washington for allowing Paine to languish in a French prison. He charged Washington with "egotism," in believing the American Revolution was "all his own doing," when in reality, Paine said, the general's actual contributions were small. Washington, he wrote, had no share in the political aspects of the Revolution, and his military achievement was conspicuous only for his "constancy."

Paine spent the next few years unhappy and longing to return to America. During this time he wrote *The Age of Reason* (published in two parts, 1794 and 1795), which soon became something of "the atheists' bible." It attacked organized religion and aroused indignation in America. It didn't sit too well in England either, where the government indicted Tom Paine for treason and declared him an outlaw.

At age sixty-five Thomas Paine returned to America, where he lived the rest of his life in near poverty, occasionally contributing essays to the Jeffersonian press—*The American Citizen* and the *Public Advertiser*. He was under almost constant assault for his deist writings, and his final years were ones of lonely, private depression. Isolated from his old associates, Paine began drinking heavily.

From July 1808 almost until his death, the aging and ill Thomas Paine lived as a boarder with the Ryder family in the Greenwich Village area of New York City. Initially he paid them ten dollars a week, until February 1809, when the rent was doubled because he needed so much attendance.

By May, Paine realized that he was dying and persuaded his longtime close friend Madame Margaret Bonneville, with whom Paine lived for a time in Paris, to take him into her house. Thomas Paine died on the morning of June 8, 1809. His death passed virtually unnoticed in the American press.

He'd hoped to be buried in a Quaker cemetery, but the Society of Friends denied his request. Paine was buried on the outskirts of a small farm he owned at New Rochelle. Only six mourners attended the funeral of the man who had once inspired millions. None of the six officially represented either the United States or France. Two of those who did attend the funeral were blacks who wanted to pay tribute to Tom Paine for his efforts to end slavery. It is not known if they were slaves or freemen.

On June 17, 1775, the mentally ill James Otis was confined at his Boston home. He eluded servants who were guarding him, borrowed a musket, and rushed off to Bunker Hill. He wasn't hurt in the fighting, but it was a sign to his family that he should be sent away to the country. The following year Otis petitioned the Revolutionary Massachusetts legislature for an amount of money he claimed due him. In the petition he called himself "James Oates," perhaps referring back to one Titus Oates, a madman who "had set all England aflame in the seventeenth century with false reports about a popish plot against the king's life."

After years of living in the country and existing on a diet of bread and honey, James Otis had become enormously fat. Not yet sixty, he had frequent premonitions of an early death. He was right.

On May 23, 1783, James Otis stood calmly watching a summer storm, cane in one hand and leaning against the doorpost. A flash of lightning crashed against the chimney, followed a roof rafter, and grounded in a door timber, where it split apart the door casing and killed James Otis. "Death," says the *Dictionary of American Biography of James Otis,* "came as he had always wished it would; only fire from heaven could release his fiery soul." His biographer, William Tudor, wrote of Otis's death:

> When God in anger saw the spot,
> On earth to Otis given,
> In thunder as from Sinai's Mount
> He snatch'd him back to heaven.

After the Battle of Ninety-Six, the Continental army primarily used Tadeusz Kosciuszko as a cavalry officer. After the Revolution, Kosciuszko returned to Poland, where over the next thirty-three years he campaigned to free his native land from Russia.

Tadeusz Kosciuszko asked France's revolutionary government for support. They refused, and without outside help he tried to lead a popular uprising against the puppet king. It failed. He was defeated, captured, and held prisoner for two years before finally being released. In 1797, Kosciuszko sailed back to America for the last time, where the new government eventually paid him $15,000 for services in the Revolution. Congress also awarded him five hundred acres of land in Ohio; he sold the land and used it to help establish the Colored School at Newark, New Jersey. Napoleon finally offered to help Kosciuszko in another revolt against the Polish king, but the "little general" wanted to control Poland once he'd liberated it. Kosciuszko refused his terms, and he spent the remainder of his life working for the restoration of government as free as he'd fought for in America. He was unsuccessful. Shortly before his death in 1817, Tadeusz Kosciuszko emancipated his serfs. He was seventy-one.

Four months after resigning his commission to protest the acquittal of an officer he'd charged with disobedience, Casimir Pulaski was back in action. He and his legion faced a force of British regulars and Loyalists at a pirate's nest called Little Egg Harbor, New Jersey, a few miles northeast of today's Atlantic City. A combined British-Loyalist attack came in the middle of the night and, when Pulaski and his dragoons arrived, they drove off the enemy.

The following month Pulaski appeared before Congress complaining he'd been given no opportunity for action. By then the fiasco at Monmouth Court House was over, and the "action" Pulaski wanted had moved south. Pulaski, on the other hand, was sent north to the village of Minisink, New York, which had been the site of a minor battle a month earlier. In late November, Pulaski complained that he'd been sent into exile at a place "which even the savages shun, and [I have] nothing but the bears to fight with."

In December 1778, the British captured Savannah, Georgia, losing just three men killed and nine others wounded. American forces lost eighty-three killed, and the British took 451 prisoners along with three ships, forty-eight cannon, twenty-three mortars, and a large quantity of supplies. The following month Augusta also fell.

British troops were moving into Virginia and North Carolina and taking aim at the largest seaport in the South, Charleston, South Carolina. There was a desperate need in the South for cavalry, and Count Pulaski said he was ready.

In February 1779, General Washington, at the insistence of Congress, ordered Pulaski to take his dragoons south. "You will, of course," Washington wrote Pulaski, "give instructions to the Officer Commanding to preserve the strictest discipline on the march and in quarters, that the inhabitants may have no reason to complain of licentious conduct in the Soldiers." Pulaski wrote to Congress that he was "dissatisfied with the present situation of his corps on account of its numbers being too small for a command equal to his rank." He and his legion were in Yorktown, Virginia, in late February "waiting to settle his accounts," according to Assistant Quartermaster General Charles Pettit. He never did clear them up.

By March, Pulaski still had not left Yorktown, and he still blamed the quartermaster. He wrote Congress claiming they had not provided adequate funds for supplies; true, he'd been given $35,000, but he wanted an additional $15,000, and not that newly printed Continental money either, but "some other," which he did not specify.

Casimir Pulaski obviously had trouble making friends. He had, it seems, no trouble making enemies. Joseph Reed of New Jersey, a cavalry officer with whom Pulaski argued verbally and on paper, complained to the Congressional Board of War that Pulaski's troops "forage indiscriminately & take whatever they want from the poor terrified Inhabitants, many of whom strongly impressed by the Terrors of military Violence in Europe, submit to the spoiling of their goods & insult of their Persons without complaining." Board spokesman Timothy Pickering told Reed he would investigate the situation. Besides, he added, Pulaski would be leaving Yorktown "in a few days."

Pulaski finally left Yorktown, but instead of heading south, he went north, to Annapolis, Maryland, where he tried to recruit troops for his legion. "Undouptely [sic]," he wrote, "by sikness or desertion I'll lose some of my men on the road, which lost [sic] added to the one I made in the last Campaign could hardly be repared in the southward the white people being very scarce there, that granted I should be very much indepted to you." It was not a successful sales pitch. Pulaski claimed he'd renamed his troops the "Maryland Legion," hoping to get Baltimore officials to cooperate. They didn't buy it, and Pulaski finally moved out toward Savannah. He arrived at Charleston on May 8.

Admiral-General Count Charles-Hector Thédat d'Estaing had sailed the French fleet south to the West Indies after a disappointing allied effort against Newport, Rhode Island, in August 1778. His orders gave him discretion whether he should aid the American rebels, and General Benjamin Lincoln appealed to Charleston for d'Estaing to do just that.

D'Estaing agreed. After all, hurricane season was beginning in the West Indies, and the farther north he was, the better. He left San Domingo on August 16, and in September, d'Estaing was off the coast of Charleston, ready to cooperate. Seeing the French fleet, Loyalists in Savannah sent word to General Clinton, asking for help. By early October a privateer had reached the general in New York with information that d'Estaing was about to strike Savannah.

In preparation for the Savannah campaign General Lincoln withdrew his Continental troops from the forts around Charleston and replaced them with militia. He ordered Pulaski to join Continental troops at Augusta and march toward Savannah, where he would coordinate with the French. On September 11, Pulaski and a few of his horsemen crossed the Savannah River west of town, where he skirmished with the redcoats. "Count Pulaski advanced with cavalry," a Boston newspaper reported, "took the enemy's picket and also surprised their captain and three privates at Ebenezer [Georgia]."

On the day Pulaski crossed the Savannah, d'Estaing began landing troops at Beaulieu, south of the city. Bad weather caused a delay, but by the 16th, Lincoln, d'Estaing, and Pulaski had joined forces, a total of between four and five thousand men, including a black regiment d'Estaing had recruited in Haiti. They faced a British force of about 3,200, plus a number of civilians and runaway slaves, who would be used to improve the town's fortifications. Six British ships were sunk in the channel, blocking it.

Savannah was Charleston all over again, only this time it was in reverse. D'Estaing called on the British garrison to surrender. Garrison commander General Augustine Provost first asked for twenty-four hours to consider surrendering, then refused; during that time he'd pulled his scattered army together. (It was the same ploy

Cornwallis would try against Washington at Yorktown, but Washington refused and Cornwallis had no recourse but to surrender.) Instead of immediately attacking Savannah as some officers (including Colonel William Moultrie of Fort Sullivan fame) suggested, d'Estaing decided on a siege. To do so, they had to haul cannon and mortars fourteen miles from the landing site, over sandy soil—it's appropriately called the "low country"—and in a heavy rain. Finally work was begun on what were called the "regular approaches"—a time-consuming method in which the besieging force digs trenches in a zigzag pattern, moves forward, digs more trenches, and moves forward again—began on October 3. French and American troops bombarded the city, which, incidentally was well inside the British fortifications. Mainly it was civilians who were killed or wounded in the barrage.

Off the coast d'Estaing's naval captains complained. Hurricane season had moved north and the fleet now was vulnerable.* French sailors, who unlike their British opponents had not taken to eating and drinking vitamin C–laden limes, were dying of scurvy at an average of thirty-five a day.

After a week d'Estaing agreed to abandon the siege and make an all-out attack on Savannah. The allies would attack in two columns, one American, the other French, at dawn on October 9.

Between the time d'Estaing demanded that Provost surrender and the time the attack began, the British constructed rugged defenses backed with plenty of cannon. They met the allied attack with storms of grapeshot and musketry.

"The American column on the right," Major Thomas Pinckney of the South Carolina militia wrote, "were to be preceded by Pulaski, with his cavalry." Pinckney added that Pulaski said to Colonel Daniel Horry, "Follow my Lancers to whom I have given my order of Attack." Pulaski was "at the head of two hundred horsemen, was in full gallop riding into the town, between the redoubts, with an intention of charging in the rear." The count "proceeded gallantly until stopped

---

* On October 10 a hurricane hit the West Indies, flattening Barbados and Martinique and sinking almost every ship in its path. Upward of 30,000 people died in what came to be called the great hurricane of 1780.

by the abatis, and before he could force through it, received his mortal wound."

Depending on the source, Casimir Pulaski was hit in either the groin by grapeshot, in the thigh by a musket ball, or in the scrotum by a combination of the two. Admiral d'Estaing noted that Pulaski "fell by his own fault as he had been at a spot where he should not have been." In any case, Pulaski's men retreated, leaving him where he'd fallen. When they realized they'd forgotten Casimir, "some of his men displayed great courage and personal attachment in returning through the firing, covered by the smoke, to the place where he lay and bore him off."

Pulaski was still alive but bleeding badly when he was taken on board the brig *Wasp,* but he didn't last long. Casimir Pulaski was thirty-one years old when he died, probably on October 11. Where he was buried is uncertain.

Colonel Horry was unable to stop the retreating cavalry. In an hour the allies lost more than one thousand men. Moses Buffington, a Tory inside Savannah, wrote his parents:

> We have had perhaps as hard Sege as Ever has Been since the Rebelion began. We were Brocked [blocked] up both by Land and water from the 10th of September until october the 18th During which time a grate part was taking up in Can[on]ading and Ball Bumbarding from Both sides the[y] throw upwards of 1000 Shells into our works Beside some thousand Balls and a quantity of Carcages [Carcasses? Cartridges?] in order to burn the town October 9th the[y] made a general atack on us about the Brake of day which Lasted about an our and half after which time the[y] thought proper to Retreat Leaving upwards of four hundred of their Best troops on the ground the Loss on our side did not Exceed fifty killed and wounded.

Actually the allies lost over 800, including about 650 French troops; the British lost no more than sixteen killed and thirty-nine wounded. At least to the British military. Since d'Estaing's artillery mainly bombarded the city of Savannah, not the British fortifications, the loss among those in the city may have been much higher.

The British drove many of the retreating American and French troops into the swamp. In disgust, d'Estaing, who had been wounded twice himself, returned to his ships and sailed back to France. In New York, Sir Henry Clinton said, "I think this is the greatest event that has happened [in] the whole war."

Many consider Count Casimir Pulaski a failure—"His American career was tragic," says the *Dictionary of American Biography*. Many others believe he was a hero. On October 11, 1853, a monument was dedicated to him in Savannah. "Whether the seas received him or not," Henry Williams said in a speech during the laying of a cornerstone of the Pulaski Monument, "or whether he lies under some spreading oak upon St. Helena's Island in our sister State or sleeps beneath the sod of Greenwich by the banks of our own beautiful streams, an hour's pilgrimage from the spot where he fell, remains to this day a mystery."

John Paul Jones was a few months past his forty-fifth birthday and living in Paris when artist Thomas Carlyle saw him:

> In Faded naval uniform, Paul Jones lingers visible here; like a wine-skin from which the wine is drawn. Like the ghost of himself! Low is his once loud bruit (his voice); scarcely audible, save with extreme tedium, in ministerial ante-chambers. . . . What changes, culminatings and declinings!
>
> Poor Paul! hunger and dispiritment track thy sinking footsteps; once or at most twice, in this Revolution-tumult the figure of thee emerges; mute, ghost-like, as "with stars dim-twinkling through."

John Paul Jones died in Paris in 1792, three weeks before a mob overran the French royal palace of the Tuileries. He was buried at St. Louis cemetery, but bodies of members of the Swiss guard who'd been killed trying to protect the king and queen were thrown into the grave with Jones.

In 1899, French and American officials began a search for Jones's body. The cemetery had been covered by houses since his death, and no one was certain where it was. It wasn't until 1905 that Jones's body was found along with the remains of the Swiss guard. The murdered guard had been stacked like so much cordwood, but three other bodies were found in separate lead coffins. Two were those of unknown civilians, but the third coffin apparently contained the remains of John Paul Jones. A report at the time said that when the third coffin was opened it contained "a remarkably well-preserved corpse whose face had an unmistakable resemblance to the portrait of Paul Jones." An autopsy reportedly confirmed that it was indeed Jones.

President Theodore Roosevelt sent a fleet of four cruisers to retrieve the remains. After an elaborate ceremony and parade featuring both French and American military personnel, Jones's coffin was transferred to the cruiser *Brooklyn*. Two weeks later the entourage, now including four battleships, sailed into Chesapeake Bay. Off Annapolis, Maryland, the body was taken ashore and placed in a temporary vault. In 1913, Jones's remains were placed in the crypt at the U.S. Naval Academy.

For years middies (Naval Academy midshipmen) sang a parody on a popular song called "Everybody Works but Father":

> Everybody works but John Paul Jones!
> He lies around all day,
> Body pickled in alcohol
> On a permanent jag, they say.
> Middies stand around him
> Doing honor to his bones;
> Everybody works in "Crabtown"
> But John Paul Jones!

As a young man Aaron Burr had been a notorious lover, and at age seventy-seven he remarried. His new wife was Betsey Bowen Jumel, a fifty-five-year-old widow. The marriage, however, lasted only four months before she left him. Betsey charged her septuagenarian husband with adultery. For her divorce Betsey had as her attorney one Alexander Hamilton, Jr., son of the man Aaron Burr had killed in a duel thirty-one years earlier. Betsey, incidentally, claimed that among her many lovers had been that same Alexander Hamilton, Sr.

Betsey's divorce from Aaron was granted on September 14, 1836. It was the same day that Aaron Burr died.

Joseph Plumb Martin finally left the army in 1784, long after the Battle of Yorktown, and a year after the Treaty of Paris ended the war on September 3, 1783. He moved to Maine, "where I have remained ever since, and where I expect to remain so long as I remain in existence." In his memoirs Martin complained that when men enlisted in the Continental army, "they were promised a hundred acres of land, each, which was to be in their own or the adjoining states." But they were "turned adrift like old worn-out horses, and nothing said about land to pasture them upon." Finally Congress approved the "Soldiers' Lands" in Ohio. In the years to come these land grants became a source of a new life for some veterans and a source of wealth for others, nonveterans who purchased soldiers' grants for a small percentage of their worth and, gambling on inflation, later sold them at sometimes huge profits.

Joseph Martin himself enlisted for a bounty of three pounds, a "gun, bayonet, cartouche box, and blanket." It was paid to his grandfather on August 3, 1777, when Martin reenlisted in the Continental army. Martin wrote that often during the war he went "one, two, three, and even four days without a morsel" of food. American troops "being tracked by the blood of their feet on the frozen ground," he said, was "literally true, and the thousandth part of their sufferings has not, nor ever will be told."

As has been the case in almost every war America has fought, after the fighting is over, people, including many in Congress, forget about the men and women who suffered for their country. America's "poor old decrepit soldiers," Martin claimed, "after all that has been served to discourage them, have found friends in the community, and I trust there are many, very many, that are sensible of the usefulness of that suffering army."

They marched home after Yorktown, that rag-tag and bob-tail army, in some cases to find their loved ones gone and new enemies waiting. While they'd been gone, civilians—both those who called themselves Patriots and Tories—had taken over their land and farms and homes.

In 1818, at age fifty-nine, Martin was destitute. "I have no real nor personal estate," he testified in court, "nor any income whatever. . . . Without [a] pension I am unable to support myself and family." The court granted him a pension of ninety-six dollars a year.

Joseph Plumb Martin died on May 2, 1850. He was eighty-nine.* A monument at his grave in Sandy Point Cemetery states simply: A Soldier of the Revolution.

About ten in the morning on Thursday, December 12, 1799, George Washington, now retired from both the army and political life, went for a ride at his Virginia plantation, Mount Vernon. He usually rode every day, even if the weather was as bad as it was that day—dripping melted snow from his cloak, his neck and hair damp from the snow. An anti-Washington report at the time claimed the general had been out cavorting with a black concubine.

On Friday the general complained of "a hoarseness, which increased in the evening; but he made light of it." By Saturday the 14th, his throat was raw and aching, and he had a violent cough. Very likely, Washington had pneumonia, but Sir Alexander Fleming, and the penicillin he invented 129 years later, were not around to save the general.

Instead, doctors gave Washington a mixture of molasses, butter, and vinegar, which itself almost killed him. The general's physicians then tried a mixture of tartar and calomel—mercury. Mercury, of course, is poisonous.

Not content with poisoning him, the physicians bled him four times, draining a total of a quart of blood. Reports written at the time said that by the afternoon the flow of blood was "slow," which you'd expect,

---

* There is a discrepancy in his memorial and his own stated date of birth. The gravestone gives his age at ninety years, six months, and nineteen days; however, he gave his birth date as November 21, 1760, making him eighty-nine years and five months at the time of his death.

considering how much they'd already taken. An average 150-pound man has about five and a quarter quarts of blood. George Washington's physicians, who admittedly were not trained in medicine in today's terms, took almost one-fifth of his blood. Twenty percent.

Three physicians attended the former president that day, and one of them, James Craik, later wrote that he didn't approve of the way his colleagues were treating Washington. Claiming he "was averse to bleeding the General," Craik wrote that if they had not bled Washington "our good friend might be alive."

They bled him and they poisoned him. At four-thirty that afternoon Washington asked his secretary, Tobias Lear, to have Martha bring him two copies of his will. She did, and he looked at both, said that one of them was useless and asked his wife of more than forty years to burn it; she did.

Washington clearly realized where his illness was heading. He told Lear: "I find that I am going. My breath cannot continue long. I believed from the first attack it would be fatal. . . ."

Then he told his secretary to "arrange and record my late military letters and papers. Arrange my accounts and settle my books. . . . Let Mr. Rawlins [another aide] finish recording my other letters, which he has begun."

The general asked Lear if there was anything he had forgotten, since "he had but a very short time." Lear tried to ease Washington's fears; no, he objected, you are not near death. Washington would have none of it. He smiled and observed "that he certainly was, and that it was the debt which we all must pay."

Once later that night, and again the following morning, he was lifted into a chair near the fire, but the effort was too much for him, and he had to be returned to bed. "I am afraid," he told Lear, "I shall fatigue you too much." When Dr. Craik asked Washington if he could sit up, the former president "held out his hand" to Lear "and was raised up." "I feel myself going," Washington said. "You had better not take any more trouble about me but let me go off quietly; I cannot last long."

At ten that morning he told his secretary, "I am just going. Have me decently buried, and do not let my body be put into the Vault in less than two days after I am dead."

He looked at Lear: "Do you understand me?"

"Yes, sir."

"'Tis well," Washington said. They were his last words.

Shortly before eleven Washington withdrew his hand from Lear's, felt his own pulse, then returned his hand to his secretary's. Dr. Craik was sitting by the fire, and he arose to comfort Washington. "The general's hand fell," Lear wrote, "and he expired without a struggle or a sigh."

No one thought to look at a clock, so it's unknown just what time George Washington died.

Martha was sitting at the foot of the bed. "Is he gone?" she asked. Lear couldn't speak but indicated that he was. "'Tis well," Martha said, almost as if she were repeating the general's words. "All is over now. . . . I shall soon follow him."

On December 18, the general's body was placed in a black-draped coffin befitting his large size and importance. As he had requested, he would be entombed near the home he loved so much.

A party of militia from Alexandria had asked to be present, and their arrival delayed the entombment. It was late afternoon when the funeral services got underway.

A vessel anchored nearby in the Potomac River fired off its cannon in salute, and the procession formed. First came rifle- and cavalrymen from the Revolution. Slaves led Washington's favorite horse down a gently sloping lawn. (Under the general's will, the last 150 slaves that Washington owned would be freed at Martha's death, May 22, 1802.) Six army colonels acted as pallbearers. The general's sword and cape rested on top of the casket. Members of the Alexandria, Virginia, Masonic Lodge, where Washington was a member, followed in the rear.

It's uncertain why, but Martha did not join the cortage, watching instead from a window in the house.

The military group split into two lines, and mourners walked between them to the vault. As the guns continued to fire from the riverboat, the rector of Alexandria's Christ Church read the final service. Pallbearers placed the coffin in the recesses of the vault, and the mourners turned and walked back up the hill to Mount Vernon.

• • •

In eulogizing Washington, Henry "Light-Horse Harry" Lee said of the general: "To the memory of the Man, first in war, first in peace, and first in the hearts of his countrymen," basically repeating a House of Representatives resolution of a week earlier. When Napoleon heard of Washington's death, he declared ten days of mourning in France. Official mourning in America continued until February 22, 1800. It would have been George Washington's sixty-eighth birthday. Unofficial grieving continued months longer. Finally, almost a year after Washington's death, the tributes came to an end, and the mourning mobs stopped parading by the vault on the banks of the Potomac.

George Washington rapidly lapsed into history and myth, with both reality and illusion quickly changing. Within a decade the general had become almost a demigod. Certainly it's strange that this transformation came so fast. At the time of his death, Washington was somewhat controversial. He had condoned, perhaps beyond his own wishes, the punishing of his enemies, which quite possibly was unconstitutional. As a Federalist he tried to silence members of the more republican (that is, the Democratic-Republican or anti-Federalist) press. When Washington sent federal troops into western Pennsylvania to disperse the Whiskey Rebellion rioters in 1794 (the rioters protested the excise tax on whiskey), opposing politicians bitterly attacked him. When he died, the Philadelphia *Aurora*, published by Benjamin Franklin's grandson, ran the following notation:

> Every heart, in unison with the freedom and happiness of the people, ought to beat high in exultation, that the name of Washington ceases from this day to give a currency to political iniquity and to legalize corruption.

Between the winter of his death and the outbreak of the Civil War in 1861, America came close to worshiping George Washington. Much of that worship must be attributed to the now-discredited Parson Weems, who began collecting tales about his hero even before the general's death.

Less than a month after Washington's death, Weems told publishers, Carey and Wayne of Philadelphia, "I've something to whisper in your lug (ear). Washington, you know, is gone! Millions are gaping to read something about him. I am very nearly primed and cocked for 'em." But Carey and Wayne were too slow for Weems, and within three weeks the self-proclaimed man of God found others to print his book:

> The True Patriot or Beauties of Washington
> Abundantly Biographical & Anecdotal
> Curious & Marvellous.

Weems traveled the country, selling his books for twenty-five cents a copy.

Meanwhile George Washington's nephew, Bushrod Washington, persuaded U.S. Chief Justice John Marshall to write an official biography. It wasn't until 1804 that the first installment of Marshall's book was printed—oddly enough, by Weems's old publisher, C. P. Wayne. In publishing terms the Chief Justice's book was a disaster, five volumes at the then-steep price of three dollars each. According to John Adams, the Marshall version of Washington's life story was not a book at all but, rather, "a Mausoleum, 100 square feet at the base and 200 feet high."

Instead of taking to this expensive literary "mausoleum," the public chose to believe Parson Weems's version of Washington. Eager for someone who was more hero than man, they devoured every fable that Weems contrived. The tale of George's mother—while pregnant with the future general, Weems claimed, Mary Ball Washington dreamed a dream "which foretold his greatness and the history of the Revolution." The cherry-tree story and the exaggeration of Washington tossing some object across some river. How George hated to fight, yet "performed feats of strength," and how a "famous Indian warrior" swore that "Washington was not born to be killed by a bullet! For I had seventeen fair fires at him with my rifle, and after all could not bring him to the ground." Not that the warrior was a poor shot.

When there were no facts upon which Parson Weems could base his stories, he turned to fantasy, making them up. Some were, like television political commercials of today, virtually impossible to disprove. For example, as unlikely as the tale is, in truth, we *do not know that the cherry-tree episode did not occur.*

Generations believed the Weems fabrications, and it would be additional generations before the true stories would be written. Finally we learned that George Washington was a man of his time, larger than life perhaps, but still a man of his time. He had his faults, both physical and emotional. He was not a marble monument. We made him one.

As the figurative monument to Washington grew, efforts rapidly mounted to build a more tangible shrine to the general. The U.S. House appropriated $200,000 for a project. A year after his death George's widow approved a proposal to build a marble mausoleum; it would be pyramidal in shape with a base one hundred feet square. Into it would go Washington's coffin. The mausoleum would be in the capital city, however, and southerners, especially Virginians, didn't like the idea of moving their home-grown hero's remains from Mount Vernon. They fought to keep the general's remains at the plantation, and they won the argument.

Every so often, however, other plans were proposed to move Washington's remains to some place north of the home he loved. As the country grew, there was talk of moving the U.S. capital to someplace more central—Columbus, Ohio, for example. That idea carried with it however, a vision of the capital moving whenever the country expanded, and with it, Washington's remains, trucked about every time America grew.

British troops burned the interior of the Capitol in 1814, and the central portion of the structure was rebuilt. A plan was laid to transfer Washington's remains to a crypt constructed in the repaired building. Again there was opposition, and again the plan was rejected.

In 1831, a new brick tomb, built on a site the general himself had selected at Mount Vernon, was completed. His remains and those of Martha were reinterred. The vault was locked and the key thrown into the Potomac.

The nation still worshipped the memory of George Washington, and in state after state, monuments were erected to the man who would be president, not king. On July 4, 1848, a cornerstone for a national monument was laid in the marshlands town named after him. The white marble obelisk would be 555 feet, 5½ inches high; each side of the square base would be 55 feet, 1½ inches long. But time, and a war in which the General's home state of Virginia was on the opposite side, frustrated the builders. For years the monument sat only half finished, and when building resumed, the marble had to come from a different source; it was of a slightly different color, the difference easily distinguished even today.

Finally, on December 6, 1884, a 3,300-pound aluminum capstone was put in place at the top of the obelisk. And on February 21, 1885, the Washington Monument was officially dedicated. An account of the ceremony says that it was a bitterly cold day, with snow on the ground and a high wind blowing.

From the observation level some 55 feet from the top of the monument, you can see for miles into the city and surrounding countryside. Look about sixteen miles due south and you can see Mount Vernon. There, between the Potomac River and the plantation house, George and Martha Washington lie in a vault whose iron gates are padlocked. Adoration of the demigod has decreased, and keepers of the vault now fear vandalism.

George Washington was branded an assassin after his defeat at Fort Necessity; after all, he killed a French diplomat. Forced into early military retirement, he became a slaveholding farmer who grew marijuana and introduced mules to America. Virtually uneducated but with a fierce ambition, he became a colonial legislator, relentlessly striving for fame but at first missing it. He was aloof, cool, and distant, giving others a sense of hidden violence.

He proposed to one woman while he was in love with another and resigned himself to marry the first when he couldn't have the second. Apparently the man known as the father of his country was biologically unable to have children.

When his home colony rose up to demand freedom, he chose to lead his people—a soldier who might not have either home or country to which he could return if the army lost. With his army saved and freedom for his people assured, he returned to the farm he loved. The people he had led to victory, however, would not allow that to happen just yet, and once more they demanded he return as their commander, this time as head of a new form of government. Washington may not have invented the position to which he was elected, but he mastered and subdued the job, giving it a dignity and strength that few had envisioned. Now, two hundred years after his death, we still don't fully understand the enigma that was George Washington.

In an oyster gray building on a hill in Richmond, Virginia, in the rotunda of the state capitol designed by Thomas Jefferson, stands a lifesize, life-like marble statue of Washington by sculptor Jean Houdon. Washington was president when Houdon began work on the statue. The sculptor had trouble getting the look just right; he wanted a look of concern, perhaps disapproval. Houdon said that finally, as he sketched and pondered Washington, a trader arrived to sell the president some mules. The trader told Washington the price, and the president's mouth tightened. Houdon had the expression he was looking for.

He portrayed Washington not in the Roman-style toga that was fashionable for statues of the time,* but showed the Great Man dressed in an old coat, two buttons missing from one side and one from the other. For years a janitor in the Virginia capitol told visitors the missing buttons were meant to show that Martha was less than a perfect housekeeper. Not so. It was simply an old military coat, almost worn out from wear while fighting for freedom.

When the statue was completed, Houdon invited Washington to see the work before it was put on display. The general stood before the statue, then went over into a corner, where he looked at it from another angle. Finally he nodded: He liked it. It was rare praise coming from George Washington.

The statue shows a face with a massive nose and jawbones, a melancholy downturn to the mouth (the price of those mules, perhaps),

* Horatio Greenough did sculpt a posthumous work of Washington wearing a toga and sandals. The general's contemporaries realized a half-naked Washington looked ridiculous. Washington, they said, "was too prudent and careful of his health to expose himself thus in a climate so uncertain as ours." The toga-clad Washington was intended to be placed in the Capitol, but objections were so loud, the plans were dropped.

wide-set and solemn eyes, looking off at a vision lesser mortals cannot imagine. Ralph Waldo Emerson said they were "heavy, laden eyes [that] stare at you, as the eyes of an ox in pasture." The mouth, Emerson said, "has gravity and depth of quiet, as if this MAN has absorbed all the serenity of America and left none for his restless, rickety, hysterical countrymen."

For more than two centuries George Washington has baffled and beguiled us. He likely will continue to do so for centuries more.

On April 5, 1869, Daniel T. Bakeman of Freedom, Cattaraugus County, New York died. Bakeman was the last of the pensioned soldiers of the Revolutionary army. With him the last of the American Revolutionaries were gone.

Epilogue:
Personal Thoughts on the American Revolution

"Tut, tut, child," said the Duchess. "Everything's got a moral if only you can find it."
—Lewis Carroll (Charles Lutwidge Dodgson),
Alice's Adventures in Wonderland, 1865

"War, children, is just a shot away, it's just a shot away".
—Michael Philip "Mick" Jagger, *Gimme Shelter,* 1969

The makers of the American Revolution—those who thought of it, who fought it, those who designed the Constitution and nation that emerged from it—were not giants. We do them a disservice by considering them to be such. They were men and women who rose above their own mediocrity and changed the world.

The American Revolution was, in many ways, the greatest war ever fought by any people. Not in the number who took part; that "honor" goes to World War II. Not in the number of American casualties; the Civil War saw many more. The American Revolution was the greatest war because of what it did to and for a people, to and for the world.

Essentially World War II put us in our place; Hitler was gone; the Japanese war party defeated. Even before the war, it was obvious the United States was the rising world power.

The Vietnam War returned the status quo. The land that had been artificially divided along political lines once more was one. After three years of fighting, the Korean War stopped, but the issues that started the war still haven't been settled.

Eight years after the hundred-hour war in the Persian Gulf War, the United States perennially stands prepared to send troops into the region to fight once more a war of despots and oil wells.

There were other wars, of course, but in the end none had the long-lasting effect of the American Revolution. Abraham Lincoln proclaimed that America had been "conceived in liberty and dedicated to the proposition that all men are created equal." Both of these clauses are, to some degree or other, incorrect.

The American Revolution to a great extent was fought for economic reasons. We did not want to be taxed by somebody else even if those taxes might be used to our own benefit. If anybody was going to dig into our pockets, it was going to be us.

Many who spoke out loudest against tyranny at the same time tyrannized others. Many of our Founding Fathers were slave holders; many others prospered from the sale and breeding of slaves. Many lived just this side of legality.

Liberty was not the seed from which we grew. It was, instead, a nutrient that allowed us to do *to* and *for* ourselves, while helping those unable to help themselves. Equality? Well, we should not look on the late eighteenth century with late-twentieth-century eyes, but there truly was no equality of races, sexes, or economic origin at the time, and we still haven't attained them.

Which brings us back to this "nongiant" belief. Those who invented America overcame their own need either to obtain or retain economic wealth. It is perhaps trite but true: They overcame themselves.

They did not give us liberty. They gave us the means to assure our own liberty.

During those times, the times that tried men's souls, as Tom Paine put it, we were a small number of people on a far-flung shore, but these nongiants brought us together. That was no small accomplishment considering problems of the times.

Those nongiants somehow got us all on the same page of history at the same time. It was and is a wonderful page, but one we must constantly fight to preserve—for ourselves and those who will follow.

They were nongiants, those men and women of our Revolution, but marvelous people who did remarkable things.

Did the Revolution ever end? Fifty-four years after the Battle of Yorktown, France's Alexis de Tocqueville wrote: "America is a land of wonders, in which everything is in constant motion and every change seems an improvement."

Epilogue

Wonders still surround us, the constant motion of change continues. The American Revolution and the Constitution are, as they say, works in progress. Those who gave us the gifts of freedom, liberty, and democracy opened to us a wondrous future. However, in looking to our future, as we must, we should not forget our past. The past, after all, is that foreign land from which we all emigrated.

Bibliography

Manuscripts:

Adams, John. Papers. Massachusetts Historical Collection.

Adams, John. "A Dissertation on the Canon and Feudal Laws." Massachusetts Historical Collection.

André, Major John. *Major André's Journal: Operations of the British Army under Lieutenant Generals Sir William Howe and Sir Henry Clinton, June, 1777, to November, 1778, to Which is Added "The Ethics of Major André's Mission."* Tarrytown, N.Y. The Bibliographical Society, 1904.

Arnold, Benedict [probably] to General Philip Schuyler. "Letters Written while on an Expedition across the State of Maine to Attack Quebec in 1775." Maine Historical Society Collection, vol. 1, 1831.

The Case of Captain Thomas Preston of the 29th Regiment. House of Lords Manuscript Collection, London.

Cornwallis, Lord General Charles. Papers. Public Records Office, London.

Darlington, William to Thomas Wharton, Jr. November 29, 1845. *Historical Society of Pennsylvania Bulletin*, vol. 1.

Gates, Horatio. Collection. New York Historical Society.

Hay, Major Samuel to Colonel William Irvine, written at Trappe, Pennsylvania, September 28, 1777. Pennsylvania Archives, 2nd series, vol. 1.

Howe, Sir William. Orderly Book. Lloyd W. Smith Collection, Morristown National Historical Park.

Hughes, John. Papers. Historical Society of Pennsylvania.

Jefferson, Thomas to William Rosco, December 27, 1820. University of Virginia Library, Charlottesville, Virginia.

Laurens, Henry, "Narrative of his Capture, of his Confinement in the Tower of London, etc., 1780, 1781, 1782." South Carolina Historical Society Collections.

Madison, James. Papers. Library of Congress.

Powell, Barbara MacDonald. *The Most Celebrated Encampment: Valley*

Forge in American Culture. Unpublished Ph.D. dissertation. Cornell University, 1983.

Quincy, Josiah, Jr. Papers. Massachusetts Historical Society.

Revere, Paul. Papers. Massachusetts Historical Papers.

Stokes Collection. New York Public Library.

U.S. Treasury Papers. Class I, bundle 442.

Washington, George to the president of the Confederation Congress, September 11, 1777. Library of Congress.

Magazines:

American Historical Review, 26 (1920–1921), 745; original in *Paris Service Hydrographique de la Marine,* vol 76, no. 2; photocopy in Research Department, Colonial Williamsburg Foundation, Williamsburg, Virginia.

Bushnell, David. "General Principles and Construction of a Sub-marine Vessel." *Transactions of the American Philosophic Society,* no. 4, 1799.

Foster, Eugene A., et al. "Jefferson Father Slave's Last Child." *Nature,* November 5, 1998.

Freehling, William W. "The Founding Father and Slavery." *American Historical Review,* no. 77, February 1972.

Gustaitis, Joseph. "One-Man Army." *American History,* October 1994.

"Instructions to the Delegates to be chosen for the County of Cumberland on Monday, the 22nd Day of April, 1776, to Sit in the General Convention of this Colony." *The William and Mary Quarterly Historical Magazine,* first series, vol. 2, 1893–1894.

Jackson, Luther P. "Virginia Negro Soldiers and Seamen in the American Revolution." *Journal of Negro History,* vol. 27, 1942.

Johnston, Henry P. "Sergeant Lee's Experience with Bushnell's Submarine Torpedo in 1776." *Magazine of History,* no. 29, 1893.

Lander, Eric S. and Ellis, Joseph. "Founding Father," *Nature,* November 5, 1998.

Massachusetts Historical Society, proceedings, 1864–1865, Boston, 1866.

Musset, Charles F., ed. "Some Political Writings of James Otis." *University of Missouri Studies,* vol. 4, 1929.

Morris, Richard B. "Then and there the child independence was born." *American Heritage,* vol. XII, no. 2, February 1962.

Nash, Gary. "Poverty and Poor Relief in Pre-Revolutionary Philadelphia." *The William and Mary Quarterly*, no. 33, 3rd series.

Pennsylvania Magazine, 1776. Now in the New York Public Library rare books division.

Proceedings of the Convention of Delegates for the Counties & Corporations in the Colony of Virginia, Held at Richmond Town, March 23, 1775. Richmond, Virginia, 1816.

Proceedings of the Massachusetts Historical Society, 1881–1882.

Revolutionary War Records, Captain Samuel Peck's Company, Douglas's Regiment. National Archives, Record Group 93.

Sargent, Winthrop. "Letters of John Andrews, Esq. of Boston, 1772–1776."

Trist, Nicholas. Papers. University of Virginia Library.

"Vital Facts." *A Chronology of the College of William and Mary*, Williamsburg, Virginia, 1963, 9th revision.

Waldo, Albigence, Valley Forge, 1777–1778. "The Diary of Albigence Waldo of the Connecticut Line." *Pennsylvania Magazine of History and Biography*, vol 21, 1897.

Wiener, Frederick Bernays. "The Signer Who Recanted." *American Heritage*, June 1975.

Newspapers:
Boston Gazette, November 15, 1779.
Chicago Tribune.
London Morning Post and Daily Advertiser, April 28, 1778.
New Hampshire Gazette.
New York Gazetter and *New Daily Advertiser.*
New York Times, November 1, 1998.
New York Times, November 4, 1998.
Niles' Weekly Register, March 7, 1818.
Pennsylvania Evening Post, January 2, 1776.
Pennsylvania Gazette, May 29, 1776.
Philadelphia Inquirer, November 3, 1998.
Virginia Gazette.

Early Works:
Adams, Charles Francis, ed. *The Works of John Adams*, 10 vols. Boston, 1850–1856.

Brock, R.A., ed. *The Official Records of Robert Dinwiddie: 1751–1758.* Richmond, Virginia, 1883.

Burgoyne, General John, to Lord George Germain, February 28, 1777. *A State of the Expedition from Canada.* London, 1780.

Carrington, H. B. *Battles of the American Revolution: 1775–1781.* New York, 1876.

Custis, George Washington Parke. *Recollections and Private Memoirs of Washington by his Adopted Son, George Washington Parke Custis.* Philadelphia, 1856.

Dawson, Henry B. *Battles of the United States, by Sea and Land: Embracing Those of the Revolutionary and Indian Wars, the War of 1812, and the Mexican War; with Official Documents and Biographies of the Most Distinguished Military and Naval Commanders,* 2 vols., New York, 1858.

DeBeauvoir, François-Jean, Chevalier de Castellux. *Travels in North America in the Years 1780, 1781, and 1782,* 2 vols., New York, 1827, reprinted 1963.

Fanning, Nathaniel. *Narrative of the Adventures of an American Navy Officer.* New York, 1806.

Fiske, John, *The American Revolution,* 2 vols., Boston, 1891, reprinted 1901.

Frothingham, Richard, *Rise of the Republic of the United States.* Boston, 1872.

Gibbes, R. W., ed. *Documentary History of the American Revolution: Consisting of Letters and Papers Relating to the Contest for Liberty, Chiefly in South Carolina, from Originals in Possession of the Editor, and Other sources: 1776–1782,* 3 vols., New York, 1853–1857.

Goss, Elbridge Henry. *The Life of Paul Revere.* Boston, 1891.

Hawkes, James. *A Retrospect of the Boston Tea-Party, with a Memoir of George T. Hewes, Survivor of the Little Band of Patriots Who Drowned the Tea in Boston Harbour in 1773. By a citizen of New York.* New York, 1834.

Henry, John Joseph. "Account of Arnold's Campaign Against Quebec, and of the Hardships and Sufferings of the Band of Heroes who Traversed the Wilderness of Maine from Cambridge to the St. Lawrence, in the Autumn of 1775." Albany, New York, 1877.

Hunt, Gaillard, ed. *Journals of the American Congress: From 1774 to 1788,* 4 vols., Washington, D.C., 1823.

Lecky, W. E. *The American Revolution: 1763–1783*. New York, 1898.

Lee, Richard Henry II. *Memoir of the Life of Richard Henry Lee*, 2 vols., Philadelphia, 1825.

Lossing, Benson J. *The Pictorial Field Book of the Revolution: Or, Illustrations, by Pen and Pencil, of the History, Biography, Scenery, Relics, and Traditions of the War for Independence*, 2 vols., New York, 1851.

Marshall, John. *The Life of George Washington*, 11 vols., Philadelphia, 1848.

Martin, Joseph Plumb. *A Narrative of some of the Adventures, Dangers, and Sufferings of a Revolutionary soldier, Interspersed with Anecdotes of Incidents That Occurred Within His Own Observations*. Hallowell, Maine, 1818, reprinted as *Private Yankee Doodle*, George F. Scheer, ed, Boston, 1962.

Mather, Increase. *Dignity and Duty of Aged Servants of the Lord*. Boston, 1716.

———. *Two discourses*. Boston, 1716.

Meyers, Albert C., ed. *Hanna Logan's Courtship*. Philadelphia, 1904.

Moore, Frank, ed. *Materials for History, Printed From Original Manuscripts*. New York, 1861.

Randall, Henry S. *The Life of Jefferson*, 3 vols., New York, 1858.

Stone, William L. trans. *Letters and Journals Relating to the War of the American Revolution*. Albany, New York, 1898, reprinted 1968.

Warren, Mercy. *History of the American Revolution*, 3 vols., Boston, 1805.

Weems, Mason Locke. *Life of George Washington With Curious Anecdotes, Equally Honorable to Himself and His Young Countrymen*. New York, 1800.

Whitemore, William H., et al, *Reports of the Record Commission of Boston*, 14 vols., Boston, 1885.

Wirt, William. *Sketches of the Life and Character of Patrick Henry*. Philadelphia, 1818.

Modern Works:

Adams, Randolph G. and Peckham, Howard H., eds. *Lexington to Fallen Timbers, 1775: Episodes from the Earliest History of Our Military Forces*. Ann Arbor, Michigan, 1942.

Adler, Mortimer J., ed. *The Revolutionary Years: Britannica's Book of the American Revolution*. Chicago, 1976.

Bibliography

Alden, John Richard. *The American Revolution*. New York, 1954.

Alverez, Walter C., M.D. *The Neuroses: Diagnoses and Management of Functional Disorders and Minor Psychoses*. Philadelphia, 1951.

Ayer, A. J. *Thomas Paine*. New York, 1988, reprinted 1990.

Bear, James A., ed. *Jefferson at Monticello*. Charlottesville, Virginia, 1967.

Boatner, Mark M. III. *Encyclopedia of the American Revolution*. New York, 1966, reprinted 1994.

Boorstin, Daniel J. *The Americans*. 3 vols., New York, 1965.

Bowen, Catherine Drinker. *Miracle at Philadelphia: The Story of the Constitutional Convention, May to September 1787*. Boston, 1966.

Boyd, Julian, ed. *The Papers of Thomas Jefferson*, 18 vols., Princeton, New Jersey, 1950–1972.

Brindenbaugh, Carl and Jessica. *Rebels and Gentlemen: Philadelphia in the Age of Franklin*. New York, 1942, reprinted 1965.

Burns, James MacGregor. *The Vineyard of Liberty*. New York, 1981.

Butterfield, L. H., Friedlaender, Marc, and Kline, Mary-Jo. *The Book of Abigail and John: Selected Letters of the Adams Family, 1762–1784*. Boston, 1975.

Carter, Edwin, ed. *The Correspondence of General Thomas Gage*, 2 vols., New Haven, Connecticut, 1931–1932.

Churchill, Winston. *A History of the English Speaking Peoples*, 6 vols., London, 1958.

Colbert, David, ed. *Eyewitness to America: 500 Years of America in the Words of Those Who Saw it Happen*. New York, 1997.

Commager, Henry Steele and Morris, Richard B. *The Spirit of 'Seventy-Six: The Story of the American Revolution As Told by Participants*. New York, 1958.

Conner, Paul W. *Poor Richard's Politics: Benjamin Franklin and His New American Order*. New York, 1997.

Crane, Verner W. *Benjamin Franklin and a Rising People*. Boston, 1954.

Cushing, Henry Alonzo, ed. *The Writings of Samuel Adams*, 4 vols., New York, 1904–1908.

Emerson, Ralph Waldo and Forbes, Waldo Emerson, eds. *Journals of Ralph Waldo Emerson*. Boston, 1912.

Emery, Noemie. *Washington: A Biography*. New York, 1976.

Handlin, Oscar and Clive, John, eds. *Gottlieb Mittelberger's Journey to Pennsylvania*. Cambridge, Massachusetts, 1960.

Fisher, Sydney George. *The Struggle for American Independence*, 2 vols., New York, 1908.

Fleming, Thomas. *Liberty! The American Revolution*. New York, 1997.

———. *1776: Year of Illusions*. New York, 1975.

———. *The Man Who Dared Lightning: A New Look at Benjamin Franklin*. New York, 1971.

Flexner, James Thomas. *Washington: The Indispensable Man*. Boston, 1933, reprinted 1984.

———. *George Washington: Anguish and Farewell (1793–1799)*. Boston, 1948.

Fortescue, Sir John, ed. *The Correspondence of King George the Third from 1760 to December 1783*, 3 vols., London, 1927–1929.

Fraser, Walter, Jr. *Patriots, Pistols and Petticoats: "Poor Sinful Charles Town" During the American Revolution*, 2nd edition Columbia, South Carolina, 1993.

Freeman, Douglas Southall. *George Washington*, 7 vols., New York, 1948–1957.

Garrison, Webb. *Great Stories of the American Revolution*. Nashville, Tennessee, 1990.

Gaylin, Willard, ed. *The Meaning of Despair: Psychoanalytic Contributions to the Understanding of Depression*. New York, 1968.

Goodwin, Rutherford. *A Brief and True Report Concerning Williamsburg in Virginia*. Richmond, Virginia, 1972.

Gorlin, R. J., Cohen, M. M., Jr., and Levin, L. S. *Syndromes of the Head and Neck*, 3rd edition New York, 1990.

Greene, Jack P. *Pursuits of Happiness: The Social Development of Early Modern British Colonies and the Formation of American Culture*. Chapel Hill, North Carolina, 1988.

Greven, Philip. *The Protestant Temperament*. New York, 1977.

Haber, Philip M., ed. *The Papers of Henry Laurens*, 3 vols., Columbia, South Carolina, 1968–1972.

Hakim, Joy. *A History of the U.S: Making Thirteen Colonies*. New York, 1993.

Hawke, David Freeman. *Franklin*. New York, 1985.

Heckham, Howard. *The Toll of Independence*. Chicago, 1947.

Heitman, Francis B. *Historical Register of Officers of the Continental Army*, revised and enlarged. Washington, D.C., 1914.

Hulton, Ann. *Letters of a Loyalist Lady: Being the letters of Ann Hulton, Sister of Henry Hulton, Commissioner of Customs at Boston, 1767–1776.* Cambridge, Massachusetts, 1927.

Hunt, Gaillard, ed. *Journals of the Continental Congress.* 34 vols., Washington, D.C., 1904–1937.

Hunt, John Gabriel, ed. *The Inaugural Addresses of the Presidents.* New York, 1995.

Jamison, J. Franklin, Johnson, Allen, and Malone, Dumas, eds. *Dictionary of American Biography,* 21 vols., New York, 1928–1943.

Kennedy, John Pendleton, ed., *Journals of the House of Burgesses of Virginia: 1761–1765.* Richmond, Virgina, 1907.

———. *Journals of the House of Burgesses of Virginia, 1773–1776.* Richmond, Virginia, 1905.

Ketchum, Richard. *Decisive Day: The Battle for Bunker Hill.* New York, 1962, reprinted 1974.

Ketchum, Richard M., ed. *The American Heritage Book of the Revolution.* New York, 1971.

Koch, Adriene and Peden, William. *The Life and Selected Writings of Thomas Jefferson.* New York, 1944.

Kulikoff, Allan. *Tobacco and Slaves: The Development of Southern Cultures in the Chesapeake, 1680–1800.* Chapel Hill, North Carolina, 1986.

Lancaster, Bruce. *The American Revolution.* New York, 1987, originally published as *The American Heritage Book of the American Revolution,* 1971.

Langguth, A. J. *Patriots: The Men Who Started the American Revolution.* New York, 1988.

MacLean, J. P. *An Historical Account of the Settlements of Scotch Highlanders in America Prior to the Peace of 1783.* Cleveland, Ohio, 1968, reprinted 1978.

McCrum, Robert, Cran, William, and MacNeil, Robert. *The Story of English.* New York, 1986.

McNeil, Keith and McNeil, Rusty. *Colonial and Revolutionary Songbook.* Riverside, California, 1996.

Madison, James. *Notes of the Debates in the Federal Convention of 1787.* New York, 1987; first published in 1840, reprinted in 1966.

Malone, Dumas. *Jefferson and His Time,* 6 vols., Boston, 1948–1977.

Marion, Robert, M.D. *Was George Washington Really the Father of Our Country?* Reading, Massachusetts, 1994.

Mapp, Alf J. *The Virginia Experiment: The Old Dominion's Role in the Making of America: 1607–1781.* Lanham, Maryland, 1985.

Mayo, Lawrence Shaw, ed. *Thomas Hutchinson: The History of the Colony and Province of Massachusetts Bay,* 3 vols., Cambridge, Massachusetts, 1936.

Miller, John C. *Sam Adams, Pioneer in Propaganda.* New York, 1936, reprinted 1960.

———. *The Origins of the American Revolution.* Boston, 1943.

Millett, Allan R. and Maslowski, Peter. *For the Common Defense: A Military History of the United States of America.* New York, 1984, revised 1994.

Morgan, Edmund S. *Virginians at Home: Family Life in the Eighteenth Century.* Williamsburg, Virginia, 1952.

———. *The Birth of the Republic: 1763–1789.* Chicago, 1956.

———. and Morgan, Helen M. *The Stamp Act Crisis: Prologue to Revolution.* Chapel Hill, North Carolina, 1953, revised 1962.

Morison, Samuel Eliot. *John Paul Jones.* Boston, 1959.

Morris, Richard B. *The American Revolution: A Short History.* New York, 1955.

Morton, Richard L. *Colonial Virginia,* 2 vols., Chapel Hill, North Carolina, 1960.

Nagel, Paul C. *The Lees of Virginia: Seven Generations of an American Family.* New York, 1990.

Nickerson, Hoffman. *The Turning Point of the Revolution: Or Burgoyne in America.* Boston, 1928.

Official Guide to Colonial Williamburg. Williamsburg, Virginia, 1985, 8th printing, 1994.

Oxford Universal Dictionary on Historical Principles. Oxford, England, 1933, revised 1955.

Paine, Thomas. *The Rights of Man.* New York, 1984.

Peterson, Harold L. *Arms and Armor in Colonial America: 1526–1783.* Harrisburg, Pennsylvania, 1956.

Quarles, Benjamin. *The Negro in the American Revolution.* Chapel Hill, North Carolina, 1961.

Revelyan, George Otto. *The American Revolution,* 6 vols., Oxford,

1909–1914, edited by Richard B. Morris as a one-volume version, 1964.

Robson, Eric. *The American Revolution in its Political and Military Aspects: 1763–1783.* New York, 1966.

Sellby, John E. *The Revolution in Virginia: 1775–1783.* Williamsburg, Virginia, 1988.

Sellers, Charles Coleman. *Patience Wright: American Spy in George III's London.* Middleton, Connecticut, 1976.

Shaw, Peter. *American Patriots and the Rituals of Revolution.* Cambridge, Massachusetts, 1981.

Shenkman, Richard. *I Love Paul Revere, Whether He Rode or Not.* New York, 1991.

———. *Legends, Lies and Cherished Myths of American History.* New York, 1988.

Smith, Page. *A New Age Now Begins: A People's History of the American Revolution,* 2 vols., New York, 1976.

Smyth, Albert. *The Writings of Benjamin Franklin,* 10 vols., New York, 1905–1907.

Szmanski, Leszek. *Casimir Pulaski: A Hero of the American Revolution.* New York, 1979, reprinted 1994.

Tourtellot, Arthur B. *Lexington and Concord: The Beginning of the War of the American Revolution.* New York, 1963, originally published as *William Diamond's Drum.*

Tyler, Alice Felt. *Freedom's Ferment: Phases of American Social History from the Colonial Period to the Outbreak of the Civil War.* Minneapolis, Minnesota, 1944.

Van Doren, Mark, ed. *Correspondence of Aaron Burr and His Daughter Theodosia.* New York, 1929.

Wallechinsky, David and Wallace, Irving. *The People's Almanac.* Garden City, New York, 1975.

Ward, Christopher. *War of the Revolution,* 2 vols., New York, 1952.

Weeler, Richard, ed. *Voices of 1776: The Story of the American Revolution in the Words of Those Who Were There.* New York, 1972.

Weisberger, Bernard A. *The American People.* New York, 1970.

Wilbur, C. Keith. *The Revolutionary Soldier: 1775–1783.* Old Saybrook, Connecticut, 1969, reprinted 1993.

Wilcox, William B., ed. *The American Revolution: Sir Henry Clinton's*

Narrative of His Campaigns: 1775–1782. New Haven, Connecticut, 1954.

Willison, George F. *Behold Virginia! The Fifth Crown.* New York, 1951.

Wright, Esmond, ed. *The Fire of Liberty: The American War of Independence Seen Through the Eyes of the Men and Women, the Statesmen and Soldiers Who fought It.* New York, 1970.

Wright, Mike. *What They Didn't Teach You About the Civil War.* Novato, California, 1996.

Wrong, George M. *Washington and His Comrades in Arms.* New Haven, Connecticut, 1921.

Wrote, L. Kevin and Zobel, Hiller, eds. *Legal Papers of John Adams,* 3 vols., Cambridge, Massachusetts, 1965.

Zobel, Hiller B. *The Boston Massacre.* New York, 1971, reprinted 1996.

Index

Index

Index